Contemporary Britain

A Geographical Perspective

A.G. Champion
Senior Lecturer in Geography
University of Newcastle upon Tyne

and

A.R. Townsend
Reader in Geography
University of Durham

Edward Arnold
A division of Hodder & Stoughton
LONDON NEW YORK MELBOURNE AUCKLAND

© 1990 A.G. Champion and A.R. Townsend

First published in Great Britain 1990

Distributed in the USA by Routledge, Chapman and Hall, Inc.
29 West 35th Street, New York, NY 10001

British Library Cataloguing in Publication Data

Champion, A. G. (Anthony Gerard)
  Contemporary Britain: a geographical perspective.
  1. Great Britain. Geographical features
  I. Title   II. Townsend, Alan R.
  914.1

  ISBN 0-7131-6580-4

Library of Congress Cataloging-in-Publication Data

Champion, A. G. (Anthony Gerard)
  Contemporary Britain: a geographical perspective/
  A.G. Champion and A.R. Townsend.
      p.   cm.
  Includes bibliographical references and index.
  ISBN 0-7131-6580-4 (pb.): $24.95 (U.S.: est.)
    1. Great Britain—Economic conditions—1945– —Regional
  disparities.   2. Great Britain—Population.   3. Labor supply—
  Great Britain—Regional disparities.   4. Regional planning—
  Great Britain.   5. Great Britain—Geography.   I. Townsend, Alan R.   II. Title.
  HC256.6.C415   1990
  330.941'0859—dc20   90-40796
                                                                          CIP

Typeset in Linotron Palatino by Rowland Phototypesetting Limited,
Bury St Edmunds, Suffolk.
Printed and bound in Great Britain for
Edward Arnold, a division of Hodder and Stoughton Limited,
Mill Road, Dunton Green, Sevenoaks, Kent TN13 2YA by
St Edmundsbury Press Limited, Bury St Edmunds, Suffolk.

Contents

Preface

At the beginning of the 1990s, Britain is emerging from the most significant decade of change in society and geography since the 1930s, and arguably since the height of the Industrial Revolution over a century ago. Neither the 'drift to the South East' of the 1950s and early 1960s, nor the urban–rural shift of the later 1960s and 1970s can rival the fundamental nature and scale of events of the last 10 years. The deep recession of 1979–83 opened up major social and spatial divisions, and these new patterns were largely reinforced by the eventual economic recovery.

De-industrialization caused massive unemployment in the 1980s, which began with inner city riots and ended with the possible identification of an 'underclass' amongst the low-skilled and the ethnic minorities. New forms of employment did emerge, often for women, but chiefly in the 'greater South East', which was eventually swamped by building applications and traffic. Unlike the 1930s, however, there is no hope of a revival of employment levels in traditional industries, as symbolized most dramatically by the complete removal of steel works at places like Consett (Co. Durham) and Shotton (Clwyd). The huge scale of this transformation was graphically illustrated by the results of the first property revaluation since 1973 (published in January 1990) which suggested 40–50 per cent *decreases* in the rate bills for factories and warehouses in northern England and increases of up to 95 per cent for shops, offices and other commercial property in London and much of southern England.

Less obviously perhaps, but equally important, this transformation has prompted changes in the way in which people look at the changing map of Britain. In the first place, more policy makers, academics and businessmen are giving attention to the international arena. This is partly because of the increasing recognition of international forces in producing changes within the UK. It is also to compare the record of Britain's economic performance and social change with that elsewhere, most notably among the other member states of the European Community, the USA and Japan. Secondly, because many view the de-industrialization of the UK as largely irreversible, there has been an upsurge of interest in the role of the service sector. This has led to more intensive investigation of its locational characteristics and its effect on regional and urban patterns of economic activity, whether financial services, tourism or other activities. Thirdly, despite – or, more likely, because of – the significance of the simple North–South division in the 1980s, the spatial focus of both academics and policy makers has partly switched from the eleven 'standard regions' (South East, North West, Scotland, etc.) to the local scale (places or 'localities' defined at the level of individual settlements). This shift reflects the much greater importance of environment and local politics, whether in business formation or concern for the quality of life and social opportunities.

It is these two sets of developments – the new patterns 'on the ground' and the emergence of new perspectives on them – which have stimulated us to produce this volume and have influenced us in selecting its contents. The basic aim is to present an account of the way in which national and international trends in economy and society have re-shaped the geography of the UK in recent years and will, we believe, continue to affect localities to the end of the twentieth century and beyond. Our main emphasis must be on the processes of economic change, especially the changing role of Britain in international production and trade, the decline of employment in manufacturing industry and blue-collar occupations, and equally the emergence of new types of employment. Other related themes are the changing levels of public expenditure and the drive towards privatization, the trends towards greater household fission and social heterogeneity, the major developments in communications and retailing, and the re-emergence of concern over environment, housing, transport infrastructure and land-use planning. In addition, because the Thatcherite vision of a 'new' Britain provided a strong undercurrent to many of these considerations, we make frequent mention of the political inputs to and policy implications of geographical change. At the same time, however, we show that in many ways the actions of Conservative governments of the 1980s served more to accelerate the changes than to initiate them.

Our views about the importance of the new developments are also reflected in the organization of the volume. Briefly, the book is arranged in four parts. The first introduces the main themes of economic and social change, setting Britain's experience into its international and long-term context. This shows how much the country's present characteristics and problems are rooted in its historical development and in its relationships with other parts of the globe. Part II describes the impact of change on the map of Britain, looking at the last quarter of a century but giving most attention to the events of the 1980s. This shows how the processes have had different implications for different places according to their inherited characteristics and to the changing role that they are playing on national and international stages. This outcome provides the grounds for distinguishing four broad types of places, which form the basis for the four chapters in Part III: large cities, prosperous sub-regions, industrial districts, and more remote rural areas. We see this as a key contribution of the book, because this division – crude though it may be, and lacking in precision at the edges – corresponds much more closely to the realities and academic perceptions of late-twentieth-century Britain than the usual regional treatment. For each type of place, we begin by describing the main features of population and employment change, then go on to examine the problems that they have caused in social and land-use terms, and finally look at the forms of policy which have been developed in response. In Part IV the concluding chapter draws on the findings of the previous sections in order to assess the future prospects for different types of places against the background of the evolving patterns of population and employment change. It ends by pointing to the key policy issues at the sub-regional level, particularly those relating to the matching of people and other resources across the country as a whole.

This structure allows us to combine both a systematic and an area-based approach to the study of Britain's emerging geography. It helps us to view local-scale changes in their wider geographical settings and to place recent trends and current issues in their longer-term historical context. We feel that it is important to give readers a reasonably detailed account of where we have come from, so that they can more fully appreciate the fundamental significance of the latest developments. Moreover, the emphasis on different types of places in Part III allows us to take advantage of the detailed research on localities which was undertaken during the 1980s, including the 'Inner Cities in Context' and 'Changing Urban and Regional Systems' initiatives funded by the Economic and Social Research Council.

It may be questioned whether the beginning of the 1990s is a good time to assess trends in the internal geography of Britain. As we note in Chapter 12, many of the issues facing the UK are national questions with an international origin, subject to uncertain political developments in western and eastern Europe and economic forces across the globe. Nevertheless, we believe that the UK has now begun to emerge from the trauma of the early 1980s. It has experienced several years of change in the same directions, undesirable though some of these are deemed to be by many people. Indeed, the background work required in the preparation of this volume has increased our appreciation of the strong consistency of trends and processes, particularly from the dramatic low-point of the early 1980s to the end of the decade. These represent the longer-term geographical shifts from North to South and from large city to smaller settlements and more rural environments.

It is, of course, impossible to be completely up to date. We have been able to include some important sets of official data which have become available within the last two months (e.g. regional estimates of employees in employment up to mid 1989 published in the November 1989 issue of the *Employment Gazette* and labour force projections to the year 2000, published in the January 1990 issue of the *Employment Gazette*). We also provide some of the first analyses of the local-level results of the 1987 Census of Employment (issued in September 1989). In addition, we refer at appropriate points to the statistical series which readers can use to monitor trends over the next few years and we make suggestions as to how this book can help to interpret the results obtained.

Needless to say, we owe a great deal to those who have given us advice and support during the preparation of this book, including all those authors and publishers who have given us permission to draw on their material (see the separate list of Acknowledgements). In particular, we received helpful comments from three anonymous readers and from colleagues in our two departments. The volume also benefits from the analysis of employment, unemployment and migration statistics on the National Online Manpower Information System (University of Durham), programmed by Michael Blakemore, Bob Nelson, Sinclair Sutherland, Frances Drake and Peter Dodds. Reference to 'LLMAs' relates to the Local Labour Market Areas of the CURDS functional regionalization of Great Britain (see Coombes *et al.*, 1982, for full details). Thanks are due to David Hume and Arthur Corner for drawing all the figures, to Marilyn Champion and Dorothy Trotter for preparing the typescript and to former research colleagues, Colin Crouch and Franc Peck, for stimulus and ideas throughout the 1980s.

A.G. Champion, Newcastle upon Tyne
A.R. Townsend, Durham
January 1990

Acknowledgements

Table 1.1: based on data of Crouch C.S. 1989: The economic geography of recession in the UK; the early 1980s and historical perspectives. Unpublished PhD Thesis, University of Durham.

Table 2.1: based on data in Atkinson, A. 1983: UK trade in manufactured goods. *Barclays Review* LVIII, 4, centre spread.

Table 2.5: based on data in Cheshire, P., Carbonaro, G. and Hay, D. 1986: Problems of urban decline and growth in EEC countries. *Urban Studies* 23, 131–49.

Figure 3.1: updated from Figure 4.1 in Tilly, L.A. and Scott, J.W. 1978: *Women, work and family.* New York: Holt, Rinehart and Winston.

Table 4.7: abridged from Table 8 in Champion, A.G. and Congdon, P.D. 1989: An analysis of the recovery of London's population change rate. *Built Environment* 13, 193–211.

Table 5.7: appeared as Table 6.1 in Townsend, A.R. and Peck, F.W. The geography of mass-redundancy (174–216) in M. Pacione (ed.) 1985 *Progress in industrial geography.* London: Croom Helm.

Table 5.8: based on data in Camley, M. 1987: Employment in the public and private sectors, 1981 to 1987. *Economic Trends* 410, 98–107 and in Fleming, A. 1988: Employment in the public and private sectors, 1982 to 1988. *Economic Trends* 414, 119–129. By permission of the Controller of HMSO.

Figure 6.1B: based on Figure 3 in Keeble, D.E. 1990: Small firms, new firms and uneven regional development in the United Kingdom. *Area* 22.

Figure 7.4B: provided by M.G. Coombes and S. Raybould, Centre for Urban and Regional Development Studies, University of Newcastle upon Tyne.

Table 7.5: modified from Table 1 in Owen, D.W. and Green, A.E. 1989: Labour market accounts for travel-to-work areas, 1981–84. *Regional Studies* 23, 69–72.

Figure 7.5: based on Figure 7.1 in Donnison, D. and Soto, P. 1980: *The good city.* London: Heinemann, 101.

Figure 10.2: updated from Martin, R. 1989: The new economics and politics of regional restructuring: the British experience. In Albrechts, L., Moulaert, F., Roberts, T. and Swyngedouw, E. *Regional planning at the crossroads.* London: Jessica Kingsley.

Table 10.3: based on data in Department of the Environment, Inner Cities Directorate 1983: *Census Information Note* No. 2: Urban deprivation. By permission of the Controller of HMSO.

Table 10.4: abridged from Robinson, F., Wren, C. and Goddard, J. 1987: *Economic development policies: an evaluative study of the Newcastle Metropolitan Region*. Oxford: Oxford University Press, Table 3.2. By permission of the Oxford University Press.

Table 10.5: based on data in Armstrong, H.W. 1988: *A comparison of industrial development initiatives of metropolitan and non metropolitan district councils in England and Wales*. Lancaster: University of Lancaster, Department of Economics.

Table 12.3: based on data in Cambridge Econometrics and Northern Ireland Economic Research Centre 1988: *Regional economic prospects, analysis and forecasts to the year 2000 for the standard planning regions of the UK* (unabridged version), Appendix C.

Table 12.4: based on Figure 4 in Begg, I. and Moore, B. *The future economic role of urban systems*, University of Cambridge, mimeo.

PART I

The Forces of Change

1

Key geographical trends

Geographers have always been interested in the relations between people and the environment. A particular interest for Britain lies in assessing which environments are most threatened by ongoing movements of population and employment, with their attendant roads, shopping centres and housing. In turn, however, the question of where population is growing – or declining – is fundamentally related to human welfare. It leads on to one of the basic processes of geographical inquiry, to study the impact of processes occurring over time on different areas. The temporal processes that we shall examine, such as the changing structure of employment, may result more from international forces than from influences in the local environment, but they may change the map of the UK at regional, sub-regional or local scale.

Uneven regional development

One of the most important features of the British outlook of the last hundred years has been its revelry in nostalgia and dislike of change. This is reflected in the highest places, such as parliament, and does not fit easily with the hectic pace of recent change in the economy. In this volume we shall concentrate on changes since 1960, and particularly since 1980. It is tempting to underestimate the scale and radical nature of changes occurring around us, socially or geographically.

One salutary reminder is that many writers see 'uneven regional development' as the norm in western industrialized society (Smith, 1984; Storper and Walker, 1989). The flow of people, profits and investment between regions produces differences in living standards between them. It is currently widely accepted that regional *divergence* in living standards within countries is the norm (Bennett, 1980, 67). For example, there remain clear differences in unemployment levels between northern and southern Italy, or different parts of France. One can go further, however, and assert that the 1980s were a period of more rapid change in UK economic geography than any previous decade of this century. Smith (1984, ix), for example, argues 'one can hardly look at the world today without perceiving that, at the hands

1

of capital, the last two decades have witnessed an emergent restructuring of geographical space more dramatic than any before', instancing de-industrialization and regional decline, changes in the distribution of popu-lation in metropolitan areas, and the nascent industrialization of the Third World.

Historical precedents of major change can well be illustrated from Britain itself, where the whole geographical pattern of the Industrial Revolution provides ample evidence of radical geographical evolution. Even in the mid eighteenth century, Britain 'exhibited a complex and shifting pattern of industrial concentration', and some areas 'became de-industrialized, like parts of East Anglia' (Pollard, 1981, 10). 'Above all, the British industrial revolution was a regional phenomenon' (Pollard, 1981, 14); but of ten pioneering regions, four declined soon after they had made their vital contribution (Cornwall, Shropshire, North Wales and the Derbyshire up-lands), while two more (Tyneside and Clydeside) had to get something like a second wind to survive as centres of expanding metal industries and shipbuilding.

50-year 'long cycles' and British regions

These impulses of expansion and decline may be related to the 'upswings' and 'downswings' of the suggested international 'Kondratieff cycle'. Experi-ence of recession in the 1980s has re-directed our attention to a longer-term temporal pattern in economic events, which was first applied to nineteenth-century international change. A Russian scholar, Kondratieff published in 1926 evidence for the view that familiar economic cycles of 3.5 to 11 years' length were superimposed on deeper 'long waves' of 47 to 60 years. He identified these in England, France, the United States and Germany from the movement of prices, interest rates, wages, foreign trade and metal production. For instance, he observed expansions of English foreign trade on about a 50-year cycle from the 1790s to 1810, from 1842 to 1873, and from 1893 to 1914, each separated by periods of consolidation.

This pattern sheds light on the evolution of many local economies, for instance the industrialization of Shropshire (in the Coalbrookdale Coalfield). Industrial development in this case was prepared in the 'down-swing' before the 1790s, largely took place in the 'upswing' from the 1790s to 1810, was overtaken by the rest of the West Midlands from 1842 to 1873, and was largely extinguished in the downswing from the 1920s to 1932. Like-wise, one may say that much of the Lancashire and Yorkshire textiles industries developed from the 1790s to 1810, and from 1842 to 1873, and declined in subsequent downswings. The heavy industry of Scotland and north-east England largely developed from 1842 to 1873. The pattern is in fact more complex than can be schematized in any one model of develop-ment (Marshall, 1987); some regions like the Midlands repeatedly found replacement industries at least until the 1966–81 downswing.

The emergence of the North–South divide

More general was the reversal in the relative fortunes of the northern and southern parts of Britain in about 1921, when many of the older industrial regions fell into relative decline in economic and population trends. Table 1.1 shows that the South East, East Anglia and the South West (as mapped at Figure 1.1) together had 46 per cent of the population of Great Britain in 1701; this share fell to its lowest level, of 38 per cent, in 1921, before recovering to 42 per cent in recent census years. The adjustment of population through migration was prompted by the existence of higher unemployment levels in northern Britain throughout the period since 1921; these peaked in the year 1932, when over 2,750,000 people were unemployed. After this, employment levels improved in all regions, but despite the beginnings of 'regional policy' from 1934 (McCrone, 1969), employment change was more favourable to the 'South' than the 'North' in all years before 1973 except 1937 and 1939 (Crouch, 1989; excluding the war years 1940–45).

Table 1.1 Population distribution, by regional grouping, 1701–1981 (per cent)

	East Anglia South East and South West	East and West Midlands	Rest	Great Britain
1701	46	16	38	100.0
1921	38.0	14.8	47.2	100.0
1971	42.0	16.8	41.2	100.0
1981	42.3	17.1	40.6	100.0

Source: Crouch, 1989

A fundamental map (Figure 1.1) shows the value of production per head (gdp *per capita*) in the standard regions. The high levels of wealth in the South East and East Anglia are the central feature of UK geography today. The depth of the North–South divide, its precise definition, and directions of change are key issues for this volume. Along with this run many other questions. For instance, are regions like East Anglia 're-industrializing'? If so, why? Major reversals occurred in the relative trends of different regions in the past; are they occurring now?

Concentration and dispersal across a finer-grained map

In practice this book requires a finer-grained view than that of Figure 1.1. Political discussion of the North–South divide in the late 1980s demonstrated examples of relative poverty in the South, notably the inner residential areas of London, and of relative affluence in the North, such as the Aberdeen area and North Yorkshire. As in the USA and, more recently, several countries of Europe, it is seen that international and national processes have impacted differentially on different *kinds* of *subregions*. The spatial expression of these differences appears at three levels of concentration and dispersal.

Figure 1.1 Regional variations in gross domestic product, 1987 (UK = 100). Data exclude production of North Sea oil etc. from Continental Shelf. Source: *Regional Trends* 1989, 135.

Core-periphery relationships

Much of the distinction between North and South since 1920 is best expressed in terms of the performance of individual sub-regions. For instance, 'new industrial regions' (Greater London, Warwickshire, Staffordshire and Worcestershire) expanded their share of net output from 28.7 per cent to 37.1 per cent over the period 1924 to 1935 (Pollard, 1983). The attraction of the London market, and the adoption of West Midlands skills by the motor and engineering industries, led to a consolidation of the economy on these core regions. This structural advantage was offset by the transfer of nearly half a million industrial jobs under government regional policy, 1945–65, to assisted areas of the 'periphery'; these areas were again defined essentially as sub-regions, namely, much of the Clyde Valley, the north-east coast of England, South Wales and Cornwall, together with Merseyside.

Urban–rural relationships

Geographers have discovered a recent tendency for rural areas to see something of a recovery in population and employment levels, no matter where they are; conversely, conurbation (metropolitan) areas have suffered a loss of population and employment, whether in London, the West Midlands or the North; while intervening areas lie along a statistical continuum. Fothergill and Gudgin (1979) demonstrated this pattern from data for the period 1959 to 1975. As there was much greater divergence in growth levels between conurbations and rural sub-regions than between the 11 constituent regions of the UK, the statistical performance of the regions is better understood and predicted by reference to their respective mixtures of conurbation and rural sub-regions than to their industrial structure.

City–suburban relationships

It is in the 'inner cities' that conurbation employment has fallen most steeply, and that greater social sorting produces concentrations of poorer people, with distinctive ethnic and family structures, as in social geography texts. Both population and employment were already falling in the former London County Council area between 1951 and 1961, and the process intensified in all cities after 1966. In contrast, suburban areas increased in relative wealth, developed more local jobs, and intensified many of the socio-economic characteristics of the 'safe' Conservative constituency.

The challenge of different kinds of places

All the evidence has led us to organize this book with reference to different kinds of places. The resolution of the different forces is studied not in terms of the 11 standard regions shown in Figure 1.1, as commonly used in statistical volumes and geographical texts on Great Britain, but in terms of types of sub-regions – the large cities, the prosperous sub-regions, the declining industrial areas, and the outer (more remote) rural areas. This is not to say that there are not important distinctions between, say, the large cities, or between declining industrial areas; individual localities may all show different social relationships (Cooke, 1989); it may be that similarities of trends in the 1960s and 1970s were in part coincidental, and that there will be salient differences in the 1990s. However, the trends of the 1960s, 1970s and 1980s have already created different planning problems.

The large cities

The modern western city remains the centre of many activities of society, but was seen as representing a large planning problem from the early 1960s. Many initial questions concerned excessive transport congestion for the users of cities, and the renewed need for planned decentralization of people and growth. By the 1980s, however, massive decline of jobs and population had led to the concentration of national socio-economic problems in inner cities, and to a very varied set of government programmes to improve the situation (Chapter 8).

The problems of coping with growth in attractive, prosperous sub-regions

The dispersal of housing and employment growth from the cities to surrounding counties occurred in many different phases, but has increasingly raised major questions in land-use planning. The rival claims of economic growth and of countryside conservation are in conflict in rural areas of the South, and some other regions (Chapter 9). Thus a political dilemma has re-emerged. Economic trends and population projections may be evaluated to assess the future position of Green Belts, and whether any of the growth of modern light industry and offices may again be diverted to areas of types we now mention.

The challenge of redundant places and 'grey areas'

The 1930s showed how individual towns (such as Jarrow) could lose the bulk of their economic livelihood, and 'deindustrialization' of the 1980s has done the same. The emphasis now has switched more to whole manufacturing and mining sub-regions (such as South Yorkshire or Merseyside), which, together with older parts of major cities, can suffer unemployment rates in excess of ten per cent with little prospect of redress. If it is difficult to restore economic vitality to the worst-hit redundant areas, it has nonetheless been argued, since the Hunt Report (Department of Economic Affairs, 1969) on 'Intermediate Areas', that the growth needs and potential of 'grey areas' were bypassed by policy. Are there any possibilities or precedents for developing the image and infrastructure of areas such as West Yorkshire, as a means of introducing some modern economic activity at least to parts of the 'urban North'? (Chapter 10)

The emerging issue of outer rural areas

Some of the most surprising issues of contemporary Britain arise in areas like Cornwall or mid Wales, which had previously been suffering from the decline of population and employment. Their more rural environments have not only attracted people there for holidays and retirement, but also induced elements of industrial growth. Some of these new elements are in conflict with the needs of local people and the preservation of the environment (Chapter 11).

The threats of increasing polarization in UK society

If these types of challenges are not resolved, then explicit political conflict and urban violence will accelerate. Like most western European nations the UK divides between 'left' and 'right': between the Labour party's view of the world, in which an emphasis on public spending on welfare and infrastructure was closely associated with post-war urban and regional planning, and a Conservative party view which in the 1980s emphasized that free-market economic growth must come before state spending. The gap between these views widened enough in the early 1980s for (what is now) the Liberal Democrat party to capture a fairly even share of the voting allegiances of different socio-economic groups and regions. This accentuated the contrast between Labour and Conservative voters, with manual socio-economic groups, public service workers, and council house tenants most likely to vote Labour, and a strong association between white-collar owner occupation and Conservative allegiance (Johnston *et al.*, 1988).

The spatial outcome of increasing socio-political polarization was an increase in the contrasts of wealth and of constituency voting between North and South, and between urban and rural areas. In 1983, the Conservatives lost their last remaining seats in Glasgow and Liverpool, and Labour's loss of all but three seats in the South (other than in London) left it in control of large contiguous areas only at the core of individual conurbations, and in the former coalfield areas of Strathclyde, the north east of England, South Yorkshire and South Wales. In 1987, the small 2.5 per cent national swing from Conservative to Labour was differentiated between North and South. The number of Conservative MPs in Scotland was reduced from 21 to 10, and the Conservatives lost their last seats in Newcastle upon Tyne, Bradford, Manchester and Leicester. However, a swing *towards* the Conservatives in London reduced Labour's representation there from 26 to 24 seats.

A strong correlation exists between party control and constituency unemployment levels, because parliamentary seats are small enough to represent distinct residential districts in larger urban areas, and because voting behaviour and unemployment are two variables which are both strongly related, in turn, to social class characteristics. The comparison can be made visually in Figure 1.2, which allocates equal space on the page to each constituency, Figure 1.2A for unemployment, and in Figure 1.2B for the 1987 election result at the same time. Although there is still some variation in the size of constituency electorates and their populations (after the redrawing of their boundaries in 1983), the simple comparison of numbers unemployed (claimants) at the 1987 election is useful. Of the worst fifth of constituencies for unemployment (127 shaded black), only 18 returned Conservative MPs, and three Alliance. Of the best fifth (127, unshaded), only 10 returned MPs other than Conservative, of which only one (Yeovil) was in England. (Indeed of the next best fifth, all but 17 returned Conservatives.) Table 1.2 shows the size of Conservative majorities in the best ten constituencies (in Surrey, Buckinghamshire, Oxfordshire and London), and the size of Labour majorities in the worst ten (located in inner cities and the North).

Voting in national elections is only the tip of the iceberg, however, in expressing the troubles of 'northern council estate' Britain. Social contrasts can take different forms in different areas, witness the tensions between the (generally poorer) Catholics and the (relatively richer) Protestants in Northern Ireland. Different political coalitions occupy power in county and district authorities in different parts of the UK, and a key question emerges from local government: if national government policy provides no remedy for the problems of economic development of so many towns and cities, is there any scope for local authorities to generate greater employment and investment themselves? These are questions which we take up later in the volume. Many of the similarities and divisions between different areas of Britain need

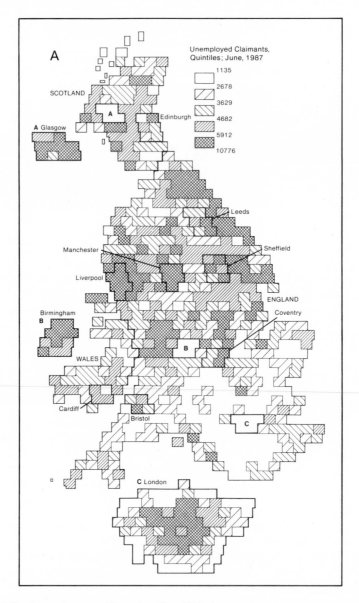

Figure 1.2 Parliamentary constituencies, Great Britain:
(A) Unemployment, June 1987, and (B) General Election results, 1987. Each constituency
is given an equal area of the cartogram. Source: NOMIS, *The Times*, *Daily Telegraph*.

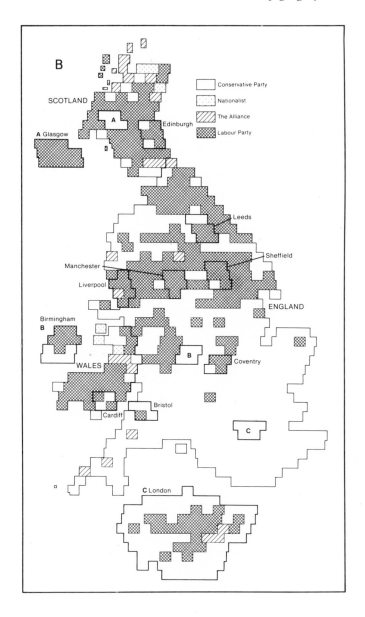

B

SCOTLAND

A Glasgow

A

Edinburgh

Conservative Party

Nationalist

The Alliance

Labour Party

Leeds

Manchester

Sheffield

Liverpool

ENGLAND

Birmingham
B

B

Coventry

WALES

Cardiff

Bristol

C

C London

Table 1.2 Constituency unemployment and General Election results, June 1987, extreme values

Lowest number Unemployed	Unemployed claimants	Conservative majority
1. Esher, Surrey	1 135	19 068
2. Mole Valley, Surrey	1 186	16 076
3. South West Surrey	1 229	14 343
4. East Surrey	1 231	18 126
5. Chesham and Amersham, Bucks	1 247	19 440
6. Surbiton, London	1 247	9 741
7. Henley, Oxon	1 353	17 082
8. Ruislip – Northwood, London	1 372	16 971
9. Beaconsfield, Bucks	1 374	21 339
10. Wantage, Oxon	1 449	12 156

Highest number Unemployed	Unemployed claimants	Labour majority
1. Manchester Central	10 776	19 867
2. Liverpool Riverside	10 764	20 689
3. Liverpool Walton	10 303	23 253
4. Hackney South and Shoreditch, London	10 225	7 522
5. Sunderland North, Tyne and Wear	10 129	14 672
6. Bootle, Merseyside	9 955	24 477
7. Sheffield Central	9 729	19 342
8. Vauxhall, London	9 680	9 019
9. Middlesbrough, Cleveland	9 653	14 958
10. Birmingham Small Heath	9 599	15 521

Source: NOMIS, *The Times*, 11 June

deeper understanding, which can be provided by a fuller review of the country's international and historical position.

Further Reading:

Kondratieff's basic statement is available in translation in Kondratieff (1978) and an extensive statement of relevant European research is to be found in Pollard (1981). An interpretation of British experience is in Marshall (1987). A refreshing view of past industrial specialisation among British coalfields is provided by Rawstron (1964) and of long-term population movements by Osborne (1964).

A summary of attention to the 'North–South' problem can be found in Lewis and Townsend (1989). A radical survey of industrial and regional change in Britain is provided by Dunford and Perrons (1983). For a recent collection of regional and policy reports (including the former 'grey areas' of the North West and Yorkshire and Humberside), see Damesick and Wood (1987).

The 'core-periphery' question was developed by Keeble (1976) and the basic statement of the 'urban–rural shift' is in Fothergill and Gudgin (1982). A useful reader on critical urban problems is provided by Anderson *et al.* (1983) and one of the few volumes in its field is Herington (1984). Analyses of the 1983 and 1987 general elections are provided by Johnston *et al.* (1988).

2
Britain's position in the wider world

'Few human geographers seem willing to come out of their national shells and take the wider view which would enable them to understand what is going on within their own countries' (Thrift, 1986, 62). This chapter concentrates on the international context, past and present, of change in the UK. We hope to say enough about the UK's international position to show that international competition, and the changing commodity composition of world trade, are the keys to understanding the changing composition and size of the UK economy. Those, in turn, are vital to understanding the growth of employment and population in different areas of the country at different dates: for instance, the earlier growth of the Atlantic ports of Glasgow, Liverpool and Bristol, or the relative prosperity of London or Aberdeen *vis-à-vis* most manufacturing areas in the 1980s. It is sometimes argued that international competitive pressures are the origins, directly or indirectly, of all the UK's economic and employment problems. We do not fully agree with this, but the issue must await Chapter 5.

The economic base of growth and decline

The 'Thatcher governments' of 1979 onwards argued that 'the world does not owe us a living'. Translated into disciplinary terms, the study of international economic geography should precede social geography and town planning. Most people live where they do because it contains factories, farms and offices, or perhaps transport facilities, educational institutions or research laboratories, which draw income into the area. Much of this income is from the surrounding region or other parts of the same country. Yet some of the income from the goods and services supplied comes directly or indirectly from other countries.

Indeed, income from other countries, and imports from other countries, may be the critical factors in the modern competitive success of local factories, farms and offices. International competition is now intense in many industries and is frequently the main factor in the rise and fall of different industries, and therefore of different areas. Much of the distribution of population was built up in a period when British industry enjoyed competitive supremacy in international trade. Now, when the USA, Japan and western Europe wrestle with each other for the domination of world markets, including those of Britain, many production areas of this country are already redundant or facing extinction. Areas of growth occur in an uneven manner as they are critically dependent on the expansion of new business in the supply of specialist goods and services, often to the international market.

Long-term perspectives

On the periphery of Europe again

It is salutary to recall that, as Europe's main offshore islands, the British Isles were historically often the last to benefit from the diffusion of innovative ideas in Europe. Estimates of past populations have tended to be revised upwards, but in the Roman period, Britain sustained a population much lower than did Italy. Most of our population stock arrived later, from northern Germany and Denmark, as shown in the place names of most of England and southern Scotland, and in the Middle Ages the Kingdom of Scotland was one of the poorest areas of Europe. Trading wealth was largely confined to southern centres of wool exports; when England joined other Atlantic states, Spain, Portugal, France and the Netherlands, in expansion to other continents, much of the resulting capital remained in the south. Scotland eventually benefited greatly from Union with England in 1707, but in the heyday of nineteenth-century expansion large parts of the western and northern periphery of Britain remained bitterly poor: the clearance of people to make way for sheep caused large-scale migration from the highlands and islands of Scotland, and a large part of the population of Ireland was forced to emigrate through the scarcity of food.

Today there is little doubt that northern and western Britain, now including industrial areas, form part of the relatively deprived 'periphery' of western Europe – with southern Spain and southern Italy. These physical extremities are important for NATO bases, and can for various reasons prove attractive for tourists. However, national averages leave Britain as a whole in a substantially inferior position to western Germany and France. Even Italy, which suffered recurrent economic stagnation from the seventeenth century to the 1950s, claims to have overtaken the UK in the value of production per head (with a population of virtually the same size). The UK's former advantages of an Atlantic position, a plentiful supply of coal (in which Italy's supplies were nugatory), and its building of an Empire (in which Italy's success was very limited by comparison) have come to nought. It remains essential to remind ourselves of the UK's imperial and industrial past, in understanding its ports, industrial concentrations and London.

Imperial power and 'workshop' of the world

The UK provides the oldest industrial landscapes of the world, a point of considerable significance in Chapters 5, 8 and 10. If we find that industries are now disappearing fairly rapidly, it is also worth realizing that they arrived on the landscape quite suddenly. There is, of course, debate as to the accuracy of the term 'Industrial Revolution' to describe the arrival of the factory system in Britain, where production often grew slowly in small workshops. Modern research shows that industry had its roots in the

previous rural life of home weavers and part-time farmers, that technological innovations (such as Abraham Darby's use of coal in smelting iron,
1709) took many decades to supplant existing methods of production and
provide for successful exports, and that early reliance on water power and
canal transport placed limits on expansion. The nineteenth-century emergence of coal-based technology, including the modern railway, was as much a
result of 'Revolution' as a cause. There was nothing pre-ordained in Britain's
supremacy, or in the industrial specialisms eventually adopted by different
coalfields (and sung by a hundred previous textbooks). However, the fact
and success of world-scale specialism are undoubted; for instance, towards
the end of the nineteenth century the Lancashire cotton industry exported
nine-tenths of its output.

Economic influence in the world was closely interrelated with political
power. 'Exports, backed by the systematic and aggressive help of government, provided the spark, and – with cotton textiles – the "leading sector" of
industry' (Hobsbawm, 1969, 50). Behind this trade lay two centuries of
growth in Europe's Atlantic trade by the leading colonial and slave-trading
ports, Bristol, Glasgow and Liverpool. Britain acquired large parts of North
America (until the independence of the USA in 1776), the West Indies, the
West African coast, and the Indian sub-continent and this was partly a
cause, partly a reinforcement of industrial growth: 'We were, or we
increasingly became, the agency of economic interchange between the
advanced and the backward, the industrial and the primary-producing, the
metropolitan and the colonial or quasi-colonial regions of the world'
(Hobsbawm, 1969, 14). This role required closer political control from the
1880s, when the competitive growth of Imperialism among European
powers led to the scramble for Africa, and to British dominance of the Latin
American market.

Iron and steel works came to rely, like cotton mills, on the Empire and a
few other developing countries. Middlesbrough steel, for instance, can still
be identified in the railway stations of India and Argentina: on the eve of the
First World War, those countries alone bought more British iron and steel
exports than the whole of Europe. By that date the Empire received nearly
half the total of British foreign investment, and Latin America a further fifth.
Britain did 'rule the waves' on the shores of most continents, and settlement
continued in 'Canada, South Africa, Australia and New Zealand. British
imperial and industrial success appeared unlimited, but in fact was already
being compromised by long-term processes of economic and political
change, which we shall outline in the next two sections. Only retrospective-
ly have we learnt that Imperial investment was not particularly profitable
overall. However, it did benefit certain social classes in certain areas. For
instance, Davis and Huttenback (1987) argue that British political and social
élites, along with merchants, particularly those based in London, received
the largest share of the benefits available from the Empire, while successfully avoiding a full share of the associated tax costs.

Long-term processes of economic change and restructuring

The competitive advance of other countries and relative decline of British production areas can largely be charted in relation to Kondratieff's 'long waves'. Kondratieff presented few data for growth from 1789 to 1814 from countries other than Britain because they had little growth to analyse. Parts of Belgium, Germany and France were economically active, but real growth came with the mid-century period of railway building. 'It seems possible to place France in the company of those countries – Germany and the US included – which at mid century experienced a "railway Kondratieff" with emphatic growth-industry capabilities' (Trebilcock, 1981). Having achieved modern technological growth in the period 1849 to 1873, several of these countries then consolidated their competitive position during the 'Victorian depression' of the 1880s. In the period of expansion from 1893 to 1914, Germany developed an extremely powerful position in the new technologies of chemicals, dyestuffs and electrical engineering.

Britain's share of world trade in manufactured goods fell to one third by 1900 and was further reduced in each of the next four decades. Germany and the USA had overtaken Britain's total levels of production by 1900 and equalled her world share of manufactured exports in the depressed conditions, or 'downswing', of the 1930s. It is commonplace now to seek the beginnings of Britain's relative world decline early in the 1880s to 1930s cycle, and to blame them on Britain's lack of adaptation to changing competitive conditions in industry. Behind this, it is claimed, lay 'complacency by the descendants of industrial pioneers', a 'disdain for trade' and 'anti-manufacturing snobbery', the 'neglect of technical education' and 'failure of the universities to supply industrial leaders' (Allen, 1979). It is held by others, however, that a large part of the relative decline was the inevitable sequel of having been a pioneer in industrialization. Either way, the outcome is a marked legacy in the economic landscape, representing today the 'continuing influence of Britain's historical international position' (Massey, 1986): by the time of the 1930s depression, some of the greatest industrial regions of Britain, the specialist production regions of textiles, steel, ships and coal exports, with their ports, had already entered a long period of continuous decline.

Adjustment to relative decline

Political realignment from Commonwealth to Europe

Success in some new industries and London's continuing world importance in finance during the 'upswing' from 1933 to 1966, together with the deep interruption of the Second World War, largely disguised the gradually declining value of the UK's old international and political role. The independence of India and Pakistan in 1947, Ghana and Malaysia in 1957, and most other African dependencies in the 1960s, were only milestones in the long, gradual process of the relative weakening of Commonwealth links, which for instance withdrew the tariff advantages of the British cotton industry in many tropical markets. But 'Commonwealth preference' was still important in the 1960s because it was granted on half the UK's imports from Commonwealth countries.

'Whether under the Labour or the Conservative Government, links with the Commonwealth were regarded as precluding too close links with the countries of Europe' (Kitzinger, 1961, 9). Repeatedly the UK passed over opportunities to join or even lead the emerging European Common Market, now the European Community (EC). This was partly because of perceptions of the political complexion and potential instability of such a body, but mainly because Common Market membership would be incompatible with the spirit of the Commonwealth. Economic arguments appeared conclusive: Britain had a special position as banker to the sterling area, and would have great difficulty in adjusting its food production and Commonwealth food imports to Common Market structures. Like many observers, UK leaders failed to appreciate that the greatest potential for post-war expansion lay in the trade of industrial goods between industrialized countries. At the foundation of the Common Market in 1958, its area received an apparently modest share of the UK's total exports, a mere 13.7 per cent: the sterling area and Canada together received nearly half. Yet the Common Market total was expanding rapidly, and the Commonwealth total was stable. The UK's exports went mostly to the low tariff countries of the market, which would raise tariffs on British goods and abolish tariffs on all goods from their partners. The Treaty of Rome, which established the Common Market, accelerated the already rapid growth of some members, so that the 1960s saw the emergence of a dynamic economy far stronger than the British, offering economies of scale in a consumer market of more than 200 million people. The UK finally overcame its internal doubts and external diplomatic problems and joined the Common Market (the EC) in 1973, along with Ireland and Denmark. The precise impact on the UK is still debated, but internal political opposition largely evaporated between the 1983 and 1987 General Elections.

Changing patterns of external trade and migration

Social and trading links have been slow to change. Throughout the twentieth century the Commonwealth countries remained the main origins and destinations of international migration. A net outflow from the UK until the 1931 Census was followed by a period of net inward migration which culminated in the early 1960s in the peak arrivals of migrants from the 'new Commonwealth', chiefly the Caribbean and the Indian sub-continent, reflecting a UK shortage of labour in the long 'post-war boom'. The subsequent period of net outward migration was dominated by the Commonwealth, but by 1985 a small growth in migration to and from the EC contributed to a net inward balance.

Though less visible, it was export competition in goods and services which had a more fundamental effect on UK towns and cities. The internal economic geography of the UK has been reworked over a century by fundamental change in the nature and orientation of exports, which has reflected the success of individual industries and their factories. Table 2.1

Table 2.1 Composition of UK merchandise exports 1900 and 1987 (per cent)

Export goods	1900	1987
Manufactured goods, including	78.7	76.4
Textiles	36.4	2.4
Metals & metal manufacturers	14.4	6.5
Machinery & transport equipment	10.3	36.1
Chemicals	4.8	13.2
Other	12.8	18.2
Non-manufactured goods, including	20.3	23.6
Coal	12.5	0.4
Petroleum	—	10.6
Other	7.8	12.6
Other	1.0	—
Total	100.0	100.0

Source: Atkinson, 1983; *Annual Abstract of Statistics*, 1989

demonstrates the principal changes so far this century in the composition of export goods. In 1900, the country was still largely dependent on exports of textiles, metals and coal, whereas by 1987 nearly half the country's exports were accounted for by 'machinery and transport equipment' and chemicals. The impact of North Sea oil on the structure of the balance of payments may actually have reduced the absolute volume of manufacturing exports. This is because it raised the real sterling exchange rate, rendering 'marginal' manufacturing exports uncompetitive. We shall return to this issue at several points later in this volume.

The geographical destinations of exports have shown a swing towards the EC. As recently as 1970 the Commonwealth accounted for 20 per cent of the value of the UK's trade in manufactured goods, but by 1982 that share had decreased to 11 per cent. Table 2.2 demonstrates changes over the seventeen years to 1987: western Europe took over half our exports for the first time in recent history; by 1987, the EC alone took virtually half, and most other destinations, except for North America, had declined in relative importance.

The tragedy is that visible trade with industrialized countries was not favourable. In 1973 the UK had the smallest dependence on EC markets of any of the nine EC members, and this was still the case ten years later. The central problem still seems to be that the UK is generally less adept than other developed economies at moving out of slow growth industries into

Table 2.2 Destination of UK exports of manufactured goods, 1970 and 1987 (per cent)

Destination	1970	1987
Western Europe, of which	45.2	58.9
EC	28.9	49.4
Other developed economies, of which	27.5	22.0
North America	14.6	16.3
Developing countries	23.3	17.2
Centrally planned economies	4.0	1.9
	100.0	100.0

Source: *Annual Abstract of Statistics*, 1971 and 1988

faster growing ones, such as scientific instruments and electronics' (Atkinson, 1983). Foreign imports into Britain continued to grow rapidly in the 1970s and 1980s while UK exports of manufactures levelled off from the late 1970s, making the UK a net importer of manufactured goods for the first time in the long history we have described (Figure 2.1). The UK's growth of total exports showed the slowest growth of any of 19 Industrial Market Economies for much of the last 25 years (World Bank, 1989); however, through the mid 1980s the decline of the UK's share of world trade was arrested at the level of about 8 per cent.

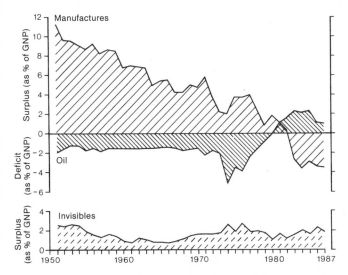

Figure 2.1 External balances on foreign trade, United Kingdom, 1951–1987. Source: *Annual Abstract of Statistics*, HMSO.

Economic level on the international ladder

The result of all these changes is two-fold, that the UK has been getting richer, but not as fast as the rest of the industrialized world. It is difficult for many to appreciate that it is now just an average 'industrialized country'. For the decade 1975–84, the OECD (Organization for Economic Co-operation and Development) reported for the UK a *decrease* in total manufacturing output of 4.3 per cent, while virtually all the other major industrial nations *increased* their output (though at a lower rate than before 1975) – Japan by 61.4 per cent, the USA by 41.6 per cent, Italy by 22.1 per cent, and West Germany by 16.0 per cent. However, from 1985 to mid 1989, UK manufacturing output increased by 19 per cent; the value of output from production industries, including North Sea oil, increased by 8 per cent, compared with 14 in OECD countries.

On the occasion of the Prime Minister's visit to the USSR in March 1987, the Soviet authorities put out a statement that the UK lay *seventeenth* in the world economic league. Using the measure of gross national product *per capita* in 1987, the World Bank (1989) also put the UK seventeenth on the world ladder, after 14 of the 19 Industrial Market Economies and two 'high income oil exporters', the United Arab Emirates and Kuwait. The UK's GNP of $10,420 *per capita* contrasted with an average for 42 'lowest income economies' of $290. However, such comparison of gross product per head of different countries at contemporary exchange rates with the dollar gives misleading results. It is possible to calculate hypothetical exchange rates to allow for the fact that specific commodities (say, bread, video cassettes etc.) are cheaper in country A than country B. Such comparisons of production on the basis of 'real income per head', or 'purchasing power parity' showed the UK in 1985 to have 64.8 per cent of the income of the USA, or 85.6 per cent of the average of six countries shown at Figure 2.2. On this basis the UK had held its own relative to the USA over 25 years but had fallen below the *average* of the six, certainly below Japan, West Germany and France; indeed Japan overtook the UK in 1972, West Germany in the early 1960s, and France in the late 1960s, but on this calculation the UK still lay ahead of Italy. In EC data for ten constituent countries, the UK ranked seventh for gdp *per capita* in both adjusted and unadjusted data. The effects of oil appeared to halt the decline in the 1980s, and it is a principal question for this book whether recovery is being, or can be, generated by the growth of services (such as financial services) provided to other countries (see below).

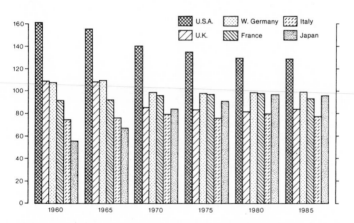

Figure 2.2 Relative gross domestic product at 'purchasing power parities', 1960–85 (average of six countries = 100). Source: EC Annual Economic Report, 1986.

International comparisons of employment

Demand in the US economy generated the net addition of 23 million new jobs in the period 1974 to 1986, fuelled partly by population growth, illegal immigration and lower increases in productivity than before. Figure 2.3 looks at a similar period for Europe. The strongest growth of total employment was reported by the USSR, in Scandinavia (which has the highest proportion of its population at work), and in a number of countries in central and eastern Europe such as Austria, Yugoslavia and Romania (a broadly similar pattern is evident for manufacturing employment). It is chiefly the

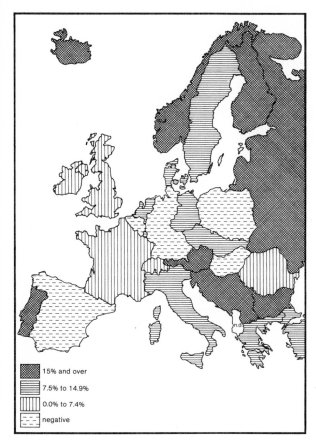

15% and over

7.5% to 14.9%

0.0% to 7.4%

negative

Figure 2.3 Change in total employment in Europe, 1971–86, by country. Source: International Labour Organisation, 1987, and OECD, 1988.

EC which failed to show any net increase of jobs in this period. The map shows falling employment in five countries: Poland, Spain, West Germany, Hungary and Belgium. The overall pattern has been attributed to a well-established preference on the part of western European firms (unlike those in the USA) to continue investing in labour-saving equipment. This may be the cause of semi-permanent structural unemployment, aggravated perhaps by excessively cautious government policies.

In the mid 1980s, unemployment in most western market countries reached its highest level since World War II. Part of this represented a disquieting pattern which had set in since the 1960s (see Table 2.3). But the immediate cause of the growth of unemployment in western Europe to a peak of 19 million in 1986 was a sharp deterioration since 1979 (Table 2.4) in Europe, but not in the USA. When, as here, figures are standardized between different countries, the UK exhibited the worst overall unemployment rates in 1982, but France and Italy were latterly suffering worse unemployment.

Table 2.3 Population and employment trends in non-Communist Europe, 1960–1987 (millions)

	1960	1975	1987
Total population aged 15 to 64	215.2	240.1	270.5
Economically active population	150.1	161.0	177.3
Employed population, including	145.8	149.8	155.3
Agriculture	36.6	23.9	19.6
Industry	53.3	56.0	48.7
Services	52.2	69.9	87.1
Unemployment: total	3.9	7.9	18.8

Note: 19 countries including Turkey
Source: *OECD Labour Force Statistics*, 1989

Table 2.4 Standardized unemployment rates for selected countries, 1968–87 (per cent)

	1968–73	1974–79	1979	1982	1987
USA	4.6	6.7	5.8	9.5	6.1
Japan	1.2	1.9	2.1	2.4	2.8
France	2.5	4.5	5.9	8.1	10.5
Italy	5.7	6.6	7.6	8.4	11.8
Germany	0.9	3.2	3.3	6.7	7.9
UK	3.3	5.0	4.6	10.4	10.3
EC	2.9	4.8	5.6	9.3	10.9

Source: *OECD Labour Force Statistics*, 1989

The European Commission can standardize unemployment data as be-tween constituent regions of their territory. Figure 2.4, for 1986, provides an intricate pattern of data but its outstanding characteristic is a distinction between 'core' and 'periphery' in the EC area. The 'core' of this unit has sometimes been seen as a 'golden triangle' based on Paris, London and Hamburg, whose prosperity was a function of accessibility to the rest of Europe. Keeble *et al.* (1982) show that the maximum value of accessibility to the European market lay in the area of the Ruhr/Benelux, and that poor access was one common causative factor in the higher unemployment rates of the peripheral regions of the Community. However, Figure 2.4 provides us with a different 'core area', suggesting perhaps there is something in Hall's (1987) identification of a larger triangle lying between Toulouse, Copenhagen and Florence. Some elements of a regular transition toward higher unemployment in the periphery appear on Figure 2.4, from eastern to western France, from south and east England to Ireland and Scotland, from northern to southern Italy, although the highest regional rates in the Community were encountered in southern Spain. If we were to present separate maps for unemployment by sex, the map for females would show southern Italy in a worse light, but female unemployment data are particu-larly prone to non-comparability because of wider differences between countries in the definitions used.

It would be valuable to study other variables across the map of the EC. Cheshire *et al.* (1986) have undertaken a multi-variate study of 103 urban regions of the EC. Through combining in 'discriminant analysis' measures of

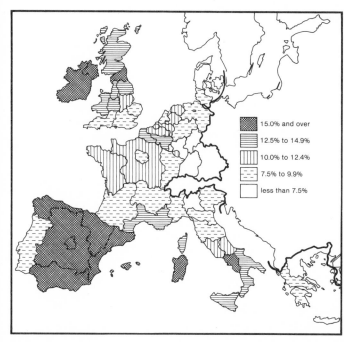

Figure 2.4 Harmonized rates of unemployment in the EC, April 1986, by region. Source: Eurostat estimates.

urban income, unemployment, migration and the demand for visitors' travel to the different centres, they rank the 103 'Functional Urban Regions' according to an index of their problems. The general pattern of results tends to confirm the impression that the UK is relatively poorly placed in the EC (in these data before the accession of Spain and Portugal). The UK had only four representatives in the first, prosperous, half of the list: Norwich (23), ·Brighton (28), London (34) and Leicester (35). Table 2.5 shows the UK's strong representation in the bottom ten places. The areas were also ranked according to 'the deterioration of their position in three constituent parts of the period 1971–84; Liverpool, Sunderland, Belfast and Glasgow appear in the bottom ten in all sub-periods. This is further evidence of a somewhat depressing saga, even for readers from the south of England.

Table 2.5 Ranking of worst Functional Urban Regions of the EC (see text)

Rank	Region	Location	Rank	Region	Location
103	Liverpool	North West	98	Naples	S. Italy
102	Sunderland	North	97	Newcastle	North
101	Glasgow	Scotland	96	Cagliari	Sardinia
100	Belfast	N. Ireland	95	Valenciennes	N. France
99	Charleroi	S. Belgium	94	Cosenza	S. Italy

Source: Cheshire, Carbonara and Hay, 1986

From leader to follower?

The relative decline of the UK economy has been accompanied by the loss of world leadership both in successive individual industries and in fields of social and welfare reform. This is only the logical concomitant of the view reported earlier, that there was a certain inevitability about the relative deterioration of the world's first industrial power. Again, we have mentioned that from the 1880s, certain advanced industries developed primarily in other countries (notably Germany and the USA) before the UK. Equally, the UK was bound to lose its leadership in relatively simple labour-intensive industries like textiles; this is the most widely spread industry in the world (Dicken, 1986), and a vital element of Third World employment. The longer-term benefit for the UK of the development of textiles in Lancashire and Yorkshire was to introduce, through the production of textile machinery, the skills of modern mechanical engineering. But even in metal-using industries leadership has been lost not only by the UK but also by Europe. Whereas as recently as 1950 half the world's ships were built in the UK (notably in Liverpool, Sunderland, Belfast and Glasgow), this role was taken by Japan (45.9 per cent in 1985), followed by western Europe (21.8 per cent), South Korea (11.5 per cent) and the Soviet Bloc (10.0 per cent). In the 1950s the UK was still second to the USA for its share of world manufacturing exports and produced half the world's export of motor cars. However, the industry was partly under US control, and in the late 1980s the only remaining motor-car manufacturer in UK hands, Rover, had only 15 per cent even of the UK market.

There are, of course, many links and parallels between economic history and the development of the government and social institutions. Town planning is of great interest in the map of contemporary Britain. It can be argued that town planning has its origins in the early cities of, say, Egypt or Mexico, or in the architecture of Renaissance Europe. 'But social ideas do not grow independently of their context. The idea of town planning was something that presented itself as an answer to a problem or group of problems which had arisen in contemporary urban life' (Ashworth, 1954, 2). Early industrialization created Victorian cities, and town planning was one of the measures adopted to correct the unhealthy and congested nature of the industrial city. Some of the first newly-planned settlements were established by Victorian industrialists themselves, but a long process of government legislation culminated in the passing, between 1945 and 1950, of comprehensive Town and Country Planning legislation, including provision for New Towns and National Parks but also a characteristically negative policy toward the expansion of cities themselves. The UK's New Towns have attracted international fame and study, and our approach to town planning became a model for the Commonwealth, Scandinavia, the Netherlands and Israel.

However, this record has been marred by the UK's relative lack of money to invest in new housing and public works and to maintain the existing stock. Successful post-war reconstruction was overtaken in the first half of the 1980s by economic depression and the European unemployment crisis. Thus, even if we look strictly inside the built-up urban area, conventional town planning has become much less relevant in the 1980s than the growth of crime and the condition of existing property for increasingly large sections of the community.

Meanwhile, the rest of Europe has moved ahead of the UK in other innovations in the urban environment. In many countries 'comparison shopping' has been largely decentralized from city centres to regional shopping centres. In the UK, such a centre was proposed in the early 1960s at Haydock Park, near the intersection of the M62 with the M6 between Liverpool and Manchester. Others were proposed on the outskirts of Leicester, Birmingham and Bristol. As retail centres they would probably have been a success, but they threatened existing centres and the needs of non-car owners: 'these and other proposals were greeted with hostility by planners and rejected largely on impact grounds' (Schiller, 1986, 13). The first free-standing regional centres in the UK are at Brent Cross, north London, and the Metro Centre, Gateshead, followed by the Meadowhall development, by the M1 near Sheffield.

In transport, too, the UK lost its early lead in rail and road development. The first European motorways were built in Germany and Italy in the 1920s and 1930s; the UK had active plans to follow them, but these were shelved on the outbreak of war, and the first British motorway was not built until 1958 (the Preston bypass). The length of motorway reached 1,000 kilometres only in 1970, but had grown to 3,110 kilometres by 1988. Italy and Switzerland electrified their main-line railways early in this century, but the UK had to wait till the 1960s for electrification from London to north-west England, and the late 1980s to Yorkshire. In 1984, 56.9 per cent of British Rail train kilometres were under electric haulage compared with 75.1 per cent in the EC as a whole. Furthermore, the leading European countries are now engaged in building new strategic lengths of fast track, which will hopefully link with the Channel Tunnel and with improvements in Belgium and the Netherlands to provide high-speed links between London, Paris, Brussels, Amsterdam and Cologne (Figure 2.5).

In contrast with the UK's decline towards the European material average, it is frequently asserted that the UK has maintained its lead in intellectual and research activity. This 'hypothesis of superior inventiveness' has some early support from the UK's discovery of penicillin, radar and the jet engine. Budworth (1986) has shown, however, that reports that 55 per cent of all 'significant' world inventions since the Second World War are of UK origin are a garbled version of a 1976 report for the United States' National Science Foundation. The total innovations counted for each country were 257 in the USA, 45 in the UK, 23 in West Germany and 17 in France. Even in the sub-class of 'radical breakthroughs', the USA outran the UK by 65 to 25 innovations. Thus, the UK was still a European leader in innovation in the 1950s and 1960s, but perhaps had a bias towards pure science rather than towards the commercial development of technological ideas that will form the next generation of industries.

Statistical data indicate that the UK has a low proportion of its 16, 17 and 18 year olds undergoing education compared with most western industrialized countries other than Spain and Portugal; however, a thorough review of eight measures of participation and spending on higher education showed

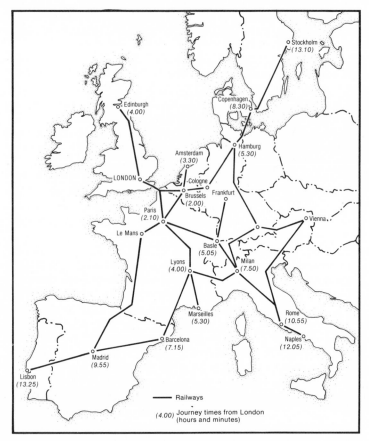

Figure 2.5 Projected high-speed European rail network, with estimated journey times from London. Source: *The Economist*, 11 March 1989, 81.

varying results on different measures (Department of Education and Science, 1987). At the same time, UK industry has been constrained by skill shortages at most times since the Second World War. It appears to be that the generally unskilled nature of the labour force helps to determine that the processes of UK industry are, by present international standards, relatively simple and low productivity ones; the country is locked into comparatively simple technology because it does not have the technical expertise to use technology to the fullest effect.

The 'New International Division of Labour'

The Transnational Corporation

The people who are in the best position to compare the costs, uses and potential of different national labour markets are often the decision-makers of Transnational Corporations (TNCs). These are companies which run or control economic activity in more than one country and can therefore, in locating new investment or abandoning old plants, take advantage of geographical differences between countries in the costs of production. (As in the usage of Dicken, 1986, the term Transnational Corporation is preferred here to the term Multinational Corporation, because there are few corporations with an equal footing in two or more leading countries, even in the EC.) The power of TNCs is very great because of the number of factories, warehouses, offices and research laboratories which they control in different countries. Of course, the UK has long been the home of large companies exploiting 'primary products' (plantation crops, furs, timber and minerals) in different parts of the Commonwealth and the world. But the 'multi-plant' manufacturing enterprise is fairly new. In 1963 the hundred largest UK enterprises controlled on average only 40 plants each *within* the UK: by 1972 this had increased to 72, and it is clear that this period of domestic expansion and takeovers was also the main period of international expansion by TNCs. They began to use their holdings in different regions and countries for different but complementary roles within their respective international patterns of plants, and thus had systematic effects on the evolution of employment patterns in different kinds of country.

In the UK the leading effect of international investment is the presence here of foreign TNCs' factories, of which the most prominent and well established remain those of US origin. American factories increased in number particularly between the wars, but the increase continued in the post-war period so that by 1977 they employed a total of 711,800 workers in the UK, or 70.2 per cent of all the employees of foreign-owned manufacturing firms. These foreign-owned firms were responsible for about 20 per cent of UK manufacturing output – a slightly lower proportion than in France, West Germany or Italy, but becoming more diverse as investment from the EC, Japan and other industrialized countries increased while that of the USA declined.

The net effect of foreign TNCs on UK unemployment is a hotly debated topic which we shall hope to resolve in later chapters. One basic reason for concern in industrialized countries is that the 'New International Division of Labour' (Froebel *et al.*, 1980) is alleged to involve a transfer of TNC manufacturing production from industrialized countries like the UK to new 'export processing zones' etc., in Third World countries such as Malaysia, and to production within the domestic markets of countries such as Brazil. On the one hand, it is argued that labour costs in advanced countries have become too high to be competitive for many industrial tasks. On the other hand, through the development of container transport, telecommunications and the division of production into simpler, semi-skilled tasks, technology has made it possible to transfer these tasks to new factories in Third World markets.

However, there are in reality few prominent cases of the direct transfer of production from the UK to the Third World. The UK evidence (Labour Research Department, 1987) confirms the view that outward investment by home-based manufacturing concerns has concentrated not in the Third World but in North America and western Europe (rather than the Commonwealth); it is the wish to have a stake in economies that are growing more rapidly than the UK which is the key factor in company decision-making. In the individual years 1980 to 1984, the proportion of investment going to Third World countries, as derived from a survey of the leading 40 UK manufacturing corporations, varied between 10 and 26 per cent.

The Labour Research Department (1987) argued that 'more and more, for large UK-based companies the UK has ceased to be the primary area of operations.' In the leading 40 corporations, overseas employment increased from 34 per cent in 1979 to 44 per cent in 1986. The overall flow of investment from UK TNCs involved the absolute and relative exporting of jobs to other countries. The 40 corporations increased their employment overseas by 125,000 between 1979 and 1986, while reducing jobs in the UK by 425,000. The UK not only remained the second largest source, after the USA, for foreign direct investment, but increased in importance after 1979 when the first Thatcher government abandoned most controls on the foreign exchange of sterling currency. Increasingly, therefore, TNCs take up international investment opportunities through international capital markets, and domestic companies have to compete for capital from the USA, Japan and other countries. Thus stock markets are no longer simply domestic institutions, one of the points we explore in the following section.

London's world status

The world's first industrial country has clearly fallen into relative decline on many measures of industrial competitiveness. How has it balanced its books with the rest of the world? The answer is that three other sectors have provided relief – the revenues of North Sea oil extraction from 1980 (an activity of limited life), the profits from selling services to other countries, and the profits on investment in other countries. A number of sub-regions of the UK, as we shall see, earn their living through providing tourist facilities or business services to other areas. The concept, however, is nowhere more relevant than for the London area itself, which has recently been reaffirmed as a home of the rapidly expanding international office sector.

The financial activities of the City of London both pre-date British industrialism and have survived its relative world decline. McRae and Cairncross (1984,2) argue that the growth of the City originated in the large volume of government borrowing in the eighteenth century to pay for Britain's foreign wars; the Industrial Revolution took place almost independently of the City, which thereby showed that it perhaps could survive on its financial wits as a major service centre.

> For the last twenty years of progressive manufacturing decline in Britain, the one optimistic assertion had been that while industry's contraction might be irreversible, at least the City of London remained the financial centre of Europe and second only perhaps to New York in the world. London's insurance and commodity markets, the inheritance of a century of British imperial and trade dominance before the First World War, remained the most truly international of their kind. British invisible foreign earnings from financial services were the largest in the world and for long had made up any deficit on visible trade.
>
> (Hamilton, 1986, 130–1)

Success was not automatic, since the country lacked the economic base and domestic resources of France and West Germany, let alone the USA or Japan. However, the ending of UK exchange controls in 1979, and government stimulation of a relaxation in trading regulations ('Big Bang' of 1986) helped to secure London's recognized position, with Tokyo and New York, among the world's three leading financial centres, which together, with their respective working days, provide for 24-hour activity in world financial markets.

The volume of the UK's resulting 'invisible earnings' is shown for 1987 in Table 2.6. On the net basis shown in the third column of this table, the UK has frequently stood second only to the USA, lying ahead of France and Germany. When we come to examine the employment trends of Greater London, we shall find that some of the most buoyant growth lies in 'business services', that is in firms providing specialist management advice, computer software, accountancy and advertising to banks, insurance firms, stock exchange partnerships and TNCs themselves. As Noyelle and Stanback (1984) have stressed, the growth of services for other firms, 'producer services', is critical in both USA and world geography; in the international division of labour, it is creating specialized centres of skilled workers in a small number of international centres of white-collar work. The UK is fortunate to have one of these 'world cities'.

Table 2.6 Leading flows of UK invisible trade, 1987 (£ millions)

	Credit	Debit	Net
Financial and related services	14 727	4 845	9 882
Travel	6 237	7 255	−1 018
Sea transport	3 341	4 465	−1 124
Civil aviation	3 270	3 764	− 494
Total	27 575	20 329	7 246

Note: the net total was reported to be negative by 1989.
Source: *Annual Abstract of Statistics*, 1989

Conclusion

What emerges from this broad review of international and historical trends is that international issues are all-important for Britain's internal geography. The country was a leader in the expansion of Europe, but holds only an average position in the European Community area as it becomes a more unified, single competitive market from 1992. In many ways, the modernization of industry and training remain critical for Britain's future in that market. The details of the harmonization of the financial system of Europe may threaten the City of London's position compared with European cities. The principal legacy of Britain's past world role lies in the important growth of the City in the 1980s, which of course benefits the provinces of Britain only indirectly.

Further reading

A recent study of European industrial development is provided by Trebilcock (1981), and data for individual countries can be updated from OECD (annual) and World Bank (annual).

The relationships between industrialism and the British Empire are reviewed in Hobsbawn (1969). The causes of Britain's relative decline are addressed in Allen (1979), and the thesis that British society, fatally, failed to embrace industrialism is developed in Weiner (1981).

Geographers' exploration of UK post-war foreign trade problems is exemplified in Hudson and Williams (1986), and critical reviews by economists of the foreign trading position are available from Kaldor (1966), and Singh (1977). An example of an industrial study is Dunnett (1980).

A translation from the original German provides a key text, Froebel *et al.* (1980). A reader on many current world issues is provided by Johnston and Taylor (1986). Dicken (1986) provides an extensive study of world industrial geography. The international role of UK financial services is explained in McRae and Cairncross (1984), and the changing US role of service employment is analysed in Noyelle and Stanback (1984).

3
Transformation towards a post-industrial society

A fundamental process of change is occurring within society both in the UK and certain other richer nations: this has been termed the emergence of 'post-industrial society' (Bell, 1973). For a century, the typical UK employee was male, engaged in manual factory work, and lived in a large industrial city or town – with many implications for leisure and health patterns. Yet we have already found in Chapter 2 that the UK has, relatively speaking, been suffering from declining international competitiveness as a place in which goods are actually made, though it has been holding its own in providing financial services on a world scale, and is prosperous enough, for example, to have a demand for hypermarkets on the international model. A pronounced shift towards decentralized smaller plants, and towards non-manufacturing activities in the economy, has already occurred.

The transformation to a 'post-industrial' society has further to go in some parts of the UK than others. Some areas, we shall find, are better characterized by the loss of manufacturing work and are 'de-industrialized', as opposed to 'post-industrial'. The latter denotes the arrival of new sources of employment and is clearly a better term for wide areas of the South East. How far will the transition spread, and how far will it solve the UK's socio-economic problems? These are central issues in this volume. Before assessing the impact of the process of change on different areas of the UK (in Parts II and III), it is essential to assess the character and pace of socio-economic change for the nation as a whole. This involves reference not only to average wealth and the structure of employment, but also to the social distribution of wealth and its spending. This must include spending by private individuals and by the state, the latter providing for 'collective consumption' of health and welfare services.

An outline of socio-economic change

Health and wealth in the UK today and yesterday

The greatest reform in access to health care was the setting up of the National Health Service in 1948. Even this has proved disappointing for its slow development of preventative medicine, but it contributed further to many changes. For instance, infant mortality, which had stood at 147 per thousand (births) at the turn of the century, was reduced to 20 per thousand in 1965 and nine per thousand in 1987. It is difficult to make broader international comparisons in social policy, but Kaim-Caudle (1973) placed the UK top among ten countries for its health service provision, though in his survey of wider social security policies the top place went more often to other countries, the Netherlands, West Germany and Denmark.

The fall in death rates was the most fundamental feature of change in the longer term. Expressed as crude annual rates per thousand, they fell from 23 in 1861–65 to 12 in 1931–35, but have since shown no further improvement due to the ageing of the population, and still stood at 11.4 in 1988. Birth rates fell somewhat later, from their peak of 35.5 per thousand in 1871–75 to 16.3 in 1931, before showing remarkable fluctuations after the war – with a peak of 18.8 per thousand in 1964, a trough of 11.9 in 1977, and a recent figure of 13.8 (1988). The delay between the long decline of death rates and that of birth rates yielded considerable 'natural increase' over much of the century.

The legacy of all these changes (Table 3.1) comprised only a very small UK rate of increase of total population in the 1970s and 1980s, but an increase in the size of school-leaving and working age groups (15–64) for much of this period, as well as a marked rise in the proportion of the population over 65, particularly of the very elderly. The latter, however, was less critical in the UK than the increase expected in other west European countries, notably West Germany. Table 3.1 and subsequent tables provide a comparison between the UK and developed countries as a whole, in the shape of averages for the EC (the present 12 countries of the European Community) and for the OECD (the EC plus 12 further countries: the USA, Canada, Australia, New Zealand, Japan, Austria, Finland, Iceland, Norway, Sweden, Switzerland and Turkey).

Table 3.1 Principal features of population change, 1961–87, UK, EC and OECD

		UK	EC	OECD
Total population (millions)	1961	52.8	282.5	648.6
	1971	55.9	305.6	722.8
	1981	56.4	319.2	786.5
	1987	56.9	323.7	819.8
Population from 15 to 64 years	1961	64.8	64.6	62.3
(as percentage of above)	1971	62.2	63.2	63.3
	1981	64.4	65.1	65.4
	1987	65.6	67.2	66.7

Source: OECD Labour Force Statistics, 1964–1984 (1986), 1967–1987 (1989)

A number of European countries, like the UK, fed a large volume of school-leavers onto the labour market in a period, the 1980s, of economic difficulty. Here the demographic fact of 1960s fertility ran directly counter to later economic events, whereas the 1990s already show a different combination of circumstances. What other relationships might exist between demographic and economic trends?

There were some suggestions that a lower rate of population increase, from the decline in the UK birth rate after 1964, was a cause of economic decline, as it reduced demand for the purchase of consumer durables. An analysis by Reddaway (1977) of the period 1961–71 showed that this view was wide of the mark; only 3 per cent of the purchase of motor cars and television sets in this period was attributable to population increase. The rest chiefly reflected greatly increased levels of *per capita* demand, in the consumer revolution of Galbraith's *Affluent Society* (1958). Four-fifths of households already had a television set by 1962 and the figure had grown to 98 per cent in 1988 (with 53 per cent having added a video recorder). With more spectacular growth in purchases of refrigerators, freezers and washing machines, the home provided physically less onerous domestic drudgery for housewives, and was more of a centre of leisure-time entertainment. Mobility increased too, as ownership of cars increased from one per ten people in 1960 to one per 3.2 at the end of 1987, or 0.85 per household. Average personal income rose in real terms by as much as 5 per cent per annum in the early 1960s, and continued to grow by an average of more than 1 per cent per year in the 1970s, resuming a level of 2–3 per cent per year in 1983–88.

The rise of unemployment up to 1986 raises many questions about the *distribution* of income in society, which we shall consider in the final part of this chapter. We can, however, be clear that the average household was spending its increased income in a very different way in 1985 compared with five decades earlier. In 1937/8 the average UK (industrial working-class) household had to spend 40.1 per cent of its income on food, compared with 30.4 per cent for all households in 1961, and only 19.0 per cent in 1987. The 1987 household had more spare income, within its weekly total of £188.62, for a wide range of other needs. Following the figure of 19.0 per cent are 16.1 per cent of income spent on housing and 14.3 per cent on transport (*Employment Gazette*, April 1989). Both these two figures have profound implications for migration, daily travel and tourism in UK sub-regions as they will be visualized in Part III, and for the growing purchase of services outside the home. Consumer expenditure does not vary greatly between regions, but the main North–South differences are outlined in Lewis and Townsend (1989).

The changing structure of work

Home and work are linked in many ways, notably because the location of work and of home are mutually related. However, different kinds of work may have different patterns of location (between countries, cities and regions), and a change in the structure of employment may thus be important for the relative economic prosperity of different countries, cities and regions. Many writers take the view that it is the changing structure of spending, described immediately above, which accounts for the changing structure of employment in modern western society. On the one hand, industry is achieving much greater productivity per worker than in previous decades, and so employing fewer production workers, yet paying much higher salaries and wages to the individual worker. On the other hand, he or she disposes this increased income over a wider range of services, many of which (it is asserted) are less capable of automation (increased productivity) than is the case in production of industrial goods. In restaurants, the Health Service or teaching, machines can be of assistance (for instance, in washing-up, diagnosis or use of videos respectively) but have not yet replaced the work of chefs, nurses or teachers. This has led to a changing ratio between service sector and industrial workers, in the same way that the number of industrial workers earlier overtook the number of workers on the land (Figure 3.1). Under the 'Fisher-Clark' hypothesis, industrialized countries have seen a progression from Primary employment (agriculture, forestry, fishing and mining) to Secondary employment (industrial activity in manufacturing and construction) and in turn to Tertiary employment (services including distribution, transport, finance and public services). In geographical terms, there has been a progression from work on the land to factory work, and in turn to jobs in shops, offices and hospitals.

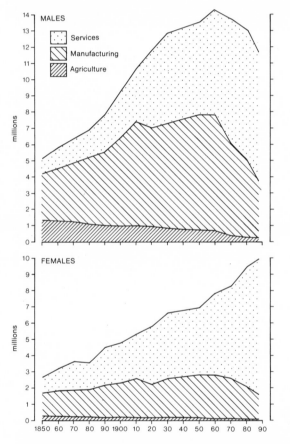

Figure 3.1 Sectoral changes in employment, Great Britain, 1850–1988. Source: Tilly and Scott, 1978; *Employment Gazette* (various).

There are several criticisms of this simple hypothesis. The most fundamental criticism challenges the contention that productivity in the service sector must necessarily remain low, because human tasks such as cooking, nursing or teaching cannot readily be replaced by machines. However, problems of measurement have led to underestimation of improvements in service-sector productivity expressed most recently in the drive towards self-service restaurants and petrol stations, and automated cash dispensers at banks. Secondly, as Gershuny and Miles (1983) stress, the nature of trading relationships between sectors is complex. On the one hand, manufactured goods like washing machines and power tools encourage consumers to provide their *own* services in the home (DIY – 'do it yourself'), while on the other, some of the large increases in service employment result from the provision of work by service enterprises for *other* firms. Thirdly, there are many historical and current variations in different developed countries' shares of employment in Primary, Secondary and Tertiary sectors (Urry, 1987b).

We may at this stage, however, rest the case on the changing structure of employment (Figure 3.1): this is basic to our study because, as we have said, Primary, Secondary and Tertiary sectors of the economy tend to have different locational patterns, and a shift from one sector to another may thus have fundamental effects on the geography of employment – and therefore of population. This process has been at work since the Industrial Revolution. Historical estimates of Table 3.2 indicate most firmly the decline in the relative importance of the Primary sector, which provided nearly a quarter of all jobs in 1841 but only 4 per cent by 1961. The Tertiary sector was already larger than the Primary in 1841 and provided virtually half of all jobs by 1961: it advanced most markedly between 1911 and 1931. The Secondary sector provided more than half of all employment between 1851 and 1921, but ended the period, as it began, with 48 per cent.

Table 3.2 Composition of the occupied population, by sector, 1841–1961 Great Britain (per cent)

	Primary	Secondary	Tertiary
1841	24	48	27
1871	17	52	31
1891	12	53	35
1911	9	55	36
1931	6	45	49
1951	5	49	46
1961	4	48	49

Source: Robertson, Briggs and Goodchild, 1982

A pronounced swing from Secondary to Tertiary employment was renewed around 1961. International comparison for the subsequent period (Table 3.3) indicates, *whatever the starting point in different countries*, a steady rate of change in the structure of employment in one direction, towards a greater share of employment in the Tertiary sector. In the OECD area as a whole, which includes the USA, service employment increased from 44 to 62 per cent of total employment, a swing of 18 'percentage points', while the EC and UK swing was of 20 points. (Despite changes of definition from Table 3.2 to 3.3, values for the UK in 1961 are closely comparable in both tables.) These are very substantial changes which are widely expected to continue in the 1990s.

Table 3.3 Composition of total employment, by sector,
1961–87, UK, EC and OECD (per cent)

		UK	EC	OECD
Agriculture	1961	4.6	20.2	20.8
	1971	3.1	13.1	13.3
	1981	2.6	9.3	9.7
	1987	2.4	7.9	8.4
Industry	1961	47.6	40.3	35.5
	1971	43.8	41.3	36.4
	1981	35.8	36.9	33.1
	1987	29.8	32.8	30.1
Services	1961	47.8	39.5	43.7
	1971	53.1	45.7	50.3
	1981	61.5	53.7	57.2
	1987	67.8	59.2	61.6

Note: Industry here includes mining & quarrying,
manufacturing, electricity, gas, water and construction
Source: *OECD Labour Force Statistics*, 1964–1984 (1986),
1967–1987 (1989)

Remarkably, the UK proportion of employment in industry fell below 30 per cent by 1987. It is when we look at data on the role of industry internationally that the emergence of a 'post-industrial society' is less clear. In the OECD area as a whole, industry's share of total employment passed its peak only in 1969, and its subsequent reduction in importance was more modest than in the UK, which, almost uniquely, has not only lost much factory employment but also suffered a net loss of factory output from 1974 to 1988. Even here, manufacturing's share of *production*, of 'gross domestic product', fell only from 30 per cent in the period 1961 to 1976 to 25 per cent in 1984 (Harris, 1987). We may conclude then that 'de-industrialization' is meaningful as a simple description of a relentless process in which the manufacturing sector suffers declining shares of total *employment*, inevitably leading to the service sector capturing a greater share, but that the process takes on a different pace and complexion in different countries and places.

Even *within* industry, however, pronounced shifts are in progress between different types of work. White-collar workers increased their share of manufacturing employment from 27.6 to 31.7 per cent between the 1971 and 1981 Censuses; that is to say that *services* provided in offices and laboratories *within* manufacturing concerns increased in relative importance and largely escaped the process of job reduction which took place on the shop floor. We may refer to the functions of manager, sales representative, typist, or industrial scientist, or for that matter fitter, as 'occupations'. Geographers have gradually realized that it may be more relevant to classify workers by their occupations than by their industries, firstly because large corporations may employ a different mix of occupations at establishments in different parts of the country (Massey, 1984), and secondly because of the different trends, incomes and social attributes attaching to manual and non-manual workers, and to different varieties of each.

We can extend this interpretation to the service (Tertiary) sector, for here *white-collar occupations* are both dominant and increasing further in relative importance. Thus, in the Health Service, nurses, doctors and technicians are tending to increase in number at the expense of more strictly manual jobs in hospital cleaning, cooking and domestic work. Again this contributes to a continuing shift from manual to non-manual occupations which is affecting most parts of the economy. This change can clearly be related to the country's net increase of average real income and the emergence of a clear majority of households which owned a car and owned their house (Table 3.4). The ownership of housing was encouraged by the Conservative governments of the 1980s, who obviously place great sociological significance on it themselves.

Table 3.4 Socio-economic characteristics of households, 1971–88, Great Britain (per cent)

	Higher status group*	Households with car(s)	Owner occupiers
1971	22	51	48
1981	27	61	56
1971–81 change	+ 5	+10	+ 8
1981	n/a	59	54
1988	n/a	65	64
1981–88 change	n/a	+ 6	+10

Note: *Households headed by persons in Socio-Economic Groups 1–5 and 13
Source: Population Census Small Area Statistics for 1971–81; General Household Survey for 1981–88

Occupation is, in turn, the principal determinant of the 'social class' or 'socio-economic' characteristics of different areas. On this basis, Table 3.4 shows that the share of economically active and retired persons in the 'higher-status groups' increased between 1971 and 1981 from 22 per cent to 27 per cent of the population. The majority of readers probably regard these features as self-evident, but they may not be aware of the speed with which UK society has changed in the last three decades, or, as we shall see, of the effects on areas which have not shared in the process. It is therefore critical to assess whether the shift towards service industries and service occupations will redress the problems of the rest of the community, accompanied by all their political and social ramifications.

New forms of employment

Gender

Many of the changes we have already discussed reflect a changed role for women, which is important for everyone's experience of contemporary Britain. In steadily increasing numbers (Figure 3.1) women have found time for paid work, itself closely involved with smaller families and, allegedly, with more labour-saving devices among consumption goods in the modern home. In many households the modern standard of living depends on married women finding jobs, often in service occupations, on a scale much greater than in the previous generation. A change of attitudes to the role of the sexes in paid work represents a revolution in the interpretation of gender, though female work remains different from male work in a variety of ways.

Recent research, however, suggests that, roughly speaking, 'we have been here before'. In the eighteenth century when the first Industrial Revolution was born, the home was a place of work for both sexes, in farmwork, handicrafts and textiles. The later growth of textile mills in the North West, Yorkshire and the East Midlands produced high rates of female participation in factory work in these areas, a relative regional difference which persisted until the 1960s (Women and Geography Study Group, 1984, 72). However, female participation rates there and in most regions fell from 1871 to 1921 (Marshall, 1986, 128). The proportion of women working in *other* people's homes, i.e. in domestic service, was a component of this and fell continuously throughout the century beginning in 1850. Some writers suggest that reduced participation in work was encouraged by Victorian moralists through an idealization of the role of the home, while others saw that in the early twentieth century 'the development of separate suburban environments in the maturing industrial/commercial city was itself of crucial importance in the establishment of the home as a separate sphere and in the enforcement of the social definition of a woman's place as being in the home' (Mackenzie and Rose, 1983, 169).

The great increase during this century has been in the paid work of married women. While the proportion of other women at work has re-mained between 40 and 60 per cent, the early decades (Table 3.5) showed 10 per cent or less of married females at work, compared with a recent (1988) figure of 55.7 per cent who were economically active. The source of the net increase of jobs has been the service sector; as shown in Figure 3.1, the number of females in manufacturing increased only marginally from 1850 to 1960, and then declined. Increased participation rates have occurred chiefly among mothers with children at school, and the immediate cause is that women are spending fewer years than before exclusively in child rearing. The fundamental reason for increased participation is sought in social

Table 3.5 Economic activity rates, by sex and marital status, 1921–88, Great Britain (per cent)

	Married Women	Other Women	Males
1921	8.7	53.8	87.1
1931	10.0	60.2	90.5
1951	21.7	55.0	87.6
1961	29.7	50.6	86.0
1971	42.2	43.7	81.4
1981	47.2	42.9	77.8
1988	55.7	44.6	75.4

Note: Based on population of 15 and over, except 1921 (12+), 1931 (14+), 1981 (16+)
Source: British Labour Statistics, Historical Abstract (1886–1968), Department of Employment and Productivity, 1971; Census of Population, 1981; 1988 Labour Force Survey, *Employment Gazette*, 1989, 183

change, and in the availability of improved washing machines, shopping facilities etc. Gershuny (1982) reported that these have saved time for working-class households and challenged the widespread contrary belief, instanced by Bowlby (1984), that technology has not in fact cut domestic labour. However, it is suggested here that the prime factor attracting women to work in the 1980s lay rather in *demand* for labour from the service sector, albeit at comparatively low rates of pay (Townsend, 1986a).

Socially, we have seen a change of almost revolutionary proportions; in terms of economics and economic geography, however, the pattern is less clear. Women's gross hourly earnings as a proportion of men's increased, under the influence of equal pay legislation, from 63.1 per cent in 1970 to 75.5 per cent in 1977. This peak was not reached again for a long period, but by 1989 it had reached 76.4 per cent (*Employment Gazette*, November 1989). Added to this differential in hourly pay was the effect of 'full-time' females working shorter hours, reducing their gross weekly earnings to 67.6 per cent of those of men. When we add to this in turn the effect of nearly half of all women working 'part-time', then the average income of all households where the married woman was working was only about 40 per cent higher than where the married woman was not working. Women's employment is thus commonly regarded as profitable only to a couple with a working husband. Where the husband is unemployed, the UK's national insurance laws make it of little financial advantage for a woman to take low-paid work. It is thus having one worker in the family that enables the other members to take low-paid work. Furthermore, Pahl (1984, 336) concluded that the contrast between households with jobs and those without extended to unpaid work around the home: 'The contrast between households with money being productive and busy and the households without money being unproductive and idle is the overwhelming conclusion . . .' Halsey arrives at a similar finding, after rejecting the view that women's work may have moderated the 'class-ridden' nature of British society:

> Sexual inequality is a dimension of social stratification in its own right. But its impact on class inequality . . . is to sharpen class division. Socially assortative mating increases the spread of income and wealth between families 'headed' by individuals (usually males) of different occupational class. Significantly also there is a high correlation between husband's and wife's unemployment.
>
> (Halsey, 1986, 36)

Changing terms of employment

In general, the rise of female employment can be seen as part of a transcending trend which divides the workforce between two broad groups. On the one hand are employers' most important workers, possessing most of the central skills on which the organization depends; on the other are auxiliary workers with fewer specific skills and less security of tenure in their jobs, the latter including most of the women workers. Most organizations, very remarkably, are heading in the direction of a stronger division between the two types:

> The emerging model is one of horizontal segmentation into a core workforce, which will conduct the organizations' key, firm-specific activities, surrounded

by a cluster of peripheral groups. Their twin purpose is to protect the core group from numerical employment fluctuations while conducting the host of non-specific and subsidiary activities which all organizations require and generate. The core group is required to be functionally flexible; the numerical flexibility secured from the use of peripheral groups provides the core group with employment security as the basis of their functional flexibility in the face of change. Peripheral groups may be made up of employees or of workers bought in on a sub-contract basis. The exploitation of a range of alternative contractual and working time arrangements permits firms to secure precisely the number and types of such secondary workers that they might require at any time.

(Atkinson, 1985, 3)

This division between 'core' and 'peripheral' workers was hastened by the concentration of redundancies, from 1979 to 1981, among male manual workers. This contributed to a fall of 423,000, from 1971 to 1981, in the number of males at work. On the other hand there was an increase in overall activity rates between 1971 and 1981 (Table 3.6), which was due to the increase (of 692,000) in working females. Yet, in that period the number of females working part-time increased by a larger amount, 974,000, so there was a decrease in female full-time work. The UK's overall 1987 activity rate of 49.6 per cent was exceeded by only one EC country, Denmark. However, the UK economically active included still large proportions who were unemployed and receiving unemployment benefit, and a proportion of females working part-time, 43.9 per cent, which was exceptionally high. It is possible to adjust the data for the high proportion of part-time workers, by assuming that two of them are equivalent to one full-time worker. When this adjustment is made, the UK's distinction disappears; it is merely an average EC country for its level of human activity in the economy, expressed in terms of 'full-time equivalents' per head of population (for details by GB region, see Table 6.11 below).

Table 3.6 Economically active as percentage of total population, 1961–87 UK, EC and OECD

	UK	EC	OECD
1961	46.8	43.8	43.3
1971	45.1	41.6	42.9
1981	47.4	42.5	45.3
1987	49.6	43.9	46.6

Source: *OECD Labour Force Statistics*, 1964–84 (1986), 1967–87 (1989) at work or seeking work

The emergence of a distinction between the full-time workforce and a large part-time group is a comparatively recent phenomenon. If we take the engineering industry, we find that 'normal' weekly hours were reduced from 58.5 in 1851 and 47 between the two world wars to a '40-hour week' in 1968. However, the regular use of overtime meant that adult male manual workers were still undertaking an average week of 44.2 hours in 1988. But holidays with pay of more than two weeks had become increasingly common from 1965 onwards. Security, high income and 'fringe benefits' such as paid holidays are seen to characterize the 'core' workforce, while the peripheral workforce has a lower income, a minimum of 'fringe benefits' and generally shorter, though variable, hours. Pahl (1984) asserts that it is the last hundred years that have been the aberration compared with the greater flexibility of both earlier periods and the present time. Many writers have asserted that the USA's high level of growth in employment since the 1970s has been achieved only by incorporating many people in the low-paid 'peripheral' workforce.

It is argued that the UK in the 1980s showed a similar transformation. The predominance of secure full-time jobs gave way under pressure of high unemployment, weakened trade unions, rising female employment, and the removal of labour market restrictions, to a more flexible workforce, which we can categorize as comprising *part-time workers* (conventionally defined as undertaking less than 30 hours per week), *home workers* or *home-based workers, temporary staff*, and the *self-employed* (frequently undertaking work sub-contracted from normal employers); some of these people may be undertaking a 'second job' in addition to their main one.

For the sake of the country's geography, it may be that the growth of 'core' workers is concentrated more in some regions and types of area than in others. We shall consider these changes in more detail in Chapter 6, and relate them to spatial data by reference principally to female and part-time employees. Their implications are important, particularly for the standards of living of 'peripheral workers'. These contribute to many *distributional* questions concerning the share of the UK's current wealth enjoyed by different social groups.

The politics of the post-industrial transformation

The distribution of income

It is important to study the changing distribution of income between social groups in the present context, because it may carry with it changes in the distribution of income between different types of place. For instance, there had been a trend, in the early 1970s, towards a more equal distribution of income between regions of the UK, but this was reversed under the Conservative government after 1979, when the share of national income received by south-east England increased in connection with the location of wealthier groups. A key point is the question whether individual socio-economic groups enjoy a better life through being concentrated together; does the overall social composition of an area enhance or reduce the prospects of individuals in a given socio-economic group? In a detailed examination of the issue, Donnison and Soto (1980) argue that, on the whole it does not, i.e. that location is more important than the social composition of an area for the individual.

Detailed trends in the distribution of income at any one time are the net result of many forces, several of which we have mentioned already. Among positive features were the growth of service-sector employment, including notably public services in the 1960s and early 1970s and financial and business services in the 1980s; the increase of North Sea oil production from 1979 to 1985; and the recovery of overall output, reflected in the real growth of disposable income from 1982 to 1989. Negative features relate principally to manual workers and the manufacturing workforce. The latter fell from 7.7 million in 1973 to 5.1 million in 1990 because of the effects of recession conditions in 1979–82, the accelerated growth in productivity after 1980 and the application of new technology. We shall see later in Part II that this decline of manufacturing employment was closely identified with the heavy growth of unemployment in the 1980s, and with its concentration in most industrial towns and cities outside the South East, places which typically had rates of unemployment of 14 to 20 per cent. This loss of income became generalized, through the play of the labour market, to less skilled families, to school-leavers, to ethnic minorities, and to the sick and disabled to create what has been described as a 'deprived underclass'. There is mounting evidence that unemployment accentuated the contrasts in health among different social classes in the UK. Features of deprivation were closely correlated with each other, socially and spatially, and caused widespread comment on the emergence of 'two nations' (Martin, 1987, 1989a).

The influence of government and politics

Viewed on the longer scale, this century saw slow progress toward a more equal distribution of income until the mid 1970s, when the process was reversed (Halsey, 1986, 39). Why was this allowed to happen; or to put it another way, why were issues of distribution within society put into second place?

Under the 'post-war consensus' the long boom in the economy allowed Conservative governments (1951–64, 1970–74) as well as Labour (1945–51, 1964–70, 1974–79) to engage in the redistribution of resources to poorer groups and areas through 'progressive taxation' (taxing income at higher rates in higher-income groups) and through expenditure on social security programmes, supplementary benefit, education, health, etc. In addition to being the party representing the interests of wealthier people, Mrs Thatcher's Conservative governments of the 1980s argued that the UK's competitive position was so difficult that the interests of production had to come firmly before redistribution.

The effect of the changes in the patterns of taxation and public spending was to accentuate an underlying inequality in income distribution. The bottom 40 per cent of households saw their share of national income fall from 8.7 per cent in 1981 to 6.0 per cent in 1986. The top fifth increased their share from 46.4 to 50.7 per cent (Table 3.7). By the mid 1980s, therefore the poor were significantly worse off, relative to the rest of the population, than ten years earlier, although in absolute terms their purchasing power improved.

In association with this trend, there was renewed attention to longstanding evidence on the effects of poverty on health, in association with government restrictions on the growth of Health Service spending. The effect of economic difficulties on health and health spending is debatable, but one conclusion was given as follows:

> There is no question that inequalities in health between rich and poor do exist and that poverty causes ill-health. But it is highly questionable whether the health gap is getting wider. The rise in long-term unemployment and the

Table 3.7 Distribution of income, by households, 1976–86, UK (per cent)

Income Measure	Households grouped by income				
	Bottom fifth	Next fifth	Middle fifth	Next fifth	Top fifth
Original income					
1976	0.8	9.4	18.8	26.6	44.4
1981	0.6	8.1	18.0	26.9	46.4
1986	0.3	5.7	16.4	26.9	50.7
Disposable income (after direct taxes)					
1976	7.0	12.6	18.2	24.1	38.1
1981	6.7	12.1	17.7	24.1	39.4
1986	5.9	11.0	16.9	24.4	42.2

Source: *Social Trends*, HMSO (1989), Table 5.18

increase in child poverty since the mid 1970s is likely to mean that the health of the lower social classes is improving more slowly than it should and would have done, rather than that it is getting worse.

(Le Grand, 1987, 22)

Le Grand's calculations stressed that upward social mobility meant there are now fewer people in manual and unskilled social classes than 20 or 30 years ago.

This major social trend has widespread implications in different kinds of geography, not least in connection with elections. There is considerable debate over the long-term significance of this trend in politics; does it have a clear effect, in turn, on the influence of the Labour party? Halsey (1986) suggested that the steady fall in Labour's percentage share of the vote from 1964 to 1983 was attributable not primarily to people of a given social class voting differently over time, but to a straightforward decline in the working-class population, which affected many parliamentary constituencies: 'The dominant class had grown from 18 per cent of the electorate in 1964 to 29 per cent in 1983 while the working-class proportion had dropped from 47 to 31 per cent' (Halsey, 1986, 88).

Accompanying this possible result of 'de-industrialization' was the growth of alternative, mainly middle-class parties including the Liberal Democrat party, SDP, Scottish and Welsh Nationalists and the Green party. The Green party reflected more widespread concern for the environment, especially in the European elections of 1989. A Gallup Survey (Heald and Wybrow, 1986, 151) had earlier reported that a majority (57 per cent) preferred protection of the environment even at the expense of holding back economic growth. On the other hand, 32 per cent felt that economic growth should be given priority even if the environment suffered to some extent. There was, however, a generation gap: young adults, aged from 18 to 34, put the environment first by a margin of 63 per cent to 28 per cent, but senior citizens were almost evenly divided. Clearly, the post-industrial world is changing attitudes as well as places. There are thus significant differences between places in voting patterns generally, and in attitudes to the debate about growth and the environment, because social and demographic groups are not evenly distributed across the country.

Conclusion

In this chapter we have considered the rapidly changing size and composition of the 'national cake'. This evolution may itself have the potential to alter Britain's geography, through providing built-in advantages for some occupations and places and relative disadvantages for others. Much of the governmental life of a western nation also concerns the politics of distribution, above all the distribution of wealth between social classes. As, however, social classes are unevenly distributed over the map of Britain, then the politics of distribution also quickly becomes a geographical matter implicitly, if not explicitly through spatial policies. Some social geographers might consider it sufficient to emphasize the national issue of distribution, leaving the spatial outcome as a secondary by-product. We, however, consider it necessary now to disaggregate the main national trends into their principal spatial components in Part II, before considering the different circumstances and politics of four broad geographical types of area of Britain in Part III.

Further reading

A prime example of geographers interpreting international socio-economic change is Dicken and Lloyd (1981). Social and economic polarization in this country are considered by geographers in Hudson and Williams (1989) and in McDowell *et al.* (1989). There are many histories of UK change by sociologists, but a good example is Halsey (1986). The individual reader can most conveniently update statistical trends for topics in this chapter by reference to *Social Trends* and *Regional Trends* (HMSO, annual) and OECD (annual).

Demographic trends are analysed by Compton (1982), and by Lawton (1982). Another useful study, which looks at the implications of demographic trends for a range of different activities at the national level, is Ermisch (1983). On health and social services, valuable perspectives are provided by two volumes: from that of British social administration by Titmuss (1976), and in terms of international comparison by geographers Joseph and Phillips (1984). The relationship with social inequality is considered in Whitehead (1987).

The best introductions by a geographer to international trends in the service industries and their various interpretations are by Daniels (1982, 1985). A refreshing view of the changing nature of work, especially in the home, is provided by Pahl (1984). New forms of employment are explored by Redclift and Mingione (1985). The first major introduction to feminist geography, including women's employment, is by the Women and Geography Study Group of the IBG (1984). Changes in women's roles are studied by Mackenzie and Rose in Anderson *et al.* (1983), and by Beechey (1986).

Inequality and the response to it are themes of many geographical and political studies. The example of a geographer's approach is provided by Knox (1982). An example from political science is Leys (1983).

PART II

The Geographical Impact

4

Population change

At a superficial level the recent history of population in Britain conveys an almost static picture. Yet under this placid surface there are strong forces of demographic restructuring at work. Chapter 3 has referred to the very low overall rate of national population growth in recent years. However, the collapse in the birth rate from its peak in the mid 1960s, which was primarily responsible for this, was itself a major event with long-term implications. Mention has already been made of the inexorable movement of the 1960s 'baby boom' through schooling age during the 1970s to entry into higher education and the labour force in the 1980s. These are not the only changes. The legacy of Britain's largest ever baby boom, dating from the early years of this century, manifested itself in the growth of the numbers of people of pensionable age in the 1960s and 1970s and the dramatic increase in the numbers of the very elderly in the 1980s. For various reasons including the growth of the elderly population, the fall in the birth rate, the increase in the number of young adults and the rising divorce rate, the long-term trend towards smaller average household size has continued and even accelerated over the past two decades. At the same time, Britain has been developing into an increasingly plural society, with a major increase in the size of the non-white ethnic groups alongside a decline in the size of the white population.

It is inconceivable that these dramatic changes in demographic structure could have taken place without a major effect on the geographical distribution of population in Britain and on its composition in different localities. In fact, they have been accompanied by a massive redistribution of population away from the largest cities to smaller settlements and more rural areas and by an acceleration of the drift from North to South. Across much of the advanced western world the 1970s are now synonymous with the phenomenon of 'counterurbanization'. This term was coined by Berry (1976) to denote a turnaround in net migration flows, away from greater concentration of population in a small number of major agglomerations, and towards a revival of population growth in more rural areas and peripheral regions. In the UK, as in many other countries, however, this trend of deconcentration slowed down in the later 1970s. By contrast, the early 1980s were dominated by the re-emergence of the drift to the South East which had been such a focus of attention in the 1950s and early 1960s. As a result, the 'inner city problem' has changed somewhat in character since it was first recognized as a major political issue in the mid 1970s. That is because the resurgence of development pressures in the more central parts of the larger cities, particularly London, has proved a very mixed blessing to the low-income residents which these areas have inherited.

These shifts in population distribution result partly from the changes in demographic structure just described, but the links are not always clear. It is migration patterns that are primarily responsible for these shifts, and they are also related to changes in residential preferences and to trends in the location of employment and housing opportunities. What is certain, however, is that these structural and geographical changes in the population have, in combination, produced a profound transformation in the population size and composition of most places in Britain over the past two decades. It is a major finding that the socio-demographic profiles of individual localities have become increasingly distinctive. It is also the case that demographic forces are looming ever larger in determining the way in which the geography of Britain is evolving. Already it is possible to identify significant differences between changes in the distribution of population and employment, but the developments of recent years have sown the seeds for potentially much greater dislocation in the future. It is this increasingly autonomous nature of population change that prompts us to tackle this subject first in our review of the broad geographical patterns underlying the changes affecting individual places. This is also the reason why, having examined the main dimensions of employment change in the next two chapters, we return to the topic of population in Chapter 7. This investigates more fully the nature and scale of the dislocation between trends in the distribution of people and jobs, and examines the barriers which appear to restrict the efficiency of the 'matching processes' in the labour and housing markets. The purpose of the remainder of this chapter is to analyse the changing structure and composition of the national population, assess the principal dimensions of population redistribution, and examine the impact which both these sources of change are having on the geography of Britain.

Key demographic trends

Overall numbers of people

The principal dimensions of overall population change in the UK are shown in Figure 4.1 Somewhat paradoxically, the total population has changed relatively little in size since the early 1970s, but this in itself represents a significant change from previous experience. Official estimates put the UK's mid-1988 population at some 57,065,000 – the highest level yet, but only 1.1 million or 2.0 per cent larger than in 1971. This compares with an average *annual* increase of 0.5–0.6 per cent in the 1950s and 1960s. Particularly dramatic was the reduction in growth rate which took place between the mid 1960s, when the annual increase reached almost 400,000, and the five years

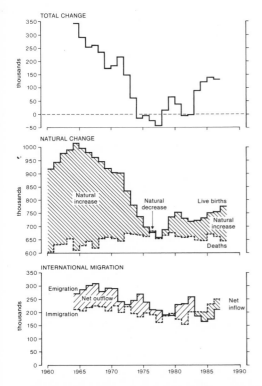

Figure 4.1 Population change and its components, UK, 1960–87. Total change is calculated as the sum of natural change and net international migration and excludes other changes such as movements of Armed Forces, the effects of changes in the definition of population, and other statistical adjustments. Source: *Annual Abstract of Statistics*, various years.

1973–78 when the national population was virtually static in size. Since the early 1980s something of an upturn has occurred, with annual increases in excess of 100,000 being recorded in the mid 1980s (Figure 4.1).

Components of national population change

The direct causes of these trends can be expressed in terms of the contribution made by births, deaths and international migration. All three components had a hand in producing the marked reduction in annual growth rate between the first half of the 1960s and the first half of the 1970s, but the dominant feature was the fall in the number of births. While the average number of deaths climbed by 37,000 a year between these two periods and the rate of net emigration from the UK is estimated to have increased by 47,000 a year, the annual average number of births fell by 222,000. The annual statistics plotted in Figure 4.1 reveal that the number of births declined by one third from a peak of over one million in 1964 to less than 660,000 in 1977. Since then the birth rate has recovered somewhat, leading to modest rates of natural increase. The mid 1980s were also associated with a switch in the direction of the international migration balance. The fairly consistent pattern of net losses recorded since the mid 1960s was replaced in 1983–88 by substantial net gains (Figure 4.1). This was brought about principally by a sharp fall in emigration by British citizens, but was reinforced by some increase in immigration by both British passport-holders and others.

Ethnic composition

The relatively small amount of movement in the national population total since the early 1970s, however, masks the considerable changes that have taken place in the composition and structure of the population. Amongst the most remarkable is the growth in Britain's ethnic minorities. Their combined size was estimated at only around 200,000 people in 1951, but was six times larger by 1971 and put at over 2.4 million by the mid 1980s (Shaw, 1988). Indeed, for some years now, Britain's non-white population has totally dominated the nation's population growth. In the fifteen years 1971–86 its increase by over 1.2 million people compared with an increase of only 672,000 in the total population of Great Britain, indicating that Britain's white population fell by some 560,000 over this period. This replacement of whites by non-whites derives partly from the general pattern of international population exchanges reigning since the late 1940s, with net outflows of British citizens and net inflows of residents from the former colonial territories. It has, however, been made more visible in recent years by the lower national birth rate and by the strong natural increase of immigrant groups, resulting from their youthful age structure and relatively high fertility. By the mid 1980s over two-thirds of Britain's non-white population was made up by just three broad cultural groups – Indians (760,000), West Indians (534,000) and Pakistanis (397,000).

Age distribution

Age patterns have also been undergoing major changes in recent years. Britain's passage through the 'demographic transition' in the nineteenth and early twentieth centuries, associated with rising life expectancy and falling fertility (Chapter 3), long ago began to change the nation's age 'pyramid' into a rectangular shape. Even so, the number of people moving through particular age groups has varied substantially over the past two or three decades. International migration has played a part since young adults and families are more than proportionately represented in these flows, but the prime factor is the variation in the size of age groups resulting from previous fluctuations in births.

As a result, the size of almost all age groups has changed substantially over the past two decades, in marked contrast to the small increase registered by the overall population. As shown in Table 4.1, the numbers of pre-school and school-age children were both about one-fifth lower in 1988 than in 1971, together contracting by some 2.7 million. Meanwhile, the number of 25–44 years olds grew by a similar amount, with both the constituent age groups expanding by 20 per cent. The largest percentage

Table 4.1 Age structure, UK, 1971–88

Age group	1971		1988		1971–88 change	
	000s	%	000s	%	000s	%
0–4	4 551	8.1	3 747	6.6	− 804	−17.7
5–14	8 916	15.9	7 013	12.3	−1 903	−21.3
15–24	8 145	14.6	8 977	15.7	+ 832	+10.2
25–34	6 971	12.5	8 387	14.7	+1 416	+20.3
35–44	6 512	11.6	7 853	13.8	+1 341	+20.6
45–59	10 201	18.2	9 264	16.2	− 937	− 9.2
60–74	7 986	14.3	7 971	14.0	− 15	− 0.2
75+	2 644	4.7	3 852	6.8	+1 208	+45.7
Under 16	14 256	25.5	11 537	20.2	−2 719	−19.1
16–PA	32 549	58.2	35 116	61.5	+2 567	+ 7.9
PA & over	9 123	16.3	10 412	18.2	+1 289	+14.1
Total	55 928	100.0	57 066	100.0	+1 138	+ 2.0

Note: PA = pensionable age (65 for men, 60 for women)
Source: calculated from *Population Trends* 57 (Autumn 1989), Table 6

increase, however, was recorded by the very elderly – the survivors of the large birth cohorts dating from the early years of this century – with the number of people aged 75 and over up by 46 per cent on their 1971 level.

These changes have had massive implications for the provision of age-specific services such as maternity facilities, school places, youth training, elderly health care and sheltered housing. Particular problems arose as the baby boom of the late 1950s and early 1960s 'came of age', with pressures on higher education, the job market and the housing stock. For instance, the number of working-age people (16–pensionable age) grew by 1.2 million between 1971 and 1981 and by a further 1.3 million in the seven years up to 1988, while the age groups spanning the period of most intense new household formation (15–44 years old) contained 3.6 million more people in 1988 than at the beginning of the 1970s.

Household size and structure

Alongside these changes in age structure, and partly related to them, have been some substantial changes in the way in which people group themselves into households. These trends are potentially very important because the number of people in a household and the composition of the households – in terms of such characteristics as sex, age and relationships to each other – both have a strong influence on the preferred type and location of housing accommodation. Any change in the size and structure of households in a particular place or for the nation as a whole will have substantial implications for housing requirements and land-use planning. Over the last two decades, households have been shrinking in size, increasing in number and becoming more varied in their type. The reduction in fertility from the mid 1960s peak has led to a decrease in the average size of family households, with a very marked drop in the number of very large households. The increase in the number of elderly people, together with a rise in the proportion living alone, has boosted the number of small households, as too has the higher divorce rate. It has also been spurred on by the growing tendency for young adults to seek accommodation away from their parents' home and, particularly in the 1980s, by the increase in the numbers of young adults resulting from the baby boom.

The overall effect on household size and composition can be gauged from the following statistics. According to the General Household Survey, the proportion of one-person households went up from 17 per cent in 1971 to 26 per cent in 1988, while that of households with six or more people fell from 6 to 2 per cent. Average household size fell from 2.91 in 1971 to 2.70 in 1981 and was down to 2.48 by 1988, a fall of 15 per cent from 1971. Not surprisingly, the increase in the number of households in Great Britain was running far ahead of the rate of population growth over this period, totalling some 20 per cent for 1971–88. In absolute terms, there were three extra households for every extra member of the population over this period, generating a very much higher level of new housing need than reflected in the overall population figures. Recent years have also seen a swing away from the traditional 'family' household. By 1988, married couples with children made up no more than 26 per cent of all households in Britain. Married couples without children, including 'empty nesters' (older families whose children have left home) as well as newly-married partners, form the largest single group of households at 36 per cent of the total, while the proportion of households comprising lone parents with children stood at 8 per cent in 1988.

Geographical implications

These key demographic developments of the past 20–30 years have had a major impact on regional and local populations in the UK. This has occurred in two ways. One is that, because in general these trends are not only national but also nationwide, the structure and composition of the population in each place in Britain has to some extent tended to change along similar lines, albeit not at precisely the same rates. Thus most places are now characterized by longer life expectancy, lower fertility, higher average age, smaller household size and more lone-parent families than they were in the early 1960s. The other notable consequence is that these changes can lead to alterations in the distribution of population between places. For instance, with lower household size, a fully built-up town must decline in population, given its essentially fixed stock of dwellings. This is particularly likely to occur for larger cities with very limited amounts of vacant land and in rural areas where environmental and other considerations have led to the imposition of strict controls on new building.

These demographic forces can also operate in more subtle ways. For instance, the 'coming of age' of a baby boom can be expected to lead to higher levels of migration towards the 'bright city lights', while the subsequent increase in the numbers of young couples is likely to lead to greater demand for family-size housing and suburban residential locations. In such ways can basic demographic developments, which are normally monitored at national level, promote changes in population distribution through their influence on migration. These work alongside other factors such as trends in the distribution of employment opportunities at both regional and more local scales and changes in the preferences of individuals about the types of places that they would like to live in.

Migration and changes in population distribution

Just as with population structure and composition, so also the patterning of people across national space is highly dynamic despite the low level of national population growth in recent years. Three principal dimensions have dominated geographical patterns of population change in the second half of the twentieth century. Though often difficult to distinguish in practice, in the simplest terms they relate to the three main spatial scales of economic and social organization. They involve, firstly, the change in the balance between Britain's two broad geographical 'nations' from North to South; secondly, the 'urban–rural shift' from larger metropolitan centres to smaller cities and towns, including those situated in the more remote and rural regions; and thirdly, suburbanization and local metropolitan decentralization within the commuting hinterlands of individual urban centres. They differ in their date of onset and in their scale and relative importance over time. The most dramatic development of the last quarter of a century has been the emergence of the urban–rural shift as a major factor in population redistribution, but in the late 1970s and early 1980s its strength waned somewhat, as too did the pace of local decentralization, whereas the North–South divide reasserted itself at this time after a period of lower significance.

Migration holds the key to understanding these shifts in population distribution. Because as recognized a century ago by Ravenstein (1885, 1889) most movement takes place over shorter distances, migration's role in population change becomes more important as the spatial scale of analysis descends. Moreover, its significance has increased in recent years relative to the role of natural increase. This is partly because the once marked regional and local differences in rates of natural increase – characterized notably by high fertility in rural areas and high mortality in towns – have diminished (Armitage, 1987). At the same time, levels of residential mobility have tended to increase in gross terms, giving the potential for more rapid and substantial net changes in population distribution. In the last twenty years the importance of migration has been reinforced by the decline in rates of natural increase; now that births and deaths are almost in balance, migration is the crucial determinant of whether population grows or contracts even at the national level. Finally, because it tends to be selective in terms of the types of people involved, migration also has the power to produce substantial and rapid changes in the population composition of individual places.

The North–South drift

For at least half a century, as outlined in Chapter 1, the dominant movement of population and employment at this 'two Britains' scale has been from

North to South. This represents a reversal of the prevailing trends of the nineteenth century and is re-establishing the broad distribution found before 1750, dominated by the national capital and the rich agricultural lowlands (Osborne, 1964; Department of the Environment, 1971). The shift of people into the Midlands and south of England slowed substantially during the later 1960s and early 1970s, but its subsequent re-emergence formed one of the key features of the 1980s, along with the 'transfer' of large parts of the Midlands into the North (Green, 1988; Lewis and Townsend, 1989; Martin, 1989a).

According to the annual data on migration and population change provided by the National Health Service Central Register and mid-year population estimates, the re-opening of the North–South divide appears to date from the first half of the 1970s. If the South is redefined to include only the four regions of the South East, South West, East Anglia and the East Midlands, then the net movement of people from North to South can be seen to have risen from a low point of only around 10,000–20,000 a year in the early 1970s to a peak of nearly 70,000 by 1985–86 (Figure 4.2). In terms of overall rate of population growth, the gap between the four regions of the South and those comprising the rest of Great Britain – which had narrowed to only 1.6 points (per thousand people a year) in 1974–77 – widened progressively through the remainder of the 1970s and into the 1980s (Table 4.2). Particularly impressive has been the major revival of the South East since the mid 1970s, but there has also been a return to strong growth in the other three regions of the South in the mid 1980s. By contrast, all northern regions suffered badly in the early 1980s and only Wales exceeded the national rate of recovery in 1984–87 (Table 4.2). Employment conditions were clearly involved (Chapter 5).

Moreover, it is not only the quantity but also the composition (or 'quality') of the North–South drift that appears to be affecting the balance between the two parts of the country. Since the 1920s concern has been expressed over the fact that it tends to be the younger and better qualified people who are

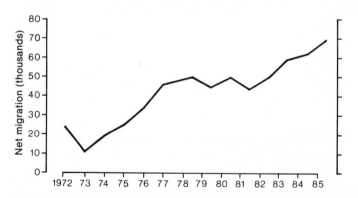

Figure 4.2 Net migration to the South from the rest of Great Britain, 1971–86. South refers to the South East, South West, East Anglia and East Midlands. Source: data for 1971–78 comprise two-year running averages estimated from Ogilvy, 1982; 1978/79 onwards from OPCS Monitors, Ref. MN.

Table 4.2 Population change, 1971–87, by standard region (annual rate per 1 000 people)

Region	1971–74	1974–77	1977–81	1981–84	1984–87
East Anglia	16.1	9.9	9.3	7.9	12.7
South West	9.5	5.5	4.7	6.1	9.5
East Midlands	8.4	3.7	4.3	1.9	5.9
South East	− 1.1	−2.4	1.0	2.0	4.0
South: total	3.0	0.5	2.6	3.1	5.8
Wales	5.4	1.8	1.1	−0.7	3.4
West Midlands	2.7	−0.8	0.6	−0.7	1.4
Yorkshire & Humberside	1.7	−0.4	−0.1	−1.0	− 0.3
North West	− 1.7	−3.2	−3.0	−3.3	− 1.3
Northern	0.2	−0.5	−2.5	−2.6	− 1.8
Scotland	0.3	−0.9	−2.2	−2.2	− 2.2
North: total	1.0	−1.1	−1.2	−1.8	− 0.4
Great Britain	2.0	−0.3	0.7	0.6	2.7
Difference between South and North	2.0	1.6	3.8	4.9	6.2

Note: Regions ranked by 1984–87 change rate
Source: calculated from mid-year estimates

leaving the less dynamic North, thus undermining the ability of the latter to rejuvenate itself. This selectivity in the migration process appears to have intensified in the 1980s. For instance, the Census shows a switch from a net outflow of young adults from Greater London to the rest of Great Britain in 1970–71 to a net inflow to London in 1980–81 (Champion and Congdon, 1988a). According to analyses based on the 1983 Labour Force Survey, migration's role in swelling the South's labour force was then restricted to non-manual workers; though unemployment rates for manual workers were markedly higher in the North than the South, there was no net migration of manual workers to the South (Hughes and McCormick, 1987a). The background and implications of this are discussed more fully in Chapter 7.

Urban–rural shift

Studies of population and employment change in the 1970s, particularly those based on the results of the 1981 Census, are dominated by the urban–rural shift. This is true not just for the UK, but applies widely across the more developed western world (Champion, 1989d). The long-established tendency for national populations to become more concentrated in large metropolitan centres and their surrounding hinterlands was found to be interrupted, if not broken: major cities were losing population not just from their older inner areas but from their whole city regions, while more remote rural areas with a history of depopulation began to record population growth for the first time for decades (Morrison and Wheeler, 1976; Vining and Strauss, 1977; Vining and Kontuly, 1978; Brown and Wardwell, 1980; Fielding, 1982).

Some evidence of the importance of the urban–rural shift in Britain is provided by Figure 4.3. Here, aggregation of 1971–81 population change data for five groups of the CURDS Local Labour Market Areas (LLMAs, see Champion *et al.*, 1987) shows the strong negative relationship between growth rate and size of place that Fielding (1982) expects if 'counter-urbanization' forces are at work. Liverpool, Glasgow and Manchester dominate the list of fastest declining LLMAs for 1971–81, not just in absolute but also in percentage terms, despite their large size, with London not far behind. By contrast, the fastest growing places were smaller cities and towns at some distance from the major metropolitan centres, most of them involving overspill arrangements under the New or Expanded Towns schemes such as Milton Keynes (Bucks.), Redditch (Hereford and Worcs.), Tamworth (Staffs.) and Peterborough (Cambs.); see Champion *et al.* (1987, 21) for further details.

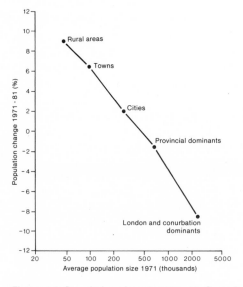

Figure 4.3 Population change 1971–81, Great Britain, by Local Labour Market Area size. LLMAs are grouped by size and urban status. Conurbation Dominants comprise Birmingham, Manchester, Glasgow, Liverpool and Newcastle upon Tyne. Provincial Dominants comprise Leeds, Bristol, Edinburgh, Nottingham and Sheffield. Source: Champion *et al.*, 1987, Table 2.3.

One of the most impressive features of 1971–81 population changes is the marked upturn in rate of population growth which was recorded by many of the more remote rural places in Britain, compared with the 1960s. Table 4.3 gives details of population change over the two decades for the twenty counties and Scottish regions which in 1981 had the lowest population densities (i.e. were the most rural). It can be seen that, whereas in the 1960s half these areas had growth rates below the national average, in the 1970s only one area – Tayside – was in this situation. Moreover, only Wiltshire experienced a cutback in growth rate between the decades that was greater

Table 4.3 Population change, 1961–81, in Britain's areas of lowest population density

Area*	Population density 1981 (persons/ha)	Population change (%)		Difference (% point)
		1961–71	1971–81	
Highlands	0.07	7.1	14.0	+ 6.9
Scottish island areas	0.15	− 7.0	21.7	+28.7
Borders	0.21	− 3.7	1.3	+ 5.0
Powys	0.22	− 3.0	11.5	+14.5
Dumfries and Galloway	0.23	− 2.2	1.4	+ 3.6
Tayside	0.52	− 0.1	− 1.5	− 1.4
Grampian	0.54	− 0.4	7.6	+ 8.0
Dyfed	0.57	0.2	4.4	+ 4.2
Gwynedd	0.60	3.2	4.3	+ 1.1
Northumberland	0.60	1.9	7.1	+ 5.2
Cumbria	0.71	1.3	2.3	+ 1.0
North Yorkshire	0.80	9.0	6.3	− 2.7
Lincolnshire	0.93	7.4	9.4	+ 2.0
Central	1.04	7.5	3.9	+ 3.6
Shropshire	1.08	13.2	11.5	+ 2.3
Cornwall	1.21	11.2	13.3	+ 2.1
Somerset	1.23	11.8	10.6	− 1.2
Norfolk	1.29	10.6	11.0	+ 0.4
Devon	1.42	9.2	6.7	− 2.5
Wiltshire	1.49	15.1	6.5	− 9.6
National average	2.39	5.3	0.6	− 4.7

Note: *County (England and Wales), and region (Scotland)
Source: OPCS (1984a), Table 1

than the national figure, while 15 of the 20 areas saw a positive movement in growth rate against the national trend. Additional evidence of the significance of rural growth is provided by population data for a classification of districts in England and Wales. The most rural category labelled 'remoter, mainly rural districts' was the only one to record an upturn in population growth rate between the 1960s and 1970s and in the latter period recorded an overall growth rate second only to districts containing New Towns (OPCS, 1981).

Annual population estimates give a rather different impression of the phasing of the pace of the urban–rural shift over time (Champion, 1981, 1987b). They indicate that it was already accelerating in the mid and late 1960s and actually reached a peak in the first three or four years of the following decade, after which it fell back substantially. This is reflected at both ends of the settlement hierarchy in Table 4.4, not only in the reduction in the growth rate of the remoter, mainly rural districts but also in the marked fall in the rate of population loss estimated for Greater London and the principal cities of the Metropolitan Counties.

On the other hand, it would be a mistake to conclude that the urban–rural shift is a spent force. In the first place, even in the early 1980s, the more rural areas were still gaining population far more rapidly than the nation as a whole, and the more general process of deconcentration from the metropolitan counties and from the largest settlements in non-metropolitan counties was still continuing apace. Secondly, the latest available informa-

Table 4.4 Population change, 1961–87, by type of district, England and Wales only (annual average rate per 1000 people)

Type of District	61–66	66–71	71–74	74–77	77–81	81–84	84–87
Greater London boroughs	− 4	− 9	−12	−12	− 7	−2	1
Inner London	− 8	−19	−21	−19	−15	−5	0
Outer London	− 1	− 2	− 6	− 7	− 3	−1	1
Metropolitan districts	2	− 0	− 4	− 5	− 4	−4	− 3
Principal cities	− 8	− 8	−11	−10	− 8	−5	− 4
Other districts	7	4	− 1	0	− 3	−3	− 2
Non-metropolitan districts	13	10	8	4	5	3	6
Cities	1	− 2	− 2	− 4	− 3	−3	− 4
Industrial areas	8	7	7	1	2	−1	1
With New Towns	23	19	16	14	14	8	9
Resort, port & retirement	14	10	9	5	5	7	13
Urban & mixed urban–rural	23	17	9	6	7	5	7
Remoter, mainly rural	8	10	15	9	7	6	11
England and Wales	6	4	2	0	1	1	3

Source: calculated from OPCS mid-year population estimates. Reprinted from Champion (1989d), Table 5.2

tion at the time of writing (November 1989) suggests that a further surge of non-metropolitan growth was underway by the mid 1980s, with the remoter, mainly rural areas and resort, port and retirement areas – along with Inner London – being the main beneficiaries of the acceleration in the national growth rate at this time (Table 4.4).

The continuing strength of the urban–rural shift is evident from Figure 4.4, albeit overlain by the drift from North to South. Population growth in the 1980s was dominated by shire counties in the southern half of England, the 'rural South', particularly those forming an arc in and around the western and northern parts of the South East region. In both 1981–84 and 1984–87 Berkshire, Buckinghamshire, Cambridgeshire, Dorset and Oxfordshire were amongst the fast-growing counties, along with Cornwall and the Isle of Wight. The biggest increases in growth rate between the two periods, however, occurred largely in counties situated at a greater distance from London, namely (in rank order) Northamptonshire, Isle of Wight, Lincolnshire, Dyfed, Gloucestershire, Devon, Dorset and Hereford & Worcester. Migration (Figure 4.5B) has played the key role in these growth patterns – indeed, to a greater extent than might be expected from the overall rates of population change, because it is also compensating for substantial natural decrease in some of the fastest growing counties, principally those noted as retirement areas like East and West Sussex, the Isle of Wight, Dorset and Devon (Figure 4.5A). The urban–rural shift is also identifiable further north, but in the context of lower regional growth and with less marked differences between county growth rates; for instance, in northern England, with Cleveland and Tyne & Wear in population decline and with Northumberland and Cumbria failing to reach the national average rate of growth in the mid 1980s.

A wide range of factors has been put forward to account for the urban–

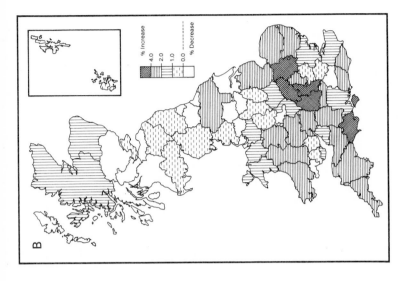

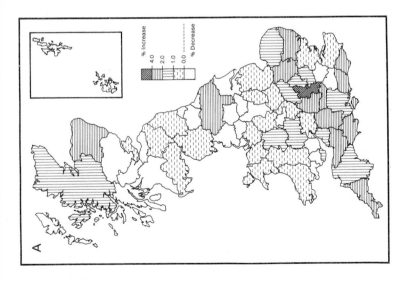

Figure 4.4 Population change, by county and Scottish region: (A) 1981–84 (B) 1984–87. Source: data supplied by Office of Population Censuses and Surveys and Registrar General Scotland.

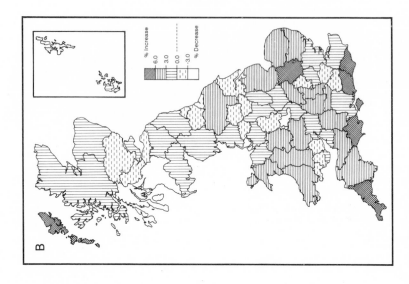

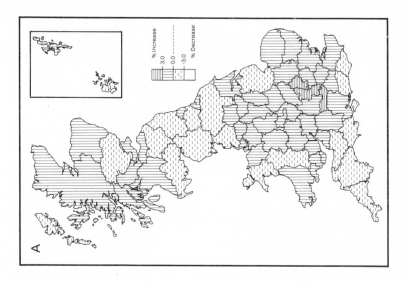

Figure 4.5 Components of population change 1981–87, by county and Scottish region: (A) Natural change (B) Net migration and other changes. Source: as for Figure 4.4.

rural shift and its phasing over time (Champion, 1987b). Retirement migration is an important component, but except for a few areas its contribution to population growth has been smaller than that of other age groups, not just pre-retirement moves but also those of younger working age and their families (Warnes and Law, 1984). For these, the main factors would seem to be a change in residential preferences and the greater availability of jobs in more rural areas. As described in more detail in Chapters 5 and 6, the latter results from the growth in employment in public-sector services in the late 1960s and early 1970s and the search by companies for less cramped factory sites and for cheaper and less unionized labour such as married women (Fothergill and Gudgin, 1982; Massey, 1984). The programme of motorway building played an important facilitating role, while direct government involvement made a substantial contribution in the form of the Location of Offices Bureau, large-scale slum clearance and the official overspill programme, the latter being expanded in the light of the mid 1960s projections of strong national population growth (Hamnett and Randolph, 1983a; Robert and Randolph, 1983). The demographic trends outlined earlier in this chapter also played a part, as the rearing of the 1960s baby-boom children increased the demand for houses with gardens and as falling average household size reduced the population capacity of cities that had only limited sites available for new housing construction.

The decrease in the pace of urban–rural movement in the late 1970s can partly be ascribed to some of the same factors working in reverse. These include the ageing of the baby boom, the run-down of the New and Expanded Towns programme, the switch from slum clearance to housing rehabilitation and the reorientation of government policy to deal with the problems of the inner city areas. This slow-down can also be related to the economic hiccoughs of the later 1970s and particularly the period of deep recession in 1979–82 (Townsend, 1983). This led to a reduction in the amount of capital available for new investment in manufacturing and to a fall in the ability of private individuals to change jobs and move houses. Both these increased again with the economic recovery of the mid 1980s, though more noticeably in the South than in the North.

As with the North–South drift, the urban–rural shift has involved certain types of people more than others, a feature which intensified as migration became more difficult after the early 1970s peak. As can be seen from the composition of net migration flows from London to the rest of Great Britain (Table 4.5), this was particularly true for income groups (as represented by socio-economic groups and housing tenure). Even in 1970–71 London's net loss of population was skewed towards non-manual workers and owner-occupiers, but the subsequent reduction in the scale of movement had its greatest effect on the proportion of public-sector tenants and of lower-income sections of the labour force, both manual and non-manual. This can be attributed in large measure to the lower demand of low-paid labour in non-metropolitan manufacturing during the recession years and to a contraction in housing opportunities for low-income groups. The latter have always found it more difficult to move out of cities than owner occupiers, because of the limited availability of private-rented accommodation outside the large cities and because of the barriers limiting transfers between council

Table 4.5 Migration between London and the rest of Great Britain, 1970–71 and 1980–81, by socio-economic grouping and housing tenure (thousands)

Characteristics at time of Census	Out-migration 70–71	Out-migration 80–81	In-migration 70–71	In-migration 80–81	Net out-migration 70–71	Net out-migration 80–81
Socio-economic groupings						
Professional/managerial	37.1	24.3	19.3	18.1	17.8	6.2
Other non-manual	71.4	38.6	44.3	37.2	27.1	1.4
Skilled manual	28.0	12.4	9.8	6.9	18.2	5.6
Other manual	21.7	11.7	12.6	11.6	9.1	0.1
Armed Forces & I.D.	7.0	12.1	6.4	8.3	0.6	3.8
All economically active	165.2	99.1	92.4	82.1	72.8	17.0
Housing tenure						
Owner occupiers	142.9	94.3	41.3	37.6	101.6	56.7
Renting from LA/NT	38.2	17.2	8.9	12.0	29.3	5.2
Other renters	48.8	25.6	68.3	42.5	− 19.5	−16.9
All in private households	229.9	137.0	118.5	92.1	111.4	44.9

Note: ID = inadequately described; LA/NT = Local Authorities and New Towns. A negative sign for net out-migration denotes net in-migration to London
Source: Migration Regional Reports of the 1971 and 1981 Censuses. Reprinted from Champion and Congdon (1989a), Table 8

housing areas. However, in the later 1970s these problems were exacerbated by the rundown of the New and Expanded Towns programme and the lower level of public-sector house-building. These problems have been compounded in the 1980s by the government's encouragement of the sale of council houses and by the rise in house prices in the owner-occupied sector, so that the acceleration in the urban–rural shift in the mid 1980s is not likely to have been caused by the lower paid. This has important implications for the social composition of both origin and destination areas as will be seen later in the chapter.

Suburbanization and local decentralization

The flight from the older inner areas to the suburbs is a long-established feature of population redistribution. It dates from the latter half of the nineteenth century when improvements in local passenger transport allowed people to reside at greater distances from their workplaces. The rate and physical extent of suburban and 'exurban' growth accelerated rapidly in the inter-war period, with the sharp increase in car ownership, but it has taken on even greater numerical and spatial dimensions since the early 1950s. It is normally defined as the intra-urban movement of population from the inner to the outer parts of the same urban region, but in more recent years it has become inextricably bound up with the patterns of inter-urban redistribution associated with the urban–rural shift. Indeed, while the latter has fuelled the rate of suburban growth for smaller cities and towns, the larger cities have experienced a reduction in their rate of suburban growth.

These trends and interrelationships can be illustrated most effectively by reference to the zone level of the Functional Regions framework, particularly the contrast between the Cores and Rings which make up the Daily Urban Systems of the 228 Functional Regions in Britain. The Cores are defined in such a way as to embrace the entire built-up area of the main settlement and therefore include the contiguous suburbs as they existed in 1971 as well as the inner city areas (see Champion *et al.*, 1987, for further details). Nevertheless, the predominance of centrifugal movement is clear and is found to have intensified markedly between the 1950s and the 1970s. As shown in Table 4.6, the growth rate for the 228 Cores, in aggregate, declined from 4.0 per cent in 1951–61 to 0.7 per cent in the following decade and slumped further to –4.2 per cent in the 1970s.

Table 4.6 Population change, Great Britain, 1951–87, by Functional Region zone

Zone	1951–61	1961–71	1971–81	1981–87
Change for period (000s)				
Core	+1 328	+ 230	−1 466	−257
Ring	+1 067	+2 006	+1 208	+500
Outer Area	+ 50	+ 327	+ 327	+178
Rural Area	− 15	+ 131	+ 228	+116
Total	+2 429	+2 693	+ 296	+536
Annual rate (per 1000 people)				
Core	+ 4.0	+ 0.7	− 4.2	−1.3
Ring	+10.5	+17.8	+ 9.1	+5.8
Outer Area	+ 1.7	+11.3	+10.1	+8.5
Rural Area	− 0.6	+ 5.4	+ 8.8	+7.0
Total	+ 5.0	+ 5.3	+ 0.6	+1.7

Source: Data for 1951–81 calculated from Population Census; 1981–87 change calculated from data provided by CACI Market Analysis

These patterns can be related to the same type of factors as described above for the urban–rural shift. This is particularly the case for the 'push element' operating in the inner city areas. These comprise several features: employment has fallen in most branches of manufacturing and in some parts of the service sector; land has been diverted from residential use by office expansion, road construction and slum clearance; more mobile people have been leaving to escape the poor physical environment and the social problems; new private house-building has been discouraged by high costs, land hoarding by local authorities and uncertainties about sales potential; and falling household size has reduced the capacity of the overall housing stock (Cameron, 1980; Evans and Eversley, 1980; Kennett and Hall, 1981; Lawless, 1981).

The effect of these push factors on the individual city regions has, however, been reinforced by limitations imposed on new population growth in their outer areas. Again falling household size has played an important role here in reducing the capacity of these areas, but equally significant have been the tight planning controls on urban development, particularly the wide Green Belts round most of the larger cities. As pointed out by Hall *et al.* (1973) and Hamnett and Randolph (1983a), much of the urban–rural shift in the more heavily populated parts of the country would seem to comprise essentially suburban movements which have been forced to become 'exurban' and inter-urban because of pressure on space. Initially, a majority of these reluctant long-distance movers commute back to their metropolitan jobs, but in the longer term many take up more local jobs – a feature that has grown as employment too has decentralized (Herington, 1984; Congdon and Champion, 1989).

The local centrifugal movements have been just as selective in their social composition as the longer-distance transfers involved in the urban–rural shift and North–South drift, indeed probably even more so. Archetypal suburbia from the 1920s contains virtually no housing for private renting. Moreover, a substantial proportion of the council housing built on low-density suburban estates in the inter-war period has now been incorporated into the owner-occupied sector and no longer provides a route for lower-income households wanting to move into the suburbs. As Hall *et al.* (1973) discovered, for most of the post-war period the political interests of both the Labour-held city authorities and the surrounding Tory-controlled shire counties were best served by restricting the outward movement of the lower-paid – considerations which, along with other factors, led to the encouragement of high-rise apartment blocks on redeveloped sites in inner urban areas. The only significant opportunities for low-income people to decentralize locally (as opposed to the longer-distance moves facilitated by the New and Expanded Towns programmes) have derived from the re-cycling of older and poorer quality housing in the inner suburbs and from the development of spare peripheral sites by city councils – the 'outer council estates' which now suffer from major social and physical problems because of inaccessibility, limited facilities, faulty design and inadequate maintenance.

In the 1980s local decentralization has been occurring at a slower pace than in the previous decade and in some cases appears to have gone into reverse. This is seen in the narrowing of the difference in growth rate between the Cores and Rings of the Functional Regions framework (Table 4.6). It is also reflected in the reduction in the population losses for the larger metropolitan centres, most notably London (Table 4.4). In fact, during the first half of the 1980s, there was virtually no distinction in growth rates between Inner and Outer London Boroughs (Champion and Congdon, 1988b). In the London case at least, this recovery can no doubt be attributed in part to the strength of its economy, the support given by central government to the Docklands redevelopment and other schemes, and the associated attraction of young professionals back to the more central parts of the city. Here and elsewhere, however, the barriers to the outward movement of the lower paid and ethnic minorities have also played a significant role, leading to further social polarization not just between inner city and suburb but also between different parts of inner city areas.

Impact on socio-demographic patterns and local population profiles

The three basic dimensions of migration, together with the major changes in national population structure and composition outlined in the earlier section of this chapter, have produced some distinctive patterns in Britain's population geography. In recent years, relatively few places have recorded growth rates around the national average. Most have either grown much more rapidly, or they have declined significantly. In terms of their population characteristics, few places can be regarded as microcosms of the nation as a whole. Because of the selective nature of migration, areas that have been growing rapidly tend to have very different population profiles from those that have been declining, the latter generally having below-average representations of young families, owner-occupiers and high-income professionals. The larger cities, as well as bearing the hallmarks of population decline, also contain above-average shares of young single adults, one-parent families and ethnic minorities. The destinations of the net migration flows, particularly at the intermediate scale of the urban–rural shift, comprise a number of relatively distinctive categories according to the nature of their growth. These include retirement areas, overspill towns, industrial centres, commuting dormitories and traditional market centres. This section highlights some of the principal types of variation between places that impinge on their economic performance and social problems.

Social polarization

Recent trends have tended to produce greater social divisions between places. The socially selective nature of migration, which the previous section identified at all three scales, has worked alongside differences in the indigenous rates of upward social mobility to produce impressive contrasts in social status and other indicators of material well-being between North and South, between rural and urban sub-regions, and between suburbs and inner cities. At the level of the 280 Local Labour Market Areas, the proportion of economically active or retired people in the higher socio-economic groups – the most sophisticated measure of social status available from the 1981 Census – displays an immense range between 43.1 per cent for St Albans and 12.5 per cent for West Bromwich (Table 4.7A). Similarly, the proportion of households with two or more cars in High Wycombe in 1981 was five times as large as for Mexborough in South Yorkshire (Table 4.7B). The county-level map of social class composition (Figure 4.6A) reveals the expected patterns of greatest prosperity in the shire counties of southeastern England and greatest relative deprivation in the more industrial areas of the rest of the country.

Educational achievement and health record

These social patterns are quite closely correlated with spatial variations in education and health. The South East is the leading region in terms of the educational qualifications of its workforce and the level of school attainment. At the 1981 Census 16.3 per cent of its employed men had successfully completed higher education, with the next highest region – the South West – managing only 13.3 per cent and the Northern Region lowest at 11.5 per cent. Similarly, the proportion of school-leavers in 1985–86 who had obtained at least one 'A' Level stood at 23.5 per cent for the South East compared with barely 16 per cent for the Northern Region.

In recent years considerable attention has been given to the 'health divide' in Britain (Black Report, 1980; Whitehead, 1987). Again this has a clear

Table 4.7 Highest and lowest Local Labour Market Areas for two social indicators, 1981

Highest LLMAs	%	Lowest LLMAs	%
A. Proportion of economically active or retired persons in SEGs 1–5 and 13			
St Albans	43.1	West Bromwich	12.5
Maidenhead	40.2	Peterlee	14.3
Haywards Heath	39.8	Mexborough	14.5
Guildford	39.6	Mansfield	16.7
Woking & Weybridge	39.4	Gelligaer	16.8
High Wycombe	38.6	Corby	16.9
Bishop's Stortford	37.4	Castleford & Pontefract	16.9
Winchester	37.1	Merthyr Tydfil	17.0
Aldershot & Farnborough	37.1	Bathgate	17.3
Horsham	36.1	Smethwick	17.3
B. Proportion of households with 2 or more cars			
High Wycombe	34.3	Mexborough	6.8
Maidenhead	33.6	South Shields	6.8
Woking & Weybridge	30.9	Sunderland	7.0
Bishop's Stortford	30.6	Peterlee	7.1
Aldershot	29.4	West Bromwich	7.5
Guildford	29.4	Coatbridge & Airdrie	7.6
St Albans	29.2	Merthyr Tydfil	7.8
Hertford & Ware	29.0	Glasgow	8.3
Stratford On Avon	28.2	Newcastle upon Tyne	8.4
Horsham	27.2	Bathgate	8.5

Source: Population Census Small Area Statistics. Reprinted from Champion *et al.* (1987), Tables 7.2 and 7.3

geographical expression at the broad regional level. The Northern Region, Scotland and Northern Ireland recorded the highest age-adjusted mortality rates in 1986, at over 13.0 per thousand, while the lowest at under 11.0 were found in East Anglia, the South West and the South East. The spatial differentials are, however, most marked at the local scales which pick out residential clusters with distinctive social mixes. For instance, major variations in health were found within the Northern Region by Townsend *et al.* (1988), who identified close links between health standards and levels of material prosperity. In a detailed study of premature mortality in North Tyneside, Phillimore (1989) has shown that people aged under 65 in the two worst-off wards are subject to mortality rates around 50 per cent higher than the national average, while in the two wards at the other extreme the rates are 30 per cent below average.

These variations in health and educational attainment are of long standing and appear to have defied attempts made under the Welfare State to obtain greater equality in access to services. They were certainly very clear twenty years ago according to the regional and county data analysed by Coates and Rawstron (1971). Moreover, they cannot be accounted for merely by reference to spatial differences in social composition. For instance, Fox and Goldblatt (1982) have noted that a clear North–South contrast in mortality rates remained even after standardizing for the socio-economic character of areas. Similarly, as observed by Bradford and Burdett (1989), larger numbers of children in southern England go through the private education system

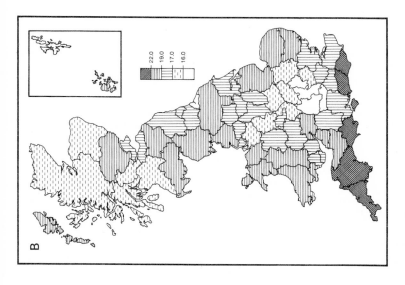

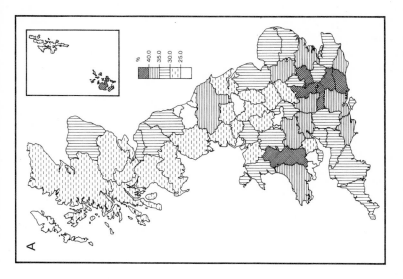

Figure 4.6 Socio-demographic variation, by county and Scottish region: (A) Population in households with head in Social Class I and II as percentage of population in all households with economically active heads, 1981; (B) Pensionable age and over (65 for males, 60 for females) as percentage of all residents, 1986. Source: (A) 1981 Census; (B) Mid-year estimates.

than would be expected from the social class patterns there. With the widening of the income range between social groups since the late 1970s and the government's emphasis on restricting public spending and encouraging privatization, there are signs that these geographical differences have widened over the past decade (see Bradford and Burdett (1989) and Curtis and Mohan (1989) for reviews).

Non-white population

As mentioned earlier in the chapter, the rapid growth of the ethnic minority populations is one of the major features of Britain's demographic development over the past three decades. It is also an extremely distinctive feature in terms of its high level of geographical polarization. It is not easy to measure at local scale because the 1981 Census did not contain an ethnicity question, but an impression can be gained from birth-place data in the Census. In 1981, six of the 280 LLMAs accounted for over half of the people in Britain that had been born in the New Commonwealth or Pakistan (NCWP). London and Leicester had almost three times the national average share, while Bradford, Slough, Birmingham and Smethwick had over twice the average (Champion *et al.*, 1987).

Using the broader measure of the proportion of the population living in a household headed by a NCWP-born person, the South East headed the regional averages in 1981, closely followed by the West Midlands region, but again the main contrasts are more local in nature. The proportion averaged one in five for Inner London as a whole, but at borough level ranged from almost 30 per cent in Haringey to under 10 per cent for Kensington and Chelsea and was in fact highest for an outer borough – Brent – at 33.5 per cent. Outside London there was only a handful of districts with over 10 per cent of their population living in households with a NCWP-born head – Luton and Slough in the South East, Birmingham, Sandwell and Wolverhampton in the West Midlands, Blackburn in Lancashire, and the City of Leicester, being the highest at 21.7 per cent in 1981. These stand out as islands within a sea of districts where the proportion is generally below 3 per cent (OPCS, 1984a). This high degree of concentration also manifests itself at the most localized scales. This is shown, for instance, by a survey of Leicester, where each individual ethnic and cultural group tends to possess its own distinctive residential territory (Leicester CC, 1983).

These patterns represent the outcome of the recent history of NCWP immigration, the lowly status of those involved and the direct or indirect effects of racial discrimination. Most of the original immigrants were recruited during the period of labour shortages in the 1950s and 1960s for particular types of jobs including the textile industry and more menial tasks in the service sector. Their local distribution was largely determined by the availability of low-cost housing. The original patterns have been reinforced by the subsequent arrival of relations and others from the same parts of the world, as well as by their high birth rate – the result of relatively high fertility and young average age. The degree of dispersion away from these concentrations has been limited by the same forces that have prevented low-income people in general from moving into suburban environments, combined with a desire for being amongst their own people in an essentially alien culture. As such, the ethnic minorities represent a major demographic strength for parts of urban Britain, though at the same time their presence may have hastened the exodus of better-off whites and certainly gives rise to a very difficult set of policy issues (Chapter 8).

Age structure

Migration processes have also given rise to distinctive age patterns around Britain, though the absolute scale of differences between places is relatively small. The principal contrast across the country is between the younger populations of the urban heartland areas and the older populations of the coastal and rural rims (Figure 4.6B). This pattern reflects both the tendency for school-leavers to leave the more rural and remote parts of the country and the fact that many people at or near retirement age see advantages in moving away from the more expensive and congested metropolitan regions. The counties with the highest proportions of 25–44 year olds form a compact block around the northern and western edges of the South East region. This results chiefly from age-selective migration from London, but also bears witness to the North–South movement of labour. It contrasts with the above-average representation of older-working-age people in much of northern England.

At the level of individual LLMAs there are some very marked differences in age structure. For instance, in 1981 almost 36 per cent of Clacton's population were of pensionable age, over twice the national average of 17.5 per cent, and people of older working age – either those taking early retirement or moving in anticipation of retirement after their children had grown up – are also strongly represented here and in similar resorts like Eastbourne, Worthing, Hastings, Llandudno and Torquay. At the other extreme, the proportion of elderly was smallest in LLMAs which have New or Expanded Towns at their core, such as Tamworth, Harlow, Basildon, Redditch and Milton Keynes, all with less than 12.0 per cent in pensionable age groups in 1981 (Champion *et al.*, 1987).

These local imbalances in age composition raise important policy issues. Mention has already been made of the significance of national trends in age structure, but it can be seen that these effects can be substantially reinforced at the regional and local level through migration. Moreover, once im-balances have been created, they tend to work their way through the higher age groups *in situ*. Thus the traditional retirement resorts have already experienced a large increase in the number of very elderly people who place extra demands on health and residential care facilities, to the extent that in places like Worthing, Hastings, Eastbourne and Clacton around one in eight people were aged 75 or over in 1981. The earlier New Towns are particularly prone to this ageing process, given that many of them were built up extremely quickly with young married couples in rented accommodation (Champion *et al.*, 1977). Places like Welwyn Garden City and Crawley have been experiencing the relentless movement of these original cohorts of migrants up the 'age pyramid'. In 1981 Welwyn possessed the largest proportion of older working people out of all the LLMAs in Britain, while

Stevenage, Thetford and Bracknell headed the list of LLMAs with the greatest percentage increases in elderly numbers over the previous decade (Champion *et al.*, 1987).

Change in labour supply

One of the most remarkable aspects of population change in recent years has been the growth and redistribution of the labour force. This has resulted partly from the increased participation of married women and the 'coming of age' of the main post-war baby boom, but has of course been influenced greatly at more local level by migration. Not surprisingly, the most rapid increase in economically active persons between 1971 and 1981 was regis-tered by the New and Expanded Towns, with Milton Keynes LLMA experiencing a massive 64 per cent growth in labour supply over the decade. By contrast, West Bromwich, Manchester, London and Liverpool all sustained losses amounting to over 10 per cent of their workforce.

Labour supply patterns have, however, become more complicated in the 1980s and are inevitably emerging as a key issue of the 1990s. On the one hand, the economic recession of the early 1980s coincided with the peaking of school-leaving rates resulting from the baby boom. This led not only to the aggravation of unemployment problems but also to the lowering of labour force participation rates through earlier retirement and fewer married women returning to work after child-rearing – a phenomenon which, not surprisingly, was particularly marked in northern cities and industrial towns. On the other, the national 'demographic time bomb' of much smaller numbers of school-leavers in the 1990s is likely to have its most severe impact on those places which experience rapid-migration of younger fami-lies during the 1950s and 1960s, namely the older New Towns and the more traditional commuting zones and most notably those in the Home Counties/Outer Metropolitan Area of South East England. We give more detailed treatment to these developments in Chapter 7.

Conclusion

The 1970s and 1980s have constituted a period of major transformation in Britain's demographic patterns, notwithstanding the almost stationary size of the national population itself. Its overall composition has been changing substantially towards older average age, smaller household size, greater labour force participation, and generally greater prosperity. Two of the most distinctive features of post-1950 Britain – the baby boom and New Common-wealth immigration – have become deeply embedded in the national population profile and will produce further upheavals within the foresee-able future. In combination, these changes have considerably altered the character of most places in Britain.

Even more important in the context of this book, however, have been the changes wrought by migration. Population redistribution over the past quarter of a century has been characterized by unprecedentedly large inter-urban flows in contrast to the dominance of relatively local rural-to-urban and suburban moves in previous decades. Against the background of almost zero national population growth in the 1970s and 1980s, this has produced a mosaic of both absolute growth and absolute decline across Britain with relatively few places maintaining a static population size. A large number of places, particularly the smaller cities and towns of southern England, have been on the receiving end of all three major migration streams, while at the other extreme the large cities, particularly those in northern England and Scotland (the 'urban north'), have acted as the main reservoir from which these flows have been drawn. As a result of different levels of personal mobility, the former types of place have tended to attract people who are younger, better qualified, more enterprising and more wealthy and have thus gained at the expense of the larger cities and less dynamic industrial areas, causing the latter a double blow in terms of both quantity and quality.

The resulting degree of demographic and socio-economic polarization at regional, sub-regional and local scales is the central feature of the many changes which have affected the geography of the UK in the second half of the twentieth century. The remaining chapters in this part of the book examine the economic forces which have contributed to these trends and the impact which population change has in its turn had on the spatial organization of economic activity. The 'explosion' of place differentiation in Britain also provides the rationale for the more locally focused treatments in Part III, which are arranged in term of types of places rather than on the basis of the standard regional units used conventionally for more detailed accounts of the geography of Britain.

Further reading

The most useful and comprehensive account of the background to recent population developments is provided by Joshi (1989). This contains chapters on fertility, the family, divorce, old age, education, housing, internal migration and ethnic minorities, as well as a chapter stressing the significance and implications of population change for planning and policy-making. The latest statistics on population change and its components can be obtained from the journal *Population Trends* (OPCS); this also includes annual reviews of trends in migration, both international and internal. A longer-term perspective on developments is available in the OPCS publications series DR, the latest available at the time of writing being *Demographic Review 1984*.

Background information on the spatial aspects of population change and related trends in demographic and social structure is provided by Compton (1982); Lawton (1982); and Champion (1983). Population trends since 1971 for different types of places are outlined by Britton (1986), while an account of vital trends is provided by Armitage (1987).

The main features of recent migration at regional and metropolitan scales are described by Stillwell and Boden (1986). Several studies focus primarily on the urban–rural shift in population distribution, including Hamnett and Randolph (1983a); Robert and Randolph (1983); and Champion (1987b). The nature of counterurbanization is examined by Champion (1989c), while one example of the reduction in big-city population losses in the 1980s is provided by Champion and Congdon (1988).

The socially selective nature of population changes and the problems which this causes are explored by Champion (1989a). Regional variations in health and education are detailed by Curtis and Mohan (1989) and Bradford and Burdett (1989). The policy implications of trends relating to health and education are explored in chapters by Whitelegg and Briault (1986).

Regional and local variations in socio-economic characteristics, labour supply, age structure and ethnic composition, particularly relating to 1981 and the changes over the previous decade, are described by Champion *et al.* (1987). Differentials in wealth and opportunity are examined by class, gender, race and geographical location by Hudson and Williams (1989). Trends in age structure across Britain are described by Warnes and Law (1984). An introduction to the geography of race is provided by Peach (1982). A fascinating case study of ethnic patterns is available in a report by Leicester City Council (1983).

5

De-industrialization

The British map of industrial employment has changed more fundamentally and dramatically than that of population. The result of this discordance is the map of continuing unemployment, only gradually moderated by net migration from industrial areas (Chapter 4). More manufacturing jobs have been lost in the UK than in any other European country. The net loss of 2.8 million from 1971 to 1989 occurred above all through the decline of the large factory. This involves a very broad range of industries, including mass production factories, older, heavier industries and manufacture by the public sector, the private sector and foreign firms; it is accompanied by job losses in supporting service industries such as docks and railways, and, with renewed vigour in the period after 1985, by coal mining. Chapter 3 (p. 29) used 'de-industrialization' as a simple description of manufacturing's declining share of total employment. In this chapter, we consider the incidence of falling employment in all sectors, but manufacturing and mining are the worst affected. In Chapter 6 we shall evaluate increase.

Which people, which industries and which places are the losers from industrial change? Chapter 3 showed a general picture of a society moving away from the basis of male manual work. A decline in the national importance of industry must also, however, induce relative decline in industrial regions. Many British readers will not feel such change directly if they are students from a more prosperous area (as is likely since higher education places are filled largely from non-manual social groups). However, the co-existence of unemployment and labour shortage in different places is a cost to the whole society. The country needs professional workers who can work on both sides of the 'North–South divide'. In political life there is a fierce interest in the poverty, unemployment and poor housing that are a legacy of Britain's industrial past.

Why did the world's first industrial country (Chapter 2) fall prey to such rapid industrial and geographical change in the 1970s and 1980s? In Chapter 2 we outlined the UK's fading international competitiveness. The singular British anomaly of failure to expand employment over the longer term in the manufacture of new information technology products was, in the view of the geographers Hall and Preston (1988, 220–1), 'a consequence of the deteriorating competitive position of British firms, associated with poor innovative performance'. However, in a more general analysis, Rowthorn (1986, 26) argued that Britain was ahead of other countries in the post-war era in maturing into a post-industrial economy, thus the decline of industrial employment was earlier and deeper. Secondly, he concluded, huge improvements in non-manufacturing trade meant that the country no longer needed a large surplus on manufactured goods. 'Between them these two factors – maturity and trade specialization – account for virtually all the decline of manufacturing employment, 1955–81. Poor industrial performance is of only minor importance in explaining this decline' (Rowthorn, 1986, 26). We must ask whether performance is less important than general structural change in individual areas as well.

The changes of the 1980s were more far-reaching than those of the 1930s. In the earlier decade, heavy unemployment in the peripheral regions was also gradually overtaken by consistent national growth. Employment expanded about 1 per cent per annum faster in the South than the North. The extra growth was in new places and industries, yet much was still generated in manufacturing employment. In the 1980s there were not only changes in product demand and in imports and exports, but large-scale changes in investment and in the occupational structure. In the 1930s, the growth of manufacturing was dramatized by the mass production methods already pioneered by Henry Ford in his US car factories. In the 1980s, British industry is seen to have evolved *away* from the self-contained mass production factory toward 'flexible production', making shorter runs for particular customers and supported by greater sub-contracting of supplies and services. The era of 'Fordism' is allegedly being replaced by a 'regime' of 'flexible accumulation' (Murray, 1988; Scott, 1988).

This chapter certainly finds evidence for the first part of the process, a diminution in importance of the traditional large factory, not least in TNCs with many plants. New and old questions follow. What does this mean for the traditional large factory *town*? Why is there a migration of industry from urban areas towards relatively rural ones? Does any of the 'blame' fall on the industrial areas and their people and institutions, or does it lie in historical factors and the national and international organization of industry? Do firms close their branch plants before their headquarters? Are foreign TNCs responsible for proportionately more redundancies and closures in Britain than are domestically-owned firms? Did the Conservative government's policies of 1979–80 accelerate job losses, and were their reductions of public-sector employment a significant contribution to the job losses of the 1980s? Does the pattern of job loss leave any support for a return to past 'regional policies', in which government steered new investment to areas experiencing higher unemployment? Is there any policy scope for local economic initiatives or for devolution of power to Scotland, Wales and the English regions? Whatever the level of national economic success, certain areas will remain disadvantaged. What is at stake is whether conurbations like Merseyside and Tyneside face a future as grim as the present Belfast.

Elements of accelerated de-industrialization

The slowing down in the world industrial economy in the 1970s changed the whole environment in which many firms worked. Reduced demand and increased competition forced down profit levels, acting as an extra spur to reduce costs through reorganizing factories and introducing new technologies. Large companies took over others and thus became more 'trans-national' in operation. This 'centralization and internationalization of capital' knew no political boundaries, and the UK in particular was prone to a loss of investment overseas and increased imports (Chapter 2).

The outstanding feature of the UK economy in the 1970s and 1980s was the extraordinary setbacks met by the manufacturing sector. The *overall output* of the economy, including services, grew at moderate rates in most years of the 1970s (not 1974 to 1975 or 1979 to 1980), before resuming accelerating rates of growth from 1981 *until mid 1989*. By contrast, the manufacturing sector suffered much deeper and more sustained losses of output (Figure 5.1). Indeed the 1974 level of output stood as a record until 1988! From 1974 to 1975 output fell by 12 per cent, followed by moderate recovery, but from 1979 to 1981 there was a reduction of no less than 17 per cent. These were 'asymmetrical cyclical troughs' because recovery of output was spread over a much longer period than its initial loss, and because many factories closed for good in the second recession. International increases in oil prices preceded both recessions, but in Britain the second was advanced and deepened by government policy. There must be doubt as to whether the Government fully intended the severity of the monetary squeeze and the

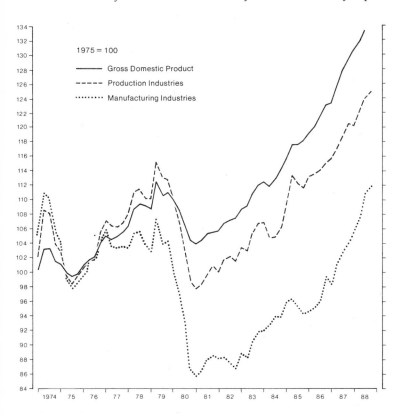

Figure 5.1 Output of the UK economy, 1974–88, including separate index for manufacturing industries (1975 = 100). Source: *Employment Gazette* (various), Table 1.8.

massive rise in the real exchange rate that impinged on the economy in those years, but it is not possible to overstate the economic shock that hit industry in 1979–1981. Some argued that the shock made industry return in the end to competitiveness, but other economists argued that subsequent growth owed more to spending North Sea oil profits on a consumer boom.

The late 1970s' level of manufacturing *investment* stood as a record until 1987. The withdrawal of investment from UK manufacturing (Table 5.1) was especially marked by comparison with other sectors in the UK and with UK investment in manufacturing overseas. Table 5.1 shows that the manufacturing sector led fixed investment in 1978, but that 'financial and business services' overtook it during the recession (and had doubled in amount by 1986). By contrast a fall in investment in 'oil and gas', principally in the North Sea, was associated with depleting reserves.

This pattern included a reduction in the number of manufacturing establishments employing ten or more people; it is here that we can begin to visualize the effects of de-industrialization on the ground. Table 5.2 shows

Table 5.1 Key indicators of economic change in the UK economy, 1978–88

Indicator	1978	1981	1988
Gross domestic product	101.0	100.0	124.5
Manufacturing production	116.7	100.0	125.6
Construction activity	116.9	100.0	126.6
Oil tonnage extracted	60.3	100.0	127.7
Volume of retail sales	96.0	100.0	139.4
Consumer expenditure	96.0	100.0	130.2
Annual fixed investment (£m, at 1980 values):			
Manufacturing	7 221	4 865	7 038
Distribution	3 158	2 972	} 13 955
Financial and business services	4 341	6 109	

Source: National Institute Economic Review, 120 (1987), 129 (1989)

Table 5.2 Number of manufacturing establishments recorded in the United Kingdom, 1971–88

Employment size	1971	1983	1988	Change 1971–88 Nos.	%
10– 19	16 617	n.a.	17 152	+ 535	+ 3.2
20– 99	27 408	23 238	23 903	−3 505	−12.8
100–199	6 140	4 732	4 768	−1 372	−22.3
200–499	4 850	3 397	3 240	−1 610	−33.2
500–999	1 650	1 120	913	− 737	−44.7
1 000 and over	1 132	658	452	− 680	−60.0
Total 20 & over	41 180	33 145	33 276	−7 904	−19.2

Note: The number of 'local manufacturing units' of the Census of Production employing less than 10 stood in 1988 at 105,936; equivalent data are not available for the earlier years. The Census units of 1983 and 1988 are broken down by reference to employment data of 1981 and 1986 respectively
Source: Business Monitor, PA 1003, 1971, 1983, 1988

that over the period 1971 to 1988 the number employing 1,000 or more workers fell by more than half to leave less than 500 such factories in the whole country. This strongly supports one of the concepts of 'the end of Fordism', the reduced importance of the mass-production factory. What is more, the table is remarkable in revealing a progressively better record for successively smaller sizes of factory (although medium-sized factories ceased to fall in number in the mid 1980s, and all figures are influenced by contracting units moving from a larger to a smaller category).

Falling industrial employment could in the past be better characterized by reference to *product sectors* such as cotton, 1945–61, or coal mining, which lost 317,000 jobs from 1961 to 1971. The greatest sources of all job losses from 1971 to 1978 lay in the manufacture of textiles, mechanical engineering and metals, but already manufacturing decline was generalized, common to many products and areas. Thus the effect of different inherited structures, that is of 'industrial structure', in differentiating the employment trends of different areas became weakened (Fothergill and Gudgin, 1982, 56). The period of most rapid decline, 1978–81, was notable for *some* disproportionate job losses, in metals, vehicles and textiles (Townsend, 1983), and in public administration. However, if we take eleven years to the date of writing (1978–89 at Table 5.3), we find that, while job losses were concentrated in manufacturing, they were again widely spread within it. Four metal-using and manufacturing industries are prominent at the head of the list, with losses of more than 200,000 jobs each. In the public sector, the coal industry and the whole sphere of public administration and defence both appear. We shall deal separately later with public service job losses, as a continuing feature of the 1980s, but the data justify us in paying prime attention to manufacturing.

Table 5.3 Leading 'classes' of economic activity with declining employment, Great Britain, 1978–89 (June)

Class	1978 000s	1989 000s	Change 1978–89 000s	%
Mechanical engineering	1 031.7	783.8	− 247.9	−24.0
Metal manufacturing and ore extraction .	391.6	157.8	− 233.8	−59.7
Coal extraction and solid fuels	307.5	101.8	− 205.7	−66.9
Electrical and electronic engineering	749.5	544.5	− 205.0	−27.4
Motor vehicles and parts	471.6	268.3	− 203.3	−43.1
Miscellaneous metal goods	514.5	334.6	− 179.9	−35.0
Textiles	388.3	217.8	− 170.5	−43.9
Food, drink and tobacco	712.0	549.9	− 162.1	−22.8
Aerospace, ships etc.	378.7	218.3	− 160.4	−42.4
Construction	1 160.8	1 041.7	− 119.1	−10.3
Footwear and clothing	397.3	283.6	− 113.7	−28.6
Public administration and defence	1 679.8	1 573.4	− 106.4	− 6.3
All sectors	22 273.5	21 952.4	− 321.1	− 1.4
Manufacturing sectors only	7 138.0	5 086.9	−2 051.1	−28.7
Males only	13 100.0	11 713.7	−1 386.3	−10.6

Source: *Employment Gazette*, November 1989 and Historical Supplements

The loss of 28.7 per cent (2.05 million) from Great Britain's factory jobs in 11 years, 1978–89, occurred through several processes. Formal *redundancy* was concentrated in the manufacturing sector; there were no less than 2,071,600 cases of confirmed redundancies in manufacturing (Townsend, 1983), out of 2,974,700 in the whole economy, 1978–87. However, some workers were made redundant several times over, even though redundancy is generally a last resort; indeed it is only one part of the complex process of *job turnover*. Martin (1984) and Meager (1984) both pointed out that, when considered as a proportion of *gross* as opposed to *net* job loss, redundancy was not the dominant process. Figure 5.2 enables us to separate recruitment and 'discharges' in manufacturing. What we find over 15 years after the 1974–75 recession was much less turnover in the factory workforce in the context of surrounding unemployment. The main impact of the 1979–80 recession was felt in a sharp drop in recruitment, which then grew slowly to match discharges only in 1987–88.

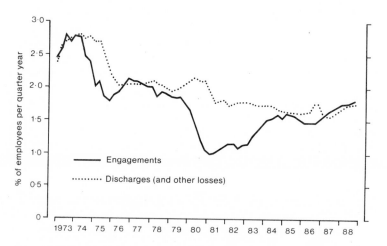

Figure 5.2 The process of manufacturing employment change, Great Britain, 1973–88. Source: *Employment Gazette* 97, December 1989, Table 1.6.

Why did it take so long for manufacturing employment to level out? If redundancy was the leading form of change to 1981, it was gains in *productivity* that made the greatest inroads from then. Many writers consider that the closure by 1981 of older large plants itself artificially improved the overall average of output per worker. In studying the period 1968–77, Davies and Caves (1987) had argued that it was the conjunction of British managerial weakness and labour organization in large plants which led to the traditional national problem of low productivity. Metcalf (1988) concludes that levels of unionization, which were higher in large plants, did affect productivity. Unionized workplaces were in 1980–84 actually more likely to suffer job losses (after standardizing by product sector) than non-unionized plants, which were more likely to enjoy job gains. These data are in line with the general concept of a trend to more 'flexible production';

they link the reduction in large plants, presented earlier, with the increase achieved in manufacturing output per person employed of 50 per cent, 1981–89.

The factory labour force *fell* by 16.6 per cent in the same period *after* the main recession, because the growth of productivity outstripped that of output, which was only 29.5 per cent. Taking the whole period 1978–89 (Table 5.3), manufacturing employment was responsible for the overall decline of male employment. In the opposite direction, the total working population increased for demographic reasons (Chapter 4), and female employment and activity rates expanded, chiefly in part-time work in the service sector. The net result was of course the high levels of unemployment of much of the 1980s.

Unemployment then was chiefly due to de-industrialization, and this was apparent in the precise timing and location of its rise in the early 1980s. It carries many accompanying social and medical problems and many possible definitions (Farmer, 1985). Nearly 40 per cent of the unemployed had been claiming benefit for at least 52 weeks in mid 1989, although 'turnover' among shorter duration claimants was by then fairly rapid. It would be wrong to suggest that the long-term male unemployed of 1989 were the same people as those made redundant from factories in earlier years, but in geography the correlation is very close.

Geographical dimensions of de-industrialization

North–South drift

The 'North–South divide' in Britain's economic patterns was increasingly recognized in the 1980s (Lewis and Townsend, 1989). We shall approach the far-reaching changes of the recent record at a number of levels, from a division of Britain into two units ('North' and 'South') down to the examples of individual factories. Theorists may argue that real factories represent a crucial level of explanation and that one cannot 'read off' local events from international and national trends. Nonetheless, the changes in employment by product sectors which we have reported at Table 5.3, that is, changes in national 'industrial structure', will go a long way to explain the concentration of de-industrialization in regions of the 'North', with all its effects on population (Chapter 4). The focus of the *inter-war* depression in Scotland, the Northern Region and Wales is universally attributed to specialization in a narrow band of declining industries, and these areas were identified as the principal target of regional policy for the subsequent decades. The early 1970s were one period of 'policy success' in which the gap between 'North' and 'South' in employment change was almost closed (see measures for 1971–78 at Table 5.4).

Most of the difference between North and South in periods between 1971 and 1984 (Table 5.4) could still be predicted from the national industrial composition of changes in employment. Data in brackets indicate the values of change that would be 'expected' if employment in all individual manufacturing industries were to undergo the same changes as in Great Britain as a whole. Thus, referring back to the period 1971–78, that method predicted a

Table 5.4 Manufacturing employment change, 1971–89, by standard region (percentage change, 'expected' values in brackets)

Region	1971–78	1978–81	1981–84	1984–87	1987–89
South: total	− 9.5(− 8.4)	−11.3(−13.1)	− 9.3(− 9.8)	− 5.8(−3.2)	−2.5
South East (excl. Greater London)	− 2.2(− 8.0)	−10.6(−12.3)	− 8.1(− 9.4)	− 4.1(−1.8)	−1.1
Greater London	−26.7(− 7.8)	−12.8(−12.6)	−16.9(− 8.4)	−15.4(−3.5)	−9.8
East Anglia	+ 5.0(− 5.1)	− 9.2(−15.9)	+ 1.9(−11.2)	− 6.7(−2.5)	−0.8
South West	− 2.6(− 8.4)	− 9.1(−11.9)	− 4.9(−11.7)	− 2.2(−5.5)	−0.3
East Midlands	− 2.8(−11.2)	−13.2(−15.6)	− 8.4(−11.2)	+ 0.0(−3.7)	+0.2
North: total	− 9.8(−10.6)	−20.0(−18.6)	−13.4(−13.0)	− 2.6(−5.0)	+1.4
West Midlands	−10.7(− 8.8)	−20.2(−19.7)	−11.4(−14.7)	− 6.4(−5.1)	+0.1
Yorkshire & Humberside	− 8.6(−12.7)	−20.0(−21.0)	−16.3(−15.0)	− 0.6(−5.1)	+0.4
North West	−11.9(−11.1)	−19.7(−16.3)	−16.1(−12.1)	− 1.2(−2.1)	+1.0
Northern Region	− 8.2(−10.3)	−19.8(−17.6)	−18.7(−14.4)	− 1.0(−4.4)	+2.9
Wales	− 4.5(−11.3)	−23.2(−21.5)	−10.9(−15.1)	+ 5.8(−7.6)	+6.6
Scotland	− 9.9(− 9.4)	−18.9(−16.6)	−13.6(−13.1)	− 6.2(−5.7)	+1.3
Difference between South and North	+ 0.3(+ 2.2)	+ 8.7(+ 5.5)	+ 4.1(+ 3.2)	− 3.2(+1.8)	−3.9
Great Britain	− 9.7(− 9.7)	−16.2(−16.2)	−10.7(−10.7)	− 2.3(−2.3)	−0.4

Note: 'Expected' values calculated by shift-share analysis at detailed level ('minimum list headings', 1971–1981, 'activity headings', 1981–87), NOMIS.
Source: Censuses of Employment, June (1971, 1978), September (1981, 1984, 1987); *Employment Gazette* estimates, November (1989) for June (1989)

difference of only 2.2 percentage points in the rate of change of North and South, and the gap was in reality almost closed by a 'differential shift' (the difference between recorded and expected) *in favour of the North*. This was due to the coincidence of the growth of 'regional policy factories' in, for instance, the Northern Region and Wales with a heavy run-down in London factories (sometimes due to property development).

The gap was re-opened with a vengeance by events after 1978, when 'the North–South divide' entered a period of widening on most economic and political measures. In 1979–83 manufacturing output declined in all regions, varying from –3.0 per cent in East Anglia to –19.3 per cent in the North West, –20.0 per cent in Wales and –23.3 per cent in the West Midlands. These three regions of the North were also the ones most hit by redundancies, but job loss in all regions of the North was close to its average of –20.0 per cent from 1978 to 1981, compared with –11.3 per cent in the South. Industrial structure can account for two-thirds of this gap, 5.5 out of 8.7 per cent, because of the North's bias towards iron and steel, motor vehicles and textiles. However, there were additional 'differential shifts', further differences in perform-ance, which were most marked in Scotland and the North West, and which remain for discussion. The aftermath of recession in 1981 to 1984 was felt most in the North, and differences in industrial structure left all its con-stituent regions likely to show heavier decline (in data in brackets) than any of those of the South. In the event, all regions of the North also experienced negative 'differential shifts' except Wales and the West Midlands in 1981 to 1984, and all regions of the South enjoyed positive 'differential shifts' except Greater London.

All these differences between North and South were in turn further amplified by the greater proportionate dependence of the overall employ-ment structure of the North on manufacturing. Not only did the North lose 1.3 million factory jobs in eleven years (31.6 per cent of employment in manufacturing and 63 per cent more than the number lost in the South) but, as a result, the growth of other sectors and female employment was slower than in the South. In 1989, 3 per cent more of the working population of the North were unemployed than in 1978.

In the second half of the 1980s, however, the North recovered a small part of the share of manufacturing employment which it had previously lost to the South. In direct contradiction of the predicted values of Table. 5.4 (in brackets) for the years 1984 to 1987, the North's factory jobs declined at a *lesser* rate than in the South. This difference continued in 1987 to 1989 as one between an estimated modest *increase* in employment, of 1.4 per cent, in the North, and a small continuing decline in the South. This favourable trend was to be attributed on the one hand to efforts at 're-industrialization', for instance of steel closure areas in the Northern Region and Wales, and on the other to a partial reversion to the pattern of 1971–78, when labour shortage in Greater London created some of the worst trends in manufacturing employment.

Urban–rural shift

A fall in manufacturing employment in the most populated urban regions (as mentioned above) was a tell-tale sign of the more systematic 'urban–rural shift' of the 1960s and 1970s. Fothergill and Gudgin (1979) pointed to the manufacturing employment growth of the 'smallest' regions, such as East Anglia, as evidence of the displacement of growth from urban to rural areas. The earlier return of growth in these regions in the 1980s signalled a *resumption* of the urban–rural shift which we have already seen in population trends (Chapter 4).

It is not clear precisely what causes this preference for rural areas. However, it is generally agreed that industrial structure plays no general part in the urban–rural shift. Economists such as Cameron (1980b) suggest a continuing 'fall in demand for urban agglomeration economies'. Many writers suggest that cities have become high-cost locations for industry, but the evidence of an increasing number of studies is contradictory. Fothergill *et al.* (1986) sustained a more basic view, that physical space is a constraining factor in conurbations; if firms have limited land for horizontal extensions, then, as more machinery brings a steady expansion of space needed per employee, they must either employ fewer workers, or move out. This 'physical' view is comparable to the effects of declining average household size on the total population of a built-up urban area with a fixed number of dwellings (Chapter 4). At any rate, the effect of the urban–rural shift, 1960–78, was to produce a remarkable gradation in manufacturing employment change across the range of areas from London to the most rural locations.

This consistent urban–rural gradient was lost in the period 1978–81. Rural areas did experience employment decline. Nonetheless, provincial 'conurbations', all in the North, suffered appreciably more than other types of area in both absolute and proportionate terms; the effect was devastating in view of their inherited history of decline and levels of unemployment. For example, the West Midlands metropolitan area lost 23.2 per cent (151,100) of its factory jobs in this period, primarily under the impact of international competition on its motor vehicle industry (Flynn and Taylor, 1986a, 1986b; Spencer *et al.*, 1986). The Rover Group alone (then British Leyland) announced 22,000 job losses, and many of the other large cases of redundancy (Townsend, 1983, 122) were among national and local suppliers of motor cylinders, castings, tyres and other components. The Strathclyde area, with half of Scotland's economy, lost 26.6 per cent (88,100) of its manufacturing jobs in a wide range of metal industries (Townsend, 1983, 99), comprising both the (then) nationalized steel and shipbuilding industries and a number of large foreign-owned plants making vehicles, computers and washing machines. Losses of these types continued through most of the 1980s.

From 1978 to 1981 the heaviest rates of manufacturing job loss were found in two types of area in the North: metropolitan areas and steel-making counties (Figure 5.3A). The worst rates of loss were in the Welsh steel-making counties of West Glamorgan (−31.4 per cent) and Clwyd (−27.7 per cent), followed by Strathclyde (−26.6 per cent), Merseyside (−24.2 per cent)

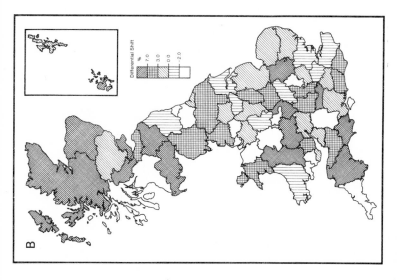

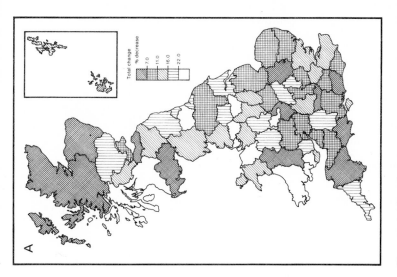

Figure 5.3 Manufacturing employment change, 1978–81: (A) Total change (B) Differential shift. Shift-share analysis conducted at level of minimum list headings of the Standard Industrial Classification, 1968. Source: Census of Employment, NOMIS.

and Durham (–23.8 per cent). These losses all exceed what would be 'expected' from the areas' detailed industrial structure (which would have forecast the greatest rates of decline in Gwent, West Glamorgan and South Yorkshire), and the balances can be mapped as 'differential shifts' (Figure 5.3B). On this basis, the worst 'performances' relative to 'expected' values were those of Strathclyde, Merseyside and West Glamorgan: the best were those of more rural areas, Powys (Chapter 11), Cambridgeshire, and Dumfries and Galloway. All counties of Great Britain (apart from Orkney) showed manufacturing decline in this period. The best industrial record, in the shape of low rates of decline, was achieved in scattered rural areas which happened to escape closures and represented survivals from the earlier, more general drift to the countryside.

In 1981–87, there was a continuing process of national job loss (Figure 5.4A; this period of decline is little known because of delays in the availability of the data that are considered here). Even after the main recession, heavy national declines occurred in mechanical engineering, motor vehicles and metals. We may extend our analysis of urban–rural shift to these years, 1981–87, by reference to Table 5.5, which disaggregates the South and North of Great Britain further into types of districts, a breakdown that is more fully explained in Chapter 7 and utilized in Chapters 8 to 11. Manufacturing employment decline reached the level of 29.7 per cent in Greater London, from 1981 to 1987, and was prevalent throughout the cities and other districts of metropolitan counties. At the other extreme, the 'remoter, mainly rural' districts and the 'mixed' urban–rural districts showed positive differential shifts in employment levels. The strong urban–rural gradient in the performance of factory employment is also evident at Figure 5.4. The worst and most significant job loss, in the overall period 1981 to 1987, was met in Cleveland (32.9 per cent; see Chapter 10), and this area demonstrates one of the severest proportionate 'differential shifts' among those mapped at Figure 5.4B, along with Greater London and Merseyside.

Reductions in manufacturing employment were even more dramatic at the LLMA level, 1971–87 (Table 5.6), and were compounded by the disproportionate dependence on manufacturing of many of Britain's provincial cities, especially Birmingham and Sheffield. On the other hand, the many other activities of London tended to offset the impact of a manufacturing recession. In general, the impact on overall unemployment tended to bear most heavily on the most peripheral conurbations (Merseyside, Tyneside and Clydeside).

The physical and social legacies of a heavy period of de-industrialization were massive, although they varied a little between areas (Chapter 11). Yet there appears to be no eventual change in the relationship between 'North–South' and 'urban–rural' dimensions. Both remained important, creating the worst conditions at their intersection, in the conurbations of the North.

Job loss in multi-plant firms

The geographical patterns of de-industrialization allow more understanding if we study the collective geographical behaviour of leading decision-takers. To many geographers the general statistical tendencies revealed above do

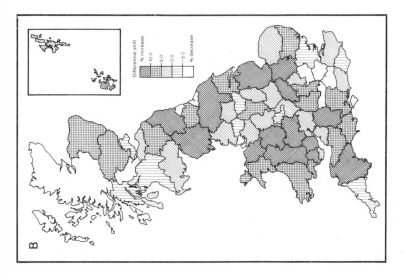

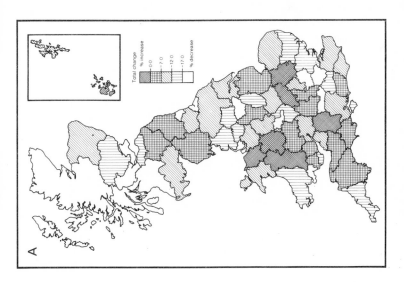

Figure 5.4 Manufacturing employment change, 1981–87: (A) Total change (B) Differential shift. Shift-share analysis conducted at the level of activity headings of the Standard Industrial Classification, 1980. Source: Census of Employment (NOMIS).

Table 5.5 Manufacturing employment change, South and North, 1981–87, by district type (percentage change)

District type	1981–84		1984–87	
	Total	Differential shift	Total	Differential shift
South				
Inner London	−14.9	−6.4	−20.5	−18.8
Outer London	−18.2	−6.9	−11.7	− 8.2
Industrial areas	−10.0	+1.9	+ 1.0	+ 3.8
Non-metropolitan cities	−10.5	+1.9	− 8.1	− 3.7
Districts with New Towns	− 7.1	+4.0	− 4.5	+ 0.2
Resort, port & retirement	− 5.0	+5.4	− 0.6	+ 2.8
Urban & mixed urban-rural	− 4.2 .	+6.3	− 3.4	− 0.3
Remoter, mainly rural	− 3.2	+7.8	+ 0.1	+ 3.4
Total	− 9.3	−0.5	− 5.8	− 2.6
North				
Other metropolitan cities	−20.5	−7.0	−10.1	− 6.0
Other metropolitan districts	−15.9	−2.5	− 2.9	+ 1.5
Industrial areas	−12.9	+0.2	+ 2.5	+ 8.0
Non-metropolitan cities	− 9.7	+0.9	− 6.1	− 0.3
Districts with New Towns	−11.7	+1.9	+ 2.1	+ 6.4
Resort, port & retirement	−19.6	−8.1	+ 9.6	+14.7
Urban & mixed urban-rural	− 8.2	+4.3	− 4.1	+ 0.4
Remoter, mainly rural	− 5.9	+5.7	+ 3.9	+ 7.6
Total	−13.4	−0.4	− 2.6	+ 2.4

Source: Shift-Share Analysis conducted at the level of individual classes 21–39 of the Standard Industrial Classification, 1980 on Census of Employment data (NOMIS)

Table 5.6 Local Labour Market Areas with largest absolute decreases in manufacturing employment, 1971–81 and 1981–87

LLMA	1971–81 000s	%	LLMA	1981–87 000s	%
London	− 389.9	−33.8	London	−212.0	−27.5
Birmingham	− 95.1	−29.6	Birmingham	− 54.2	−23.8
Glasgow	− 78.2	−38.0	Liverpool	− 37.1	−36.1
Manchester	− 76.9	−35.1	Sheffield	− 32.3	−35.6
Liverpool	− 63.6	−38.3	Glasgow	− 31.9	−24.7
Coventry	− 54.0	−39.0	Bristol	− 28.3	−31.8
Sheffield	− 47.6	−34.6	Manchester	− 26.4	−18.5
Leeds	− 41.2	−32.8	Newcastle upon Tyne	− 23.9	−24.0
Newcastle upon Tyne	− 33.3	−25.2	Nottingham	− 13.3	−13.8
Nottingham	− 32.6	−25.5	Wolverhampton	− 13.2	−23.5
Great Britain	−1 918.3	−24.3	Great Britain	−895.7	−14.9

Note: See also Table 6.6 for equivalent increases
Source: Census of Employment, NOMIS

not *explain* anything, and the use of industrial structure in this context is seen only as a first step in the analysis of spatial change. A large proportion of closure and redundancy decisions are made by relatively few employers. In the critical period, 1976–81, Table 5.7 shows that no less than 264,200 job losses were reported by only 20 transnational corporations (TNCs) and nationalized industries. Of course, these occurred in all parts of the country and include some apparently random choice of plants for closure. It might be possible, however, by sampling these and other 'corporations', to discover elements of spatial regularity, and a rationale, in the choice of locations for closures and reductions. In particular, of course, we would be interested in explanation of the differential shifts of Figures 5.3 and 5.4 through closures, etc., working against the North and urban areas, particularly against problem conurbations of the urban North (e.g. Strathclyde, Merseyside, West Glamorgan).

Why should a multi-plant corporation close one plant rather than another? The immediate answer might well be that one is making a financial profit and the other a loss. There is a recognized question in the USA as to

Table 5.7 The leading 20 job losers in the UK: losses reported at known locations, October 1976–September 1981

			Numbers of affected			
Rank	Corporation – Main product	Reported Losses	Reports	Locations	Counties	Regions
1N	BSC – Steel	76 800	86	48	22	8
2N	BL – Vehicles	36 400	42	21	11	7
3	Courtaulds – Textiles	23 200	77	49	18	10
4N	British Shipbuilders – Ships	15 600	37	23	12	6
5	GKN – Vehicle parts	13 100	41	20	11	5
6F	Peugeot-Citroën – Vehicles	10 700	12	5	3	3
7	ICI – Chemicals	9 300	17	16	9	5
8	Plessey – Telecommunications	9 200	12	5	3	3
9F	General Motors – Vehicles	7 900	11	5	4	2
10	Burton – Clothing	7 400	17	9	5	3
11	Lonrho – Varied holdings	6 300	11	4	3	3
12	GEC – Electrical goods	6 200	18	14	13	8
13	Dunlop – Rubber goods	6 100	8	6	6	5
14F	Massey Ferguson – Agricultural machines	5 800	9	4	4	4
15F	Singer – Sewing machines	5 700	5	1	1	1
16	Imperial – Food and drink	5 300	14	13	11	8
17F	Hoover – Domestic appliances	5 100	14	5	3	3
18	Thorn-EMI – Electrical goods	5 000	11	9	7	4
19	Tootal – Textiles	4 700	28	19	5	5
20	Metal Box – Metal containers	4 400	26	21	16	9
	Total	264 200				

Note: N – nationalized group then owned by British Government
       F – foreign-owned corporation
'Counties' include Northern Ireland, and regions of Scotland, as single units
Source: Monitoring and classification of *Financial Times* reports, October 1976–September 1981

Why Corporations Close Profitable Plants? (Bluestone and Harrison, 1980). The answer is that greater corporate profits may be made by releasing assets by sale of machinery, land and buildings, and by investing them in another sector (e.g. offices), or by building or re-equipping another, substitute factory elsewhere. The last strategy is known as 'investment and technical change' in Massey and Meegan's *Anatomy of Job Loss* (1982), in distinction from strategies of 'intensification' (improvement of productivity) and 'rationalization' (selective reductions) at existing sites. Watts and Stafford (1986) refer to the overall motivation of seeking higher profits elsewhere as 'opportunistic redeployment', in contrast to 'forced redeployment' through overall financial losses.

The imperative of financial difficulty, forcing corporations to cut their losses through closing capacity, was the dominant mode of UK job losses in the early 1980s. Even the strongest economic determinists, however, admit the existence of and varying scope for choice in many varied mixtures of strategies (this is the main content of Massey and Meegan, 1982). The UK shows some examples of 'investment and technical change', notably Times Newspapers' construction of an advanced new plant at Wapping, East London, and abandonment of their Fleet Street premises. However, 'selective rationalization' was sufficiently widespread for Townsend and Peck (1985c) and Watts and Stafford (1986, 216) to draw up typologies of plants' locational and other characteristics that might affect the probabilities of closure.

Direct *commercial* influences are clearly involved where the corporation closes excess capacity in a particular product, or withdraws from that market entirely. *Technological* influences may be important where the plant or machinery is old, or where new technology is unsuccessful. *Labour relations* also influence closures; some examples can be found in which corporations close plants where relations are poor, or, we may infer, where little opposition is expected. *Organizational factors* derive from the historical and sociological ties between different sites of a corporation. Geographically, this may bring in the concept of *relative location*, for instance, the distance in travel time between the corporate headquarters and a branch factory.

North–South drift; job loss in multi-plant firms

Research has shown that closures tended to occur in the North (as above). Job losses additional to 'structural shifts' occurred because of the relative status, and often age of product, of branch factories within their respective multi-plant firms, and only rarely because of their absolute location in Britain. By the 1970s the large part of industrial capacity of peripheral regions was 'externally controlled' from other regions (principally London), both through company acquisitions and through the effects of regional policy in concentrating new investment in large 'Fordist' plants in 'assisted areas'. A detailed study of the 515,700 job losses attributed in 1,468 *Financial Times* reports, 1977–81, to named corporations (Townsend and Peck, 1985b, 201) showed no less than 322,800 in then 'assisted areas', including 138,000 in Special Development Areas (SDAs). Covering most of Strathclyde, Tyne and Wear, Durham, Cleveland, Merseyside, West and Mid Glamorgan, these SDAs sustained twice their share of national redundancies in these data.

This suggests that individual multi-plant firms closed their branch plants in peripheral regions before their respective headquarters, usually in the South. In support of this view, more detailed evidence (Townsend and Peck, 1985b, 205) showed that a majority (12) of the leading 20 job-losing corporations allocated a greater proportion of their respective decisions for job losses to 'assisted areas' in 1977–79 than in 1980–81. This change was particularly marked in the electrical engineering industry, involving closure of large branch plants typically employing semi-skilled workers, as in Plessey (see below), GEC, Hoover and Thorn-EMI. Likewise, most closures by multi-plant firms in 'assisted areas' after 1977 were the first closures by the respective firms in this country and in that product heading. (The same data sets do not support any alternative view that 'multi-plant firms close their conurbation plants first'.)

The main finding then is to support the oft-cited hypothesis that 'multi-plant firms close their branch plants first'. Previous findings over this hypothesis had been contradictory. However, the result is matched by US research (Howland, 1988), which covered closures in three national industries from 1975 to 1982. The study found, as we have implied for the UK, that *local economic conditions were not to blame*, as they had little impact on plant closures. By contrast, 'the only variables to consistently predict the probability a plant will close is the plant's status as a branch, subsidiary, headquarters, or independent, and for independents, the firm's age. The likelihood of a branch plant or subsidiary closing is much higher than that of an independent or headquarters' (Howland, 1988, 193).

There had already been indications that the established branches in 'assisted areas' were becoming obsolescent or employing fewer workers in the 1970s, and that new branches were vulnerable. It can be calculated that at least 47,000 jobs in 'regional policy factories' were lost in 1977–81. The US and UK evidence naturally then brings into question the continued use of regional policies in Europe, which characteristically bring branch plants to assisted areas. However, at least 80 per cent of such jobs were not lost but were retained at least for another day, many in viable foreign TNCs, and it would not be logical to criticize the whole policy because of setbacks.

The deepest investigation of UK branch closures was prepared by Fothergill and Guy (1990). They interviewed ex-managers and others associated with 118 closures by externally controlled manufacturing plants in Northern Ireland, Tyneside, Leicestershire and South Hampshire, 1980–86. The reason for reducing capacity was attributed to long-term shifts in demand rather than recession-related factors. Most frequently the group had several alternative plants to consider for closure rather than an obvious choice. In three quarters of the job losses it was the role of the factory which was important rather than its operation or location. It was both the product and the size of plant that were critical. The implication of the study was that assisted areas are not of themselves 'uneconomic places'; the rate of closure in assisted areas was higher simply because they had attracted investment in expanding products in the 1960s which were at the stage of losing markets twenty years later.

The study of individual multi-plant firms

Individual multi-plant firms interact with each other in their decisions, chiefly through competition but also through collusion in agreeing, for instance, to close competing plants (Peck and Townsend, 1986). It is, however, feasible for the reader to study the geographical pattern of individual multi-plant firms in public libraries by use of directories and the index maintained since 1981 by the *Financial Times*. Company brochures on Courtaulds plc, the leading private corporation for job losses with 23,200 at Table 5.7 (above), showed that while it had 300 textile and other plants spread across the UK in 1976, by 1981 this stock fell by 20 per cent in 'assisted areas' but only 5 per cent in non-assisted areas.

Studies of five individual multi-plant firms by Peck and Townsend (1984, 1987) showed how their reductions in employment were fundamentally related to changes in fairly specific market niches, but how the effect of any one factor in the future of a factory was usually *contingent* upon others. In turn, the way in which different product lines were structured within *divisions* provided a key to the complex origins of job losses. The way in which the TNC frames its international marketing strategy could also determine the way in which labour shedding occurred.

Plessey plc was the eighth most important corporation in Table 5.7, and continued to consolidate its activities through mergers in the 1980s before themselves falling prey to takeover activity in 1989. The company first emerged in the Second World War, supplying electrical components for the RAF, and much of its advanced scientific work for the Ministry of Defence in 'Electronic Systems' remained (like that of very many Defence suppliers) in the South, co-ordinated from national headquarters in Ilford (Greater London).

Expansion and contraction in northern 'assisted areas' were, for market and technological reasons, the main features of change in this corporation. The Liverpool factory employed 12,000 workers in the 1960s and was supported by new 'overspill' branches in the 1960s and 1970s in north-west and north-east England. By 1977, however, national orders for electro-mechanical telephone exchange equipment were halved, the Liverpool workforce was reduced to 5,000 and branches were closed in Sunderland (2,100 redundancies) and the North West. In addition, international com-petition forced the company to sell Garrard Engineering to a Third World (Brazilian) firm which eventually transferred all production to the assisted area of Manaus, on the Amazon, with 4,000 job losses in Swindon between 1975 and 1982.

Shares in electronics companies were among the few attractive ones in the early 1980s, but by 1988 the National Economic Development Council was reporting that rationalization to meet foreign competition in this sector was overdue. After totally re-equipping their Liverpool factory to make ex-change equipment to a new electronic specification ('System X'), Plessey were forced in October 1987 to establish a joint company with GEC. This resulted in the elimination of duplication through the concentration of System X manufacture at Liverpool and Coventry, and 1,800 redundancies at Nottingham, Liverpool and three ex-GEC sites in the North (the *Guardian*,

7 May 1988), followed by a closure in County Durham. In turn, however, there followed a long-running battle to acquire Plessey by GEC and the German firm Siemens. The European Commission finally gave approval for the £2 billion bid to go ahead in August 1989, having required that part of Plessey's activities should continue under their own name. This short case-study shows the extent to which a multi-plant set of factories is vulnerable to continuing change.

The collective role of foreign transnational corporations

So far, we have tended to support one general notion, the vulnerability of branch plants. What about the notorious role of 'the multinationals' in the closure of branch plants in the UK? We have already considered UK-owned TNCs but can now consider foreign-owned manufacturing plants. As they are a clearly established data subset in the Census of Production, their collective performance can therefore be compared directly with that of UK manufacturing companies in the UK. In the years of heaviest recession (measured in this case as 1977–81), the rate of loss of jobs in foreign-owned establishments was on average *lower* than that of all UK privately-owned establishments. This applied in all regions except two, but still reflected higher rates of loss in the North than the South. All employment size bands showed a more favourable performance for the foreign plants than their UK equivalents (in both cases, the smaller the plant the better the performance), except that factories with 1,000 or more workers shed proportionately more labour (Townsend and Peck, 1986). At the sub-regional level losses were determined by the location of inter-war and post-war investment. Therefore they were *not major features of metropolitan counties*, although Strathclyde suffered disproportionate losses from the closure of the vehicle plants of Peugeot-Citroën and Massey-Ferguson.

However, the difference in performance between foreign- and UK-owned plants disappears if we take a longer time-span. By 1985 the total employment of foreign-owned plants had fallen to 677,100, dominated by ownership in the USA (416,300) and the EC (95,100); by mechanical engineering and vehicles (205,600); and by the South East (240,200). In 1985–86 a further reduction in employment, to 621,000, was more rapid than in UK-owned plants and showed a net reduction in jobs of a full third compared with 1978, *slightly more* than UK industry. In aggregate then, the run-down of employment in foreign-owned plants was steadier than in domestic industry, reflecting more the international average of changes in the economy and productivity. Figure 5.5 demonstrates the regional distribution of employment reductions from 1978 to 1986, led by the South East, the North West and Scotland. Where foreign-owned corporations created serious unemployment, it arose from their characteristic concentration of investment in large sites. One of the most spectacular of such closures was that of the American-owned Caterpillar tractor factory in Strathclyde in 1987, which was announced with great suddenness from the Detroit headquarters simply because of the corporation's international overcapacity. It was asked, how do we respond when what appears to most commentators to be a

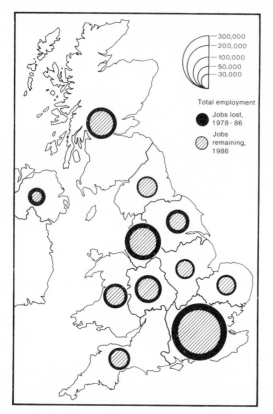

Figure 5.5 Employment change in foreign-owned factories, 1978–86, by region. Source: Censuses of Production.

profitable plant is closed on the basis of criteria that have nothing to do with the plant itself?

Private investment trends and the regions

External control, whether from abroad or from the South, was widely seen again in the later 1980s as a threat to the North. One concern is simply the common withdrawal of headquarters functions from the North when a firm is taken over from the South (Watts, 1989). The issue should be considered more widely than that, though Ashcroft and Love (1988) showed that acquisition of Scottish firms tended on average to increase sales and have no effect on overall employment. However, they thought that these aspects were outweighed by the loss of headquarters functions and their multipliers from Scotland, and concluded that UK mergers policy was blind to some of these issues. In the UK it was repeatedly suggested, during the mounting tide of national mergers of the mid 1980s, that any benefits to corporations and shareholders were being exaggerated through creative accounting. On the other hand, the European Commission could see many essential benefits accruing from the possible birth of European TNCs in the battle against the penetration of Japanese imports and factories.

As regards outward investment, it is difficult to assess the effect on *individual regions* of the outflow from the UK's own TNCs. There are very few reported cases of new investment in Third World countries directly replacing UK closures (as with Garrard Engineering, above). In fact, there is general agreement that the country's leading corporations were increasing overseas employment in other industrial countries (Chapter 2, 25–6) at the same time as reducing it in Britain. It is in the West Midlands (Gaffakin and Nickson, 1984) and the North West (Lloyd and Shutt, 1985) that researchers have correlated massive domestic job losses in leading regional corporations with net increases in respective overseas employment.

The public sector and privatization (including public services)

Even in private industry, some of the largest job losses of the 1980s have resulted from government policies, whether through economies in defence spending (with effects on British Aerospace and Westland Helicopters), changes in orders for power stations (with effects on Northern Engineering Industries), or job losses before and after privatization of nationalized industries (as with the 'break up' of the British Leyland and British Ship-builders groups).

Public-sector spending and employment were themselves heavily and deliberately constrained by the Conservative policy of 'rolling back the frontiers of the state', which to many trade-unionists was part of the same process as de-industrialization. In 1978, 69.5 per cent of the one million jobs of the nationalized manufacturing and mining concerns were in the North, many in large, male-employing urban establishments. However, the immense job losses inflicted on the British Steel Corporation in 1980 were followed by shipbuilding redundancies in naval dockyards on the south coast as well as in northern yards. Policies to contain employment levels affected railway employment in all areas and extended far into the public service sector; here the greatest loss of Health Service and local authority work to private contractors and hospitals was in the South.

Part of the problem may be that the Labour government of 1974–79 was unduly protecting jobs in northern nationalized industries, but Labour was then criticized for halting the growth of public-sector services. The Conservative approach to the employment levels of the public sector, and ultimately to the 'privatization' of much of it, was rooted in 'the assumption that the public sector is wasteful, inefficient and unproductive' (Le Grand and Robinson, 1984, 30). The growth of the Welfare State was seen to have developed diseconomies of scale and was seen to be securing staff interests rather than the public's. In particular, free from the risk of takeover or bankruptcy, staff were able to pursue their own working practices; thus 'for the government, the power given by unions to public ownership is part of the problem of nationalization' (Kay *et al.*, 1986, 299). However, international comparative reviews do not credit all private-sector corporations with better efficiency than public, and 'The real purpose of contracting out, as with state industry privatization, is as much to weaken the unions' monopoly as to save money' (*The Economist*, 17 September 1983, 53).

Public-sector employment ceased to become a growth sector across the map of Britain from 1977. Total public-sector employment rose steadily from 5.9 million in 1961 to 7.4 million in 1977 before showing reductions each year at least until 1988. In many fields, however, the use of cash limits, monitoring and sub-contracting served only to *stabilize* employment levels (Table 5.8) in the face of growing demand (for instance for health services, unemployment benefit or policing), and permanent reductions were shown principally for the civil service and nationalized industries. Data for the latter are, of course, affected by privatization itself, but it appears from government figures (*see* Note) that sale of corporations accounted for over 400,000 of the 1.14 million jobs lost from nationalized industries between 1978 and 1988 (prior to the sale of water and electricity). There were others in the period before each privatization when financial losses were being reduced or written off as part of a continuing process of rationalizing older, basic industries.

Table 5.8 Employment in the public and private sectors, 1978–88, UK

| | Total employment (000s) | | | 1978–88 | |
	1978	1981	1988	000s	%
Private sector	17 668	17 159*	19 077*	+1 409	+ 7.8
Public sector	7 331	7 185*	6 327*	−1 004	−13.7
Nationalized corporations	2 061	1 867*	924*	−1 137	−55.2
Central government	2 338	2 419	2 322	− 16	− 0.7
Civil service	900	878	778	− 122	−13.6
Health Service	1 120	1 207	1 288	+ 108	+ 9.6
Armed Forces	318	334	316	− 2	− 0.6
Local authorities	2 932	2 899	3 081	+ 149	+ 5.1
Education	1 512	1 454	1 504	− 8	− 0.5
Other	1 420	1 445	1 577	+ 157	+11.1

Note: *These figures are affected by the sale of, principally, British Aerospace (1981) 73 000 employees; Britoil and Associated British Ports (1982/3) 14 000 employees; British Telecom and Trust Ports (GB) (1984) 250 000 employees; British Gas (1986) 89 000 employees; and British Airways (1987) 36 000 employees; and by the classification of London Regional Transport (55 000 employees) as a nationalized corporation in 1984
Source: Camley, 1987; Fleming, 1988

Coal and energy

The miners' strike of 1984–85 correctly anticipated an accelerated run-down of employment by British Coal. This in turn was involved with government policies for promoting the nuclear generation of electricity, opencast mining and the privatization of electricity generation, with the threatened increased use of cheap imported coal. It had been the growth of then cheap oil supplies in the 1960s which caused the main post-war reduction of coal-mining employment, from 700,000 in 1955 to 287,000 in 1971. However, the increase in oil prices in the 1970s gave fresh support to the coal industry, major new pits were initiated in North Yorkshire and Leicestershire and job losses were still moderate when manufacturing fell under the impact of recession in 1980. In the statistical period, 1978–81, losses continued to be greatest in

Scotland, the North and Wales; they were only 4 per cent in Yorkshire and 2 per cent in the East Midlands.

This explains the shock felt when from 1981 to 1984 losses increased to 17 per cent in Yorkshire and 14 per cent in the East Midlands, again reflecting a 'southward movement' of industrial problems. The miners' strike drew attention to the social costs of pit closures in mining villages, but the government case gave barely any recognition to this and no connection was made with regional policy. After the strike, British Coal was free to reduce its workforce from 221,000 to below 100,000 (June 1989), but was producing almost the same quantity of coal because of a 60 per cent increase in productivity (Figure 5.6A). Job losses from 1984 to 1989 amounted to 41,000 in Yorkshire and Humberside and 25,000 in the East Midlands.

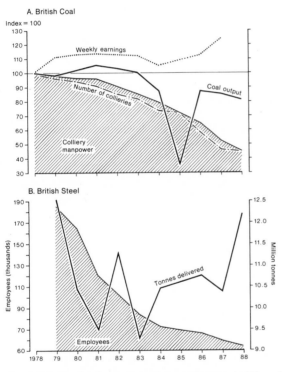

Figure 5.6 Production and employment trends in (A) coal, 1978–88, and (B) steel, 1979–88. Source: *The Economist*, 16 January 1988; *The Guardian*, 7 July 1988.

The process made for a much slower reduction in unemployment than elsewhere in the Yorkshire, Derbyshire and Nottinghamshire Coalfields, and there were fears of the industry being cut to 35,000–40,000 men, with the possible ending of mining in Scotland, Wales and the North East. It was argued, for instance, that the privatization of the electricity industry, hitherto stable in employment, could lead to the loss of 30,000 jobs in coal and more in electricity. However, the preceding privatization of gas had shown only moderate job losses, and the government lobby argued that privatization of coal itself could make marginal collieries economically viable if they had a 'leaner management' and supervisory structure.

Nationalized manufacturing

The regional impact of policy for nationalized industries since the war has been considerable (Hudson, 1985). Most localities with nationalized factories felt the impact of hardening government policies in the 1980s, but effects were selective in space and time as different public corporations received political attention at different dates. In Conservative thinking, the production of internationally tradable goods is the least appropriate activity for public ownership, and the end of nationalized manufacture in the UK is in sight at the time of writing (late 1989).

The methodology of Massey and Meegan (1982) is relevant to the British Steel Corporation in that 'investment and technical change' in new works such as Redcar (Cleveland) were accompanied by closure of many older works such as Consett (Co. Durham), Shotton (Clwyd) and Bilston (W. Midlands). The closure of Shotton Works, with 8,200 jobs in 1981, was the largest factory closure in Europe, but Britain's programme of steel industry cuts, led by Ian MacGregor in the period 1979 to 1981, was also the largest in Europe. Productivity improvements led to further losses of jobs, cut from 190,000 in 1979 to 51,600 in 1988 (Figure 5.6B), and to a return to profitability and private ownership, although the survival of the Ravenscraig Works (Strathclyde), threatened in 1990, was owed to political factors. In the transport equipment industries, British Shipbuilders showed different levels of rationalization in different divisions (Peck and Townsend, 1984), and was eventually sold off or closed, yard by yard. The Navy's own dockyard at Devonport, Plymouth, was handed over to private management in 1987, with 3,300 of the 11,500 jobs to go by 1990 (the *Guardian*, June 11 1988) and, again, little preparation of land for replacement industries. Smaller cuts were made through the reduction, privatization or closure of most of British Rail's workshops. Even in the aerospace industry, employment fell by a quarter in the period 1981 to 1988, following the privatization of British Aerospace in 1981; its acquisition of the Rover Group and the Royal Ordnance Factories also led to controversial closures, staff reductions and sales of land.

Public-sector services

It is possible to study the 'anatomy of service job loss' (Buck, 1988). However, the only sizeable national job losses in services in the 1980s were in the public sector, chiefly in the railways and ports, industries associated functionally and locationally with the decline of heavy industry itself. However, the reduction in railway employment was offset by the growth of activity in the Post Office, and changes in bus service employment were less than feared at the time of 'deregulation' (1987).

Likewise, it is a myth that the National Health Service suffered overall 'cuts' in overall employment levels in the 1980s. It was job growth that was reduced after 1981 by the Conservative government's imposition of cash limits on Health Authorities (Table 5.8). This in itself was serious in the contexts of delivering the Service and of heavy unemployment. In most Health Authority areas, increased employment of nurses was offset by reductions in the use of ancillary manual staff, even prior to the government's imposed requirement for Authorities to put this work out to tender. In the event, catering and laundry work was not a field in which private sector contractors made many successful bids, and there was a tendency for bids to be less serious or successful in northern areas than in the South (Mohan, 1988a). Combined, however, with the rationalization of facilities and the closure of older hospitals in areas of declining population, the policy became politically contentious and the source of local job losses in inner city areas. This was accentuated in London itself by a progressive policy of resource allocation, in which investment was gradually transferred from relatively over-provided regions to under-provided regions (such as the Midlands and North) (Mohan, 1988a, 1988b). (At the same time the number of nurses working in private hospitals, homes and clinics virtually doubled from 1982 to 1986, when 69 per cent worked in the South.)

The pattern of only selective reductions continues if we widen the field to comprise education, health and other services, which expanded employment in all regions from 1984 to 1989. Local authority employment increased by 2.5 per cent over the same period, despite a reduction in refuse collection and disposal, the main field till then of tendering to private-sector firms; 'although most of these firms claim to have a national presence, the great bulk of their work is in the South East and coverage of other areas is often patchy' (Le Grand and Robinson, 1984, 60). Likewise the first major reductions in civil service employment had occurred in Greater London itself, which experienced a greater absolute and proportionate loss in 1978–81 (19,200 or 12.4 per cent) than all regions. The pressure of higher salaries, labour shortages and office rents was by 1989 causing more government departments to think of moving sections of work to the North, as some had done in the 1960s and 1970s.

Overall geographical effects

The systematic questioning of the efficiency and importance of each kind of public-sector job had a searching effect on a previously fairly stable geographical pattern of employment. From what has been said, we would expect the heaviest proportionate effects of the government's many methods of reducing employment to fall on the North. It is possible to assemble total estimates of public-sector employment by region and county, but only up to 1987. If we group together all the industries that were predominantly in public ownership on the departure of the Labour government, we find that their total employment was thrown into decline in the North from 1978 to 1981, but that it continued to grow in the South. In Figure 5.7 we combine the employment of all industries that were mainly in public ownership in *1981*. Their total employment fell by 250,000 (4 per cent) from 1981 to 1987. Due to losses in manufacturing, utilities, transport and communication, job reductions occurred in 38 of the 66 counties, with some

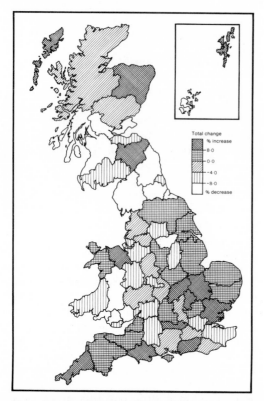

Figure 5.7 Employment change, 1981–87, in public sector industries as in 1981. Data relate to the best fit of SIC Groups to nationalized industries and public services of 1981. Source: Census of Employment (NOMIS).

of the greatest percentage reductions in counties affected by changes in the coal, shipbuilding and steel industries.

This imbalance raises many questions about the behaviour of a Conservative government towards different areas of the country. To what extent was it a responsibility of government to anticipate the loss of large units of traditional male work, whether in Plymouth, Swindon, Sheffield or Glasgow? In the event, organizations were established to try to bring new jobs to areas of coal and steel closures, but we shall see in Chapter 10 that these were mainly token operations in relation to the size of the problem. Less obvious were the far-reaching effects of stopping the previous expansion of employment in health and education, which had been crucial to the growth of income and female activity rates especially in under-provided areas of the North.

Emerging trends in the pattern of de-industrialization

The containment of employment growth in public services exposed the more starkly the effects of the greatest phase of industrial retrenchment in post-war British economic history. This was no mere cyclical event: it effected a permanent reduction in the relative economic importance of manufacturing, the male worker and the North. The searing impact of recession left behind the raw legacy of redundant sites and workers in all of the northern conurbations, above all because it was followed by a period of *jobless growth* in industry (1982–87). Some products and places provide a few exceptions to this pattern, as we shall discover in the next chapter, and there were considerable, if patchy and delayed, efforts towards 're-industrialization' (Chapter 10), which created the estimated increase of manufacturing employment across all regions of the North from 1987 to 1989, averaging 1.4 per cent, probably arrested by 1990.

In assessing the possible impact of future recessions it is as well to ask 'who is to blame?' for the northern depression of the 1980s. With the question put in that way, a group of students mentioned 'the national government', 'local government', 'the EC', 'transnational corporations', 'capitalism', 'the unions', 'regional policy', and 'the people themselves'. They actually failed to mention the main point of this chapter (Table 5.4), that the great bulk of factory job loss resulted from changes in production and employment in manufacturing *as a whole*, with only secondary variation resulting from the performance of its different parts. True, each sub-period was historically specific: while the years 1978–81 showed equally bad rates of manufacturing job loss in all the major areas of the North of Britain (Table 5.4), the aftermath in 1981–84 revealed the worst continuing rates in northern England (the Northern Region, Yorkshire & Humberside and the North West). Some of these lesser variations are due to the timing of government policy changes in the public sector.

However, negative differential shifts in the North have been associated with some of the reinforcing institutional factors mentioned by the students. Industrial structures of the North are important because they are also associated with different occupational structures, including a relative lack of professional and managerial workers, research and development facilities, and experience in developing new technologies, business support services and small firms (Northern Region Strategy Team, 1977). Branch plants in the North may continue therefore to be overlooked by both UK and TNC multi-plant corporations in the allocation of forward investment. In the 'spatial division of labour', the labour-intensive mass-production branch has a weaker role than in the 1960s and is partly replaced by TNC investment in the Third World. The number of factories employing over 1,000 in the North fell from 706 in 1971 to 282 in 1985.

Even where TNCs have been attracted by regional policy to locate new investments of the 1980s in assisted areas, the yield of additional jobs has been meagre. The Ford Motor Company itself placed one of its largest world investments, a new European engine plant, alongside its existing plant at Bridgend (Mid Glamorgan). This investment of £728 million was expected in 1988 to provide only 3,000 additional jobs, mainly in component firms. The introduction of Japanese plants to South Wales, and later to north-east England (led by Nissan), was widely seen chiefly as a spur to UK firms to 'improve' their working practices and productivity, although Dunning (1986) estimated that Japanese employment in the UK could increase to

22,000 by the end of the 1980s and to a possible 250,000 by the year 2000.

The motor industry is seen as a prototype for the 'post-Fordist regime of flexible accumulation', involving both fewer workers at principal factories and a much more varied supply of components for different models and markets. It is difficult as yet to relate these views to changes in the *map* of factory employment in Britain (critical as they are in political economy). It is acknowledged that Britain and the USA have been slower in evolving decentralized, flexible manufacturing systems than have Japan or Italy. It might be argued that the supply of components to factories on a 'just-in-time' basis might prompt adjacent location in a linked region of manufacturing, but, from reports to date, this does not have to follow. Geographers have studied the recent adaptations of local industries, such as Manchester clothing (Gibbs, 1987), but these appear to be more concerned with the survival of firms, with the same or a smaller workforce, than to do with major 're-industrialization'. Pinch *et al.* (1989) reported that the scale of development of flexible employment strategies had 'been exaggerated in the past by media hype and to some extent by the enthusiasm of academics'. Gertler (1988) concluded that the motor industry model had over-influenced academic writing and that the 'post-Fordist vision' was not a new era of production but the 'intensification and development of historical trends established long ago' (Gertler, 1988, 430). These include the improvement of productivity in general, which gathered pace in Britain prior to 1989.

Internationally one must recognize that greater success has attended more decentralized firms making products for smaller market niches. 'The most successful manufacturing regions have been ones which have linked flexible manufacturing systems with innovative organization and an emphasis on "customization", design and quality' (Murray, 1988, 11). The example of the less traditional manufacturing regions of Italy has been well used in the literature. Ginzberg and Vojta (1986) maintained that TNCs are losing their competitive edge in trade and technology and must decentralize to overcome diseconomies of scale. Robertson (1986) also argued that big companies and the public sector cannot afford to go on employing large numbers of people, as the cost of co-ordinating their activities rises and as pensions become more expensive. His view was that the breaking down of large organizations was delayed only by the political power of European governments and workers' movements. Perhaps then Britain is only losing from its delay in moving to 'post-Fordism', and creating the flexible small modern factory.

This chapter has brought together many of the negative features of economic change in 1980s Britain. It is probably significant that manufacturing employment fell at a slower rate in the North than in the South from 1984 to 1987, and was estimated to have increased from 1987 to 1989. This favourable turn was first evident in Wales, and then in the Northern Region, and was largely due to special measures for the worst-hit steel closure areas. However, we have found few indications of any change in the relentless economic decline of areas such as Merseyside or Belfast. Their future may be to show the worst urban decay and deviance in a depressed and divided society; at best, they will remain well behind the South and much of Europe in sharing the gains of an advanced material culture. But perhaps we are looking entirely in the wrong place for any significant employment gains in industry. It may be, firstly, that the increased output of manufacturing is yielding marked increases in what industrial workers (though fewer in number) spend in the service sector, and so supporting more jobs there. It may be, secondly, that the era of 'flexible accumulation' takes the form, not so much of sub-contracting between small firms within manufacturing, but rather of more work put out to service sector firms. It may be, thirdly, that the gains from more flexible forms of employment contracts are also accruing in female part-time work in the service sector. Certainly the private services sector is growing in output and employment and suffered little from recession. The question for us now is whether these new forms of growth are occurring in the same geographical labour market areas as those of factory and public sector job losses. It is this question that is crucial to Chapter 6.

Further reading

Many different aspects of this topic in Britain are covered in Martin and Rowthorn (1986), and several are further advanced in Massey and Allen (1988). The nature of industrial change is dealt with through a variety of approaches in Massey (1984); in Amin and Goddard (1986); and by Keeble (1987). The later debate over the nature of production is exemplified in Scott (1988). Unemployment may be investigated through Farmer (1985) and Routh (1986). A vivid social view is exemplified by Coffield *et al.* (1986).

Many social and political implications are spelt out in Lewis and Townsend (1989). The contrast between urban and rural trends is evident in Fothergill *et al.* (1986), and the particular case of London manufacturing in Buck *et al.* (1986).

A full survey of major redundancies is in Townsend (1983) and in Townsend and Peck (1985b). Theoretical interpretation of factory employment reductions was provided by Massey and Meegan (1982) and by Watts and Stafford (1986). However, many of the issues of UK branch closures in the early 1980s are resolved in Fothergill and Guy (1990).

Factors in the international control of industry are presented by Taylor and Thrift (1986), by Young *et al.* (1987), and by Gordon (1987). The regional role of nationalized industries is criticized by Hudson (1985). An unusual overall view is provided by Humphrys (1987). An example from a growing literature is Ascher (1987).

6

New sources of employment

Insofar as there is job growth it is in the service sectors. Therefore we should be devoting most of our creative efforts no longer to asking what happened to manufacturing – a question now all-too-well answered by a number of geographers – but rather what is happening to the services; in particular, where it is happening. The main question is: how successful are countries, cities and regions in replacing lost manufacturing jobs by new service jobs?

(Hall, 1987, 95)

This chapter is devoted to sectors of the economy which proved their ability in the 1980s not only to expand output but also to increase employment. This leads us to consider the service sector in general and to give particular attention to its various elements of growth. Moreover, just as the previous chapter needed to refer to parts of the service sector in studying employment decline, so this one turns later to those limited kinds of manufacturing which recorded job growth.

Very gradually during the 1980s, employment growth gained the upper hand over decline through the expansion of certain sectors and kinds of jobs. This trend, initially highly concentrated in geographical terms, slowly reached out to affect a wider range of areas, but in a way which only reinforced the *relative* disadvantages of manufacturing areas in the 'urban North'. There must be some weight given to the view that in allowing full scope for the revival of financial services, government policy neglected manufacturing investment (Chapter 2). However, the changing geography of the UK's employment between 1981 and 1990 had ample precedent in the restructuring of the American economy.

United States precedent

In the USA, all the permanent new jobs, 1977–86, were created in services and construction; these accounted for the whole of the net gain of 17.4 million jobs, a gain of 20.4 per cent overall (Table 6.1). The service sector, excluding construction, increased its share of total employment from 67.6 per cent to 72.4 per cent. The UK has *followed* the United States' direction and rate of movement in these ratios fairly faithfully since the 1960s, so it is valuable to study the sectoral and geographical composition of the increases in US service employment. Table 6.1 shows only a modest gain in employment in public administration and defence and in transport and utilities, but there were substantial increases in all other service sectors, notably in hotels,

Table 6.1 Change in employment in the USA, by broad industry groupings, 1977–86 (May)

Industry grouping	1977 000s	1986 000s	Change 000s	%
Agriculture	3 500	3 400	− 100	− 2.9
Mining	843	786	− 57	− 6.8
Manufacturing	19 469	19 173	− 296	− 1.5
Construction	3 859	5 001	+ 1 142	+29.6
Wholesale distribution	5 054	6 947	+ 1 893	+37.5
Retail distribution	13 816	17 903	+ 4 087	+29.6
Hotels	1 063	1 373	+ 310	+29.2
Transport and communication, energy and water	4 576	5 267	+ 691	+15.1
Banking, insurance and finance	9 498	14 520	+ 5 022	+52.9
Public administration & defence	15 342	16 801	+ 1 459	+ 9.5
Education and health	6 015	7 937	+ 1 922	+32.0
Other services	2 385	3 759	+ 1 373	+57.6
Total	85 420	102 866	+17 447	+20.4

Source: US government estimates, rearranged to provide approximate comparison with later tables for Great Britain

retail and wholesale distribution and banking, insurance and finance. The latter included an increase of 2.5 million workers (113.1 per cent) in 'business services'.

Activities which provide services to other businesses – chiefly banking, insurance, finance and wholesaling – are referred to in this chapter as *producer services*. They have been found to be important for the replacement of manufacturing jobs for three reasons. Firstly, the businesses involved may be doing work which was previously carried out within manufacturing corporations. Secondly, they may be concentrated in particular locations; thus, unlike most other services, they bring income into an area and may therefore form part of its 'economic base'. Thirdly, a good supply of producer services in an area may itself promote the success and growth of manufacturing in the same area. The growth of producer services themselves not only buttressed the power of the USA's 'world cities' (New York, Chicago and Los Angeles), but also created headquarters functions to replace the jobs lost by some major manufacturing cities like Detroit and Pittsburgh (Noyelle and Stanback, 1984), and contributed there to inner-city redevelopment.

There are numerous high-wage jobs in finance, advertising, accounting and other producer services. However, the *quality* of the new service jobs is by no means uniform, and it is argued that many services are providing only low-wage, low-productivity jobs which do not fully compensate for previous losses. For instance, Harrison (1982) argued that the much-heralded revival of the New England economy, after early 'de-industrialization', derived from insecure, low-wage employment. Friedmann (1985) argued that employment in leading world cities was increasingly being divided between high-salaried managerial and professional élites on the one hand, and low-skilled, blue-collar workers, including foreign immigrants

(Hispanics in the USA), on the other, creating 'polarization' in social geography.

Changes in the sources of new British employment

If we ask what jobs were growing in the UK of the 1980s, we find that new patterns of spending and investment called forth a different sectoral pattern of growth from before, one which has only gradually become familiar in the geographical and planning literature. Table 6.2 is based on a continuous statistical series, 1971–89, for total employees. (Our discussion in this chapter is focused firstly on employees and therefore excludes self-employed workers prior to the inclusion of the broad estimates for the latter in the final section). The table identifies the broad industries that were responsible for the recovery of overall employment levels in the 1980s. The pattern can be compared directly with the US experience shown in Table 6.1; decreases there (1977–86) were concentrated as in Great Britain, 1981 to 1989, in agriculture, mining and manufacturing, while transport and energy showed only modest increases. Jobs in service sectors increased less quickly in Britain than the US. Yet, apart from transport, all British service sectors showed an expansion of employment levels in 1981–89.

Banking, insurance and finance, the main producer services, showed the highest absolute and relative rates of expansion in employment in both countries and were by far the largest single source of British employment growth after 1981, followed by 'other services', which comprises items such as cleaning services, social welfare and recreation. The services in which

Table 6.2 Change in employment in Great Britain, by broad industry groupings, 1971–89 (June)

Industry grouping	1971 000s	1971–81 000s	%	1981–89 000s	%	1989 000s
Production industries						
Agriculture, forestry & fishing	421	− 78	−18.5	− 59	−17.2	284
Energy & water supply	790	− 90	−11.4	− 240	−34.3	460
Manufacturing	7 890	−1 791	−22.7	−1 012	−16.6	5 087
Construction	1 159	− 57	− 4.9	− 60	− 5.4	1 042
Services						
Wholesale distribution	972	+ 140	+14.4	+ 79	+ 7.1	1 191
Retailing	1 954	+ 97	+ 5.0	+ 94	+ 4.6	2 145
Hotels & catering	687	+ 243	+35.4	+ 161	+17.3	1 091
Transport & communication	1 532	− 128	− 8.4	− 81	− 5.8	1 323
Banking, insurance & finance	1 318	+ 394	+29.9	+ 876	+51.2	2 588
Public administration & defence	1 730	+ 114	+ 6.6	+ 77	+ 4.2	1 921
Education and health	2 215	+ 591	+26.7	+ 331	+11.8	3 137
Other services	978	+ 304	+31.1	+ 402	+31.4	1 684
Total	21 648	− 262	− 1.2	+ 566	+ 2.6	21 952

Note: Data relate to employees only and exclude self-employment
Source: *Employment Gazette*, November 1989, Historical Supplement No. 2, and Table 1.2

employment growth was most notably reduced were education, health and public administration. They expanded by no less than a million jobs between 1961 and 1971, and by 705,000 in 1971–81, but made a more modest contribution thereafter; this was partly due to the demographic decline in school-rolls, but partly, again, to the deliberate restriction of public expenditure by government.

The broad pattern has important exceptions when analysed on a finer scale. For instance, 17 out of 122 manufacturing industries had more employees in 1981 than in 1961, led by electronic components, plastics and computers; three out of 19 showed a net growth in employment from 1981 to 1989 (for which year only restricted estimates exist): data processing machinery and office equipment, timber and furniture, and plastics. Clearly there is a linkage between the expansion and computerization of offices and their manufacturing suppliers.

The dynamics of UK service sector trends

In recommending greater world consideration of services in promoting development, Riddle (1986) argued that

> Viewing services as unable to generate ripple effects overlooks the performance of service industries during times of economic recession. The evidence indicates that many service industries appear 'recession resistant'; if affected they tend to be affected later in the recessionary period and less seriously than manufacturing industries.
>
> (Riddle, 1986, 100)

In fact, service industries as a whole continued to increase their employment in Great Britain during the recessions of the 1970s, growing from 11.4 million in 1971 to 13.1 million at the end of 1978. The major recession of 1979–82 merely arrested any further growth until the spring of 1983, when expansion resumed, to reach a total of 15.1 million by June 1989. However, the more recent growth was not in the same sectors, or therefore types of locations, as before.

Availability of profits induced a different balance of investments after the recession from that of the years before it. Earlier data showed that fixed investment in 1978 had been led by the manufacturing sector, followed by 'financial and business services', the distributive sectors and 'oil and gas', in that order. During the recession 'financial and business services' (part of the producer services) overtook manufacturing, and by 1986 were showing a level of investment almost twice that of 1978, while manufacturing investment was 20 per cent lower, and 'oil and gas' had also fallen, because of depletion of reserves and price changes. By 1986, then, the focus of expansion in the economy had transferred to a significant degree from the 'productive sector' to services.

This switch provided several sources of new growth in employment. Most notable among these were producer services, which have generally shown continued employment increases, despite the advancing technology of office automation. As was shown in Chapter 2, the expansion of financial services offices in or near the City of London was very large. A second form of growth by producer services has been the increased *sub-contracting* of services to specialist suppliers or, in more permanent form, the *externaliz-ation* of work to service firms. As in the USA, manufacturing corporations have come increasingly to rely on specialist firms not only for the supply of skills in finance, advertising, accounting and computing, but also for the supply of security guards, office cleaning, catering, etc. Activities previously undertaken 'in house' within, say, the engineering industry are now scat-tered over several different headings of employment in the service sector.

The distributive sector is a second field of expansion in fixed investment, visible in new hypermarkets, supermarkets and distributive warehouses. Town planners met what was called a 'new wave' of investment in non-food 'superstores' seeking large sites not available in the town centre, and these were accompanied by investment in the third field, of leisure facilities. In considering *The Condition of Postmodernity*, Harvey (1989, 157) notes that 'the need to accelerate turnover time in consumption has led to a shift in emphasis from the production of goods . . . to the production of events (such as spectacles that have an almost instantaneous turnover time)'.

The location of service employment growth

Where did service expansion occur? There is a familiar temptation to say that, as service jobs are 'merely' servicing other industries and households, they will locate in proximity to them, and their geography needs little more comment. In fact, service industries *may* earn their livelihood from distant markets (at home or overseas), and may therefore locate independently of other sectors. The role of wider markets was fully recognized even in traditional texts, which regarded a capital city, an international port or financial centre, or a tourist resort as having as valid an 'economic base' for urban growth as a manufacturing area. Producer services have in their own right now won the attention of UK economic geographers in the 1980s (Marshall *et al.*, 1989). This section examines locational trends in banking, insurance and finance, tourism and retailing, these being principal sectors of interest in 1980s discussion and in Table 6.2.

Banking, insurance and finance: trends and location

The number of employees in banking, insurance and finance stood almost unchanged from 1973 to 1977 at between 1.4 and 1.5 million, but *increased* during the recession years and showed accelerated growth from 1982 to 1989, when it reached 2.6 million. In general, the restraint on growth, where and when it has applied, has resulted from the application of new informa-tion technology, computers and word processors. Within the sector, bank-ing showed only a modest growth of employment, notably moderate in the North and North West, and it was expected that information technology would prompt the establishment of computer centres in small towns and suburbs (Marshall and Bachtler, 1984). The concentration of functions, often at regional computer centres, has also contributed to net reductions, in certain years, in the number of insurance workers (Lewis, 1987).

Examined more closely, however, employment in fact expanded less in the traditional core of banking and insurance than in ancillary activities, such as foreign exchange and credit cards. The outstanding growth of 'business services', statistically part of 'banking, insurance and finance', is relatively new. It is a diffuse group led by computer services (computer bureaux, consultancies, time hire and software houses), a miscellaneous group including management, market research and public relations consultants, duplicating and copying agencies, employment agencies and credit bureaux, and architects and technical services.

To understand their geography, we must ask why all these specialist offices should have developed strongly in the 1980s. Some clearly are of a technical character and are most economically undertaken by specialists. Yet there was also a clear trend for a growing number of large organizations (whether 'national' or 'transnational') to contract out these specialist services to other producer services firms rather than to add to their administrative burdens by retaining them 'in house'. The trend also seems to be the result of a reaction to the conditions of recession and a consequent general desire on the part of many firms to streamline their administrative state.

Most financial services are in fact concentrated in regional, national and international centres of white-collar work, thereby securing the agglomeration economies resulting from staff training, transport facilities and a host of local linkages and opportunities for meeting. This growing use of specialist services increased the degree of regional clustering in the office sector. The established distribution of office employment in the UK focuses on one cluster in and around London, with high 'location quotients' shown in Table 6.3, and on lesser clusters in provincial cities such as Birmingham and Glasgow. Once office employment was recognized as a significant feature of

Table 6.3 Employment in banking, insurance and finance, 1981–89 (June), by region

Region	Location Quotient 1981	Employment 1981 000s	Employment 1989 000s	Employment change 1981–89 000s	%	Share of GDP 1987 %
South East	1.45	844	1 352	+508	+60.1	26.5
Greater London	1.96	568	847	+279	+49.1	33.4
Remainder	0.96	276	505	+229	+83.0	21.4
East Anglia	0.82	45	75	+ 30	+66.7	14.8
South West	0.92	113	199	+ 86	+76.1	17.4
East Midlands	0.65	77	106	+ 29	+37.7	10.6
West Midlands	0.75	123	176	+ 53	+43.1	14.4
Yorkshire & Humberside	0.71	105	137	+ 32	+30.5	13.6
North West	0.85	168	226	+ 58	+34.5	14.7
North	0.66	59	79	+ 20	+33.9	11.9
Wales	0.65	50	67	+ 17	+34.0	12.9
Scotland	0.81	129	172	+ 43	+33.3	15.0
Great Britain	1.00	1 712	2 588	+876	+51.2	18.7

Note: Data relate to Industrial Division 8 and to employees only, excluding self-employed. GDP = Gross Domestic Product
Source: *Employment Gazette*, November 1989, and Historical Supplement No. 2; *Regional Trends*, 1989

regional development in the late 1960s, there had been recurrent hopes that the provincial cities would receive a larger share of office development. Administrative means were employed (and revived in 1989) to encourage the decentralization of civil service offices from London. The past record demonstrates that, in the main, only large civil service offices were transferred beyond the boundaries of the South East.

A note of optimism was struck, however, by Leyshon and Thrift (1989) in suggesting that 'South goes North'. They found considerable evidence of fresh growth of financial and business services taking place in northern cities during the 1980s. London firms had expanded employment in provincial cities. Local firms had found more business through dealing with bankruptcies and financial restructuring in the recession, or through abstracting customers from London, itself increasingly preoccupied with international deals. Their evidence, which ran up to 1984, is certainly clear for certain sub-sectors. However, Table 6.4 provides data from the 1987 Census of Employment, where it becomes clear that, among the North's leading cities, only Edinburgh expanded more rapidly than the national average from 1981.

The stronger dispersal has been within the South to centres such as

Table 6.4 Local Labour Market Areas with largest increases in employment in banking, insurance and finance, 1971–81 and 1981–87

LLMA	1971–81 000s	%	LLMA	1981–87 000s	%
A Largest absolute increases					
London	+ 79.9	+ 15.2	London	+212.6	+ 36.1
Birmingham	+ 14.5	+ 36.1	Birmingham	+ 14.4	+ 28.1
Bristol	+ 11.5	+ 64.5	Manchester	+ 13.5	+ 25.9
Leeds	+ 9.2	+ 50.1	Edinburgh	+ 12.0	+ 40.3
Glasgow	+ 8.9	+ 25.3	Bristol	+ 9.4	+ 32.1
Newcastle upon Tyne	+ 7.6	+ 50.8	Bournemouth	+ 8.9	+ 62.5
Edinburgh	+ 7.2	+ 31.1	Reading	+ 8.6	+ 64.2
Sheffield	+ 6.7	+ 68.3	Glasgow	+ 7.1	+ 16.7
Portsmouth	+ 6.4	+103.6	Southampton	+ 7.0	+ 49.7
Bournemouth	+ 5.9	+ 73.1	Leeds	+ 6.6	+ 24.0
Great Britain	+453.9	+ 36.2	Great Britain	+604.0	+ 35.4
B Largest relative increase					
Andover	+ 1.6	+380.1	Newbury	+ 4.2	+188.5
Milton Keynes	+ 3.7	+295.7	Hemel Hempstead	+ 3.2	+139.3
Redditch	+ 1.7	+290.5	Hinckley	+ 0.8	+115.3
Northwich	+ 1.5	+255.8	Milton Keynes	+ 5.8	+107.0
Swindon	+ 5.5	+255.5	Monmouth	+ 0.8	+105.6
Winchester	+ 2.3	+201.8	Woodbridge	+ 0.6	+103.1
Slough	+ 4.8	+184.8	Dover	+ 0.7	+101.7
Basildon	+ 2.3	+184.3	Andover	+ 1.8	+ 99.1
Coatbridge & Airdrie	+ 0.9	+159.2	Redruth & Camborne	+ 0.8	+ 98.5
Coalville	+ 0.5	+147.6	Bracknell	+ 3.1	+ 96.9
Great Britain	+453.9	+ 36.2	Great Britain	+604.0	+ 35.4

Source: Census of Employment, NOMIS

Bournemouth (Hants.), Milton Keynes (Bucks.) or Newbury (Berks.). From 1963 to 1977 at least 50,000 jobs were decentralized from the City of London to parts of the Home Counties, and they have continued to grow there, along with a reduced flow of new arrivals from London. The net effect of these developments, together with the numerous mergers of UK firms under London head offices and the attraction of London's airports to international finance, has been to concentrate relatively *more* of the UK financial office sector in the South East and adjoining regions (Table 6.3). From 1981 to 1989 the South East itself increased its share of employment marginally from 49.3 to 52.5 per cent, while no region of northern Britain attained the national rate of expansion of 51.2 per cent. (Most fell in the range from 30 to 35 per cent.) Many of the highest *rates* of growth were in the southern regions of the South East (excluding Greater London), East Anglia and the South West (Table 6.3), located in a continuous group of counties around London from West Sussex to Cambridgeshire (Figure 6.1A) and particularly in New and Expanded Towns such as Andover, Bracknell, Hemel Hempstead, Milton Keynes and Swindon (Table 6.4). Figure 6.1B shows how the growth of new enterprises in finance and similar businesses is located in a similar group of mainly southern counties.

Conurbations and industrial counties tended to show some of the lowest rates of increase in employment in banking, insurance and finance. Indeed London itself falls significantly *below* that of the rest of the South East (Table 6.3). Within London the outer boroughs generally experienced strong growth in this sector between 1981 and 1987, while contraction or low rates of increase were characteristic of many inner boroughs. However, the City of London area expanded by 39,600 employees (22.2 per cent) in those years, chiefly in services ancillary to banking, miscellaneous business services and legal services. The City of Westminster expanded by 34,800 (31.7 per cent), above all in miscellaneous business services.

Much new growth is bypassing the inner cities and relocating in the suburbs or free-standing towns. Even when it occurs near inner cities, as in London's Docklands, the jobs are somewhat irrelevant to local employment problems. Parts of the financial sector are expanding in many LLMAs like consumer services. But many national offices are located in a sub-regional pattern which is negatively correlated with that of unemployment. Producer services in general are clearly helping to exacerbate the distinction between the core and the periphery within the British economy, and it is possible for government to alter the pattern of growth only at the margin. Thus there are clear limitations to the contribution of the biggest growth industry in tackling the UK's problems of uneven development.

Tourism and leisure: trends and location

We really must throw off the image of tourism as a second class industry which is not part of the real economy. The fact is that tourism in Britain has a turnover of £15 billion a year. It earns massive amounts of foreign currency. It employs around 1 million people and at present 50,000 new jobs are created each year.

(N. Fowler, Secretary of State for Employment,
Employment Gazette, 1987, 361. The figure of 50,000
was revised in his department's later data; see overleaf)

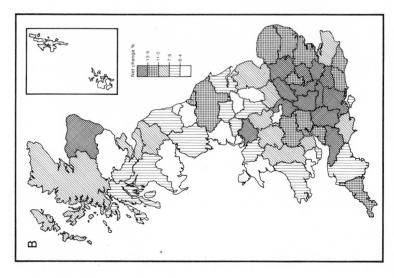

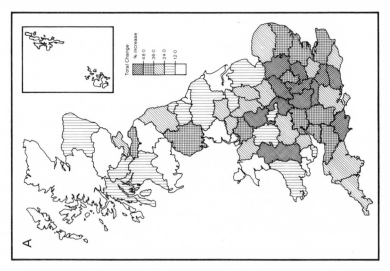

Figure 6.1 Trends in finance and business services: (A) Employment change in finance, etc., including banking, insurance and business services, 1981–87; (B) Change in the number of finance, property and business service firms per 1,000 employees, 1980–88. Source: (A) Census of Employment, NOMIS; (B) Keeble, 1990, Figure 3.

Tourism is a 'consumer service', yet it can add significantly to the income and employment of countries, regions, counties and towns, especially when, as taken here, 'residential-tourism' (comprising overnight accommodation and supporting services, including conference trade) is augmented by 'day-tourism' (car excursions, etc.). In the 1980s central government spurred on national efforts to attract international visitors, while a majority of local authorities entered into competition to persuade visitors to come to their own areas. These were not only traditional resorts, defending their basic trade. They also included big cities, building conference centres on the US model; former ports, developing marinas; industrial towns, promoting interest in their industrial archaeology; historic towns, improving the presentation of their assets; and rural areas developing and signposting 'visitor centres', along with growth of farm tourism and riding stables. The result was to strengthen invisible exports and expand manual work. Yet the policy met many criticisms; it was accused of creating dependence on a vulnerable 'ice-cream economy', of stimulating only low-paid, part-time, poorly unionized work, and of inflicting the social costs of congestion on summertime central London.

The number of overseas visitors to the UK more than doubled between 1972 and 1989 from 7.5 to 17.2 million, though this was far outstripped by an increase to 31.1 million in visits by UK residents overseas. This growth of outward tourism had a profound effect on traditional resorts little visited by overseas visitors, such as Morecambe (Urry, 1987), the Thanet Coast (Buck *et al.*, 1989), and Torbay, where hotel employment fell heavily. Growth in the UK domestic industry derived from the increasing number of people taking more than one holiday per year, from sports participation and activity-based holidays on canals etc., and from 'eating out'. Tourist attractions such as zoos and stately homes increased from about 800 in 1960 to pass the level of 2,000 by 1983.

The contribution to total employment is widely qualified by perceptions of low-wage, temporary, seasonal and part-time work. In the core of the industry, 'hotels and catering' (SIC Class 66), 54,600 of the additional 151,500 employees in 1981–89 were female part-time workers, and no less than 19,100 of these were barmaids etc. However, these data provide only a first approximation to the size of the tourist industry. On the one hand, they include local (non-tourist) employment in public houses etc.; on the other, they exclude further direct employment in museums, visitor centres and some transport services, and indirect growth in a wider group of sectors from which goods and services are bought. Estimates of total tourist employment in Great Britain in the mid 1980s varied between 1.1 and 1.7 million (Johnson and Thomas, 1990).

To analyse geographical change in the 1980s, we use the government's grouping of 'tourism-related industries', which expanded by 128,000 jobs (11 per cent) from 1981 to 1987. Table 6.5 utilizes the 1987 Census of Employment, rather than previous estimates which were used in the quotation at the beginning of this section, and which fuelled over-optimistic speculation about the potential of tourist jobs. There is also the basic point that these figures aggregate tourist activity with internal consumer spending. The South East excluding London stands out with East Anglia and the

Table 6.5 Employment in 'tourism-related industries', 1981–87 (September), by region

Region	Location Quotient 1981	Employment 1981 000s	Employment 1987 000s	Employment 1981–87 000s	%
South East	0.90	352.7	417.3	+ 64.6	+18.3
Greater London	0.94	180.9	198.4	+ 17.5	+ 9.7
Remainder	0.86	171.8	218.9	+ 47.1	+27.4
East Anglia	0.87	32.2	42.0	+ 9.9	+30.7
South West	1.29	107.9	116.0	+ 8.1	+ 7.5
East Midlands	0.80	63.4	79.9	+ 16.4	+25.9
West Midlands	0.83	91.9	99.5	+ 7.6	+ 8.3
Yorkshire & Humberside	0.98	97.7	110.5	+ 12.8	+13.1
North West	1.08	143.4	145.1	+ 1.8	+ 1.2
North	1.23	74.6	75.0	+ 0.4	+ 0.6
Wales	1.12	56.7	62.3	+ 5.5	+ 9.8
Scotland	1.25	135.1	135.8	+ 0.7	+ 0.5
Great Britain	1.00	1 155.6	1 283.3	+127.7	+11.0

Note: Data relate to the sum of Employment Groups 661, 662, 663, 665, 667, 977, 979
Source: Census of Employment, NOMIS

East Midlands as a prominent area of 1981–87 growth in this grouping. A wide arc of counties from West Sussex to Suffolk conform to this pattern (Figure 6.2), but again it is difficult to distinguish the effects of the area's income and life-style from those of tourism. Four south coast counties with traditional resorts admittedly showed employment decline. Considering, however, that over 40 per cent of foreign visitors' nights are spent in London, it is remarkable that London's employment grew by less than the national average in the 1980s (Table 6.5), notwithstanding substantial growth of employment in eating places, take-away establishments and pubs. The conclusion must be that 'tourism-related' employment is largely a misnomer, and responds more to trends in residential population than residential tourism.

In all, the South accounts for 59 per cent of nights spent away from home by domestic tourists, while the share of Wales and Scotland has declined over the last decade. The North has six of the country's top 20 tourist attractions – in rank order, Blackpool Pleasure Beach, Albert Dock (Liverpool), Alton Towers (Staffs.), York Minster, Pleasureland (Southport) and Blackpool Tower (Lancs.). Locally, such centres may exert strong effects on traffic and employment patterns, but employ only hundreds rather than thousands. Most northern regions of Britain showed very modest increases in tourism-related employment, reflecting trends in population and traditional tourism. The highest rates of employment growth there occurred in Yorkshire and Humberside (Table 6.5). However, analysis shows that much of this was in pubs and canteens, while even in the hotel trade the most significant expansion was in business centres such as Sheffield.

The evidence from these data and from local authority experience leads one to be sanguine about central government hopes over the quantity and quality of jobs provided by tourism. The government's published statistics, showing an estimated increase of 77,000 from mid 1987 to mid 1989, are too

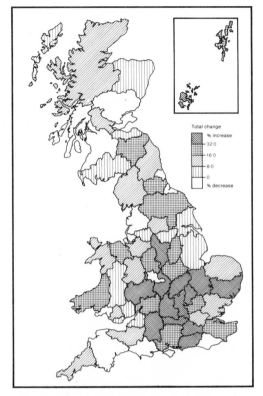

Figure 6.2 Employment change in 'tourism-related industries', 1981–87. Standard government grouping comprising SIC Groups 661, 662, 663, 665, 667, 977 and 979. Source: Census of Employment, NOMIS.

wide in scope to isolate tourism. The effects of tourist growth on London's recorded employment are not obvious, and the prospects of traditional resort areas are not good. Even where tourist growth areas such as Surrey, Oxfordshire or North Yorkshire are identified, there is usually a fair distance between them and the country's employment 'black spots'. However, forecasts of the future growth of leisure spending have led 1990 to be dubbed 'European Tourism Year' and it would be wise to allow for further large employment gains from leisure spending in the 1990s. Certainly, the sector is important in sustaining female activity rates, in releasing the income of residents into the local economy, and in sustaining the economies of an increasing number of LLMAs.

Retail activity

The retail sector was one of dynamic investment and change in the 1980s. A recovery in the growth of sales after 1982 led to the conventional supermarket being overtaken by the building of new 'superstores' and the 'third-wave' of 'out-of-town' retail warehouses. Yet such is the growth of productivity in the industry – a growth of 250 per cent in sales per full-time equivalent employee from 1961 to 1984 – that the net effect of this investment on employment was fairly small. As a consumer service, retailing is merely responding to changes in the distribution of people and income, mainly by following people in the process of decentralizing from city centres.

The effect on employment, therefore, was essentially one of redistribution, between places, between different parts of retailing and between different types of worker in the industry. Retailing continues to employ nearly one in ten of the workforce (after a small growth of employees in the 1970s offset the decline of self-employed traders), but the overall increase of employees from 1981 to 1989 was one of 4.6 per cent (Table 6.2). The numbers engaged in selling household goods, clothing and footwear increased at the expense of confectioners, tobacconists and chemists. The principal regional increases occurred, in line with population trends, in the South West, East Anglia and the South East. This increase was dominated by the West End of London, with its international attractions, but the trend was clearly one of decentralization.

These changes entail social issues. This was a principal sector for the growth of part-time employment for both sexes between 1971 and 1981 (Townsend, 1986a). Future employment trends partly depend on the relative recruitment of young people and married women (part-timers with children), but the general pattern of forecasts extending into the 1990s (Rajan, 1987) was to expect no significant changes. Improvement is critical, however, in the sphere of town planning, where the rational planning of city centres is now impossible because of the volatile behaviour of the large retailing chains. In turn, the GLC (1985) stressed how many of the new developments were both irrelevant and inimical to the needs of the poorer households without cars.

Growth of employment in manufacturing?

This chapter has so far considered the growth of employees in the service sector as the prime feature of the 1980s. It should not be forgotten, however, that there were some sectors of manufacturing growth running against the trend of the 1980s. How much do they amend the pattern so far reported?

Manufacturing output grew by 31 per cent from 1981 to 1989, albeit largely offsetting production lost from 1979 to 1981 and lacking any net growth of jobs (Chapter 5). Any gross job gains were in part cyclical, notably in the West Midlands' motor vehicle and pottery industries. Others, however, tended to parallel the growth of service industries in the prosperous sub-regions of the South. The reader will be aware of discussion of economic growth in 'high-technology industry' in the 'M4 corridor' and in terms of the 'Cambridge phenomenon'. *Net employment decline at the national scale need not rule out significant increases in some geographical areas.* Indeed, the most active past period of regional policy coincided with falling employment in the country's factories at large. The 'anatomy of job loss' (Massey and Meegan, 1982) explicitly recognizes a form of job loss, 'investment and technical change', in which new productive capacity may replace old plant, possibly at a new location.

Thus the 1980s growth and recovery of manufacturing output were enough to generate job increases in a *minority* of sectors and areas, which become more numerous as we take progressively narrower geographical and sectoral approaches and proceed further into the 1980s. In 1981–84, manufacturing employment growth was recorded by only three of the 21 'classes' of manufacturing employees, led by computers and office machinery, one of the regions, East Anglia, and 66 of the 280 LLMAs, led by Stoke-on-Trent (Staffs.), Cambridge, and Milton Keynes (Bucks.). From 1984 to 1987, again only three 'classes' expanded, together with two regions, Wales and the East Midlands, and 134 LLMAs, led principally by towns in the North. The years 1987–89 are covered (at the time of writing) only by regional sample estimates, but this period of exceptional economic growth was marked by small increases of manufacturing employees in all regions except, remarkably, the South East. The relative improvement of the North was very marginal; as mentioned in Chapter 5, it was associated with different government efforts for individual hard-hit LLMAs, which we may now identify.

The overall sub-regional picture of geographical changes in manufacturing employment for the period 1981–87 was presented in Figure 5.4 (above, p.81), while Table 6.6 shows the LLMAs with the largest absolute increases in manufacturing jobs for 1971–81 and 1981–87. Growth in 1981 to 1987 was confined to the counties of Powys, Clwyd, Shropshire, Northamptonshire, Wiltshire and Cambridgeshire, and was led by the LLMAs of Wrexham (Clwyd), Telford (Shropshire) and Milton Keynes (Bucks.). These do not all belong to the same generic type, but owe their high ranking to at least three different factors. Firstly, the momentum of town development schemes is illustrated by the appearance in the lists of the New Towns of Telford (Shropshire) and Milton Keynes (Bucks.) and of planned overspill towns such as Basingstoke (Hants.) and Thetford (Suffolk), where the expansion and letting of relatively new factories has added extra increments of growth. Secondly, official efforts aimed at the re-industrialization of steel closure towns had already borne some modest fruit in the growth of Corby (North-

Table 6.6 Local Labour Market Areas with largest absolute increases in manufacturing employment, 1971–81 and 1981–87

LLMA	1971–81 000s	%	LLMA	1981–87 000s	%
Cheltenham	+3.4	+ 18.8	Wrexham	+4.2	+27.0
Dingwall	+3.4	+287.2	Telford	+3.2	+16.8
Whitehaven	+2.7	+ 29.2	Milton Keynes	+3.0	+15.9
Worthing	+2.6	+ 22.8	Heanor	+2.9	+16.9
Thetford	+2.2	+ 30.2	Swindon	+2.8	+11.8
Inverness	+2.1	+ 99.0	Basingstoke	+2.4	+16.5
Milton Keynes	+2.1	+ 12.7	Corby	+2.4	+26.5
Barnstaple	+1.9	+ 41.1	Peterlee	+1.8	+32.9
Aldershot/Farnborough	+1.9	+ 10.2	Bury St Edmunds	+1.6	+24.1
Cambridge	+1.8	+ 7.4	Shotton	+1.6	+11.0
Great Britain	−1 918.3	− 24.3	Great Britain	−895.7	−14.9

Source: Census of Employment, NOMIS

ants.) and Shotton (Clwyd), recovering from the collapse of a staple industry during the depths of the recession and building on a very low 1981 base, from their difficult positions of 1981. In each case, the attraction of firms was helped by 'assisted area' status under regional policy, but this status was elsewhere insufficient to induce much net growth in this period. Thirdly, the table reasserts that the growth of small towns in rural areas, such as Bridlington and Barnstaple, can be of national statistical significance, although the remarkable tendency shown in the 1970s for net growth to occur in the furthest-flung Development Areas (such as Inverness, Whitehaven and Barnstaple) was not so evident in the 1980s.

Growth clearly avoided the conurbations in these periods, but did it remain a characteristic of rural areas? If we take the 'outer, mainly rural' areas of OPCS (Chapter 11), we find their average performance in Britain, 1981–87, was good compared with the national average, but still constituted a small average decrease in employment. The performance of such areas was still attributed by Fothergill *et al.* (1985) to the lower cost of factory floorspace outside urban areas during a period of capital intensification in manufacturing investment, rather than to evidence on other costs (where results are conflicting) or to availability of labour. The urban–rural dimension of change has continued in a relative sense. However, the urban–rural shift slowed down, at least for a period, in the wake of recession, in a sector where employment is declining. 'This means in practice that rural areas may sustain their level of manufacturing employment, or even increase it a little, unlike the rest of the country, but manufacturing cannot be expected to be the main source of new jobs in rural towns' (Fothergill *et al.*, 1985, 158).

High-technology industry

'High-technology' industry is widely seen as a focus of new property development and a source of new jobs. On the one hand, the post-war period saw the growth of a bunch of new industries based on the new technology of the previous twenty years, but by the early 1970s these industries had reached a stage of industrial maturity and market stagnation. On the other hand, Rothwell (1982), for example, saw possibilities for a new wave of growth (in the manner of Kondratieff cycles, Chapter 2), based on infant technologies including electronic office equipment, advanced information technology, robotics, biotechnology, medical electronics, energy-related technology and agro-chemicals. Many writers heralded the development of the advanced semiconductor industry of 'Silicon Valley', California, and made comparisons with UK experience.

Yet, 'contrary to the conventional belief, high technology is actually a reasonable potent contributor to job decline' (Hall, 1987, 95). It contributed a serious decline of 5.5 per cent (66,900) in Great Britain, 1981–87, a reduction which was concentrated in conurbations and more urbanized counties. A persistent reason was the restructuring of products, production and markets for telephone systems and television sets, involving groups like Plessey and Philips (Peck and Townsend, 1984, 1987). The market for scientific staff remained active, however, and generally stayed in the South. A study of advertisements for posts in the *New Scientist* (Simpson and Smith, 1986) showed the greatest density of posts (per head of population) in Oxfordshire, Cambridgeshire, Berkshire and Surrey. Begg and Cameron (1987) noted the concentration on the South, and were concerned over a progressive widening of the gap between North and South in high-technology industry. High-income male employment continues to be generated principally in southern areas, supported by the provision of modern, environmentally attractive premises, proximity to international airports such as Heathrow and Gatwick, and access to research laboratories, typically established during and since the war in a broad arc of the 'home counties' from Hertfordshire to Surrey. An example of science park development largely related to a university is the 'Cambridge phenomenon', which is estimated to have generated 6,000 jobs over the 1979–87 period, with high income and local multipliers.

The prime example of consistent sectoral growth, as mentioned earlier, is that of 'electronic data-processing equipment', principally computers but also including much of their peripheral equipment, terminals and hardware. In 1981, its largest absolute concentrations lay in Greater London, Hertfordshire, Berkshire and Hampshire, but with important concentrations, due to the history of UK firms, in Manchester and Staffordshire. The increase of 13,400 jobs in Great Britain between 1981 and 1987 (23.6 per cent), was spread between three pairs of counties, the leaders Hampshire and Essex, followed by Greater Manchester and the West Midlands, and in turn by Strathclyde and Gwent, although high percentage increases resulted from new branches in, for instance, Shropshire (Telford New Town). This example tends to confirm that industries needing large-scale expansions of production still look to the financial inducement of 'assisted areas' and the environment of New Towns in different regions (notably Livingston, Lothian Region). In a study of the British computer industry, Kelly (1987) argued that Cambridge and Scotland represented two particular 'types' of 'Technology-Orientated Complex', one related to the university and the other to government policy. Evidence which he put forward, however, showed convergence between the industry structures in the two areas over the last decade. This result from Scotland is relatively encouraging for individual sub-regions outside the South. However, patterns of new firm formation all tend to emphasize southern counties, reflecting expansion by units serving each other and wider markets, rather than relocation from other regions to serve local consumer markets.

Growth of small firms in manufacturing

A popular contemporary view of the 1980s was that small firms, often identified with manufacturing, were enjoying a remarkable recovery and helping to lay the foundations of a new geography of the 1990s. It has often been said that many politicians, and even academic commentators, suspend their critical faculties at the mention of either 'hi-tech industry' or 'small firms'. In this section we will concentrate primarily on small firms in manufacturing industry. Growth was remarkable, given the fact that the number of small manufacturing establishments in the UK halved between the 1930s and the 1960s. The Conservative government of 1979 onwards extended administrative and financial help to small firms in all areas and frequently saw them as a cornerstone of policies for reducing unemployment. It is now widely believed that small firms contribute to regional development through providing both inputs and, in some industries, competition for larger firms.

International evidence fed the government's view. Birch (1979) reported that 66 per cent of the increase in employment in the USA between 1969 and 1976 was in firms employing less than 20 workers. In France, West Germany and the UK, the later 1970s and early 1980s witnessed a striking and consistent relationship between rate of change in employment and size of manufacturing plant; the greater the size of establishment in an area, the greater the average rate of employment loss; the smaller the establishment, the greater the rate of employment gain (Keeble and Wever, 1986, 25; Townsend and Peck, 1985c). Detailed research for the European Commission (Storey and Johnson, 1985) accordingly showed that small and medium-sized enterprises were increasing their share of employment in most Community countries.

It is the *net pace* of growth in employment in small and new manufacturing enterprises that is critical. Data for Britain for the period 1980–88 showed a *net* increase in the number of firms registered for VAT purposes in production industry (manufacturing plus energy and water supply). Geographical analysis of the changes showed that the increase was surprisingly widespread. There were important variations within regions, showing generally a higher 'net firm formation rate' in rural counties than in urban; for instance, higher in the Welsh Marches and rural Wales than in South Wales, and in a line of counties from Somerset and Dorset to Cambridgeshire. There is no doubt about the presence of a North–South distinction when regions are ranked by their net firm formation rates. The highest rates are generally found in the three southern regions which have no conurbations, East Anglia, South West and East Midlands, while the lowest rates were recorded by Yorkshire & Humberside, the North West, the Northern Region and Scotland. The point applies strongly in the growth of service firms, as shown above in Figure 6.1B.

A number of different explanations have been offered. One stresses how the southern counties offer greater access to finance (Mason, 1987), subcontracting opportunities, recruitment of key staff and technical information. Another stresses benefits from the availability of founders with previous management experience, who will be more numerous where there is a greater existing density of small and medium-sized establishments. Mason (1985) tends to favour the latter, 'structural', argument; but the North West had nearly the average representation of smaller factories but low formation rates.

This pattern leads then to the first of several qualifications about the value of new manufacturing firms. This is simply that, far from offsetting the decline of depressed (mainly northern) regions and cities, they are developing disproportionately in the South. As summarized by Gould and Keeble (1984, 193), the number of surviving new firms created per 1,000 manufacturing employees per year varied between 0.08 in Scotland and 0.57 in Cambridgeshire and Greater Manchester. However, even in East Anglia,

Gould and Keeble (1984, 191) concluded that, as in all previous studies, 'new firms have had only a very small impact on job generation'.

Secondly, relatively few new industrial firms succeed; in production industry only a third of firms remain registered after ten years, and half the eventual jobs are created by the most successful 4 per cent of starters (Storey *et al.*, 1987). Furthermore, expansion was partly due to the effects of recession; redundant workers started businesses who otherwise would not have done so, and they were helped by the government's Enterprise Allowance Scheme, which may displace existing jobs. Lastly, there are questions about the quality of employment provided, as regards wage levels, lower levels of union organization and the division between skilled, and cheap and flexible, labour.

There has then been some misunderstanding about the extent to which new firms will provide good jobs, or indeed wish to expand output and employment. Storey *et al.* (1987) suggest that government aid should be targeted on firms with better prospects. A policy towards small business has to admit that it may have only a modest impact over a period of one or two decades. For much of the 1980s, the growth of small manufacturing firms was insufficient to offset more than a fraction of job losses in established industry. This was recognized by the former West Midlands County Council and Greater London Council in their preferred policy emphasis on medium-sized firms.

Sources of employment growth in the 1980s; an overall view

Relationships between sectors

We will now bring together all the different elements of growth of employees so far considered in this chapter, and ask how they fit together on regional, county and LLMA scales. Do the different elements, from services and manufacturing and in different forms of employment, compensate for each other's performance in individual areas, or do they (as a general reading of this chapter would suggest) tend only to reinforce each other? Is the South predominant in all types of growth, or are there pockets of growth elsewhere, as for instance in the North's small towns? We must ask to what extent are the performances of different individual sectors causally related within areas? Alternatively, is it the features of the external social and built environment which induce growth or decline in individual regions, for instance in East Anglia's factories and producer services?

A detailed combing of the Census of Employment can demonstrate some consistent rankings for manufacturing, producer services and consumer services. However, in the counties around London the rapid growth of producer services, arising from past and contemporary decentralization from London and from indigenous growth, clearly outstrips the growth of factory employment as such, and largely represents an independent input to the basic arithmetic of change. We therefore agree with Gillespie and Green (1987) that there is marked deconcentration of producer services within regions.

More precise 'multipliers' might be expected between, on the one hand, the primary sectors, manufacturing and producer services, taken together as the 'economic base' (on the assumption that the majority of establishments depend on external markets), and the rest of employment ('dependent services') on the other. Of course, many individual establishments will have activities which fail to meet the assumption. During the worst years of recession in 1978–81, there was a generally indifferent spatial response among 'dependent services' to manufacturing job loss in the same area. (There is, however, evidence of a timelag, in that the performance of 'dependent services' in 1981–84 showed a discriminating relationship to the regionally variable performance of the 'economic base' in *1978–81*). A further test is provided in Table 6.7, for 1981–87. The identity of leading areas of growth in the 'economic base' is seen to be of fundamental importance, and correlates more closely with the areas of greatest increases in total employment. In this comparison, nine leading growth areas appear in both columns, and are prominent examples of the prosperous areas considered in Chapter 9.

Table 6.7 Local Labour Market Areas with largest absolute increases in 'economic base' and total employment, 1981–87

'Economic base' LLMA	000s	%	Total employment LLMA	000s	%
Milton Keynes	+ 14.7	+43.1	Reading	+ 20.0	+14.6
Cambridge	+ 12.4	+23.8	Milton Keynes	+ 18.5	+29.9
Northampton	+ 10.6	+16.9	Northampton	+ 18.4	+17.4
Aldershot &			Cambridge	+ 15.7	+15.0
Farnborough	+ 9.2	+20.4	Oxford	+ 15.6	+10.5
Oxford	+ 8.8	+13.0	Bournemouth	+ 15.0	+ 9.9
Swindon	+ 8.3	+16.4	Aldershot &		
Newbury	+ 7.2	+52.4	Farnborough	+ 14.6	+15.6
Bournemouth	+ 7.2	+ 9.5	Swindon	+ 14.0	+15.7
High Wycombe	+ 6.9	+12.4	Norwich	+ 12.4	+ 8.4
Norwich	+ 6.5	+ 8.1	High Wycombe	+ 11.9	+13.0
Great Britain	−405.5	− 3.5	Great Britain	+178.8	+ 0.9

Note: 'Economic base' comprises Divisions 0–4 of Standard Industrial Classification, 1980 *plus* 'producer services' as defined in Marshall (1988)
Source: Census of Employment, NOMIS

Growth areas in the North?

All ten LLMAs listed in Table 6.7 lie in the South. The next 40 LLMAs, by order of size of the employment increases in their 'economic base', include only ten LLMAs in the North. By order of total employment change, the North accounts for only 12 LLMAs in the top 50. These comprise both assisted manufacturing areas such as Wrexham (Clwyd) and Irvine (Strathclyde) and service centres such as York and Northallerton (N. Yorks.). Are there any areas with a continuous record of growth in the North? Townsend (1986b) argued that centres such as Preston (Lancs.) and Chester represented (initially surprising but) genuine northern centres of relative prosperity in the period 1978–81; they would have appeared in a table like

Table 6.7 for that period, but thereafter lost their position as a result of the delayed impact of recession on the areas surrounding them.

It remains generally true that overall growth, 1981–87, was at its greatest, on average, in free-standing service centres such as Harrogate (N. Yorks.) or Shrewsbury (Shropshire) rather than in larger urban centres or in more rural areas. Thus it is true that what growth there is in the North tends to occur in medium-sized centres and not at all in the cities. However, the generalization cannot be consistently applied, not least because all categories of area performed worse than in the South.

The conclusion appears to be that sub-regional growth tends to benefit larger centres such as Oxford, but that, in more depressed northern conditions, such 'growth centres' cannot sustain momentum in the absence of more general growth in surrounding areas. There remain suggestions, however, that the *smallest* LLMAs are continuing to perform better than their respective regions. In these analyses, we have so far considered 'employees' as a uniform mass (differentiated only by sector or activity). It remains possible to incorporate the effects of different *kinds* of activity before summarizing at the regional level.

New kinds of employment?

Crude numbers of employees may provide a less accurate measure of change, industrially, socially and geographically, than in the past: in this section we ask how other measures may modify the geographical pattern obtained so far. There is widespread agreement about the *direction* of employment change in the 1980s, in the shape of an intensification of trends described in Chapter 3 away from male full-time factory employees (especially those working in large establishments), not only towards services but also towards self-employment, small firms, part-time and female employment, with workers often engaged on temporary contracts and working flexible hours. A common cause of all these trends has been the relative weakness of labour and unions in opposing cost-cutting measures by employers, notably through subcontracting and through attaining flexibility in meeting demand by retaining more 'peripheral' workers on temporary contracts. These apply most strongly to service sectors and have been proposed officially for the civil service.

The *pace* of these changes is debated. For some business critics, 'they did not cut very deeply in most firms, and therefore the outcome was more likely to be marginal, *ad hoc*, and tentative, rather than a purposeful and strategic thrust to achieve flexibility' (Atkinson and Meager, 1986). Nevertheless, radical critics saw the growing distinction between 'core' and 'peripheral' workers as sufficient to cause social polarization between advantaged and disadvantaged workers in individual places. The detection of such trends in conventional statistics is not straightforward. But in any case, we must assess how far 'new forms of employment' are reflected in or distort the conventional measures (of 'total employees in employment') used so far in this volume.

Male and female employment

Female employment has replaced male to a considerable extent in recent years. From 1981 to 1989, the number of female employees at work increased by 1,132,000 (12.4 per cent), and the number of males fell by 564,000 (4.6 per cent). Much of the increase of female employment was a by-product of growth in financial offices, hotels and catering. In coming to conclusions about the spatial pattern of growth, and particularly in the next chapter about the implications for housing and migration, it is essential to view our results through the 'gender division of labour'. Figure 6.3 adopts a common scale on which to view these changes at a county level.

The 1981–87 evidence on male employment (with its higher average income levels) underpins the concept of a 'western arc' around London; excluding Kent, Essex, Hertfordshire and London itself, a continuous area of increase in male employment stretches from West Sussex to Wiltshire and Dorset, Northamptonshire, Cambridgeshire and Suffolk, with outliers in Hereford & Worcester, Shropshire, Powys, Clwyd, Cumbria and the Western Isles. At the LLMA level (Table 6.8), all the leading cases of growth (by absolute values) lie in this western arc, whereas Aberdeen had previously been an outlier before the slackened rate of investment in North Sea oil. The areas of expanding male employment thus yield a provisional definition of the country's 'growth areas'.

The map of female employment (Figure 6.3) shows much more general increases, with areas of decline identifying the more extreme cases of industrial problems (e.g. in central Scotland, Cleveland and the West Midlands conurbation). Some of the largest increases (Table 6.8) were in the western arc, but were not always in proportion to male growth there. The effect of this comparison is to say that growth of male jobs, which are on average higher-paid than female, concentrated more in the rural South than figures for total employees have so far told us.

Full-time and part-time employment

There is a heavy overlap between the categories of female and part-time employees. The growth of part-time work in the 1980s was widely recognized. Indeed, the UK is 'ahead' of most of western Europe in this field. In most other European countries, part-time staff have the same rights as full-time. In the UK, national insurance and employment laws provide more opportunities for employers to save money by employing part-time staff in lieu of full-time. In turn, economical part-time labour is useful in providing flexible adjustment to peaks of demand, for instance in the evening or Saturday opening of supermarkets. Part-time employment has proved attractive to a particular type of workers – married women. In the 1988 Labour Force Survey (*Employment Gazette*, 1989, 185), no less than 55.7 per cent of married women were economically active, and of these 53.0 per cent were working part-time (by their own assessment). Over three-quarters of them, particularly housewives with children at school, said that they had not wanted a full-time job.

The increase of part-time employees, of whom 82.5 per cent are women,

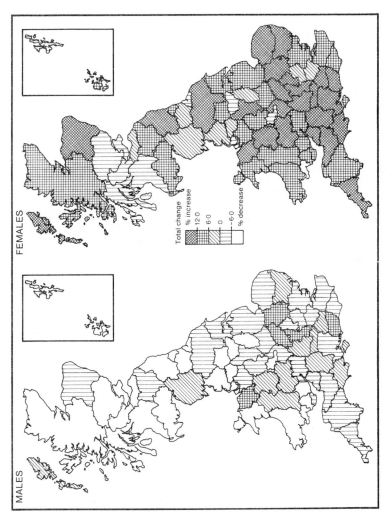

Figure 6.3 Total employment change by gender, 1981–87. Source: Census of Employment, NOMIS.

Table 6.8 Local Labour Market Areas with largest absolute increases in male and female employment, 1981–87

Males LLMA	000s	%	Females LLMA	000s	%
Milton Keynes	+7.8	+21.5	London	+ 95.8	+ 5.8
Reading	+7.3	+ 9.5	Newcastle upon Tyne	+ 15.7	+10.7
Cambridge	+6.8	+11.4	Southampton	+ 13.7	+18.6
Northampton	+6.8	+11.5	Reading	+ 12.7	+21.0
Swindon	+6.6	+13.1	Northampton	+ 11.6	+25.0
Aldershot/Farnborough	+6.2	+12.5	Bournemouth	+ 11.1	+16.2
Oxford	+6.0	+ 7.5	Milton Keynes	+ 10.6	+41.8
Newbury	+5.7	+37.7	Norwich	+ 10.3	+16.3
High Wycombe	+5.0	+10.0	Leicester	+ 9.9	+10.0
Basingstoke	+4.5	+16.5	Oxford	+ 9.5	+14.1
Great Britain	−548.2	− 4.5	Great Britain	+725.5	+ 8.1

Source: Census of Employment, NOMIS

has occurred partly through the substitution of part-time for full-time jobs. Townsend (1986a) estimated that at least half the increase of over one million part-time jobs in 1971–81 (Table 6.9) occurred through substitution. The rest depended on the favourable distribution of part-time work between sectors of the economy. Part-time work was unimportant in manufacturing, which was declining. Part-time work expanded mainly in the public sectors of the Health Service and education in the 1970s, but from 1981 to 1989 these two were each overtaken by the banking, finance and insurance group, and a miscellaneous group of services such as social welfare, while increases were also important in hotels and catering and retailing.

The patterns of growth of part-time employment are different from what we have seen so far, in that are they spread over most areas of Great Britain.

Table 6.9 Change in full-time employees, part-time employees and self-employment, Great Britain 1971–89 (thousands)

	Employees in employment		Part-time			Self Employment
	Total	Full-time	Males	Females	Total	
1971	21 648	18 307	584	2 757	3 341	1 953
1981	21 309	16 810	718	3 781	4 499	2 071
1989	21 952	16 716	917	4 319	5 236	3 050
Absolute change						
1971–81	−339	−1 497	+134	+1 024	+1 158	+118
1981–89	+643	−94	+199	+ 538	+737	+979
Percentage change						
1971–81	−1.6	−8.2	+22.9	+37.1	+34.7	+6.0
1981–89	+3.0	−0.6	+27.7	+14.2	+16.3	+47.3

Note: In addition, government statistics for June 1989 identified 469 000 people on 'work related government training programmes', 308 000 armed forces, making with the above a 'workforce in employment' of 25 780 000. Data relate to June, except for 1981 which are for September
Source: *Employment Gazette*, November 1989, and Historical Supplement No. 2, 1989

In the 1960s and 1970s part-time work contributed heavily to a 'convergence' of female activity rates, through disproportionate growth in Wales, Scotland and the North. Thus by 1981 all regions except the South West had between 19.6 and 21.6 per cent of all employees working part-time. From 1981 to 1989, an overall growth of 16.3 per cent (737,000) occurred in part-time employment, with the highest rates of growth in East Anglia, Wales and the East Midlands, followed by the North and Yorkshire and Humberside. Table 6.10 demonstrates the leading areas of part-time employment increase (in this case up to 1987), as defined in the Census of Employment to cover people working less than 30 hours per week. The leading areas are from virtually all regions. The largest absolute increase occurred in provincial service centres (such as Newcastle upon Tyne), only with some bias towards medium-sized southern centres such as Southampton and Norwich. The largest percentage increases tended to occur in medium- and small-sized areas of the North. At the level of counties (and Regions of Scotland), Figure 6.4 demonstrates for the period 1981–87 a bias in favour of peripheral 'rural' counties such as Devon, and against some conurbation areas. A correlation between population trends and the growth of part-time employees was established for the period 1971–81 (Townsend, 1986a), and is due to their work, as in retailing or schools, in servicing local populations in their respective functional regions. This is a symptom of growth in East Anglia, Northamptonshire and Warwickshire.

Table 6.10 Local Labour Market Areas with largest absolute increases in part-time employment, 1971–81 and 1981–87

LLMA	1971–81 000s	%	LLMA	1981–87 000s	%
London	+83.7	+ 13.2	Newcastle upon Tyne	+ 19.4	+29.2
Glasgow	+20.7	+ 28.9	Bradford	+ 13.0	+41.0
Manchester	+19.3	+ 21.1	Manchester	+ 10.6	+ 9.6
Southampton	+16.8	+ 67.2	London	+ 9.3	+ 1.3
Bristol	+16.6	+ 33.4	Southampton	+ 9.2	+22.1
Edinburgh	+15.5	+ 31.3	Coventry	+ 8.0	+21.2
Newcastle upon Tyne	+15.1	+ 29.5	Derby	+ 8.0	+29.2
Aberdeen	+14.6	+ 79.8	Cardiff	+ 8.0	+22.3
Winchester	+14.2	+376.5	Huddersfield	+ 7.9	+60.4
Bournemouth	+14.2	+ 58.4	Norwich	+ 7.7	+24.1
Great Britain	+1 089.4	+ 32.6	Great Britain	+569.3	+12.9

Source: Census of Employment, NOMIS

If we were to plot the distribution of change in full-time jobs, then only 25 of the 66 spatial units of the map would show positive increases. When stripped of part-time increases, only Buckinghamshire, Northamptonshire, Cambridgeshire and West Sussex show positive changes in employment, 1981 to 1987. The overall rates of change are particularly depressed in the South West and South Wales. The effect of allowing for part-time employment is, then, again to sharpen a contrast between the growth of full-time work in the rural South, and the more widely-spread growth of part-time (lower-paid) jobs.

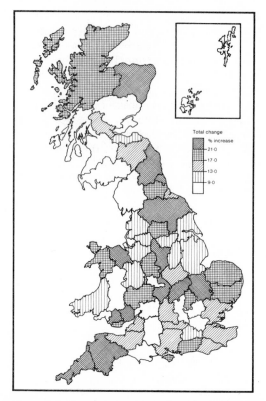

Figure 6.4 Change in total part-time employment, 1981–87. Source: Census of Employment, NOMIS. Data refers to employees working less than 30 hours per week.

It is also misleading to combine full-time and part-time jobs on an equal basis, as is done in nearly all conventional statistics and commentaries. There is now widespread realization that adjustment must be made to allow for the shorter hours of work of part-timers. In health and education, established ratios for different grades are regularly used to measure staff trends in terms of 'full-time equivalents'. Robertson *et al.* (1982) accept a ratio of 2:1 full-time: part-time as a 'fairly accurate average' across all sectors. Thus in Table 6.11 part-time employees have been counted as 'half-employees' in columns five and six to produce more realistic estimates of total employment change, expressed in terms of 'full-time equivalents'. Part-time employment increases averaged 15 per cent in both North and South. Because part-time employment thus contributes proportionately more to the otherwise unfavourable trends of poorer regions, the effect of our adjustment is to *sharpen* North–South differences. On this basis, the years 1981 to 1989 showed a 3.8 per cent reduction of employment in the North, before allowing for the self-employed.

Table 6.11 Regional employment change, 1981–89, including composite total of full-time equivalents

Region	Employees in employment — Total number of employees 000s	%	of whom Part-time 000s	%	Full-time equivalents 000s	%	Self-employed 000s	%	Composite total of full-time equivalents 000s	%
South East	+414	+ 5.7	+175	+11.4	+327	+ 5.0	+389	+55.3	+ 668	+ 9.4
Greater London	+ 14	+ 0.4	+ 8	+ 0.1	+ 10	+ 0.3	+132	+48.2	+ 125	+ 3.6
Remainder	+400	+10.9	+165	+18.4	+317	+ 9.8	+257	+59.8	+ 543	+15.0
East Anglia	+ 83	+12.2	+ 42	+28.5	+ 62	+10.2	+ 52	+59.1	+ 108	+15.7
South West	+130	+ 8.4	+ 70	+19.0	+ 95	+ 7.0	+ 80	+35.6	+ 164	+10.5
East Midlands	+ 78	+ 5.3	+ 75	+24.5	+ 41	+ 3.1	+ 61	+41.8	+ 94	+ 6.1
South	+705	+ 6.4	+362	+15.3	+524	+ 5.4	+582	+50.0	+1033	+ 9.5
West Midlands	− 3	− 0.1	+ 56	+13.6	− 31	− 1.7	+ 80	+46.8	+ 39	+ 2.0
Yorks. & Humb.	− 51	− 2.8	+ 76	+19.0	− 89	− 5.4	+ 75	+45.5	+ 24	− 1.3
North West	− 55	− 2.2	+ 58	+11.2	− 84	− 3.8	+ 78	+35.8	+ 17	− 0.7
North	− 29	− 2.6	+ 49	+21.5	− 54	− 5.3	+ 31	+36.5	+ 27	− 2.5
Wales	+ 18	+ 1.9	+ 50	+26.8	− 7	− 0.1	+ 34	+29.3	+ 22	+ 2.3
Scotland	− 74	− 3.7	+ 36	+ 8.9	− 92	− 5.1	+ 69	+45.1	− 32	− 1.6
North	−194	− 1.9	+324	+15.1	−356	− 3.8	+367	+40.4	− 38	− 0.4
Great Britain	+514	+ 2.4	+685	+15.2	+168	+ 0.9	+948	+45.8	+ 995	+ 4.7

Note: Data for September 1981 and March 1989. 'Composite total' comprises full-time equivalent employees in employment (full-time, plus part-time × 0.5), plus self-employed (× factors to allow for the proportions of self-employed who are estimated to work part-time)
Source: *Employment Gazette*, November 1989, Historical Supplement No. 2

Self-employment

There is also widespread recognition of the growth of self-employment in the 1980s. Because of the difficulty of collecting data for this sector, the conventional statistics used so far in this chapter (principally based on the Census of Employment) have excluded this kind of work. However, broad regional estimates of self-employment are now regularly made (*Employment Gazette*, 1989, Historical Supplement No. 2) and are included in Table 6.11.

Geographically, the detailed location of the self-employed is known only from the Census of Population, whose 1981 results are mapped at Figure 6.5. Because self-employment represents nearly half the total employment of the primary sector, its share of total employment is often at its highest in peripheral or coastal counties of the South West, Wales, rural Scotland and eastern England, and lowest in industrial counties such as the West Midlands, Cleveland or Strathclyde. However, at the regional level (Creigh *et al.*, 1986) little of the variation in self-employment is attributable to industrial structure, and the further relationship with unemployment is unsystematic.

When we consider the 1980s growth of self-employment, we might think

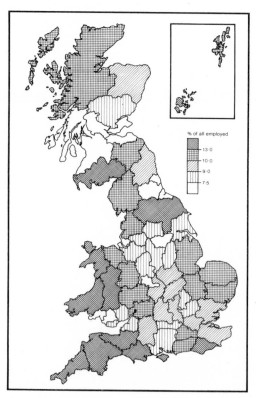

Figure 6.5 The distribution of self-employment, 1981. Source: Census of Population 1981, NOMIS.

that in areas of high unemployment the limited opportunities for gaining employment in the 1980s will have 'artificially' induced work-seekers into self-employment, including some of those with redundancy payments to invest. This factor appears to be partly cancelled out by the poorer business environment of these areas. In fact the rapid growth of the self-employed, amounting to a remarkable addition of 948,000 between 1981 and 1989, was in the dominant sub-sectors of construction, distribution, hotels, catering and miscellaneous services. As shown in Table 6.11, the greatest proportionate growth of self-employment occurred both in the South East and East Anglia, with Scotland as the main example of growth among the more depressed peripheral regions.

We may therefore make a further refinement to Table 6.11 by combining the column for self-employment with that for 'full-time equivalents' (*see* Note). The overall effect, when this 'composite total' is compared with the basic count of full-time and part-time employees in column one, is to double the apparent rate of national increase, 1981 to 1989, from 2.4 to 4.7 per cent. The composite total provides the least 'improvement' for the North, Wales and the East Midlands. One important effect of the combined calculations is to give a firmer view of the net growth of employment in the South East and South West, and to reaffirm the leading role of East Anglia in British employment changes. In all, the 'composite total' attributes the addition of a million jobs to the economy of the South (a rate of increase approaching 10 per cent), while the North retains a small decrease in employment levels, even after eliminating the statistical period 1978 to 1981, which was dominated by declining sectors (Chapter 5).

Conclusions

What broad conclusions can be drawn from the growth of the functionally 'peripheral' workforce at the expense of the 'core', and what relevance have such trends to the geography of contemporary Britain? Of the regular workforce, Hakim (1987, 93) asserted that by the mid 1980s the labour force divided into two-thirds 'permanent' and one-third 'flexible'. On this measure, one-quarter of all men in work and half of all women in work were then in the sector offering numerical flexibility through being on temporary or part-time contracts. Data for 1988, however, showed only 5.6 per cent of workers as temporary. Hakim admits, moreover, that the thesis of a major change to flexible employment is not conclusively proven in case studies: in any case issues such as homeworking, second jobs, and the black economy are of more immediate interest to sociologists than geographers. However, it is significant that *the balance of new employment in northern Britain is more heavily weighted towards part-time employment and some forms of self-employment than elsewhere, and less weighted towards new firm formation in manufacturing or services.* These new sources of employment are nowhere more evident than in the service sector.

Table 6.11 has refined our assessment of overall regional growth in the 1980s. Recurrent poor performances by the Northern Region, Scotland, Yorkshire and Humberside and the North West suggest a restoration of 'North–South' differences as *traditionally defined.* Perhaps surprisingly,

Wales and the West Midlands, frequently grouped with the North West as the worst affected regions during recession years of the early 1980s, do show some cyclical recovery and have more in common with Greater London in this table. Within the North there are cases of buoyant employment growth in centres such as Edinburgh or York, but with insufficient weight to affect heavily the overall outcome for their respective regions. Within the South, however, internal regional boundaries are less significant and it is distance from London which is the dominant element in employment growth. Repeatedly, we have found that the most successful economic base in the 1980s is found as far from London as Dorset, Wiltshire, Oxfordshire, Northamptonshire and Cambridgeshire. The modern connotations of Oxford and Cambridge are much more successful than those of major provincial cities in a service-led economy.

Further reading

Possible international precedents for UK growth are evident in the analyses of Noyelle and Stanback (1984). Comparisons of UK and US patterns of investment are made in Hall and Markusen (1985), and in Breheny and Hall (1987). Wider international comparison of employment trends is provided in Hall (1987). International data of this kind can be updated from OECD (annual). European trends are deduced in Keeble *et al.* (1983), and in Keeble and Wever (1986).

A comprehensive reader was prepared by geographers under the editorship of Lever (1987). The underlying advantages of non-metropolitan growth were developed by Fothergill *et al.* (1984). Spatial implications of new technology are considered by Rothwell (1982) and in Howells (1984). A growing literature on its field is reviewed by Mason and Harrison (1985), and an example of recent conclusions is provided by Storey *et al.* (1987).

The implications of incorporating service employment growth into economic geography and planning were prominently appraised by Gottmann (1961). An example of international awareness of the question is Riddle (1986). Many conceptual and analytical issues are developed by Gershuny and Miles (1983) and by Urry (1987). Analysis and forecasts for the UK were reported in Rajan (1987).

Reviews on the growth of service industries are provided by Daniels (1979, 1985b, 1986); Dawson (1982); and by Damesick (1986).

The identification and role of producer services have evolved through work including Wood (1986); Gillespie and Green (1987); Marshall (1985); and Marshall *et al.* (1988). Examples of material on other service sectors are Burkart and Medlik (1981) and Dawson (1980).

The effects of contemporary trends on people and places are part of an emerging social sciences literature. Some prospective 'locality studies' on 'tertiarized and managerial labour markets' were collated by Cooke (1986). Changing patterns of female and part-time employment are analysed in Martin and Roberts (1984); Beechey and Perkins (1987); and Townsend (1986). Questioning of the merits of modern employment trends is exemplified in Harrison (1982).

7
Changing dynamics of localities

Until recently, different parts of Britain appeared to have become more and more similar in terms of economic, political and social life . . . Britain in the 1970s was a great deal more homogeneous than it had been in 1945. At the end of the 1980s, such a claim would be almost unbelievable.
                                                    Lewis and Townsend (1989), xi

The three previous chapters in Part II have documented the major changes which have taken place in the geography of population and employment in Britain since the early 1970s. As noted in the quotation above, the key feature has been the widening of differences between regions and localities in stark contrast to the general tendency in earlier parts of the post-1945 period. Particularly notable has been the re-opening of the North–South divide during the late 1970s and 1980s, as the North suffered worse from the contraction of manufacturing employment during the main period of recession and the South benefitted disproportionately from the strong growth of employment in business services which dominated the subsequent national recovery. The urban–rural shift, too, was increasingly evident again in the 1980s, essentially because of the same processes – the larger manufacturing base to be eroded in the major metropolitan concentrations and the greater preference of the new forms of business for medium-sized cities and more rural areas. Though the fortunes of individual places have been conditioned by a variety of more specific factors, there has emerged a broad geography of growth and decline which reflects places' positions in relation to the interaction of these two major dimensions. As a result, the localities facing the most severe economic difficulties are generally to be found in the 'urban North' and the main concentration of most privileged places lies in the non-metropolitan South.

The purpose of this chapter is to present a more detailed picture of this 'new map of Britain' and, in so doing, prepare a framework within which the experience of different types of localities can be set. We begin by describing the main features of labour market change at regional and local scales. The outcome of the battle between the forces of de-industrialization and new job growth (see Chapter 5 and 6 respectively) is outlined in terms of overall patterns of employment change and then matched against the trends in the distribution of population (Chapter 4). The changes in the map of officially-defined 'unemployment' constitute the best known result of the mismatch between trends in people and jobs, but it is found that changes in the proportions of people who are employed or seeking work (labour force participation rates) have also played a very significant role. The next section of the chapter focuses on the dynamics of labour market change in a quest to discover why such large geographical differences have arisen. Given that the last two chapters have concentrated on the changing distribution of employment, particular attention is given here to factors affecting labour supply, most notably those which appear to limit people's ability to move house for job reasons. These processes, and the patterns of labour market change described in the previous section, both provide a clear indication of the way in which Britain's space-economy has become increasingly compartmentalized in recent years. This observation provides the cue for the final section which introduces the broad classification of localities that forms the basis of Part III.

Regional and local labour market trends in the 1980s

Employment in the 1980s

This section summarizes the evidence on trends in total employment between 1979 and 1989. The geographical differentials resulting from the developments described in Chapters 5 and 6 are abundantly clear from Table 7.1. The scale of the contrast between the North and South of Great Britain is particularly remarkable. During the main period of economic recession in 1979–83 the total number of people in work, defined as the employed together with the self-employed and including part-time as well as full-time workers, declined by 1.75 million, a fall of 7.1 per cent over the four-year

Table 7.1 Change in total employment, 1979–89, by region

Region	1989 000s	1979–83 000s	%	1983–89 000s	%	1979–89 000s	%
South East	8 799	− 312	− 3.8	+ 987	+12.6	+ 675	+ 8.3
East Anglia	906	+ 1	+ 0.1	+ 124	+15.9	+ 125	+16.0
South West	2 023	− 16	− 0.9	+ 295	+17.1	+ 279	+16.0
East Midlands	1 765	− 88	− 5.3	+ 182	+11.5	+ 94	+ 5.6
South	13 493	− 415	− 3.4	+1 588	+13.3	+1 173	+ 9.5
West Midlands	2 283	− 263	−11.0	+ 164	+ 7.7	− 99	− 4.2
Yorkshire & Humberside	2 045	− 204	− 9.5	+ 104	+ 5.4	− 100	− 4.7
North West	2 711	− 364	−12.6	+ 185	+ 7.3	− 179	− 6.2
Northern	1 205	− 177	−13.4	+ 57	+ 5.0	− 120	− 9.1
Wales	1 116	− 143	−12.4	+ 102	+10.1	− 41	− 3.5
Scotland	2 148	− 184	− 8.1	+ 70	+ 3.4	− 114	− 5.0
North	11 508	−1 335	−11.0	+ 682	+ 6.3	− 653	− 5.4
Great Britain	25 002	−1 749	− 7.1	+2 270	+10.0	+ 521	+ 2.1
South-North difference	1 985	920	7.6	906	7.0	1 826	14.7

Note: Data relate to June each year. The 1989 data are provisional. 'Total employment' refers to employees plus self-employed, but excludes work-related government training. 'South–North difference' is calculated by subtracting the North's levels and rates from those of the South
Source: calculated from *Employment Gazette* Historical Supplement No. 2, November 1989

period. Over three-quarters of these losses were sustained by the six regions of the North, despite the fact that at the beginning of this period they accounted for less than half of all the jobs in Britain. This represented a rate of loss of one in nine of the 1979 job level in the North. By contrast, the rate of net job loss recorded by the South over the same period was less than half the national average, accounting for only one job in every 30. The situation of the South at this time would appear even more favourable if the boundary between the two halves of the country followed the line between the Severn Estuary and the Wash and excluded the more poorly performing northern parts of the East Midlands from the South.

Table 7.1 also confirms the remarkable recovery made by both halves of Britain during the rest of this decade, so that not only the North as a whole but also each of its constituent regions was able to record job increases over the six-year period. Even so, the differential in employment growth rates between North and South in 1983–89 was little smaller than in the previous period. The North's increase of 682,000 jobs represented less than a third of the national increase, under half the number of jobs added by the four southern regions in aggregate and, indeed, considerably less than the number gained by the South East region alone (Table 7.1). The result of these six years of change was therefore not any narrowing of the North–South gap, but merely a small reduction in its pace of widening. By 1989 the South had almost 2 million more people in work than the North, compared to only 0.16 million extra ten years earlier. This gap between the two parts of Britain widened at an average rate of 230,000 a year in 1979–83 and by around 150,000 a year in 1983–89. Moreover, it is notable that, in contrast to the regions of the South, none of the six northern regions had been able to get back to their 1979 employment levels by the end of the decade. With one in eleven fewer jobs in 1989 than 1979, the Northern region appears to have been particularly severely disadvantaged by the events of the decade, but the North West and Scotland also remained 5 per cent or more down on their 1979 positions (Table 7.1).

The regional data in Table 7.1 also provides some evidence of the continuation of the urban–rural shift. This is particularly the case in southern Britain, where the urbanized regions of East Anglia and the South West both weathered the recession years remarkably well and subsequently saw their number of people in work grow by nearly 3 per cent a year during the remainder of the decade. It is, however, seen much more clearly at the sub-regional scale of Figure 7.1, which shows changes in the number of employees (i.e. excluding the self-employed), between the 1981 and 1987 Censuses of Employment.

All the statistical areas containing the principal metropolitan centres, including Greater London and Strathclyde, recorded overall employment decline during this six-year period, as did a number of other industrial and mining areas in South Wales, northern England and central Scotland (Fig. 7.1). Not surprisingly in view of the various aspects of employment growth outlined in Chapter 6, the major concentration of fastest-growing counties is found in the western arc around London, extending from West Sussex in the south through Berkshire, Buckinghamshire and Oxfordshire and over the regional boundary into the East Midlands and East Anglia. Growth rates of

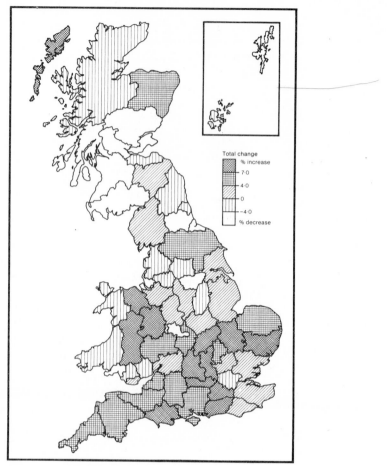

Figure 7.1 Change in total employees in employment, 1981–87. Source: Census of Employment, NOMIS.

over 4 per cent for 1981–87 also penetrate deep into the South West and into the more rural counties of the West Midlands and Welsh Marches.

Further north, too, some of the more rural counties appear relatively buoyant, particularly where they lie between major urban concentrations as does North Yorkshire (Fig. 7.1). Apart from Grampian and the small Western Isles, however, the general impression from west Wales, northern England and Scotland is that in Britain's more peripheral regions, urban and rural areas alike, have experienced economic difficulties in the 1980s. This represents a significant difference from the previous decade when the urban–rural shift was as strong here as elsewhere (Champion *et al.*, 1987, chapter 5; Owen *et al.*, 1986). The limited economic resilience of much of the rural North, particularly in comparison with the South, helps – along with the severity of recession in northern towns – to account for the poor position of the more peripheral regions revealed by the 1979–89 comparisons shown in Table 7.1.

Changing patterns of unemployment

Not surprisingly, these major trends in employment have been accompanied by large changes in the unemployment rate (Table 7.2). The single most notable feature of the past decade was the massive rise in joblessness nationwide during the first two or three years of the recession. The overall rate, which had stood at 3.9 per cent of the workforce in 1979, had doubled to 8.0 per cent in 1981, but then peaked at 11.1 per cent in 1986 before falling back to 6.2 per cent in 1989.

All regions followed this broad temporal pattern of massive increase and subsequent fall, but they vary in the extent by which they rose during the early 1980s and in the subsequent progress back down towards their earlier levels (Table 7.2). At one extreme the 1986 figures for East Anglia and the South West were 5.5 percentage points above their 1979 level, closely followed by the South East with a rise of around 5.8. Amongst the six northern regions the increase amounted to between 7.8 percentage points for Scotland and 9.1 points for the Northern Region.

Between 1986 and 1988 all regions shared fairly evenly in the national fall in unemployment rate by around 5 percentage points (Table 7.2). In terms of the decline in *numbers* unemployed, however, this made for a markedly larger reduction than average for the three southernmost regions, along with the West Midlands (final column of Table 7.2). The result was a widening of the relative difference in unemployment rates along the North–South dimension. The June 1989 rates for Scotland, the Northern Region and the North West were at least twice the overall rate for the South. Indeed, by this time the rates for East Anglia, the South West and the South East were getting back close to their levels of ten years earlier, whereas for Scotland

Table 7.2 Unemployment, 1979–89, by region

| Region | Unemployment rate | | | | Change | Change in no. unemployed | |
	1979 %	1981 %	1986 %	1989 %	1979–89 % point	1979–86 %	1986–89 %
South East	2.6	5.4	8.4	4.0	+1.4	+250.4	−51.3
East Anglia	3.1	6.3	8.6	3.6	+0.5	+213.4	−55.9
South West	4.0	6.8	9.5	4.7	+0.7	+167.2	−49.4
East Midlands	3.3	7.5	10.1	5.7	+2.4	+234.3	−42.5
South	2.9	6.0	8.8	4.3	+1.4	+228.9	−49.9
West Midlands	3.9	10.0	12.9	6.6	+2.7	+231.8	−48.8
Yorks. & Humb.	4.0	8.9	12.7	7.6	+3.6	+225.2	−39.8
North West	5.0	10.2	13.9	8.6	+3.6	+176.5	−38.1
Northern	6.4	11.7	15.5	10.0	+3.6	+138.1	−35.2
Wales	5.3	10.6	13.8	7.8	+2.5	+158.6	−42.5
Scotland	5.6	10.0	13.4	9.5	+3.9	+139.7	−29.3
North	4.9	10.1	13.6	8.3	+3.4	+176.6	−38.8
Great Britain	3.9	8.0	11.1	6.2	+2.3	+195.8	−43.3
South–North difference	2.0	4.1	4.8	4.0	+2.0	—	—

Note: Data relate to June each year, standardized to the September 1989 definition of benefit claimants
Source: Department of Employment, NOMIS

and the three most northerly regions of England, the rates were still at least 3.6 percentage points adrift.

The county-level analysis in Figure 7.2 confirms the way in which the changes of the recession period reinforced the pre-existing patterns of unemployment and led to the widening of unemployment rate differentials in the decade to 1989, while it also underlines the extent of urban–rural contrasts. In general, the impact of overall unemployment before 1979 had already tended to bear most heavily on the most peripheral conurbations of Merseyside, Tyneside and Clydeside, though Cleveland, Cornwall and Clwyd were also amongst the highest unemployment rates at this time (Figure 7.2). Over the subsequent ten years a range of counties had the serious social burden of having the statistically most significant increases in unemployment, primarily the metropolitan counties of the 'manufacturing heartland' (West Midlands, West Yorkshire, Greater Manchester) in 1978–81 but including Greater London, Cleveland and Derbyshire in 1981–84 and branching out to embrace energy-producing areas like South Yorkshire, Grampian, Fife, Lothian and Nottinghamshire as the 1980s progressed.

Nevertheless, by 1989, when there had been at least some modest recovery everywhere, the incidence of unemployment was not far different from that in 1979, with the leading areas (after the Western Isles of Scotland) being Merseyside, Cleveland, Strathclyde, Tyne and Wear, Mid-Glamorgan and South Yorkshire (Figure 7.2). Ten years of additional 'layers' of unemployment had changed the rank order in detail, with the effect of coal and steel redundancies in South Yorkshire being one major example, but the main impression is of consistency. The labour market legacies of the heavy de-industrialization described in Chapter 5 were massive, yet there appears to have been no eventual change in the relationship between 'North–South' and 'urban–rural' dimensions. Both remained important, creating the worst conditions at the intersection of the two dimensions – in the conurbations of the urban North – and bestowing their most beneficial effects on the broad 'western arc' in the South outside Greater London.

Other components of labour market change

While there are clearly many parallels between the geographies of employment and unemployment change with regard to their general patterns, it would be a serious mistake to consider them as mirror images of each other. Some simple examples can easily illustrate this point. Between 1979 and 1983 the number of people in work (employees and self-employed) in the South East dropped by 312,000, but unemployment rose by 430,000, while over the same period the figures for the Northern Region were a decline of 177,000 in work but an increase in unemployment of only 107,000. Even more dramatic differences between these two elements of labour market change characterized the subsequent economic recovery, when the growth in total employment was not nearly matched by the fall in numbers unemployed. For instance, between 1983 and 1988 the South East gained over 820,000 people in work between 1983 and 1988 but saw its number of unemployed fall by only 150,000. It should be stressed that the unemployment figures

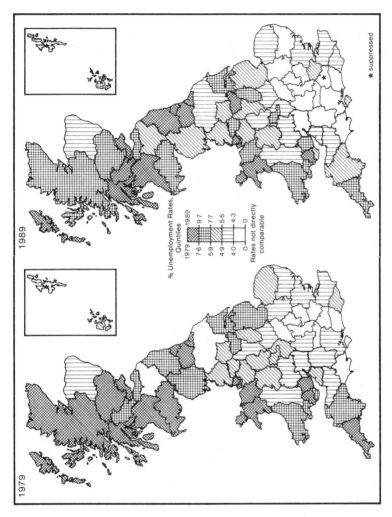

Figure 7.2 Unemployment rate, 1979 and 1989 (June). Source: Department of Employment, NOMIS.

quoted here are not affected by the many changes made in the eligibility rates for benefit claimants, since they have been revised on the basis of a consistent definition (see the note in Table 7.2). Instead, the main reasons for this discordance between employment and unemployment relate to changes in labour force participation (often referred to as 'economic activity rates') together with population trends resulting from natural change and migration.

Several factors influence the degree to which people are economically active. One long-established reason is known as the 'discouraged worker' effect, whereby poor job opportunities deter people from offering their services on the labour market. In the past this feature has been considered to be particularly characteristic of married women, who tend to enter and leave the labour force much more readily than other groups, with more of them moving directly between employment and 'economic inactivity' and fewer registering as unemployed. Chapter 6 has described the extent to which female employment grew during the 1980s, especially in the form of part-time work which is more prone to this type of labour market mobility. Other sources of change in labour force participation rates have also become numerically more important during the past decade, including early retirement and longer spells of full-time education and training.

During the past two decades, there have been major changes in economic activity rates, with a marked contrast between the trends for males and females (particularly married women). For Britain as a whole, the proportion of male civilians aged 16 or over who were economically active fell from 80.5 per cent in 1971 to 73.7 per cent in 1987, while the proportion of economically active women rose from 43.9 to 50.0 per cent over the same period (Table 7.3). The impact of the recession is evident in both sets of figures, with the fall in male rates being particularly steep between 1979 and 1983 and with the rise in female rates being more rapid in the 1970s than subsequently and indeed being temporarily reversed in the early 1980s. Similarly, regional differences in the extent of these changes reflect at least in part the relative buoyancy of their economies. Between 1971 and 1987 the South East, East Anglia and the South West all recorded considerably smaller reductions in male rates than the national average, while the steepest falls occurred in Wales and the West Midlands. Meanwhile, over the same period the largest increases in the economically-active proportion of females took place in East Anglia and the South West, and the smallest in the West Midlands, the North West and Scotland.

The specific contribution of these changes in activity rate to the growth of the labour force between 1971 and 1987 is shown in Table 7.4. At national level it can be seen that the higher female rates more than offset the lower male rates in their effect on overall labour supply, producing an increase in labour force equivalent to 1.8 per cent of its 1971 level. The chief interest, however, is the regional variation in the effect of activity rate changes. Four of the six regions of northern Britain experienced a reduction in overall participation rates between 1971 and 1987. This occurred either through faster than average falls in male rates (most notably in Wales), or lower than average rises in female activity (most notably in the West Midlands and North West), and in most cases, a combination of both these. At the other

Table 7.3 Male and female economic activity rates, 1971–87 by region

	Economic activity rate (%)				Change (% point)
Sex/Region	1971	1979	1983	1987	1971–87
Males					
South East	80.8	77.8	75.7	75.5	− 5.3
East Anglia	76.5	75.1	72.3	71.1	− 5.4
South West	75.2	72.7	70.3	71.1	− 4.1
East Midlands	81.4	79.0	75.0	75.1	− 6.3
West Midlands	84.0	79.9	75.2	75.2	− 8.8
Yorkshire & Humb.	80.6	77.7	73.9	72.5	− 8.1
North West	81.8	77.3	74.0	73.4	− 8.4
Northern	80.7	77.7	73.3	72.7	− 8.0
Wales	78.4	75.7	69.3	68.0	−10.4
Scotland	80.5	78.6	74.8	73.1	− 7.4
Great Britain	80.5	77.5	74.2	73.7	− 6.8
Females					
South East	46.2	48.2	48.4	52.2	+ 6.0
East Anglia	39.6	45.1	47.4	50.0	+10.4
South West	38.5	44.0	44.7	49.9	+11.4
East Midlands	44.1	47.4	48.1	50.2	+ 6.1
West Midlands	46.6	49.5	47.0	49.8	+ 3.2
Yorkshire & Humb.	42.7	46.8	47.2	48.4	+ 5.7
North West	45.3	48.6	47.2	50.1	+ 4.8
Northern	41.1	45.7	44.8	48.8	+ 7.7
Wales	36.7	41.9	41.2	43.5	+ 6.8
Scotland	43.6	49.8	47.0	47.8	+ 4.2
Great Britain	43.9	47.4	47.0	50.0	+ 6.1

Note: Rates expressed as percentage of home population aged 16 or over who are in the civilian labour force
Source: *Regional Trends* 23 (1988), Table 9.5 and 24 (1989), Table 10.5

Table 7.4 Components of change in the civilian labour force, 1971–87, by region

Region	Activity rate effect	Population effect	Total change
South East	2.8	5.8	8.6
East Anglia	8.8	23.7	32.5
South West	10.1	16.4	26.6
East Midlands	1.7	14.3	16.0
West Midlands	− 1.7	6.1	4.4
Yorkshire & Humberside	1.0	5.8	6.8
North West	− 0.9	2.0	1.1
Northern	2.4	3.6	6.0
Wales	− 0.9	7.5	6.6
Scotland	− 0.4	6.3	5.9
Great Britain	1.8	7.3	9.1

Note: Expressed as % of the 1971 labour force
Source: *Regional Trends* 24 (1989), Table 10.4

extreme, for East Anglia and the South West, the activity rate changes over the period 1971–87 had the effect of adding to their labour supply by 9–10 per cent (Table 7.4).

Besides the activity rate effect, there are two further factors which affect the relationship between employment and unemployment trends. In Table 7.4 these are subsumed under the single heading of 'population effect'. One is the 'natural change' in the population insofar as it relates to the labour market, principally the size of the age cohorts entering and leaving the labour market at school-leaving and retirement ages respectively, and the other is the effect of population movement on labour supply. Given the marked increase in the school-leaving age group resulting from the post-war 'baby boom' as well as the stronger currents of migration recorded within Britain over the past two decades (see Chapter 4), it is not surprising to find from Table 7.4 that the population effect is strongly positive at national level and that it exhibits marked regional variations. In particular, it was responsible for increasing East Anglia's labour force by some 24 per cent between 1971 and 1987 and those of the South West and East Midlands by around 15 per cent. At the same time, it is noteworthy that the population effect was positive in all regions, since the effects of net out-migration from most of the regions of the North as well as from the South East over this period were more than offset by the natural increase of their working-age populations.

Labour market accounts

The principal message of the previous section is that labour market changes comprise a number of separate ingredients which are likely to fluctuate over time and vary from place to place in their importance. In particular, it has been suggested that there need be no strong correlation between employment change and unemployment trends because the effect of the former on the latter can be cushioned by adjustments in labour force participation rates and by migration (and commuting) and will also be conditioned by the level of natural change in the working-age population.

One way of looking at the interplay between these ingredients is through the medium of 'labour market accounts'. This approach was originally developed at Cambridge University to study the components of labour market change at regional level (Department of Applied Economics, 1980), but it has subsequently been applied at county level by Champion et al. (1982) and to LLMAs by Owen et al. (1984). All these studies adopted the 'employment shortfall' perspective according to which a 'shortfall' arises if the increase in the number of jobs is insufficient to match the growth in labour supply resulting from the natural increase and the rise in participation rates. Such a 'shortfall' can be resolved either through net out-migration of the labour force or through an increase in unemployment.

The results of the Cambridge analysis, which relate to the period 1966–78, provide useful background to the developments of the 1980s. The UK as a whole experienced a 2.6 per cent increase in labour force as a result of natural change and a further 2.1 per cent increase due to a rise in participation rates. Because this 4.7 per cent increase in labour supply occurred at the same time as a 1.4 per cent decline in employment, there was an employment shortfall of around 6 per cent. The latter problem was ameliorated by a 1.4 per cent reduction in labour supply through net emigration, but still caused 4.6 per cent of the labour force to transfer into the ranks of the unemployed by 1978. At regional level, it was found that in only East Anglia and the South West did the demand for labour rise faster than the indigenous supply and give rise to an employment surplus. In these two cases, migration appeared to over-respond because it added considerably more people to the labour force that was needed to meet the deficit of workers, while rather surprisingly the East Midlands and Wales also experienced net in-migration of labour over this period in spite of having a job shortfall. The result was a much more even increase in unemployment across the country than could have been expected on the basis of the geography of employment growth alone, made possible largely through the role of migration as an 'equalizer of misery'.

The most recent application of the accounts methodology is that by Owen and Green (1989). Using aggregations of Travel to Work Areas (TTWAs), this work demonstrates the importance of both the North–South divide and urban–rural shifts in the labour market change between 1981 and 1984. Table 7.5 presents their results, though it should be noted that their original table has been modified by rearranging the constituent elements of the shortfall and response. The labour market response now contains three components – net out-migration, change in participation and change in unemployment – and in the final column of Table 7.5 the last two are added together to represent the effect of the change in the proportion of people in work. All components are expressed in terms of their size relative to the numbers of economically active people in the relevant TTWA type at the start of the study period in 1981.

Immediately evident from Table 7.5 is the contrast between North and South. The aggregate of TTWAs comprising the North recorded a natural increase in labour supply between 1981 and 1984 that was equivalent to 1.9 per cent of the economically active population in 1981. Combined with the significant decline in employment over this three-year period, this produced a major shortfall in jobs over and above the job deficiency already existing in 1981. By contrast, over this period, the South saw its number of jobs not only grow but rise more rapidly than the increase in labour force produced by natural change, resulting in a job surplus.

In terms of the three components of labour market response, the brunt of the North's job shortfall was borne by the effect of a fall in the proportion of people at work, primarily by an increase in officially recorded unemployment but also by a significant fall in labour force participation. By contrast, the migration component played very little role in alleviating the North's job shortfall. For the South, the effects of net in-migration from the North and from the rest of the world more than matched the job surplus, but the overall rise in participation rates there formed an even more important contribution to increased labour supply. At first glance, the resulting rise in unemployment in the South suggests that 'the misery' has been more evenly spread, but when consideration is broadened to include changes in *non*-employment as well as official unemployment, the scale of the contrast between North and South is clear, with a major fall in the proportion in work in the

Table 7.5 Labour market accounts for types of Travel-to-Work Areas, 1981–84

TTWA type (1)	Components of job shortfall			Labour market responses			Fall in proportion in work (8) (6)–(7)
	Natural change (2)	Employment change (3)	Total job shortfall (4)	Net out-migration (5)	Unemployment change (6)	Participation change (7)	
Great Britain	1.7	0.4	1.3	−0.4	2.1	0.4	1.7
South	1.5	2.6	−1.1	−1.3	1.7	1.6	0.2
North	1.9	−1.6	3.5	0.3	2.5	−0.7	3.2
Million Cities	1.1	−1.2	2.3	0.7	2.4	0.8	1.6
Large Dominants	1.5	−0.1	1.6	−0.3	2.2	0.2	2.0
Subdominant Cities	2.2	1.2	1.0	−0.2	1.7	0.5	1.2
Medium-sized Centres	1.7	0.7	1.0	−1.0	1.9	−0.1	2.0
Subdominant Towns	2.1	1.3	0.8	−0.9	1.8	0.1	1.7
Small Towns	1.8	1.5	0.3	−1.9	2.5	0.3	2.2
Rural Areas	1.8	2.0	−0.2	−2.7	2.6	0.2	2.4
South							
Million Cities	0.6	−0.1	0.7	0.2	2.4	2.0	0.4
Large Dominants	1.6	2.9	−1.3	−1.4	1.5	1.4	0.1
Subdominant Cities	2.2	4.5	−2.3	−1.0	0.7	2.0	−1.3
Medium-sized Centres	1.4	3.2	−1.8	−2.7	2.1	1.2	0.9
Subdominant Towns	2.3	4.7	−2.4	−2.8	1.4	1.1	0.3
Small Towns	1.8	2.9	−1.1	−2.7	2.7	1.1	1.6
Rural Areas	1.8	4.0	−2.2	−3.0	1.4	0.6	0.8
North							
Million Cities	2.0	−2.8	4.8	1.5	2.3	−0.9	3.1
Large Dominants	1.5	−2.1	3.6	0.4	2.6	−0.5	3.1
Subdominant Cities	2.3	−2.2	4.5	0.6	2.7	−1.1	3.8
Medium-sized Centres	1.9	−0.7	2.6	0.0	1.9	−0.8	2.7
Subdominant Towns	2.0	−0.9	2.9	−0.2	2.1	−0.5	2.6
Small Towns	1.9	0.1	1.8	−1.1	2.4	−0.5	2.9
Rural Areas	1.9	0.1	1.8	−2.3	3.7	−0.4	4.1

Note: All values are expressed as percentages of the total economically active population in 1981. The job shortfall (column 4) = (2) − (3) = (5) + (6) − (7). Figures may not sum because of rounding. *Source:* modified from Owen and Green (1989), Table 1 former and virtually no change in the South even after allowing for the redistributive effects of migration (Table 7.5, final column).

Urban–rural contrasts are also very evident from Owen and Green's calculations, not just in statistics relating to size classes across Britain as a whole (the second panel of Table 7.5) but also to a considerable extent within both South and North separately (the last two panels). In the table the TTWA groups are arranged in order of descending size and urban status. Across the country as a whole, there is found to be a strong urban–rural gradient in terms of job shortfall. This is primarily a reflection of differences in the rate of employment growth because the level of natural change in 1981–84 exhibits relatively little variation between the two groups. The urban–rural shift in population through migration is also marked and has swollen the labour force of Small Towns and Rural Areas to such an extent that both these also experienced large increases in unemployment. This latter feature is particularly evident in northern Britain, where there are very strong urban-rural differences in employment change, job shortfall and changes in labour supply due to migration. In the South, on the other hand, the major contrast is between London (the only TTWA in the Million City Group here) and the rest of the TTWA groups, for over this period this is the only group which is characterized by a substantial job shortfall and which did not experience strong employment growth and net in-migration.

As well as allowing the role of the various components of labour market change to be disentangled, this analysis also permits the relative importance of the North–South and urban–rural dimensions to be assessed, at least for the earlier part of the 1980s. The evidence of Table 7.5 suggests that, while both dimensions were operating at this time, the North–South divide was the more powerful. Even though the urban–rural dimension is represented by seven categories, it does not exhibit such a wide range as the simple North–South distinction on the key indicators of job shortfall, employment change, and fall in proportion in work (compare the first two panels of Table 7.5). Indeed, on these three components there is virtually no overlap between the levels recorded by the TTWA size categories in the North and those in the South; even the best performing type in the North has done worse than the worst performing type in the South. Particularly noteworthy is the fall in overall labour force participation rate in all northern categories in contrast to its rise in all southern ones (bottom two panels of Table 7.5). This conclusion, however, does not apply to the migration component. According to Table 7.5, the variation in migration response along the urban–rural gradient is much wider than for the North–South dimension. In the latter context it is remarkable how limited a role migration has played in helping to adjust for the major job shortfall experienced by the North. This aspect is examined in more detail in the next section.

Migration and the matching of people and jobs

Migration is both a cause and an effect of the changes which have taken place in the nature of localities in Britain. On the one hand, it has produced a major reduction in the population of the larger cities and generated widespread growth for medium-sized and smaller places. As noted in Chapter 4, this deconcentration has not only changed the size of these places' populations, but, as a result of the selective nature of the migration process, has also altered their socio-demographic character. On the other hand, while the rate of net North–South movement increased between the mid 1970s and the mid 1980s, the small numbers involved in comparison with the scale of the North's job shortfall at this time can be associated with marked changes in the northern labour market, including lower levels of labour force participation and higher rates of official unemployment. The purpose of this section therefore is to examine in more detail the role of migration as a component of labour market change and, more specifically, to investigate the factors which influence its effectiveness in matching the supply of workers to the availability of jobs at regional and local scales.

Migration as a labour market equilibriator

A high political profile has been accorded to migration for some years now. In an interview recorded during the period of deep recession, the Prime Minister, Margaret Thatcher, was quoted as saying, '. . . there must be some mobility of labour. If people today are not willing to move as their fathers did, the economy cannot thrive. . . . The great prosperity of this country in the last century would never have come about, had people not been ready to face the upheaval of converting themselves from a mainly rural to a largely industrial country' (*The Times*, 21 July 1980). This view was given its most famous expression the following year at the Conservative party conference, when Norman Tebbit, then Secretary of State for Employment, alluded to the fact that in the 1930s his unemployed father 'got on his bike and looked for work and kept on looking until he found it.' Those statements reflected a belief that economic recovery was being jeopardized by people's lack of geographical mobility. In this context the exhortation 'Get on your bike' has become synonymous with labour migration from areas of unemployment to areas where jobs are available – an issue which achieved even greater salience as parts of southern Britain began to encounter labour supply problems in the mid 1980s (see, for instance, Parsons, 1987).

Indeed, conventional wisdom supports this line of argument, viewing migration as one of the principal equilibriating mechanisms in the labour market. According to neo-classical models, migration should work to eradicate spatial variations in the matching of people and jobs, particularly as evidenced by geographical differences in unemployment levels and wage rates (see Clark *et al.*, 1986, and Minford, 1985, for reviews). In theory, an individual will migrate at a point where net income to be gained by a move exceeds the value of net income derived in the home area. For an unemployed person, this threshold is assumed to be reached readily because it is believed that most jobs will offer higher income than unemployment benefit payments. However, migration is also considered an attractive option for employed people because of the tendency for wages to be bid up in areas of relative labour scarcity. Because of this latter factor, theory also predicts that, as well as a shift of workers to the jobs, there will be a movement of capital in the opposite direction as employers relocate their operations to take advantage of lower wage rates in areas with less pressure on labour supplies – and, in addition, to take advantage of the lower land and rental costs normally found in such places.

Clearly from what has been observed earlier in this chapter, this mechanism appears to have worked more satisfactorily in some contexts than in others. At the urban–rural scale the 1980s witnessed a continued shift in job opportunities away from high-cost metropolitan environments towards small and medium-sized local labour markets – a redistribution which was fairly closely paralleled by the movement of people. At the scale of the North–South divide, however, we have seen that these equilibrating mechanisms appear almost entirely to have collapsed in the early 1980s, with any northward shift of capital being entirely inadequate to compensate for the regional differential in job losses and with the relatively limited southward drift of population hardly denting the job surpluses which developed in the North in the main recession years.

The net redistribution of people from North to South has not always been so limited. The 'drift to the South East' became a major political issue during the economic recovery of the 1930s and again during the 'never had it so good' era of the later 1950s and early 1960s (Osborne, 1964; Lawton, 1983). Gordon (1988) demonstrated clearly the magnitude of the transformation which has taken place since that time. He compared the estimated actual rates of labour migration with calculations of the scale of movement required to maintain the same differentials in unemployment and participation rates. For the period 1951–71 the actual rate of net out-migration from the North was, at 69,000 a year, only marginally lower than the 'required rate' of 74,000. For the period 1971–88, however, the required rate of North–South movement had moved up to 94,000 a year, but the actual rate has slumped to 38,000 on average. The biggest dislocation was found for the recession period 1978–85, when the required rate stood at 159,000 a year and the actual rate fluctuated between 45, and 57,000.

The explanation for this lack of population redistribution from North to South appears to lie chiefly with the limited mobility of manual workers. In an analysis based on the 1983 Labour Force Survey, Hughes and McCormick (1987) found that there was no net flow of manual workers from the six more depressed regions of the country to the four most prosperous ones. This was in spite of the much higher unemployment rates amongst manual workers in all the northern regions. At this time migration's role in swelling the South's labour force appeared to be restricted to non-manual workers, for whom the South provided 61 per cent of inter-regional movers' destinations while accounting for only 52 per cent of moves by place of origin. Indeed, for the non-manual population, migration's equilibrating effect was shown to be quite strong in that there were relatively small variations in unemployment rates across the country for this sector.

These observations on the limited net movement from North to South may seem surprising when set in the context of the fact that Britain is characterized by a large volume of migration each year. Though levels of residential mobility vary over time according to economic conditions, even at the height of the recession the 1981 Census recorded that almost one in ten of the population changed their address over the previous twelve months. The resolution of this paradox lies in the nature of these movements. As was originally observed by Ravenstein (1885, 1889) and subsequently confirmed by the value of gravity models in predicting population movements (e.g. Gleave and Cordey-Hayes, 1977), it is short-distance migration that predominates. In 1980/81, 69 per cent of people changing address moved less than 10 km and only 13 per cent moved more than 80 km. Moreover, in comparison with 1970/71, there had been a particularly sharp fall in the numbers moving over longer distances. These are the more strongly motivated by employment-related reasons in contrast to the housing, social and environmental factors which bear more heavily on movements over shorter distances (OPCS, 1983).

Housing and other barriers to labour migration

The key question relates to the low level of long-distance migration, particularly between northern and southern halves of the country and more notably amongst manual workers. One approach is to answer it in terms of the constraints operating on potential movers. This focuses on the individual migrant and views the labour migration process as a sequence of obstacles or 'hurdles', each of which must be cleared before a successful move can take place. The first of these hurdles is the problem of obtaining information about vacancies, with job search and labour recruitment methods varying significantly by occupation, industry and gender. Completing the job search process successfully involves a whole series of hurdles – applying for a job, being invited for interview, attending an interview, and finally, being offered an acceptable job. Next there is the hurdle of moving to a new area, a step in which the availability, cost and quality of housing form major considerations. Finally comes the challenge of settling down and remaining in the destination area beyond the short term, putting down roots and building up a new network of social relationships and activities to replace the ones left behind (Green et al., 1986).

Every migrant faces these hurdles, but the size of the hurdles, and the ease with which they may be surmounted, varies from individual to individual in accordance with their differing circumstances. In particular, they constitute much more serious obstacles to the less skilled and the unemployed. In relation to information sources, for instance, the less skilled place considerable reliance on informal networks such as friends and relatives, which are very largely local in orientation, in contrast to skilled non-manual groups with their eyes on national newspapers and professional journals. Even the official employment services such as Job Centres have traditionally provided information mainly about local jobs, though the opening of the National Vacancy Circulation System (NATVACS) in 1984 provided the potential for wider dissemination of employment opportunities round the country. A whole series of schemes has been tried at one time or another to help people find and take up new jobs, but they have involved relatively small numbers.

Of all the hurdles, however, housing is perhaps the most widely recognized barrier (Champion et al., 1987b; Minford et al., 1987; Bover et al., 1988). There are problems both over the volume and type of housing. As is clear from the evidence submitted to an inquiry chaired by the Duke of Edinburgh (National Federation of Housing Associations, 1985a, 1985b), the availability of accommodation varies dramatically between different parts of the country. London was shown to be facing particularly serious housing problems, reflected in high rates of homelessness, extensive use of temporary accommodation, the lengthening of waiting lists for council housing, and massive pressures within the private rented sector. The inquiry also identified the growth areas of the South East and the 'M4 Corridor' to Bristol as facing particular shortages. Part of this problem relates to the rate of new construction which adds only about 1 per cent to the stock each year, rendering impossible a major redistribution of housing in the short term. It is also the case that planning controls restrict the scale of new building permitted in the most rapidly growing parts of the country, especially in the outer parts of the South East where political battles have raged throughout the post-war period and became particularly intense in the 1980s (see Chapter 9 for a fuller discussion).

As regards type of accommodation, the most crucial aspect bearing on labour mobility has been the literal decimation of the private-rented sector which accounted for over 90 per cent of stock on the eve of the First World War and is now down to below one-tenth for the UK as a whole (Figure 7.3). This sector has traditionally played a very important role in labour mobility, either as a permanent solution to individuals' housing problems or as a stepping-stone on the path towards house purchase or renting from the council. This is reflected in this sector's high turnover rates and large proportion of newcomers moving for job reasons (Table 7.6). The reduction in its stock has therefore been a serious blow for potential migrants. Attempts made by the government in the 1980s to revive this sector have so far (1989) failed to stem its decline, though some increase in accommodation provided by housing associations has been achieved.

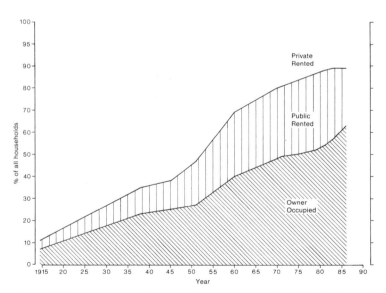

Figure 7.3 Tenure composition of the housing stock, Great Britain, 1914–86. Source: *Social Trends*, various issues.

Table 7.6 Measures of residential mobility, by housing tenure

Measures	Owner occupied	Council rented	Private rented	All tenures
1 All movers as % of households in each tenure, 1977–78	8.6	9.2	20.7	10.6
2 % tenure with moving households, 1981	5.4	6.9	11.4	6.6
3 % all movers out of tenure who moved for job reasons, England, 1977–78	27.2	8.6	25.5	22.4
4 % all movers into tenure who moved for job reasons, England, 1977–78	24.3	8.7	35.0	22.4
5 % all movers out of tenure who moved 20 miles or more, England, 1977–78	30.5	10.0	17.5	20.8
6 % all movers into tenure who moved 20 miles or more, England, 1977–78	26.6	6.3	27.4	20.8
7 % of tenure with household moving between Districts, 1981	2.4	0.9	5.2	2.4
8 % of tenure with households moving between Districts and whose heads were seeking work, 1981	0.1	0.1	9.1	0.2

Note: 'Tenure' refers to present tenure unless stated otherwise. 'Moves' refers to continuing households moving within last 12 months. Data for England and Wales, except where stated otherwise
Source: 1 and 3–6 from *Recently Moving Households* (PCS, 1983); 2, 7 and 8 from 1981 Population Census

The importance of the private-rented sector also derives from the lack of long-distance mobility in the local authority sector (Table 7.6). As shown by Hughes and McCormick (1981, 1985), local authority tenants are less likely than other tenure types to undertake an inter-regional move, regardless of their level of education, age or occupation. This is because most districts operate allocation rules which give priority to people who have lived longest in their administrative areas and have been on the waiting list for some time. Special mechanisms such as the Tenants Exchange Scheme and the National Mobility Scheme have had only marginal effect in facilitating long-distance movements by council tenants (Green *et al.*, 1986). Part of the problem is the fact that the smaller cities and towns of southern England which have constituted the strongest growth areas in recent years contain relatively few council houses. This deficiency has been aggravated since the late 1970s both by the very low rate of new council house building permitted by central government and by the sale of council houses to sitting tenants at discount prices, the so-called 'right to buy' sales which have proceeded particularly quickly in these areas (Dunn *et al.*, 1987; Kleinman and Whitehead, 1987). The suburbs and shire counties of the South have therefore become increasingly the preserve of owner occupiers.

Owner occupation was promoted very strongly by the Conservative government during the 1980s not only in the 'right to buy' programme but also through the continuation of income tax relief on mortgage interest payments and through subsidizing schemes for sale by housing associations. On the face of it, this trend should guarantee greater geographical mobility, because according to the available statistics house-owners' propensity to move is almost as high as that of private-sector tenants (Table 7.6). However, the fact that home owners are so mobile over long distances is undoubtedly due, first, to their need to consider a national labour market in terms of their mainly professional skills and, secondly, to the help which many types of employer are prepared to give with moving costs, particularly for staff moving to new jobs within the same organization. According to Salt (1985), an impressive 58 per cent of employed inter-regional migrants recorded by the 1981 Labour Force Survey did not change their employer. Since many of the people recruited into owner occupation in the 1980s do not possess these characteristics or advantages, the average level of mobility in this sector is likely to have fallen.

Another reason for suggesting that owner occupation is not the universal panacea for labour immobility shot to prominence in the mid 1980s – the widening of regional and local differentials in house prices. Cycles in regional house price differentials are nothing new, but during the 1980s they threatened to take on a qualitatively different form (Hamnett, 1983, 1989). The rise in London house prices by some 66 per cent between 1983 and 1986 can be attributed largely to the growth of financial and related business services, which as shown in Chapter 6 was essentially a London-based phenomenon and developed only weakly in the provincial capitals. By 1986 a major gap had opened up between Greater London and the Outer Metropolitan Area, on the one hand, and northern England on the other (Table 7.7). As a result, northern owner-occupiers became increasingly trapped, as they were not prepared to make the sacrifice in terms of size and quality of dwelling that movement from a low-cost to a high-cost area

Table 7.7 Mean house price, 1983–89, by region

Region	1983 £	ratio	1986 £	ratio	1989 £	ratio
Outer Metropolitan Area	39 090	139	59 880	151	98 485	149
Greater London	36 160	128	60 100	152	92 045	139
Outer South East	32 560	115	48 010	121	83 341	126
South West	29 450	104	41 470	105	74 116	112
East Anglia	28 290	100	40 180	101	73 390	111
United Kingdom	28 200	100	39 640	100	66 179	100
West Midlands	24 700	88	31 140	79	61 627	93
East Midlands	22 710	81	30 880	78	55 647	84
North West	22 930	81	29 760	75	53 137	80
Yorkshire & Humberside	21 670	77	27 230	69	52 131	79
Wales	23 330	83	29 810	75	50 357	76
Scotland	27 580	98	33 740	85	46 855	71
Northern region	22 690	80	27 310	69	43 402	66
Northern Ireland	23 050	82	28 350	72	27 599	42
Range Excl. N. Ireland	17 420	62	32 870	83	55 083	83

Note: The regions are ranked in order of 1989 houseprice. The data relate to the July–September quarter of each year
Source: Nationwide Anglia Building Society bulletins

required. This trap also operated in the opposite direction, in that southerners were loathe to move northwards if they were contemplating the need to return at some stage in the future (Champion *et al.*, 1987). Indeed, in the mid 1980s, virtually the only groups that stood to gain in the longer term by moving northward across the house-price divide were retirement migrants or people making their final career move. Subsequently, as the property boom diffused outwards from the South East, this particular hurdle began to diminish in scale once again, but the absolute range in prices between places was markedly wider by the end of the 1980s (Table 7.7).

Clearly, in one form or another, housing considerations add up to a formidable set of obstacles facing potential labour migrants. One symptom of this problem has been the growth of long-distance commuting on a weekly basis – not a new phenomenon, but one which in the past has been primarily associated with the construction industry and more remote sites rather than with office workers in central London. According to Hogarth and Daniel (1987, 1988), the number of people commuting weekly from north-east England to the South grew substantially in the mid 1980s. Moreover, in a sample survey, it was found that over half were in professional and managerial occupations, the majority were not young adults but family men, and for the most part they did not view this as a transitional stage in moving house to the South but as a fairly permanent arrangement – completely the opposite of the stereotype and dubbed 'Britain's new industrial gypsies' by the Labour MP, John Smith (quoted by Hogarth and Daniel, 1988, 2).

Demand deficiency and the restructuring of the space economy

Compelling though the housing-based explanation of lower labour mobility in the 1980s may seem to be, however, we should not neglect the changes which have taken place since the early 1970s in the demand for labour, both in terms of the overall availability of jobs and in relation to the type of work involved. One obvious point is that during the height of the recession in the early 1980s the shortage of jobs was so great across the nation that it made little sense for unemployed northerners to seek work in the South. Yet even at this time there existed some pockets of very low unemployment in the South like Crawley in West Sussex and Winchester in Hampshire (Champion *et al.*, 1987). It also appears that there were many firms which had difficulty in recruiting labour with particular types of skills from anywhere in the country (Atkinson and McGill, 1981). The absence of large-scale inward migration from the North could be explained directly by reference to lack of requisite skills among the northern unemployed, just as much as in terms of housing problems. Similar reasoning can help to account for the apparent reluctance of firms to consider relocation from South to North, as well as explain their much greater preference to decentralize over shorter distances.

The key to understanding this failure of the labour market to come into balance through flows of labour and capital lies in the historically specific nature of the national recovery. As described in Chapter 6, the latter very largely involved 'new forms of employment' and was anything but 'national' in its incidence. The prime motive force was the restructuring of London's economy within the context of the major growth of international trade in financial and related business services (Marshall, 1989; Thrift *et al.*, 1987). Large areas of the rest of the South became locked into the expansion of this 'information economy', not just as providers of accommodation for the growing army of commuters to central London, but also as suitable locations for 'back-office' functions. Moreover, this trend towards greater geographical concentration was reinforced by the developments taking place in the detailed organization of large companies, involving the recasting of their labour requirements on a more flexible basis (see Chapter 6).

These changes in the pattern of labour demand, consequent upon the restructuring of the British economy and the reorganization of large companies, appear to accord well with migration trends. They certainly help to explain the lack of net North-to-South movement by manual workers noted by Hughes and McCormick (1987). They can also account for the surge of net inward migration from overseas observed in the first half of the 1980s, which involved predominantly skilled manpower and was very largely orientated towards London and the South East. Moreover, they are consistent with the fall in gross levels of inter-regional labour mobility generally (see Chapter 4).

There is also clear empirical evidence of the dominant role that London and the South East play in national migration patterns and of the overall outcome of these flows in producing an upgrading of the social composition of the South. Studies by Johnson *et al.*, (1974), Flowerdew and Salt (1979), Kennett (1983) and Owen and Green (1989) have demonstrated the pivotal role which the London metropolitan labour market has in 'processing' migrants. School leavers and young adults are drawn to London from all over the country, while in net terms the outflow from London at older ages is concentrated very much on the rest of the South East and adjoining parts of the South West, East Anglia and East Midlands. Using the detailed statistics available from the OPCS Longitudinal Study, Fielding (1989) confirms that the South East acts as a kind of escalator for the upwardly socially mobile who constitute a large proportion of the in-migrants, so that migration contributes to the social 'embourgeoisement' of the region. At the same time, however, he notes that, among the migrants to the South East, there have been many who joined the urban underclass by becoming part of the region's unemployed, suggesting that migration patterns are also causing a polarization of the region's social class structure.

From the evidence of this section it would seem that the distinctive North–South and urban–rural dimensions of migration patterns in 1980s Britain can be understood in terms of both the changing nature of labour demand and the constraints imposed by housing and job-search considerations. In practice, these two groups of factors are interlinked and, to some extent, mutually reinforcing. The high cost and limited availability of housing in the South stem directly from the economic buoyancy of this core region, but at the same time they act like a filter in favour of more skilled and better-off in-migrants who then further enrich the region as a reservoir of high-level manpower. Similarly, places that are relatively accessible to London – which now include most of the South – are attractive for the growth of the new forms of employment and, partly as a result, do not suffer from the major differential in house prices that deters temporary moves from London into the North. All in all, the past two decades have brought a significant increase in the degree of compartmentalization in the UK's space economy, contrasting sharply with the prevailing tendency of regional and local equalization characteristic of the earlier part of the post-war period.

The changing map of Britain

The patterns and processes of urban and regional change described above provide the basis for dividing up the nation's localities into a small number of basic types. One of the distinctive features of the new spatial division of labour is the departure from the traditional pattern of regional specialization, such as the textile industry of Lancashire and Yorkshire or the heavy engineering of north-east England. In its stead has developed the articulation of space around an essentially urban-centred framework within which individual places take on characteristics according to the type and level of occupational functions which they are able to perform in the wider national and international space-economy, whether as centres of high-level control, research and development, or mass production, or indeed as places specializing in consumption such as retirement or tourist areas (Massey, 1984; Cooke, 1989).

At the same time, our treatment cannot ignore the major changes wrought by the dramatic events of the 1980s, for these have not only given rise to very distinctive sets of problems in different geographical contexts but have also exposed very sharply the strengths and weaknesses of individual localities in relation to the new forms of growth. This final section of Part II therefore begins by summarizing the recent dynamics of growth and decline across Britain, then describes the results of classifications of localities, which largely reflect their inherited characteristics, and concludes by outlining the four-fold typology which we use in Part III to structure our treatment of the local outcomes resulting from the interaction between new and old.

The geography of growth and decline in the 1980s

Such has been the explosion of interest since the 1970s in the state of places within the nation that there now exists a wealth of studies which draw together the main features of recent changes. These studies have built upon the earlier research concerned with local variations in 'economic health' and 'levels of living' in the USA and Britain (e.g. Thompson *et al.*, 1962; Knox, 1974) and have seen their most popular expression in the ranking of cities on the basis of 'quality of life' or 'affluence' (e.g. Boyer and Savageau, 1985; Brown, 1988; Findlay *et al.*, 1988). For present purposes the most appropriate studies are those relating to the underlying strength of the local economies, measured in terms of either past performance or enterprise potential.

The ranking of places on the basis of local economic performance in the 1980s (Champion and Green, 1989; Green and Champion, 1989) provides convincing confirmation of the significance of the North–South divide in influencing growth patterns around Britain. In particular, the 'amalgamated index' (Figure 7.4A) showed that all the highest-scoring places were located on or south of a line running from the Severn estuary to Lincolnshire and formed a continuous crescent around London from Crawley, Chichester (W. Sussex) and Winchester (Hants.) in the south to Cambridge, Newmarket (Suffolk) and Thetford (Norfolk) in the north. Conversely, almost all the places with scores below the median lay north of this line, with particularly poor rankings being found for the principal industrial concentrations, several coalfield areas and a number of remoter rural areas.

At the same time, this study also drew attention to the considerable degree of variation in performance *within* regions. Several places in the South were ranked below the national median, including Clacton (Essex), Deal and Thanet (Kent) in the South East as well as more isolated parts of East Anglia and the South West. Meanwhile, within the North a number of more dynamic and prosperous places were identified, particularly medium-sized and smaller centres such as Harrogate (N. Yorks.) and Macclesfield (Cheshire) but also including larger cities like Edinburgh and Aberdeen.

Similar conclusions have been drawn by Coombes and Raybould (1989) on the basis of an index of 'local enterprise activity potential' (LEAP). They have analysed the establishment of new firms using Value Added Tax registration records and correlating the rate of new firm formation with the underlying characteristics of areas, thereby providing a framework for predicting geographical variations in business activity. Their most recent results are presented in Figure 7.4B. At the extremes the South East emerges particularly strongly, while the places with the lowest LEAP scores are concentrated in central Scotland, north-east England, Merseyside, Humberside, South Yorkshire and South Wales.

The locality-based complexion of Britain

These patterns of recent performance and future potential are superimposed on an inherited mosaic of strengths and weaknesses. In practice, these two aspects are interlinked because the legacy of the past – whether actual or perceived – contributes to the relative attractiveness of places for new rounds of investment. Moreover, as stressed in Chapter 6, it is the extent to which the growth of the new can substitute for the loss of the old that forms one of the most powerful determinants of the changing character of localities in the last two decades of the twentieth century.

There are available a number of classifications of places in Britain that we could draw upon in order to give a detailed picture of the space-economy on which these patterns of growth and decline have been superimposed. Some derive from *a priori* rationalization, such as the CURDS 19-fold typology of LLMAs (see Champion *et al.*, 1987, chapter 1). Others are derived directly from the analysis of data assembled for the individual localities, most commonly extracted from the Population Census and subjected to a form of classification procedure such as cluster analysis or principal components analysis. The pioneering study on British towns by Moser and Scott (1961) was of this latter type and has formed the model for many subsequent schemes.

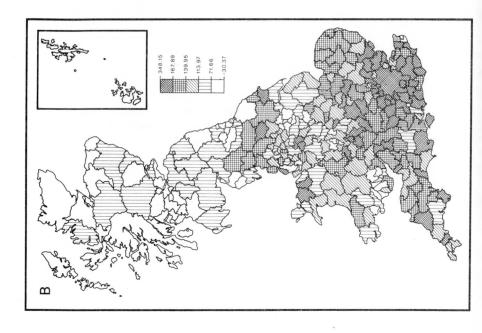

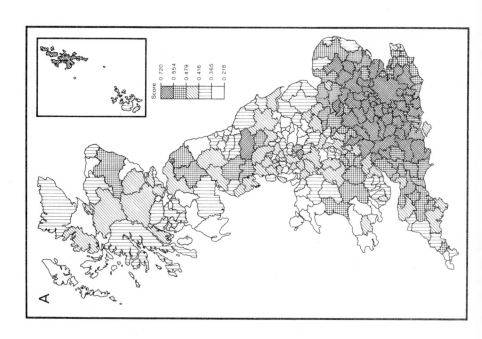

Three of these data-crunching studies are quite sufficient to indicate the nature of this inheritance. In their study 'Which local authorities are alike?', Webber and Craig (1976) distinguished a total of 30 clusters which could be grouped into six broader 'families'. Classifications produced by Donnison and Soto (1980) and Openshaw and Charlton (1984) both deal only with urban areas and both opt for thirteen clusters. There is a strong measure of consistency between these three studies in terms of the types of urban places distinguished. Common features include (though not under precisely the same titles) major cities and regional service centres, inner conurbation areas, mining settlements, textile and engineering towns, residential sub-urbs and satellite towns, new towns and other overspill areas, resorts and the Scottish dimension. Moreover, there is a remarkable degree of spatial regularity in the patterns exhibited by the separate types of places, reflecting to a large extent their origins in the former spatial division of labour. Even though the industrial sector constitutes only one of the sets of variables used in these classifications, it appears to be associated strongly with many other characteristics which thus have similarly distinctive patterns at regional and urban scales.

By way of a summary of these inherited patterns, the study by Donnison and Soto (1980) is particularly instructive because their classification was based on successive steps in splitting up the initial 'population' of urban areas. The resultant dendrogram (Figure 7.5) reveals the nature of the groupings and the characteristics on which each split was performed. In their own words,

> This analysis shows that British cities can be divided into two major groups: the industrial, working class towns, mainly in the North, depending heavily on manufacturing . . . ; and the more prosperous white collar towns, mainly in the South, depending heavily on private service industries and government . . . They might be described as 'traditional Britain' and 'new Britain'; the first industrial revolution, and the second.
>
> (Donnison and Soto, 1980, 101)

A four-fold typology of localities in Britain

The geography of growth and decline in the 1980s and the nature of Britain's inherited spatial patterns, together with the evidence reviewed earlier in the chapter, provide the basis on which we have elected to subdivide the country geographically in order to profile different types of places. For manageability in relation to the scale and aims of this book, it seemed unwise to recognize as many as thirteen types (before including rural Britain). In the end, we have opted for a more generalized framework based on the classification of local authority districts used by OPCS (1981, 1988) for the presentation of population change data for England and Wales. We have extended this classification to Scotland by reference to the same criteria (with

---

Figure 7.4 Local economic performance and potential, by Local Labour Market Areas: (A) Amalgamated Index; (B) Index of Local Enterprise Activity Potential (LEAP). Source: (A) A.G. Champion and A.E. Green; (B) M. Coombes and S. Raybould, personal communications.

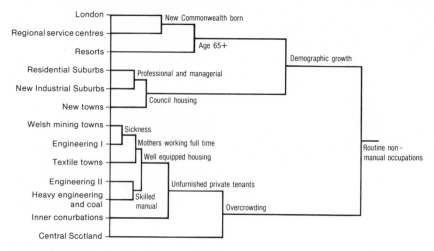

Figure 7.5 Dendrogram of cluster analysis of British towns. Source: Donnison and Soto, 1980, Figure 7.1.

the Central Clydeside Conurbation being treated as the equivalent of the English Metropolitan Counties) and have arranged the district types under four broad headings. The latter and their composition in terms of the separate OPCS district types are shown in Table 7.8, along with key statistics on population and employment change.

The first group comprises *London and the other major cities*, the latter being the principal cities of the Metropolitan Counties and Central Clydeside Conurbation, namely (in order of district population size) Birmingham, Leeds, Glasgow, Liverpool, Manchester, Sheffield and Newcastle upon Tyne. As a group, these are distinctive for their rapid rate of population decline since the 1960s, the massive scale of their inner cities and related problems, and their pivotal role – in theory, if not always in practice – in terms of the high-level transactional activities in the new information economy. In many respects, of course, London is unique, but by treating these cities together in Chapter 8, it is possible to obtain a clearer impression of the strengths and weaknesses of both the national capital and its provincial equivalents.

Our second broad type comprises the major part of 'new Britain', termed here the *prosperous sub-regions*. As outlined in Chapter 9, this is the largest of the four types in terms of number of districts and people and in terms of the diversity of places embraced within it. In relation to the OPCS classification, this includes a great number of the larger centres in the 'shire counties', which generally have strong economic bases and serve as centres within relatively prosperous wider regions. This broad group also includes two more specific types: districts with New Towns, which grew particularly strongly in the 1960s and 1970s, and resort, port and retirement districts, which in the 1980s were the most dynamic of all the OPCS categories in population terms. The largest component of the prosperous sub-regions however, comprises a long list of districts which the OPCS now refers to as

Table 7.8 Population change, 1971–88, and employment change, 1981–87, by types of local authority districts

District type	population			employment	
	1988 000s	1971–81 %	1981–88 %	1987 000s	1981–87 %
Large cities	10 865	−10.4	−2.4	5 452	−4.2
London (*South*)	6 735	− 9.6	−1.0	3 506	−1.5
Other principal cities (*North*)	4 130	−11.6	−4.5	1 946	−8.7
Prosperous sub-regions	22 182	+ 5.2	+3.2	8 465	+3.8
South	14 975	+ 6.1	+4.2	5 666	+6.1
North	7 207	+ 3.4	+1.3	2 799	−0.5
Non-metropolitan cities	5 431	− 3.0	−2.3	2 826	−0.1
Districts with New Towns	2 821	+15.1	+5.1	1 079	+4.2
Resort, port & retirement	3 611	+ 5.8	+7.2	1 105	+3.9
Urban & mixed urban/rural	10 319	+ 7.5	+4.4	3 455	+7.1
Industrial districts	16 021	+ 0.6	−0.8	5 464	−3.3
South	2 676	+ 4.8	+2.5	1 022	+1.1
North	13 344	− 0.1	−1.4	4 442	−4.2
Other metropolitan districts	8 572	− 1.4	−1.5	2 888	−4.6
Industrial areas	7 448	+ 3.2	+0.1	2 576	−1.7
Remoter, mainly rural	6 419	+10.2	+6.1	1 897	+5.0
South	3 596	+11.4	+7.4	1 102	+7.2
North	2 823	+ 8.7	+4.5	795	+2.1
Great Britain	55 486	+ 0.8	+1.3	21 271	−0.2
South	27 982	+ 2.1	+3.1	11 275	+3.1
North	27 505	− 0.5	−0.6	9 996	−3.7

Note: Due to rounding, certain items do not sum to column totals. 'South' comprises the South East, South West, East Anglia and East Midlands, 'North' the rest of Great Britain.
Source: OPCS, Registrar General Scotland, Census of Employment NOMIS.

'urban and mixed urban/rural', made up of all the other smaller urban centres and more accessible rural areas. As can be seen from Table 7.8, the prosperous sub-regions are, in aggregate, dominated by the South, with over two-thirds of their population being accounted for by the four standard regions of the South East, South West, East Anglia and the East Midlands and with this southern element being by far the faster growing, particularly in relation to employment. It is here that Britain's strongest development pressures have been concentrated in the last two decades, raising major strategic planning issues as well as more general environmental problems.

Industrial areas form the third major type. This is a very distinctive element in existing classifications and, in the OPCS classification, is most neatly captured by combining the remaining districts of the Metropolitan Counties (i.e. all except the principal city of each one) with the 'industrial districts' of the shire counties. As such, this third type is predominantly northern in distribution, with only 2.7 million of its total 16 million people in 1988 being accounted for by the four regions of the South. Along with our first category of metropolitan centres, it is the one which was most severely battered by the de-industrialization of the late 1970s and early 1980s. It does, however, include a wide range of experience in terms of these places' ability to recover from this trauma and attract new forms of employment, which forms a major theme of Chapter 10.

Finally, the *remoter, mainly rural districts* are distinctive, first of all, by virtue of their rural nature, particularly low population density and absence of larger urban centres – the reason why these were ignored entirely by two of the locality classifications mentioned earlier and by many other books on Britain. They emerged as a clearly separate element of Webber and Craig's original (1976) schema, being also characterized by relatively high levels of agricultural employment and proportions of people aged over 65. These areas, however, experienced surprisingly strong growth of jobs and younger people during the 1970s – a pattern of dynamism which became more muted towards the end of that decade but which has re-emerged in the mid 1980s, though with a much sharper contrast between North and South. In fact, in terms of population and jobs, this type is more strongly represented in the South, where it shares some of the strengths and planning issues faced by the 'prosperous sub-regions'. However, in Chapter 11, we focus principally on those areas in this category which have the most distinctive characteristics of low density settlement, extreme remoteness and dependence on traditionally rural production activities.

Conclusion

In sum, we recognize four basic types of localities as emerging from the traumatic events which affected Britain in the 1980s. To a large extent, this division reflects the interplay of the two primary dimensions of geographical change in contemporary Britain – the North–South divide, which dominated the map of job prospects throughout the decade, and the urban–rural shift, which has continued to form the most prominent element in population redistribution despite the smaller scale of the exodus from the larger cities in the late 1970s and early 1980s. Nevertheless, our typology does not constitute a neat division into urban South, rural South, urban North and rural North, but is more flexible in geographical terms, as will become clear in Part III. In particular, this framework recognizes the distinctive trends, labour functions and policy issues characteristic of localities at the two ends of the settlement-size spectrum (the large cities and remoter rural areas of Chapters 8 and 11 respectively). Moreover, by splitting the remainder of the country broadly into more and less prosperous sub-regions (Chapters 9 and 10 respectively), it acknowledges the existence of some 'booming towns' in the North, and vice versa, and provides an opportunity for exploring these patterns more systematically.

Further reading

The patterns of employment change and trends in unemployment rate described in the first part of this chapter are based on the latest data available to the authors from the Department of Employment. Interested readers can keep up to date with trends in officially defined unemployment by reference to the monthly issues of the *Employment Gazette*. Data on employment change are revised quarterly at the level of the standard region, but more local data are available only from the Census of Employment, the next being taken in 1989 and 1991 with results probably being published in 1991 and 1993.

Context for the most recent trends in labour demand can be obtained from Lewis and Townsend (1989); Massey and Allen (1988); Martin and Rowthorn (1986); and Champion *et al.* (1987). The two most relevant exercises in labour market accounting are: Owen *et al.* (1984), and Owen and Green (1989).

The role of migration as a labour market equilibriator is discussed by Minford (1985) and Green *et al.* (1986). Housing factors are considered by Champion *et al.* (1987); Minford *et al.* (1987); and Owen and Green (1989).

The geography of growth and decline in the 1980s is described by Champion and Green (1989). Economic potential is assessed by Coombes and Raybould (1989). Previous classifications of localities in Britain can be found in: Webber and Craig (1976); Donnison and Soto (1980); and Openshaw and Charlton (1984).

PART III

Local Outcomes and Government Responses

8

Large cities

The purpose of Part III is to examine the local impact of the economic and social changes that have been described in the first two parts of this book. The emphasis is on distinctive types of locality as they exist on the ground and on places as environments for people to live in. The principal themes therefore are the changing size and social structure of these types of localities and the range of opportunities available for employment, services, leisure and so on. The principal issues discussed are those of the perceived inadequacies of these environments, the policies adopted in an attempt to improve conditions, and the implications of recent and current developments for future prospects. The main questions which we are seeking to answer are: In what ways have different types of places – different in their history of development and thereby their inherited characteristics as well as in location – been affected by the major upheavals of the 1980s? How successfully have they grappled with the opportunities and challenges which these changes have thrown up? What do these outcomes promise for the future role of these places and the well-being of their people?

As outlined at the end of Chapter 7, our analysis of the geography of contemporary Britain suggests a broad four-fold typology of localities as being the minimum necessary for portraying the diversity of living conditions found across the nation. The large cities form an obvious starting point. Academics and policy-makers in this country, as in the majority of the developed world, have become increasingly concerned with the phenomenon of urban decline over the past quarter of a century. The forces of physical deconcentration, industrial restructuring and social re-sorting, described in Part II, have combined to work against these large, old urban centres, with their dense concentrations of population and employment and their obsolescent infrastructure and economic base. Moreover, such is their importance in the national space-economy that whatever happens to them has major implications for other types of localities, as the subsequent chapters in Part III will show.

Eight cities

For the purposes of this chapter, we focus our attention on London and the urban cores of the provincial conurbations. In detail, our list of cities comprises Greater London, the principal cities of the six (former) metropolitan counties in England – Birmingham, Manchester, Liverpool, Leeds, Sheffield and Newcastle upon Tyne – and their equivalent in the Central Clydeside Conurbation, Glasgow (Figure 8.1). These eight cities are distinctive by virtue of their size, their density of settlement, their scale of recent decline, the existence of a clear 'inner city' dimension to their social problems, and the welter of policy initiatives geared towards their rejuvenation. In the words of Cameron (1980, 1), these are 'the "heavy-weights" of the British urban system'. They grew to dominate national manufacturing, trade and servicing during the nineteenth century (Briggs, 1968), but more recently they have come to be considered as synonymous with 'urban decline' (Clark, 1989).

This is not to say that they are identical – far from it, for they exhibit differences in size, history of development, spatial structure, ethnic composition and current administrative status, among other features. London is obviously very different from the other seven in terms of its size, with 6.7 million residents in 1988, compared to the second city, Birmingham, with only 994,000. London's other distinguishing features include its long history as national capital and major port, its status as one of the 'big three' world cities in financial affairs, and the fact that since the abolition of the Greater London Council (GLC) in 1986 it has no single administrative authority to manage its local affairs (Hall, 1989). Liverpool, Glasgow and Newcastle, to some extent like London, built up their early prosperity on the basis of shipping and trade, whereas the other 'regional cities' grew up originally as centres of specialized manufacturing (see Chapter 2). Glasgow and Liverpool drew large Irish populations in the nineteenth century, but along with Newcastle and Sheffield they have proved far less attractive for immigrants in recent decades and as a result contain relatively few people of New Commonwealth origin. Birmingham, Manchester, Liverpool and Glasgow are located at the core of major conurbations, whereas Newcastle, Leeds and Sheffield form part of smaller and less massive concentrations (Gordon, 1986). Today only Glasgow, within the Strathclyde Region, acts as the administrative centre for its wider metropolitan region. Nevertheless, 'there is sufficient similarity in the nature of the forces shaping the pattern of conurbation development' to warrant studying these places as a single category (Cameron, 1980, 12–13).

At the same time, the experience of these cities has some relevance for other elements of urban Britain, especially for other sizeable cities. The eight cities do not have the monopoly of urban decline, ethnic minorities or riots, as will become apparent in subsequent chapters. For instance, as a declining port and fishing centre, Hull shares some of the problems of economic adjustment faced by Liverpool, while Teesside has had to come to terms with the recent rationalization of the steel industry in ways similar to Sheffield. Other non-conurbation cities like Nottingham, Leicester and Bristol contain significant 'inner city' concentrations of the elderly, low-paid

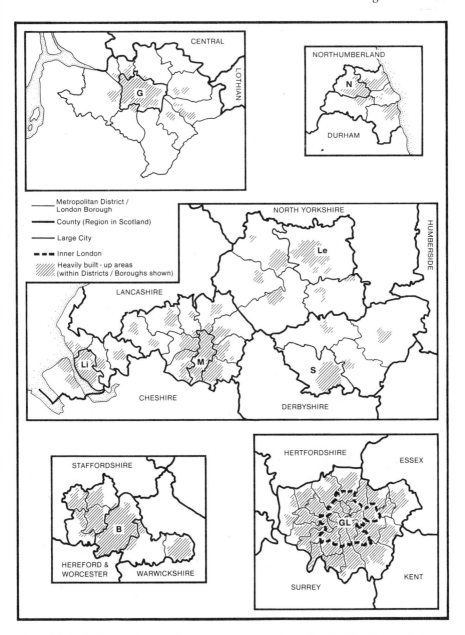

Figure 8.1 Eight large cities and their metropolitan contexts. Key to cities: B Birmingham, in West Midlands; G Glasgow, in 'Central Clydeside Conurbation' within Strathclyde Region; GL Greater London (pecked line shows Inner London); Le Leeds, in West Yorkshire; Li Liverpool, in Merseyside; M Manchester, in Greater Manchester; N Newcastle upon Tyne, in Tyne and Wear; S Sheffield, in South Yorkshire. See Figure 10.1 for location of large cities.

and ethnic minorities. Between them, however, the eight cities covered in this chapter possess a combination of characteristics and problems which is both quantitatively and qualitatively different from those of the other three locality types identified.

Our primary focus is on the geographical areas administered by the respective local authorities, except – as just mentioned – in the case of London, which is the responsibility of 32 boroughs and the City of London. These are the areas highlighted in Figure 8.1. Where appropriate and possible, the statistical information presented below relates to these units. The reason for this is that, whereas in Part II we were more interested in broad nationwide patterns and the analysis of trends for which the county scale and labour-market-area framework were more relevant, here we are principally concerned with policy issues and impacts and thus with the administrative framework through which community needs are anticipated and public solutions are normally delivered. As such, therefore, we are dealing with what in the USA is termed the 'central city' of a wider metropolitan region. This essentially comprises the metropolitan core consisting of the city centre and inner urban area, along with some of the suburbs and peripheral council estates, but excludes virtually all of the satellite towns and other settlements in the surrounding commuting ring. Even so, it will be important to bear in mind the broader geographical context of these cities because this can have a considerable bearing on their past performance and their ability to cope with current problems.

The dimensions of urban decline

'British cities are in decline', states David Clark baldly at the beginning of his recent study *Urban Decline* (Clark, 1989, 1). 'Traditionally cities were centres of growth and prosperity within the space-economy. Today, they have become areas of concentrated economic decline' (*ibid.*, 46). In one sense, there is nothing new about identifying pockets or periods of decline. For instance, Asa Briggs (1968) observed that the *City* of London first lost population in the decade 1801–11, while the crowded wards of Liverpool's city centre reached their population peak at the 1851 Census. Hall (1987), too, has highlighted the severe difficulties faced by cities during the economic recession a century ago in the late 1880s, while business confidence is judged to have reached its zenith on Tyneside and Clydeside in the 1890s (Barke, 1986; Wannop, 1986). Nevertheless, the last two decades are remarkable in terms of the scale of contraction in numbers of people and jobs and the speed with which these changes have taken place.

Population losses

Table 8.1 shows the rates of overall population change experienced by these eight cities since the turn of the century, using their present-day boundaries. Their aggregate population peaked in 1951, having increased by 2.7 million or 25 per cent since 1901. Over this period only two of the eight cities had passed their peak census population (Liverpool and Manchester, both in

Table 8.1 Population change for eight large cities, 1901–88

City	1988 population 000s	Change rate for period 1901–51 %	51–61 %	61–71 %	71–81 %	81–88 %
Birmingham	993.7	+49.1	+1.9	− 7.2	− 8.3	−2.4
Glasgow	703.2	+24.9	−2.9	−13.8	−22.0	−9.2
Leeds	709.6	+19.3	+2.5	+ 3.6	− 4.6	−1.2
Liverpool	469.6	+10.9	−5.5	−18.2	−16.4	−9.2
London	6 735.4	+25.9	−2.5	− 6.8	− 9.9	−1.0
Manchester	445.9	+ 8.3	−5.9	−17.9	−17.5	−3.6
Newcastle upon Tyne	279.6	+26.1	−2.3	− 8.4	− 9.9	−1.6
Sheffield	528.3	+23.0	+0.4	− 2.1	− 6.1	−3.6
Eight cities total	10 865.3	+25.0	−2.1	− 7.9	−10.9	−2.4
Great Britain	55 486.4	+32.1	+5.0	+ 5.3	+ 0.6	+1.3

Note: Enumerated population for 1901–81; mid-year estimates of usually resident population for 1981–88 change and 1988 population
Source: 1981 Census for Greater London 1901–81 and other cities 1961–81; Rhind (1983) for other cities 1901–61; and OPCS/GRO (Scotland) for 1981–88

1931), while three cities reached a higher census figure later than mid century (Birmingham and Sheffield in 1961 and Leeds in 1971).

In the three decades after 1951 the scale of overall population loss accelerated markedly. The population of the eight cities, in aggregate, dropped by some 290,000 or 2.1 per cent in 1951–61, but this rate of loss leapt to 7.9 per cent in the following decade and further to 10.9 per cent in the 1970s. London's absolute decline rose from 204,000 to 540,000 and then to 739,000 through the three decades, an overall contraction by 1.5 million people or 18 per cent. In relative terms the impact was even greater for some of the provincial cities, with reductions of *over a third* for Manchester, Liverpool and Glasgow between 1951 and 1981 and with Glasgow losing over one-fifth population in the single decade 1971–81 (Table 8.1).

The escalation of large-city population losses over this period resulted partly from the intensification of decline in particular parts of the cities, but also from a widening of the zones affected. This is most readily demonstrated for London, where the incidence of population loss advanced progressively outwards from the centre. According to Morrey (1973), the population of the three Central Boroughs (Camden, Kensington and Chelsea, and Westminster) peaked in 1881, while the remainder of Inner London reached its highest Census-year population in 1921. Until 1939 the Outer Boroughs were growing strongly enough to outweigh the losses elsewhere and maintained London's overall growth, but they in turn reached a peak around 1951 and joined the pattern of decline (Champion and Congdon, 1988a).

The underlying reasons for the depopulation of the large cities have been outlined in Chapter 4. They relate almost entirely to the forces of decentralization and counterurbanization – the erosion of housing land by commercial expansion, road schemes and slum clearance; a shortage of new space for house-building; falling average household size; rising incomes, greater car availability and the rise of house ownership; increasing congestion and deteriorating living conditions in the large cities; the planned dispersal of people and jobs to New and Expanded Towns; and the 'voluntary' outward movement of manufacturing and consumer-services firms. It is also true, however, that the dramatic fall in the birth rate after 1965 seriously weakened the ability of the large cities to offset their already high migration losses (Champion, 1983).

Many of these factors appear cumulative and self-reinforcing, as some service-sector jobs followed residential population into the suburbs (Hall *et al.*, 1973). The socially selective nature of this exodus further undermined the quality of life and service provision in the central cities (Eversley, 1972). Population losses were partially compensated for by the arrival of immigrants from the New Commonwealth and by the influx of young job seekers from elsewhere in Britain, but this process merely served to aggravate the differentials between inner city areas and the newer suburbs. On arrival, immigrants were tightly constrained in their location by the availability of cheap housing, particularly private-rented accommodation among the West Indians but also the cheap terrace houses which Asian families sought to buy (Peach, 1975). Subsequently the ethnic minorities generally became more widespread, but this has been more a reflection of their increasing numbers and the even faster outward movement of indigenous people than any major tendency towards greater social and cultural mixing (Jones, 1970; Peach, 1982).

On the other hand, the apparently relentless nature of urban decentralization appears to be challenged by more recent experience. As mentioned in Chapter 4, official estimates indicate a substantial slow-down in the rate of large-city depopulation since the mid 1970s (Champion, 1987b, 1989a). For the eight cities together, the annual average rate of loss for 1981–88 was 3.2 per thousand, less than a third of its 1970s level. There is also evidence of considerable new property investment in metropolitan cores and of the 'gentrification' of housing in certain inner locations (Lee, 1983; Law *et al.*, 1988; Hamnett and Randolph, 1988). On the other hand, the population recovery was patchy, with the substantial improvements recorded by Newcastle, Manchester and particularly London contrasting strongly with the continued high rate of population loss experienced by Glasgow and Liverpool (Table 8.1). Moreover, according to Gordon (1988b) and Robson (1988), any respite should be considered a purely temporary phenomenon induced by a general reduction in residential mobility arising from the economic recession of the early 1980s.

Economic restructuring

The signs of economic collapse in the large cities appeared later than for population, with job growth continuing well into the post-war period in most cities, but when decline began to set in, it did so even more dramatically. As with population, decentralization was the predominant force at work in the 1960s and early 1970s, but the most severe contraction took place as a result of the national shake-out of manufacturing industry during the recession years after 1974, and particularly in 1979–82 (see Chapter 5). The job growth which occurred over this period in certain branches of the service sector (Chapter 6) was totally unable to compensate for the losses, though some cities were beginning to record net increases by the late 1980s as part of the national economic recovery.

The scale of decentralization is clear from the calculations of Begg *et al.* (1986). The central and inner areas of the six largest conurbations, after a small gain in the 1950s, lost almost 1.2 million jobs between 1961 and 1981, a contraction of about 15 per cent in each of the two decades (Table 8.2). Their outer areas were considerably more buoyant than this during the early post-war period, but even in the 1960s they were barely able to maintain job levels, with the growth in services being only just sufficient to outweigh the losses in manufacturing and other sectors. Between 1971 and 1981 the outer and inner areas almost matched each other in losing over one-third of their remaining jobs in manufacturing, reflecting the basic weakness of industry across the whole metropolitan economy (Table 8.2).

Table 8.2 Employment change in the conurbations, 1951–81

Period/sector	Central and inner areas		Outer areas		Overall conurbations		Great Britain
	000s	%	000s	%	000s	%	(%)
1951–61							
Total employment	+ 43	+ 1.0	+231	+ 6.0	+274	+ 3.4	(+ 7.0)
of which:							
Manufacturing	−143	− 8.0	+ 84	+ 5.0	− 59	− 1.7	(+ 5.0)
Services	+205	+ 6.7	+164	+ 9.3	+369	+ 7.7	(+10.6)
1961–71							
Total employment	−643	−14.8	+ 19	+ 0.6	−624	− 8.3	(+ 1.3)
of which:							
Manufacturing	−428	−26.1	−217	−10.3	−645	−17.2	(− 3.9)
Services	−272	− 8.5	+262	+13.6	− 10	− 0.2	(+ 8.6)
1971–81							
Total employment	−538	−14.6	−236	− 7.1	−774	−11.0	(− 2.7)
of which:							
Manufacturing	−447	−36.8	−480	−32.6	−927	−34.5	(−24.5)
Services	−183	− 6.8	+272	+12.7	+ 89	+ 1.8	(+11.1)

Note: the conurbations are London, West Midlands, Greater Manchester, Merseyside, Tyneside and Clydeside.
Source: derived or calculated from Begg *et al.* (1986), Table 2.7

From what was said in Chapter 5, the major reduction in manufacturing jobs in the large cities is hardly surprising. Danson *et al.* (1980) have shown from shift-share analysis of 1952–76 employment trends that this reduction occurred almost entirely as a result of specific local factors rather than because of poor mix of industrial sectors, though clearly the 'national component' was of key importance by the end of the 1970s. Space constraints are generally recognized to be of major importance, particularly in the context of progressive falls in the density of workers per unit of floorspace and the growing preference for single-storey factories (Fothergill *et al.*, 1986). A second factor is the compulsory removal of substantial areas of old, cheap factories and workshops by planning authorities intent on road improvements or generally in improving the physical appearance of inner areas. As shown by Robson and Pace (1983) in relation to the west end of

Newcastle, these premises once housed labour-intensive operations and traditionally acted in an industrial 'seed bed' role. Moreover, city planning authorities have tended to 'zone out' industry in favour of 'tidier' activities including residential and educational uses, as well as commercial and leisure developments.

Corporate structure, as opposed to industrial structure, also provides part of the explanation, given the high proportion of manufacturing plant now owned by multi-site companies in the large cities. During phases of rationalization the inner city plants were among the first to be closed, because of space constraints and obsolete infrastructure or because of the higher value of the site in alternative use. As a result, 'cities have become increasingly unattractive locations in which to retain existing investments' (Robson, 1988, 92). Equally fundamental is the low rate of new firm formation, which has resulted from similar factors along with the shortage of entrepreneurial spirit arising from the growth of large corporate structures and the out-migration of potential businessmen (Storey, 1982; Lloyd and Mason, 1984).

Less expected, however, is the poor showing of the large cities in terms of the growth of jobs in the expanding sectors of the economy. Out of the five largest cities studied by Hall (1987), only one – Birmingham – exceeded the 10.8 per cent national rate of job growth in the service sector between 1971 and 1981. Liverpool, Glasgow, Inner London and Manchester all suffered substantial losses in the 'goods-handling' services, often with their depots in inner areas around the city centre. Even in the much more rapidly expanding 'information-handling' services (basically banking, insurance etc., together with public services), these four cities could not match the national average rise of 20.3 per cent. Particularly astonishing is London's mere 6 per cent increase, albeit on a large existing base, leading Hall (1987, 105) to comment that 'London may be a world city passing out of the world league'.

The latest available local employment data, however, shows London in a better light. As shown in Chapter 6, between 1981 and 1987 London recorded a larger absolute increase in employment in banking, insurance and finance than any other LLMA in Britain (Table 6.3), along with the largest increase in female employment and the fourth largest in part-time employment (Tables 6.8 and 6.10). The details of 1981–87 job changes for the Greater London area are given in Table 8.3 and highlighted in Figure 8.2. They confirm London's predominant role in the financial sector, and particularly business services, linked to the deregulation of the Stock Exchange and the build-up to the 'Big Bang' of 1986 (Breheny and Congdon, 1989). The dynamism of this sector helped to offset London's above-national-average loss of jobs in manufacturing and transport and its slower than average growth in distribution and 'other services'. As a result, London managed an overall rate of employment change for 1981–87 only marginally lower than the national average.

Most of the seven large cities in the provinces have been somewhat left behind in this process, as well as suffering larger losses than London in some other sectors. In relation to the latter, the trends in manufacturing are particularly impressive and depressing, with the average loss of over a quarter of jobs in this six-year period coming on top of the major contractions noted for the previous two decades in Table 8.2. Liverpool, Newcastle and

Table 8.3 Employment change for eight large cities, 1981–87 (per cent)

City	Total (0–9)	Manu-facturing (2–4)	Services (6–9)	Distrib-ution (6)	Transport & comm. (7)	Business services (839)
Birmingham	− 9.0	−27.3	+ 3.1	− 8.1	−12.6	+21.2
Glasgow	− 7.8	−27.7	− 1.2	−14.2	−28.4	+46.7
Liverpool	−20.4	−44.2	−13.2	−28.4	−34.7	+50.3
Leeds	− 2.3	−15.0	+ 5.4	+ 4.8	− 8.5	+25.9
Manchester	− 4.1	−17.9	+ 0.0	− 8.5	− 7.6	+69.3
Newcastle	− 0.4	−43.7	+15.0	−10.3	−18.0	+93.5
Sheffield	−16.1	−38.2	− 2.7	−16.9	− 9.3	+14.6
Seven cities	− 8.7	−28.6	+ 0.3	−10.9	−18.8	+38.7
London	− 1.6	−29.6	+ 6.9	+ 0.6	−14.7	+70.9
Eight cities	− 4.2	−29.1	+ 4.7	− 3.5	−16.0	+64.4
Great Britain	− 0.2	−15.7	+ 9.4	+ 3.7	− 8.4	+80.6

Note: Numbers in brackets in the column headings refer to the 1980 Standard Industrial Classification. 'Business services' comprise part of 'Banking, finance, etc.'
Source: Census of Employment, NOMIS

Sheffield were the most severely affected, with the loss of around two in five of the manufacturing jobs left after the period of deep recession in 1979–81. The traumatic effects of this decline have been compounded by the substantial shedding of labour by the service sector, with the loss of one in ten jobs from the distribution sectors of the seven cities and almost one in five from transport and communications. The worst affected in both these sectors was Liverpool, which also saw a net decline of jobs in the financial sector, and altogether lost one in five of all its jobs between 1981 and 1987 (Figure 8.2). Sheffield and Manchester shared with Liverpool a sluggish performance in the financial sector, though none of these provincial cities achieved the national rate of increase, no doubt partly because their office sector has depended to a considerable extent on a declining industrial and goods-trading role (Marshall, 1983; Marshall *et al.*, 1985). Nevertheless, since the mid 1980s it seems that the producer services sector has been undergoing

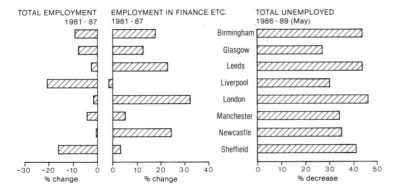

Figure 8.2 1980s changes in employment and unemployment for the eight large cities.
Source: Census of Employment, Department of Employment, NOMIS.

something of a revival in provincial cities, partly because of London's preoccupation with international finance, and that a few major cities like Birmingham, Leeds and Manchester, along with other important regional centres like Edinburgh, Cardiff, Bristol and Norwich, have benefited (Leyshon and Thrift, 1989).

Variations in growth may result from local factors of metropolitan structure. In particular, Law (1985) has suggested that Manchester is at a disadvantage compared to Birmingham and Glasgow because of difficulties of car parking and access to the city centre and because of its extensive ring of established and well-connected towns. Inner London, too, has had to compete with subsidiary centres not merely within Greater London, like Croydon, but also across the wider South East (Damesick, 1982). Much of this outer development, however, performs a supporting role in the form of back-office functions for the higher-level operations conducted in the City (Gillespie and Green, 1987; Marshall, 1989).

The social implications of decline

Britain's large cities are therefore facing the dual handicaps of long-established decentralization and large-scale de-industrialization. Little wonder that these large cities face some of the most intractable social problems in Britain today – and indeed in Europe (see Chapter 2). Moreover, these problems are compounded by the fact that many of their residents are at a disadvantage in the labour force because of various factors such as deficiencies in skills and education, discrimination on the grounds of gender and race, and work-travel difficulties imposed by residential location and inadequate transport facilities. In the words of the Archbishop's report *Faith in the City*, this adds up to a situation of 'grave and fundamental injustice' in what it designates as Urban Priority Areas (Church of England, 1985, xv).

The scale of social deprivation

There are many different ways of measuring deprivation, but there is great consistency in the general results of social monitoring. This point is made explicitly by Begg and Eversley in their examination of social deprivation for the ESRC's Inner Cities Research Programme. In their words (Begg and Eversley, 1986, 80), 'Though the exact rank order differs according to which method we use to measure intensity of deprivation, size of the deprived population, and the relationship to surrounding areas, the same areas always emerge. Glasgow old core and peripheral, the inner areas of Merseyside, Manchester-Salford, Birmingham, the rest of West Midlands, Tyne and Wear, Teesside, Leeds and Bradford, Sheffield, Leicester, and large parts of Inner London always appear.'

Moreover, the scale of inner city deprivation has been increasing over the post-war period. Not surprisingly, in view of the account in the previous section, unemployment indicates this trend very clearly. The six inner city areas studied by Begg *et al.* (1986) saw the unemployment rate of their inhabitants double from an average of 3.8 to 7.5 per cent between 1961 and 1971 and then virtually double again to 14.8 per cent in 1981. Though much of this increase reflected the national trend, the relative degree of disadvantage of the inner cities also increased, for their rate was 51 per cent above the national unemployment rate in 1981 compared with being only one-third higher in 1951.

During the 1980s spatial differences in unemployment appear to have widened further, both between cities and within them. Between 1986 and 1989 the largest reductions in numbers of unemployed occurred in London, Birmingham, Leeds and Sheffield, down by two-fifths, whereas at the other extreme, Glasgow and Liverpool recorded falls of only 25–30 per cent (Figure 8.2). At the local scale, Congdon has shown that the range of unemployment rates across London wards widened significantly between 1980 and 1987 and that this trend was echoed to some extent in mortality rates, as also observed by Townsend *et al.* (1987). At the level of the individual household, too, social polarization has been proceeding apace in London, with data from the Family Expenditure Survey showing a drop of over £7.50 a week (–14 per cent) in disposable income for the worst-off decile of households between 1981 and 1985 compared with an increase of £23.50 (+6.8 per cent) for the best-off decile – truly 'a city divided' (LSPU, 1986).

Facets of deprivation

Various geographical and social factors have been at work alongside the overall drop in job opportunities. In the first place, inner city residents have come under increasing competition in the labour market from commuters from outside the inner city, who in 1981 accounted for 39 per cent of the employment of the inner cities compared with only 20 per cent thirty years before (Begg *et al.*, 1986). Secondly, many of the large number of workers made redundant in inner city areas and some of the school-leavers do not possess the skills and education required for vacancies in the growing service-sector activities (Buck *et al.*, 1986). Thirdly, because of their limited financial means, many of the unemployed have often been forced to take accommodation in areas with least jobs and fewest facilities, including public transport services, and therefore face difficult and costly work journeys (Meadows *et al.*, 1988). This problem has been made worse by the contraction in low-income housing stock, which has thereby become more heavily concentrated in the least privileged areas where sales have been fewest (Hamnett and Randolph, 1983b, 1986; Wilmott and Murie, 1988).

These difficulties have been compounded in many cases by active discrimination which has placed the burden of deprivation disproportionately on certain groups of people. According to Townsend *et al.* (1987), those without formal qualifications, the young, women (especially single parents), non-whites (particularly those of Afro-Caribbean origin) and the disabled, have all tended to be at a significant disadvantage in the London labour market. These factors usually act in a multiplicative way, so that in 1981 37 per cent of West Indians aged 16–19 were out of work in London compared to a rate of 19 per cent for all those of West Indian origin and an overall unemployment rate of 5.5 per cent (Hollis, 1982; GLC, 1986). In the 1980s homelessness has emerged alongside joblessness as a key indicator of social malaise, reflecting in its incidence both the degree of pressure on local housing markets and the distribution of the most vulnerable social groups such as the young leaving care, ex-psychiatric patients and refugees (Bramley *et al.*, 1988). This phenomenon, too, is particularly well documented in relation to London, where the number of households accepted as homeless rose from some 14,000 in 1978 to nearly 25,000 in 1984 (Conway, 1985; Greve *et al.*, 1986). By 1987 the number of homeless households in Britain as a whole had risen to 128,200, the majority in the large cities and with 29,700 in London alone.

At the same time, it should be stressed that the inner cities are not the only places in which deprivation occurs (Bentham, 1983). This much was recognized by Sally Holtermann fifteen years ago: 'Most of the deprived do not live in deprived areas and most of those who live in deprived areas are not themselves deprived' (Holtermann, 1975). The point is, however, even truer today, partly because deprivation has spread outwards from the traditional inner areas, for instance into Outer London boroughs such as Brent and Ealing (Kinnear and Klausner, 1986) and into peripheral council estates like Drumchapel and Easterhouse in Glasgow and Kirkby on Merseyside (McGregor and Mather, 1986; Lewis and Morgan, 1986). It is also partly because social patterns in some inner urban areas have become more varied, as for instance through the gentrification of parts of Islington and Docklands in London (Hamnett and Williams, 1980).

The spiral of decline in inner city areas

Nevertheless, it is in the inner areas of the large cities where the most severe social problems remain. The structural and spatial developments of the 1970s and 1980s have led to 'a growing polarization of society characterized by concentrated poverty, dependence, unemployment and deterioration of the built environment for those left behind in the cities' (Begg *et al.*, 1986, 36). It is in such circumstances that a cumulative spiral of decline can easily set in, as outlined in the following scenario. 'Falling populations are in every case associated with falling job opportunities. Both public and private investment is withdrawn. As the population loses purchasing power, retail trades and personal services decline. Private house-building virtually ceases. Professional services deteriorate as individual practitioners choose greener pastures. It becomes increasingly difficult to staff educational, social and health services' (Eversley and Begg, 1986, 79). It is out of such conditions that despair is born and riots may occur (Hamnett, 1983a).

These are considerations which politicians ignore at their peril, as President Kennedy recognized in the US context thirty years ago (Robson, 1987, 215). In the words of a British Minister for the Inner Cities, 'Many of the most able and enterprising have left to contribute to the new prosperity elsewhere, leaving behind them a serious social imbalance and hastening the spiral of decline. No government can ignore these problems. A society which thinks it can tolerate extreme differences in the opportunities available to people in different areas is asking for resentment and social tension' (Trippier, 1989).

The political and policy responses to inner city problems

The growth of political concern

The political reaction to inner city issues has developed in three main stages. The first initiatives took place immediately after Enoch Powell's 'Rivers of Blood' speech in April 1968. They included the introduction of the Urban Programme (UP) and the setting up of a series of urban experiments including the Community Development Projects by the Labour Government of the later 1960s and the Inner Area Studies by the Conservative government in the early 1970s. The second major surge of attention followed the government's explicit recognition of the primacy of the inner city problem, as announced by the then Secretary of State for the Environment, Peter Shore, in 1976. As well as signalling the winding up of the planned overspill schemes, this heralded a major enhancement of the UP and the introduction of a range of new measures in the 1978 Inner Urban Areas Act, which incorporated many of the ideas being developed by local authorities as set out most clearly in the Tyne and Wear Act of 1976.

The third phase developed in the wake of the 1981 riots and gave the Department of the Environment even wider responsibilities for inner city regeneration and for co-ordinating the roles of the other central government departments including Industry and Employment. The lead was taken by Michael Heseltine, who became effectively the 'minister for Merseyside' where some of the worst violence had occurred and where local government was then controlled by the extreme Left. In a well-publicized drive, central government appointed a task force to deal with Liverpool's problems and brought together a group of businessmen to explore ways of attracting private investment to the inner city. Various measures followed from these actions, most notably the introduction of Urban Development Grants in 1982 (see next section).

The inner city finally – if briefly – reached the top of the political agenda in 1987, when the Prime Minister, Margaret Thatcher, announced on General Election night that this was to be the number one priority of the Conservative party's third consecutive term in power at Westminster. In her own words, 'On Monday we have a big job to do in some of those inner cities' (Robson, 1988). In practice, however, it was not until the following year that 'Action for Cities' was announced and even then, by the Government's own admission, it contained no new policy initiatives and therefore required no extra parliamentary legislation (Cabinet Office, 1988).

The development of policies for the inner city

The policy response since the mid 1970s has comprised a complex succession of new instruments and experiments (Lawless, 1988; Young, 1989). The Inner Urban Areas Act of 1978 led to the establishment of seven Inner City Partnerships, which involved the linking up of representatives of central and local government to plan the expenditure of a large part of the enhanced UP in defined areas on the ground. All these were in the large cities in England – London Docklands, Lambeth, Hackney/Islington, Birmingham,

Liverpool, Manchester/Salford and Newcastle/Gateshead. Separate arrangements had previously been devised in Scotland for the Glasgow Eastern Area Renewal project (GEAR).

The first Conservative administration introduced the Urban Development Corporation (UDC) and Enterprise Zone (EZ) in 1980. The first two UDCs started operations in the docklands of London and Liverpool in 1981 and subsequent designations included sites in Newcastle (Tyne and Wear UDC), Leeds and Manchester in 1987 and the Lower Don Valley in Sheffield in 1988. The first 11 EZs were set up in 1981–82, with a second tranche of 14 zones in 1983–84, but with the exception of the Isle of Dogs (London), Belfast and Tyneside (partly in Newcastle but mainly in Gateshead) these were not located in large cities but mainly in smaller industrial towns (see Figure 10.4).

Other initiatives included the introduction of Urban Development Grant (UDG) in 1982, which was designed to lever private sector investment into inner urban development. UDG was complemented by Urban Regeneration Grant (URG) in 1987, both being replaced by City Grant in 1988. City Action Teams (CATs) were introduced in 1985 and, along with Inner City Task Forces, had the aim of co-ordinating central government expenditure and instilling greater confidence into the private sector. Initiatives in the educational field included City Technology Colleges (CTC) and school/industry compacts, funded jointly by Whitehall and the private sector and designed to increase training opportunities and education-business contacts.

Altogether, by the late 1980s, a wide, if not bewildering, array of policy initiatives, large and small, was *available* for tackling the problems of the large cities and particularly their inner areas. Indeed the main purpose of the 'Action for Cities' brochure and the associated publicity drive in 1988 was to increase general awareness of the range of central government support and indicate more clearly how the private sector could benefit from it and thereby help the cities (Cabinet Office, 1988, especially 30–1: 'What companies can do' and 'How Government helps companies'). Table 8.4 lists the main contents of 'Action for Cities'. They embrace three levels of intensity: instruments which are targeted to very specific areas within individual cities, such as the UDCs, EZs and CATs; arrangements which are available more generally for designated cities, such as the UP and City Grant; and nationwide programmes that may or may not have an enhanced component for inner city areas such as the Loan Guarantee Scheme, the Youth Training Scheme, the National Land Register, the revival of private-rented housing, road construction programmes and so on. Even this long list fails to mention some other relevant measures, not least the various grants administered by the Department of Trade and Industry to the assisted areas and similar funding under the European Regional Development Fund, which covers most of the large Northern cities and for which London became eligible for the first time in 1989.

Changes in aims and methods

This whole package of measures represents a very significant change of emphasis from that of the mid 1970s, both in the aims of inner city policy and

Table 8.4 Central government measures for the inner cities, existing and proposed, 1988

Priorities	Aims/means

'Helping businesses succeed'
Aims: Encourage enterprise and new businesses.
        Help existing businesses to grow stronger.
Means: Enterprise Allowance Scheme
         Managed Workshops
         Small Firms Service
         Loan Guarantee Scheme
         PICKUP Programme
         Grants for Local Enterprise Agencies
         Regional Enterprise grants

'Preparing for work'
Aims: Improve people's job prospects, motivation and skills
Means: Better schools (national core curriculum, opting-out)
         City Technology Colleges
         Schools/Industry Compacts
         Youth Training Scheme
         Jobclub places
         Restart interviews
         REPLAN programme

'Developing cities'
Aims: Make areas attractive to residents and to business by
                    – tackling dereliction
                    – bringing buildings into use
                    – preparing sites and encouraging development
Means: Urban Development Corporations
         City Grant
         National land registers
         Enterprise Zones and Simplified Planning Zones
         New transport investment

'Better homes and attractive cities'
Aims: Improve the quality of housing
        Make inner city areas safe and attractive places to live and work
Means: Revive the private-rented sector
         Encourage Housing Associations
         Provide wider range of housing for sale (Right to Buy, Shared Ownership)
         Improve council estates (Priority Estates Project, Estates Action)
         Give council tenants choice (Tenants' Choice Scheme)
         Housing Action Trusts
         Urban Programme Grants
         Safer Cities schemes
         'Greening the cities'

'Making it happen'
Aims: Coordinate efforts more effectively
        Give clear lead to private sector
Means: Urban Development Corporations
         City Action Teams
         Inner city Task Forces
         'Action for Cities' investment programme

Source: *Action for Cities*, Cabinet Office, 1988

in the methods used to achieve them. The shift in aims has evolved relatively slowly. Urban policy began with the mainly physical emphasis embodied in the slum clearance and comprehensive redevelopment schemes of the early post-war period and broadened out in the late 1960s to embrace social and community considerations in the UP and Educational Priority Areas. Subsequently, concern shifted to underlying economic issues and employment problems, following the results of the experimental projects in the mid 1970s. On the other hand, the new areas of concern have not entirely erased the earlier aims, but instead have tended to complement them. This is reflected in the breadth of objectives shown in Table 8.4, which include more attractive environment, better housing and safer cities as well as stimulating enterprise and improving people's job prospects.

The change in methods has, by contrast, been more rapid and complete, primarily involving the replacement of the local authorities by the private sector as the main vehicle of urban regeneration and the principal partner of central government (Brindley and Stoker, 1988; Young, 1989). The basic UDC concept follows the successful model established by the New Town Development Corporations. Note that, whereas UDG used to be administered by the local authorities, City Grant is handled directly by central government. Successive Thatcher governments have increasingly seen the private sector as their natural ally in fighting urban decay.

Even so, the role of local government in urban regeneration should not be ignored. Firstly, it was the local authority sector which took the lead in the economic regeneration of older urban areas, most notably in the Tyne and Wear Act of 1976 (Cameron and Gillard, 1983) and in the initiative of some county councils is setting up Enterprise Boards in the late 1970s, most notably Greater London and West Midlands (Young and Mason, 1983; Mawson and Miller, 1986). Secondly, the local authorities still possess a considerable range of responsibilities in relation to education, housing, social services and environmental quality, which are crucial to both the needs of businessmen and the well-being of residents. Thirdly, and by no means least, there are a growing number of successful partnerships between local government and the private sector, not just the major city centre redevelopment schemes of the 1960s and 1970s (Holliday, 1983) but also pioneering attempts at inner city regeneration like the Phoenix initiative in Manchester and the Lower Don Valley scheme in Sheffield, both of which were appropriated by central government as 'mini-UDCs' in 1988 (Lawless, 1986; Pearson, 1986; Law, 1988).

The impact of inner-city policies

Evaluation of government policy is fraught with problems. In particular, it is very difficult to calculate how much would have happened in the absence of public intervention and, in relation to spatially targeted policies, what developments have merely been displaced from elsewhere. The lasting results are more important than any short-term impact, but are even more tricky to pin down because of all the other changes going on. Here we concentrate on attempts at evaluating two principal approaches to inner city revival and summarize the main conclusions of some broader assessments that have been made.

Urban Development Corporations (UDCs)

The UDCs embody all the principal features of the new approach to urban regeneration which the Conservative government developed in the 1980s. They are single-purpose agencies set up by central government to reclaim specific sites of derelict or under-used land, they are provided with substantial public funds with the aim of 'levering' private investment into these areas, they are controlled by non-elected boards which are accountable only to Whitehall and Parliament, and they have their own land-use planning powers in order to allow speedy progress (Lawless, 1988; Stoker, 1989). By 1989 ten UDCs had been designated, covering over 1700 hectares and taking a central grant of over £200m a year. The first two – London Docklands (LDDC) and Merseyside (MDC), both set up in 1981 – have already been the subject of extensive monitoring and evaluation. The government has argued that UDCs are 'the most important attack ever made on urban decay' (Cabinet Office, 1988, 12), but some others have been more restrained in their praise.

In the case of London Docklands (Figure 8.3), there is certainly no denying that a substantial degree of development has taken place since 1981. By 1988 600 hectares of derelict land had been reclaimed, 480,000 m^2 of commercial and industrial floorspace had been completed with a further 550,000 m^2 underway, work had started on over 15,000 homes of which 8,782 had been completed, and new infrastructure projects, notably the Docklands Light Railway and London City Airport, had been constructed (House of Commons, 1988; National Audit Office, 1988). Furthermore, an estimated 20,000 jobs (net) had been created by the 1,200 firms which had moved to the Docklands, chiefly in the Isle of Dogs Enterprise Zone, and £430m of government grant had generated £4,400m of investment from the private sector – a 'leverage ratio' of ten to one (LDDC, 1988; Trippier, 1989). On the negative side, however, there has been sharp criticism of the LDDC's high-handed approach to local authorities and community groups, in that it has overruled local planning strategy and has tended to concentrate on high-skill job and up-market housing orientated to the City of London rather than provide for redundant dockers and other unemployed and low-income residents (Ambrose, 1986; Klausner, 1987; Docklands Consultative Committee, 1988; Lawless, 1988; Stoker, 1989).

The experience of the MDC has turned out very different, in that its achievements have been comparatively limited but its relationships with local groups have been moderately good (Wray, 1987; Parkinson, 1988; Boaden, 1989). Though it got to grips swiftly with the complicated task of reclaiming and servicing the disused dockland area, by 1987 the MDC had attracted less than £20m of private investment compared with its own expenditure of nearly £140m. Moreover, at this time, only about one-third of available industrial and commercial floorspace owned by the MDC was occupied and there had been little progress in the provision of housing. Indeed, industrial prospects had already appeared so bleak that in 1985 the

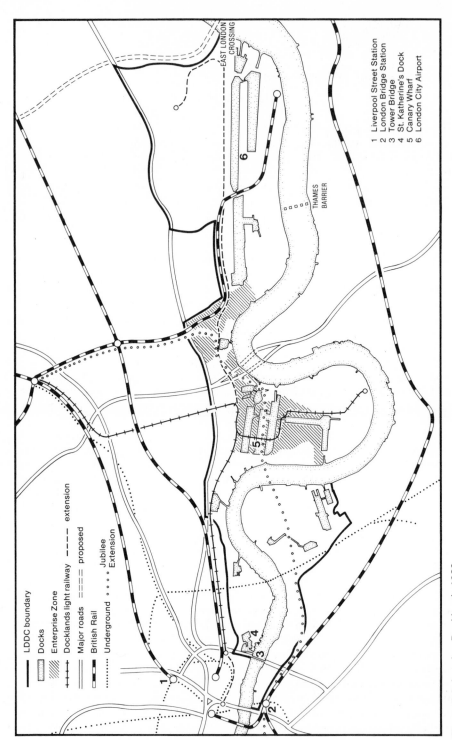

Figure 8.3 London Docklands 1989.

LDDC boundary
Docks
Enterprise Zone
Docklands light railway ----- extension
Major roads ===== proposed
British Rail
Underground ∘∘∘∘ Jubilee
Extension

EAST LONDON
CROSSING

THAMES
BARRIER

1 Liverpool Street Station
2 London Bridge Station
3 Tower Bridge
4 St. Katherine's Dock
5 Canary Wharf
6 London City Airport

MDC switched its emphasis to a tourism/leisure-led strategy for the Liverpool waterfront, but the limited financial returns on flagship projects like the renewal of Albert Dock and the International Garden Festival have not been a good omen. In terms of management style, the MDC has been criticized for lack of dynamism, poor marketing strategy and oversensitivity to local feelings, for instance in discouraging a major retail development in deference to Liverpool's concern over its effect on the city centre (National Audit Office, 1988). Nevertheless, the sub-regional economic context for the MDC is far removed from the situation in London Docklands, reinforced by the fact that Liverpool's one Enterprise Zone was located outside the MDC area at Speke.

Glasgow Eastern Area Renewal (GEAR)

The GEAR operation is the archetypal, and biggest, example of the more traditional approach to urban regeneration. Set up in 1976, it pre-dated the main surge of political concern for urban problems in England. Though the underlying aim was for a 'new town in town' after the abandonment of a proposed New Town at Stonehouse, a Development Corporation approach was ruled out in favour of a multi-agency structure primarily involving Glasgow District Council, Strathclyde Regional Council, and the Scottish Special Housing Association, but working under the general direction of the Scottish Development Agency and including financial input from the Housing Corporation, the area health board and other bodies. The emphasis, as a result, was far broader than for the UDCs, with six basic objectives – stemming population decline, generating employment, improving the environment, increasing residents' employability, overcoming their social disadvantages, and fostering residents' commitment and confidence (SDA, 1980).

The achievements of GEAR need to be seen in the light of the area's inheritance of some of the worst social, economic and physical conditions in the UK. For example, its population declined by 61 per cent between 1961 and 1978, nearly two-thirds of those remaining were classified as dependent, male adult unemployment was over four times the national average in 1976, and the area was situated in a wider labour market which was even more depressed than Liverpool's (Pacione, 1981). Altogether, well over £300m of public funds had been committed to capital projects in the area by 1988, of which some 60 per cent was devoted to housing, 15 per cent to infrastructure, transport, education and other services, 13 per cent to land assembly and factory building, and 9 per cent to various forms of environmental improvement. The results have been patchy. There have been clear advances in the physical environment and significant improvements in the level of public services and community facilities, but rather limited progress has been made in relation to economic regeneration and unemployment (Moore and Booth, 1986). Nevertheless, as evidenced by substantial private housing investment, GEAR has helped to give new confidence both to the area and to the whole city, providing a platform for imaginative projects such as its Garden Festival in 1988 and 'Europe's City of Culture' celebration in 1990. Moreover, it has proved the value of comprehensive regeneration as opposed to wholesale clearance and rebuilding, as well as the merits of decentralized management styles (Donnison and Middleton, 1987).

Evaluation of inner city policies

Assessments of the full range of inner city policies, including the UDCs and GEAR, indicate a 'curate's egg' of outcomes (Robson, 1988). The most significant achievements, as well as the most visible, have been in physical terms, with the reclamation of substantial areas of derelict land and buildings. There have been some success stories in housing renovation and environmental works, which have helped to instill greater confidence amongst private housebuilders. Considerable numbers of new businesses and jobs came to the inner cities during the 1980s, but performance has varied between places. A particularly marked contrast exists between the strong growth in London Docklands and the much slower progress made in northern cities, especially Liverpool, Glasgow and Sheffield.

Far less success seems to have been achieved in the social arena, as evidenced by the continuing high levels of deprivation mentioned earlier in the chapter. Many of the newly created jobs have gone to in-commuters rather than local residents, while the extra development pressures and private housebuilding have tightened up housing markets and heightened social tensions by juxtaposing the two extremes of the income spectrum. Where relative deprivation in inner city areas did fall during the late 1970s and early 1980s, it was often accompanied by the deterioration of conditions in surrounding areas of older suburbs or on the peripheral council estates. Meanwhile, the fall in unemployment during the late 1980s seemed more closely related to the general improvement in the national economy than to any of the policies specifically targeted on the inner cities. Clearly, a property-based approach to urban regeneration can, at best, provide only indirect benefits to the majority of local people and may serve to exacerbate their problems, at least in the short-term.

Key challenges and bottle-necks in land-use planning

The continuation of concentrated deprivation into the 1990s suggests that some powerful underlying forces are not being addressed squarely by government policies. Most critical in relation to the absolute scale of these problems is undoubtedly the state of the national economy and its regional components and the way in which de-industrialization and restructuring have had some of their most devastating impacts on inner-city areas. This is an aspect to which we will return in Chapter 12. In the meantime, however, it is important to recognize that the prospects for improvements here depend to a considerable extent on conditions elsewhere in the cities and in their wider regions. In the words of Kennett and Hall (1981, 9), 'The inner city problem can only be understood in relation to the wider metropolitan area'. This interdependence takes many forms and can impose all kinds of constraints on the metropolitan cores. There is space here to mention no more than three, and these only briefly – land, housing and transport.

Land

Shortage and high price of land have been, and continue to be, one of the principal obstacles to the regeneration of the large cities. With falling household size, lower employment densities and the general trend towards higher space standards, cities have been unable to prevent the loss of people and jobs, because even where their boundaries have been drawn comparatively generously (as for Leeds, Sheffield and Newcastle), the amount of spare land available for development has been very limited (Clark, 1989). The extensive areas of idle land in the inner areas are potentially a major resource, as the developments in London Docklands have demonstrated, but its very existence reflects the scale of the problems faced in bringing it back into use (Burrows, 1978; Coleman, 1980). These problems are not only physical in terms of the need to clear obsolete structures and decontaminate sites used previously by noxious industries, but also involve the challenges of land assembly, including fragmented land ownership and high land prices (Adams *et al.*, 1987, 1988).

The government's introduction of public land registers and its policy of forcing the sale of land held by local authorities and other public-sector bodies have helped to get the land market moving, as have the powers given to the UDCs in some of the worst affected locations. On the other hand, the Conservative party's antipathy towards tackling the land-values issue, reflected in its repeal of the three major pieces of relevant postwar legislation introduced by Labour governments since the Second World War (most recently the 1975 Community Land Act), allows the government very little scope for dealing with the artificially high level of vacant land prices. As a result, the extent of vacant and derelict land remains large, threatening to undermine the confidence generated by successful reclamation projects (Adams *et al.*, 1987; Chisholm and Kivell, 1987).

Housing

A key feature of the housing problem in large cities is the way in which a significant proportion of their lower-income residents are 'trapped' in large estates of badly designed and poorly maintained council houses and flats or in the often more cramped and even less physically sound properties of the declining private-rented sector (Malpass, 1986; Thomas, 1986). As mentioned in Chapter 7, the rundown of the New and Expanded Towns programme, the fall in the level of local authority house-building since the late 1970s, and the large scale of 'right to buy' sales of council houses in the 1980s have significantly reduced the housing opportunities for lower-income households, including single-parent families and ethnic minorities, and curtailed their ability to move in search of work and better living conditions (Conway and Ramsay, 1986).

During the 1980s a range of measures was introduced by central government to tackle this problem. These include financial support for low-cost home ownership, the reduction of restrictions on private landlords, the extension of the role of Housing Associations, and a 'widening of choice' for council tenants (Cabinet Office, 1988). Moreover, following studies of the design and management of multi-storey housing (Coleman, 1984, 1985, 1987; Power, 1984, 1987), the government launched a series of experiments aimed at improving the security and appearance of these areas and at giving residents greater say in their own affairs, including the Priority Estates Project, Estate Action and Housing Action Trusts (Power, 1982; Cabinet Office, 1988).

Nevertheless, the extent of high-rise public-sector housing in the large cities is colossal. In the mid 1980s the overall bill for council housing repairs nationwide was estimated at a huge £18 billion (DOE, 1985; Cantle, 1986). The task of making housing more attractive in inner cities and peripheral estates is therefore extremely daunting and cannot be carried out overnight. Indeed, the situation has been made worse by the government's cutbacks in financial support for local authority housing, contrasting with its strong encouragement of the owner-occupied sector through tax relief and other means (Karn *et al.*, 1985; Booth and Crook, 1986; Forrest and Murie, 1988). It is also aggravated by the tightness of planning controls on urban development, which contribute to the high price of building land for public and private sectors alike.

Transport

The problem of traffic congestion in and around the large cities once again hit the headlines during the late 1980s, a quarter of a century on from the Buchanan Report *Traffic in Towns* (Buchanan *et al.*, 1963). Post-war policies aimed at maintaining a strong role for the city centre in British cities; for instance, through controls on suburban and out-of-town retail and office development, emphasis on radial road routes in preference to suburban ringways, improvement in commuter rail services, and investment in underground services such as the Victoria and Jubilee lines in London, the Tyneside Metro and the Glasgow system's renovation (Davies and Champion, 1983). These maintained a successful role for city centres, but this in itself created problems which were then brought to a head by the surge in extra traffic resulting from the nation's economic recovery in the mid 1980s. The situation was further aggravated by the marked lack of investment during the previous decade, which was a function of successful conservationist campaigns against major road schemes as well as of the government's desire to restrict capital spending in its fight against inflation.

At this time there was a remarkable reversal of the long-term decline in public-transport commuting into central London (Green, 1989). Also national forecasts were suggesting at least a doubling in road traffic between 1990 and 2025 (Department of Transport, 1989). The government eventually responded by sanctioning studies for new railways in London, including east–west and north–south links in the central area and a new East London line to complement the woefully inadequate Docklands Light Railway (Figure 8.4). The government also announced a £12 billion programme of road construction nationwide (see Chapter 12). At the time of writing (November 1989), it is uncertain how much of this investment will occur in the near future. Agreement has been reached with the private sector on an extension to the Jubilee line into the Docklands via London Bridge, but

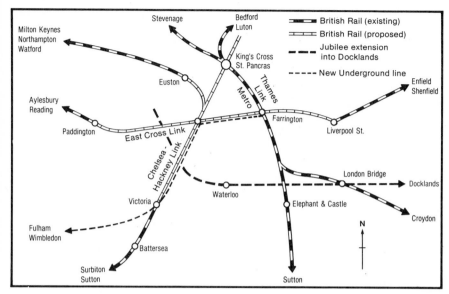

Figure 8.4 Proposed new rail lines in Central London 1988/89.

decisions on the Crossrail links have been postponed and the sum for the roads programme has been pared back by the Treasury. In any case, it is questionable how far new transport facilities inside the large cities can reduce the competitive disadvantages of inner-city locations. It is likely to be extremely difficult to make large improvements in transport in high-density urban environments without taking land from other uses and increasing pollution and other negative side-effects. The recent revival of proposals to cope with economic growth in central areas by restricting parking or charging for car usage merely illustrates the interdependent nature of transport, housing, employment and other land-use issues and underlines the need for a broader strategic perspective in government policy-making.

The eclipse of strategic thinking

Substantial though the land, housing and transport obstacles in themselves are to the continued regeneration and growth of the large cities, they are aggravated by nature of the institutional context in which relevant policies have to be formulated and implemented. The purpose of this final section is to show that the large cities now have even less political power to determine their future than they had forty years ago. As a result, there has been only a limited capacity for policy co-ordination and guidance both within the cities and in relation to the wider metropolitan context.

The weakness of local government

'Cities have never enjoyed the status and power in local government that their size and economic importance justifies' (Clark, 1989, 103). Even when the modern system of local government was introduced nationwide a hundred years ago, the city authorities were given considerably less freedom of action by central government than, say, their equivalents in the USA. Over the decades since then, their ability to control events has been weakened significantly by the failure of their administrative boundaries to expand in line with their physical growth and by the increasing tendency for Whitehall to use the town hall merely as its executive arm.

The changes which have affected the large cities most severely, however, have occurred since the early 1970s and can be summarized under three headings. One is the decision in the 1974/75 reorganization of local government to downgrade the major provincial cities from independent status (unitary bodies with powers similar to counties) to second-tier authorities within larger counties, though some of these powers were returned to the large cities at the abolition of the Metropolitan County Councils in 1986. Secondly, a wide range of traditional local government functions has been handed over to separate boards or private agencies. Last but not least, central government has assumed an increasing range of powers over local government finance in an attempt to reduce public spending and impose its own will on local affairs.

Lack of co-ordination

A major effect of this progressive centralization of government power has been a reduction in the degree of co-ordination and consistency in public policy. One of the principal strengths of the local government system is its multi-functional nature, with a broad remit set through the democratic process and a balance between physical, economic and social objectives. The 1970s saw a major push towards more comprehensive planning and integrated decision-making, including experiments in corporate planning and area management, which led to greater awareness of such problems as duplication, incompatibility and omission. The more recent hiving-off of responsibilities from local authorities to non-elected single-purpose agencies has, however, served to weaken this role.

The scope for co-ordination has also been reduced by the proliferation of central government initiatives and by the Thatcher government's insistence on bypassing the local authorities and dealing directly with the private sector. In a wide-ranging review of inner city policies, Robson is highly critical of 'the adversarial nature of our parliamentary democracy' and 'the tunnel vision of our policy makers', which have led to 'a frustrating mosaic of missed opportunities' and to measures which are 'piecemeal, *ad hoc*, and subject to the law of one hand taking away what the other was giving' (Robson, 1988, 95–6). One example cited is the way in which on Clydeside and Merseyside during the 1970s regional assistance administered by the Department of Trade and Industry favoured the conurbation's outer areas rather than supporting the drive towards inner–city regeneration. In another instance, the Department of the Environment awarded the London boroughs designated under the Urban Programme some £300m between 1979/80 and 1983/4 but took away from them £1,530m through reductions in Rate Support Grant over the same period (Lever and Moore, 1986, 145).

More recently, the wide range of measures included in the 'Action for Cities' programme, and more particularly the large number of departments and agencies responsible for them, suggest great potential for inconsistency. The City Action Teams and Task Forces, where they exist, are unlikely to be strong enough to prevent this.

It is in the broader metropolitan context, however, that some of the most fundamental problems of co-ordination can be found, particularly in balancing the needs of the large cities against those of the surrounding districts. This is not a new problem, in that the 1947 Town and Country Planning Act separated the large cities from their counties for planning purposes and gave central government the power to adjudicate over conflicts between city and hinterland (Hall *et al.* 1973; Rodgers, 1986). For the eight large cities this problem was largely resolved by the establishment of the GLC in 1965, the six English metropolitan counties in 1974, and the Scottish regions in 1975, but the abolition of the new English arrangements in 1986 left Glasgow as the only large city with a city-region scale of government (Wannop, 1986).

Under the 1985 Local Government Act, each of the 32 London Boroughs and the 36 Metropolitan Districts (of the former Metropolitan Counties) is required to produce a Unitary Development Plan for its own area within the framework of strategic guidance provided by the Secretary of State for the Environment. This guidance has to be provided on matters relating to the development and use of land which needs to be dealt with on a metropolitan-wide basis. According to the relevant document for London, issued in July 1989, these matters include 'business, industrial, retail and tourist development, road and rail infrastructure and the relationship between transport and land use; provision for additional housing for the next decade; protection of the Green Belt, Metropolitan Open Land and other open spaces; conservation of the natural and the built environment; and preservation of the character of the River Thames' (Department of the Environment, 1989b) – all key problems in the rejuvenation of the large cities, as mentioned above, yet dealt with in a mere 27-page advice note. No wonder that the new arrangements have been criticized as a poor substitute for strategic planning by metropolitan government (Clark, 1989) and that an 'air of indifference' is seen to hang over the planning of London (Grigson, 1989).

The need for choice and commitment

The reduction in local government powers in metropolitan areas and the 'strange death of strategic planning' in 1980s Britain (Breheny and Hall, 1986) bode ill for the future of the large cities, because the time has come for some hard decisions. In the face of the prospect of continued urban decline, Clark (1989) outlines three alternative strategies. One is to make a much more concerted effort at reviving the cities, which as revealed by the achievements of American cities like Baltimore and Pittsburgh (Law, 1988) requires not only specially targeted programmes but a fundamental re-appraisal of the aims and impacts of the full range of mainstream government spending. The second is to relax the spatial constraints on cities and allow them to 'recapture' the surrounding areas. This could be approached either through boundary extensions, or more feasibly through the introduction of effective metropolitan-wide government. This would allow decisions to be made for the whole functioning urban unit and thereby give the large cities the status and power which their size and importance within the nation merits. The third option is to recognize the true strength of the forces of deconcentration and regional restructuring and therefore develop policies which facilitate the rundown of cities, helping them to take on the new roles which long-term forces dictate and to tackle the inevitable problems of social adjustment in the meantime. The future of the large cities is probably the single most important issue of domestic policy facing Britain as it moves towards the twenty-first century. Since it affects the planning context for all other types of regions and localities, it is a subject to which we return in the final chapter of this book.

Further reading

Four books provide particularly useful historical perspectives on the growth of the large cities and the development of their present-day problems. Briggs (1968) traces their nineteenth-century growth, including case studies on Manchester, Leeds, Birmingham and London. Gordon (1986) examines the transformation of the UK's provincial centres during the twentieth century, including chapters on Birmingham, Manchester, Liverpool/Merseyside, Glasgow/Clydeside, Newcastle/Tyneside and Leeds. Cameron (1980) reviews economic and social trends in Britain's conurbations since the Second World War and examines the major issues faced at the end of the 1970s, including chapters on their economies, housing, transport, education, poverty, unemployment, finance and government. The story is taken through to the end of the 1980s by Clark (1989), which deals particularly with depopulation, economic decline and local government changes.

There is now a vast literature concerned with the economic and social problems of inner urban areas. Hall (1981) summarizes the findings of a working party on inner cities set up by the Social Science Research Council (now the Economic and Social Research Council, ESRC). The ESRC subsequently commissioned a larger research programme, which led to a series of publications including two volumes of 'cross-cutting' studies by Hausner (1986, 1987). This research also involved five case studies, four of which include large cities: Lever and Moore (1986); Buck *et al*. (1986); Spencer *et al*. (1986); and Robinson *et al*. (1987). These studies were also released as a collective volume in Hausner (1987) and in summary versions in Hausner (1987). The situation facing people in inner city areas was also investigated thoroughly by the Archbishop's Commission and reported in Church of England (1985).

The most comprehensive and up-to-date description and critique of inner city policy is provided by Robson (1988), and for an extremely useful outline of the development of policy, see Lawless (1988). As regards individual measures, the Urban Development Corporations are featured in several studies including Stoker (1989); Ambrose (1986), Chapter 8 on London's docklands; and Parkinson (1988). The GEAR programme is described and evaluated in Donnison and Middleton (1987). The role of UDG is assessed by Jonson (1988). The 'Action for Cities' package is reviewed by Young (1989).

Some of the major challenges currently faced by the large cities are described in Robson (1987). This includes chapters on the task of neighbourhood revitalization, the problems of housing design, and the difficulties of land assembly, as well as a case study of Glasgow. More detailed studies on housing problems and policies are Coleman (1985); Malpass (1986); and Thomas (1986). Problems of land assembly and land dereliction are covered by Adams *et al*. (1988); Civic Trust (1988); and Chisholm and Kivell (1987). Issues relating to transport, planning and conservation are addressed in Carmen (1988).

Key questions concerning the prospects for the large cities relate to the viability of their city centres, the strength of their wider metropolitan economies and to their political and institutional contexts. General treatments of these subjects can be found in Sims (1982); Davies and Champion (1983); Rose (1986); Law *et al.* (1988); Hall (1987); Rose and Page (1982); and Clark (1989). City case studies of current and future trends, in addition to those mentioned above, are: Hall (1989); Robinson (1988); Parkinson (1985); and Keating (1988).

9

Prosperous sub-regions

The focus of this chapter is on what has loosely been termed 'the UK's Sunbelt'. The prosperous sub-regions form almost the direct antithesis of the large cities, in that, by and large, they are structured around medium-sized and smaller urban centres, they have a relatively minor legacy of nineteenth-century industrial activity, they are characterized by above-average representation of more wealthy households, and above all they have experienced remarkable growth of both people and jobs in recent years. They have benefited from one or more of the chief patterns of population redistribution which have worked against the large cities, including the North–South drift, the urban–rural shift and local metropolitan decentralization. They also tend to possess certain favourable characteristics; above all, more attractive environments and more space than the large cities and the industrial areas, and better accessibility than the outer rural areas. With their innovatory images in enterprise, working practices, commuting patterns and life styles, they are widely seen as leading the way in Britain towards a new 'post-industrial' pattern of settlement.

Such images, however, tend to gloss over a large number of important features and issues which this chapter will also examine in some detail. Most fundamental is that the four local authority district types which we identify here as comprising the 'prosperous sub-regions' are a large and varied collection. Not only do they vary markedly in terms of their inherited characteristics, but they also differ widely in the sources of their recent growth. Secondly, it would be wrong to assume that, by virtue of their wealth and dynamism, they are largely free of problems. Rapid growth tends to result in as many problems as does rapid decline; it is merely the nature of the problems that is different. The principal issues for the prosperous sub-regions relate to the challenge of adjusting to new circumstances, which at the individual level can be as hard for the 'locals' as for the 'incomers' and which at the broader community level include the pressures on land, housing, transport infrastructure and other services. Finally, we seek to dispel the myth that the prosperous sub-regions are the creation of untrammelled market forces. On the contrary, the public sector – in one form or another – has had a significant hand both in bringing about their success and in contributing to their problems, so any assessment of evolving patterns must give just as serious consideration to the future form of government policies here as for other types of localities.

The identity of the prosperous sub-regions

The prosperous sub-regions form the largest of the four locality types identified at the end of Chapter 7. Defined according to an extended version of the OPCS (1981) classification of local authority districts, they comprise all of 'non-metropolitan' Britain (i.e. outside the boundaries of Greater London, the six English metropolitan counties and the Central Clydeside Conurbation) except for the 'industrial districts' (dealt with in Chapter 10) and the 'remoter, mainly rural, districts' (Chapter 11). In all, they number 195 of Britain's 459 districts and, according to 1988 estimates, account for 22.2 million people, i.e. almost exactly two-fifths of the national total (Table 7.8).

Given their number and importance, it is not surprising to find that they exhibit a substantial measure of diversity. Indeed, this grouping comprises four separate categories of the OPCS classification: namely (non-metropolitan) cities, districts with New Towns, 'resort, port and retirement districts' and '(other) urban and mixed urban–rural districts', referred to subsequently in this chapter in abbreviated form as Cities, New Towns, Resorts and Mixed. Based on measures of urban status and population composition derived from the 1971 Census, this typology indicates a number of distinct factors behind their prosperity and rapid growth, including functions as regional administrative and service centres, programmes for decentralizing people and industry from the conurbations, the influx of the more mobile elderly, and the attraction of people with city-based jobs to suburban and exurban addresses. These diverse origins continue to be reflected to some extent in the socio-demographic profiles of these places, such as a stronger representation of the elderly and professional groups in the resorts and a bias towards youth and skilled manual work in the New Towns. On the other hand, over the last two decades, many of these traditional contrasts have faded, while new features relating to more recent sources of growth have emerged.

The fact that they are unevenly distributed across the country is also not unexpected, given the clear urban and regional differences in population and employment change described in Part II, but the degree of concentration is extremely impressive. In all, the four regions of the South account for 133 of the 195 districts, including all but eight of the Resorts and three-quarters of the Mixed category (Table 9.1). The detailed geographical patterning (Figure 9.1) prompts two further observations. In the first place, the South East region outside London is composed almost entirely of prosperous sub-regions, so it is primarily within this part of Britain that the processes underlying their economic strength can be identified most readily and that their impacts on individuals and communities can be most graphically illustrated. Secondly, this type of locality is represented in all the other regions, raising the question as to how similar to the South they are in terms of sources of growth and scale of problems.

Dimensions of population change

The main features of population change are presented in Table 9.1. All the indicators point to the steadily increasing importance of this type of locality

Table 9.1 Population, 1988, and population change, 1901–88, for prosperous sub-regions

District type (no. of districts)	1988 population		Population change (%)			
	000s	Share (%)	1901–51	1951–71	1971–81	1981–88
Non-metropolitan cities (32)	5 431	24.5	+25.8	+ 3.3	− 3.0	−2.2
South (17)	2 838	12.8	+27.8	+ 3.6	− 2.8	−2.3
North (15)	2 593	11.5	+23.7	+ 3.0	− 3.2	−2.2
Districts with New Towns (25)	2 821	12.7	+47.1	+ 52.4	+15.1	+5.1
South (11)	1 276	5.8	+67.0	+115.6	+17.7	+9.0
North (14)	1 545	7.0	+40.0	+ 25.3	+13.2	+2.0
Resorts, ports and retirement (36)	3 611	16.3	+65.0	+ 20.7	+ 5.8	+7.2
South (28)	2 890	13.0	+61.9	+ 22.6	+ 6.6	+8.2
North (8)	722	3.3	+76.4	+ 14.2	+ 2.9	+3.4
Urban and mixed urban–rural (102)	10 319	46.5	+64.9	+ 42.0	+ 7.5	+4.4
South (77)	7 972	35.9	+73.6	+ 47.2	+ 8.0	+4.5
North (25)	2 347	10.6	+44.2	+ 27.0	+ 5.9	+4.2
All prosperous sub-regions (195)	22 182	100.0	+47.5	+ 26.2	+ 5.2	+3.2
South (133)	14 975	67.5	+55.4	+ 33.0	+ 6.1	+4.2
North (62)	7 207	32.5	+35.9	+ 14.7	+ 3.4	+1.3
Great Britain	55 486	—	+32.1	+ 10.5	+ 0.8	+1.3

Note: Enumerated population for 1901–71; mid-year estimates of usually resident population for 1971–88
Source: calculated from Rhind (1983) for 1901–71; OPCS/GRO (Scotland) for 1971–88

for the country as a whole and to its particularly strong growth in the South. The prosperous sub-regions accounted for 44 per cent of Britain's overall population increase during the first half of the century, and for 82 per cent in 1951–71. For 1971–88 the further increase of 1.75 million was equivalent to 159 per cent; i.e. this settlement category not only accounted for the entire national increase (albeit running at a lower level because of the fall in birth rate) but also cornered a significant part of the losses sustained by other parts of Britain, notably the large cities and most of the industrial areas.

The faster growth of the prosperous sub-regions in the southern half of the country is a long-established feature, but has become more marked in recent years. Between 1901 and 1988 the South accounted for over four-fifths of the gain recorded by the prosperous sub-regions, but the North's share fell from almost one-third in the first half of the century to barely one-fifth over the period 1951–81 and only 13 per cent in 1981–88. The meagre contribution of the North is not only a result of its having fewer prosperous sub-regions, but also directly reflects the below-average performance in the North of the New Towns and Resorts (Table 9.1).

The most notable recent development, however, has been the outward shift of the zone of strong population growth within the South. Notwithstanding the impressive recovery of London's population growth rate (see Chapter 8), the major changes of the 1980s have occurred in the outer parts of the South East, especially on the western and northern edges, and in

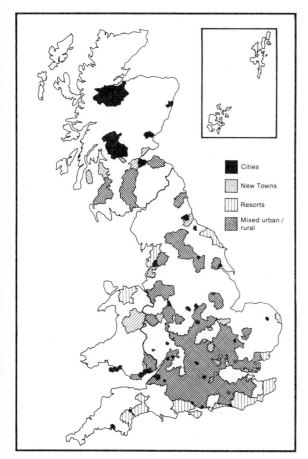

Figure 9.1 Prosperous sub-regions of Great Britain. Full titles of the four district categories are: Cities = Non-metropolitan Cities; New Towns = Districts with New Towns; Resorts = Resort, port and retirement districts; Mixed urban/rural = Urban and mixed urban/rural. Source: see text.

adjacent counties across the regional boundary. Net migration from London to the Rest of the South East (ROSE) doubled between the early and late 1980s, while the South East's overall exchanges with the rest of the UK switched from slight net inflow to strong net outflow, principally as a result of the region's overflow to neighbouring regions.

The scale of these recent changes is remarkable. Defined on a LLMA basis, the place leading this surge, Milton Keynes, is estimated to have added almost 50,000 to its population in just six years, 1981–87, an increase of 30 per cent. Not far behind in terms of absolute numbers was Bournemouth LLMA (up by 44,000), followed by Reading and Oxford (with an extra 30,000 each) and Northampton and Peterborough (an extra 23,000 each). Other southern LLMAs with 1981–87 growth rates exceeding 10 per cent include Huntingdon, Clacton, Weston-super-Mare, Newton Abbot, Newbury and Bishops Stortford. Even at the broader county level, gains of one in ten have been recorded by Cambridgeshire, Isle of Wight, Buckinghamshire and Dorset, with the rates for Berkshire, East Sussex, Northamptonshire and Oxfordshire also averaging over 1 per cent a year in the 1980s (see Fig. 4.4).

These patterns of population change clearly indicate the dominance of the 'Greater South East' in the contemporary geography of Britain, notably the extensive 'western crescent' wrapping itself round the London region from Dorset in the South West through northern Hampshire, Berkshire and Oxfordshire and on to the Milton Keynes, Northampton and Peterborough sub-regions. In part, they reflect the channelling effect of planned overspill schemes, including the New Towns, but they also suggest the fundamental role of locational and environmental factors. One of the chief 'surprises' of the 1980s is the strong growth of the 'resort, port and retirement' category in the South, following decades of being out-performed by the New Towns and the Mixed districts (Table 9.1). Being predominantly South Coast towns (Figure 9.1), most places in this category have the advantages not only of being at the greatest distance from London that is possible in that direction, but also of being perceived to have attractive physical settings and generally high standards of inherited townscape and social prestige.

Dynamics of economic growth

The scale of recent change in the prosperous sub-regions is even more impressive in relation to the economy and employment than it is for population. It is not just a question of the sheer growth in the numbers of jobs in the 1980s, remarkable though this is in the context of national economic difficulties. It is also significantly bound up with the quality of these jobs and the speed with which new types of jobs have been replacing older ones, particularly the way in which lower-level activities have been squeezed out of the stronger labour market areas by employment commanding greater skills and higher pay. This tendency is particularly well developed in the South, where the overall effect of recent trends is to reinforce the diversity of the local economy and provide an even stronger basis for future expansion.

Scale and composition of employment change

In the past, much of the population growth and wealth accruing to the prosperous sub-regions has not been related directly to local sources of economic opportunity. Many of these areas, particularly in the Mixed category, comprise the classic dormitory areas for commuters. This is especially true in the South East for those working in London, but is also found in many similarly accessible places round the conurbations of the Midlands and northern England (Figure 9.1). Moreover, there is ample evidence that long-distance commuting to metropolitan centres, especially central London, grew markedly in the mid 1980s after a period of decline (Chapter 8). It is also the case that retirement migration – one of the other traditional sources of growth in the prosperous sub-regions – accelerated during the decade (Chapter 4).

Notwithstanding these points, however, job growth has in fact been proceeding very rapidly in the prosperous sub-regions. Some of the main features have been documented in Part II. Most notable is the continuous ring of counties round the west and north of the Greater South East which experienced job growth of 7 per cent or over between 1981 and 1987, including rates of over 14 per cent for Northamptonshire and Buckinghamshire (Fig. 7.1). At the LLMA scale some very substantial increases were recorded, with Reading gaining 20,000 jobs, Milton Keynes and Northampton over 18,000, and Cambridge, Oxford and Bournemouth over 15,000 (Table 6.7). In terms of rates, Newbury topped the national ranking of LLMAs, with a 40 per cent increase in jobs in this six-year period, followed by Milton Keynes (30 per cent).

Table 9.2 presents information specifically for the prosperous sub-regions, both in aggregate and split between southern and northern representatives. The success of these areas in gaining jobs over the period 1981–87 is clear, with a 4 per cent growth contrasting with the national stagnation. While the prosperous sub-regions followed the national trend in terms of the decline in male employment and the contraction of the energy/water, manufacturing, construction and transport divisions, they performed more strongly than the country as a whole on each measure. The most impressive statistics relate to the growth of female employment, the partially related increase in the number of part-time jobs and the substantial growth in the three largest service-sector divisions – distribution, banking, insurance and finance, and other services (Table 9.2).

At the same time, it needs to be pointed out that the degree of 'prosperity' in these areas is, in many ways, a relative concept. For instance, between 1981 and 1987 the prosperous sub-regions in the North did not gain jobs in

Table 9.2 Employment change, 1981–87, for prosperous sub-regions

	1981 000s	1987 000s	1981–87 change 000s	%	(GB) (%)
Total employment	8 154.9	8 465.4	+310.5	+ 3.8	(− 0.1)
Male	4 575.6	4 508.9	− 66.7	− 1.5	(− 5.5)
Female	3 579.3	3 956.4	+377.1	+ 10.5	(+ 6.9)
Full-time	6 274.5	6 332.2	+ 57.7	+ 0.9	(− 3.2)
Part-time	1 880.4	2 133.1	+252.6	+ 13.4	(+11.2)
Energy, mining, water	207.5	178.8	− 28.7	− 13.8	(−28.2)
Manufacturing	2 226.6	1 974.2	−252.4	− 11.3	(−15.7)
Construction	413.1	384.0	− 29.1	− 7.0	(− 8.1)
Distribution	1 647.4	1 773.2	+125.8	+ 7.6	(+ 3.7)
Transport & communications	492.8	473.8	− 19.0	− 3.9	(− 8.4)
Banking, finance etc.	605.4	857.9	+252.5	+ 41.7	(+33.4)
of which					
Business services	80.5	165.8	+ 85.3	+106.1	(+80.6)
Other services	2 411.5	2 687.3	+275.8	+ 11.4	(+10.7)
Total: South	5 342.8	5 666.4	+323.6	+ 6.1	(+ 3.2)
Total: North	2 812.1	2 799.0	− 13.1	− 0.5	(− 3.7)

Note: the final column shows 1981–87 change in total employment for Great Britain.
Figures may not sum because of rounding
Source: Census of Employment, NOMIS

aggregate, but instead recorded a small degree of decline (Table 9.2). This is a much more satisfactory situation than for the North as a whole (which lost 3.7 per cent of its jobs over this period), but stands in marked contrast to the overall experience of the equivalent areas in the four southern regions. Besides suffering from an industrial structure which contained above-average proportions of the extractive and manufacturing sectors, the northern representatives performed more poorly than the South in each of the industrial groupings shown (Figure 9.2). These points are particularly true for the banking and finance division, for which more detailed statistics are provided in Table 9.3; in each comparison, the northern district type had the lower proportion of jobs in 1981 and subsequently recorded the lower rate of increase, with the biggest contrast being for the Resorts.

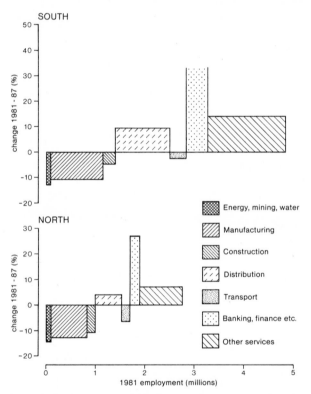

Figure 9.2 Employment, 1981, and employment change, 1981–87, by industrial division, for North/South groupings of prosperous sub-regions. Source: Census of Employment, NOMIS.

Sources of economic growth

For most of the 1980s, commentators trying to explain the concentration of economic growth in the British 'Sunbelt' focused their attention on the role of high-technology industry and drew parallels between the M4 corridor, stretching from London to South Wales, and California's 'Silicon Valley'.

Table 9.3 Employment in banking, finance, insurance, etc., and business services, 1981–87, for groups of prosperous sub-regions

Group		% total jobs 1981		% change 1981–87	
		Banking etc	Business services	Banking etc	Business services
Non-metropolitan cities	South	9.2	1.2	+ 32.6	+ 63.6
	North	8.0	0.8	+ 23.5	+ 85.6
Districts with New Towns	South	7.0	1.5	+ 64.3	+118.8
	North	4.1	0.6	+ 33.1	+129.3
Resorts, ports & retirement	South	7.7	0.5	+ 44.3	+155.4
	North	7.4	0.3	+ 8.9	+122.0
Urban & mixed urban–rural	South	7.3	1.2	+ 58.6	+128.8
	North	5.5	0.8	+ 39.4	+ 93.5
All prosperous sub-regions	South	7.9	1.1	+ 48.2	+109.5
	North	6.5	0.7	+ 27.0	+ 95.7

Source: Census of Employment, NOMIS

More detailed research has, however, challenged this image of 'high-tech' industry and has also demonstrated the diversity of the specific economic stimuli which have underpinned the growth of jobs and people in the prosperous sub-regions of the South.

In relation to 'high-tech' industry, Hall *et al.* (1987) have helped to blow away the myths surrounding the nature and scale of its contribution to growth in the prosperous sub-regions. They find no evidence of a discrete 'M4 corridor' and instead identify a 'western crescent' with relatively high representation of 'high-tech' manufacturing employment. This zone conforms quite closely with the area of most rapid employment and population growth noted above, though, as already pointed out in Chapter 6, 'high tech' itself is in aggregate a net loser of jobs rather than a direct employment generator. The real significance of this sector seems to be in the stimulus which it gives to other firms, for instance through the subcontracting of work as in the Bristol aerospace industry (Boddy, 1987b) and through the creation and perpetuation of an innovative business and research environment, such as that labelled the 'Cambridge phenomenon' (SQP, 1985).

The deconcentration of manufacturing industry has in the past been a major source of employment growth in the prosperous sub-regions. Indeed, the origins of the 'western crescent' of 'high tech' can be traced to the decentralization of the electronics industry from inner to north-west London in advance of its more recent dispersal further out along this radial sector (Keeble, 1968; Hall *et al.*, 1987). Keeble (1980) demonstrated the widespread nature of manufacturing employment growth across non-metropolitan Britain which took place during the 1960s and 1970s. At this time, much of this increase could be attributed to the policy of planned industrial dispersal to the New and Expanded Towns (Champion *et al.*, 1977). Elsewhere it was due as much to new firms and the branch plants of large corporations as it was to the physical relocation of existing operations from the congested metropolis (Fothergill and Gudgin, 1982). By the 1980s, however, the manufacturing sector no longer remained a significant source of net employment growth for most of the prosperous sub-regions, reflecting not only national trends in productivity in this sector but also the squeeze put on land and labour by the growth of higher-level activities.

By far the largest contribution to job gains in the prosperous sub-regions, particularly since the early 1970s, has been made by the service sector. This has several different elements to it. One long-established trend is the decentralization of head offices, which between the mid 1960s and the end of the 1970s was supported by government policy in the shape of the Location of Offices Bureau and the Office Development Permit system. This gave many places a foundation on which they have subsequently been able to capitalize; for example, the lead which the relocation of Eagle Star's head-quarters in 1966 gave to Cheltenham (Cowen *et al.*, 1989) and the effect which the concentration of insurance company relocations in Bristol had on stimulating a range of ancillary activities such as insurance broking (Boddy *et al.*, 1986). Corporate restructuring has aided this process, as for instance in Southampton, where several manufacturing firms have converted their factory sites into higher-level management and research activities and two international finance companies have set up their UK headquarters (Mason *et al.*, 1989).

Restructuring has also been responsible for two other major sources of employment growth in these areas – the relocation of 'back-office' functions and the phenomenal recent rise of firms specializing in business services (see Chapter 6). The last twenty years have seen major intra-regional shifts in producer-services employment to medium-sized and smaller cities in the Greater South East, motivated by the high price of floorspace and rising costs of labour in London and facilitated by advances in communications technology (Gillespie and Green, 1987; Marshall, 1988). For example, office firms moving out of London have generated considerable numbers of jobs in Reading, Bristol, Brighton and Bournemouth-Poole (Leyshon and Thrift, 1989). In recent years, too, many firms have established branch offices in the cities that have been developing as major areas of business activity and centres for high-level corporate functions; for instance, the rapid growth of accountancy jobs in Southampton during the 1980s (Morris, 1988; Mason *et al.*, 1989).

This business-related expansion also has its counterpart in the increase in jobs arising from the consumer-services multiplier. In a sense, this is the most obvious and least novel element of recent employment growth, because traditional local activities in these relatively rich farming areas, together with commuters and retirees, had already spawned a substantial presence of central-place functions even before the Second World War. Nevertheless, consumer spending has pushed ahead markedly since then, not least in the 1980s as reflected in the rise of almost 10 per cent in employment in distribution in the southern prosperous areas between 1981 and 1987 (Table 9.2) and the strong growth of 'tourism-related industries' in the counties of the western crescent (Figure 6.2). Thrift *et al.* (1987) graphical-ly outlined the way in which the huge salary rises being awarded in the City of London in the run up to the 'Big Bang' filtered through into the wider economy of southern England, for instance in terms of house purchase and private education. Moreover, this growth in 'critical mass' of consumer spending has encouraged many large suppliers with a network of area or regional offices to consolidate their activities in or around the larger regional centres like Southampton, Oxford and Bristol, allowing these sub-regions greater independence from national headquarters in London (Boddy *et al.*, 1986; Mason *et al.*, 1989).

The role of the public sector

While the sources of economic growth described so far are essentially private-sector developments, it is important to note that in many cases they have been encouraged by public-sector activities, with government acting as a facilitator and perpetuator of these trends and even as an innovator on occasions. The provision of transport infrastructure has been of fundamental importance, with the M4 and High Speed Train being cited by Boddy (1987a) as central to Bristol's strong growth and with Hall *et al.* (1987) stressing the importance of motorway and airport access for 'high-tech' industry. The opening of the M11, the selection of Stansted for airport growth, and the electrification of lines on British Rail's Anglia Region have helped to open up the Colchester/Ipswich and Cambridge/Bishop's Stortford axes and push the range of Londonward commuting and business travel further north. To a large extent, these types of investments, together with the provision of public services such as education, health and the utilities, tend to follow market forces, but their eventual effect is to reinforce the underlying trends.

Nevertheless, the prosperous sub-regions also furnish much evidence of the public sector acting in a more direct fashion. Reference has just been made to the New and Expanded Towns programme and the office relocation measures. Indeed, central government and quangos (quasi-autonomous non-governmental organizations) have themselves engaged in office dispersal. Cheltenham has been a particular beneficiary of the latter, with its selection for GCHQ (Government Communications Headquarters) in 1951, the Countryside Commission in 1970, and more recently the admissions systems for both Universities and Polytechnics (Cowen *et al.*, 1989).

In addition, the public sector has given unintentional boosts to the prosperous sub-regions (particularly in the South) that have continued to operate strongly during the 1980s even after the decision to wind up the planned overspill programme. The effect of the high priority given to defence by successive governments, and particularly by the Conservative administrations of the 1980s, is especially notable. The concentration of Britain's leading 'high-tech' firms in London and the western crescent owes much to ease of access to the corridors of power in Whitehall and to the government's many research establishments and defence bases in central southern England (Hall *et al.*, 1987). The relative resilience of the aerospace industry in places like Bristol and Stevenage has largely been based on defence contracts – which incidentally have dwarfed the scale of government grants for assisting industrial development in northern Britain (Boddy *et al.*, 1986; Philpott and Kraithman, 1986).

Impacts on localities and individuals

Growth in both demographic and economic terms has produced far-reaching changes, both on macro and on micro scales. It has produced a transformation of the social characteristics and orientation of the localities and has altered their spatial relationships with other places, most notably the large cities. At the individual level, people in the prosperous sub-regions are generally privileged relative to other types of area and have become better off, as reflected in the growth of the Conservative vote there (see Chapter 1). At the same time, households and businesses have suffered from the nature and speed of these changes, and increasingly growth has been leading to problems of economic overheating and environmental pressure. Here too, interestingly, the public sector has played an important role, because, as we will show, its strict control over land-use change has generally served to protect and enhance the environmental quality of the prosperous sub-regions and thereby helped to increase their attractiveness for the new forms of economic growth, contrary to the underlying planning goals.

The restructuring of social and spatial relations

The most direct outcomes of recent population and employment changes for localities are the urbanization of the 'countryside', the upgrading of social composition, and the creation of the 'outer city'. Perhaps the key element is that the prosperous sub-regions are, in general, no longer dominated by agricultural interests in the way that they were 25 years ago. Indeed, at that time, much of the economic life of their towns and cities was geared to providing goods and services for the surrounding rural communities and to purchasing and processing its products. Each sizeable place, not just large cities like Lincoln, Northampton, Norwich and York, but also smaller centres such as Canterbury and Hereford, had its livestock market, corn dealers and agricultural suppliers. Apart from the most obvious dormitory towns orientated towards the large metropolitan centres, particularly places like Woking and High Wycombe in the Home Counties round London, most of the sub-regions were relatively independent of each other in terms of commuting movements and tended to be inward-looking and localized in their daily activities, while in much of the deep countryside like rural Oxfordshire an essentially feudal social structure of landowner/farmer and agricultural worker was still in evidence (Newby, 1980).

The urbanization of the prosperous sub-regions and their countryside is most apparent in physical and quantitative terms. In particular, house-building has been proceeding very strongly, not least during the property boom of the mid 1980s. In the South East outside London, it is estimated that almost 350,000 new houses were completed in the years 1981–87. This figure represents an addition of 9 per cent to the overall stock and includes 32,000 houses or almost 16 per cent extra in Buckinghamshire, 33,000 or 13.7 per cent in Berkshire, 58,000 or 10.6 per cent in Hampshire and 18,000 or 9.4 per cent in Oxfordshire (SERPLAN, 1989a). New commercial and retailing schemes, associated urban development and motorway and other road building have also contributed to changing the physical appearance of these areas, even though Green Belt restrictions and other planning controls have limited the scale of agricultural land losses and prevented large-scale incursions into the countryside.

The urban impact has also been evident in other forms. It is seen in the increase in vacant and under-used land in urban-fringe locations (Coleman, 1976). The London Green Belt has been especially affected by the growth of 'horsiculture', 'quasi-farming', tax farming and the like, by the purchase of land by property and finance companies for speculative and investment purposes, and by the acquisition of rural mansions and redundant institutional buildings like isolation hospitals for commercial or residential use (Thomas, 1970; Munton, 1983). The pace of change accelerated during the 1980s, partly due to central government's policy of encouraging the rationalization of land holdings by the public sector and the utility industries, including the gas and water authorities and British Rail. Moreover, the farming industry has come under increasing pressure to diversify its activities as part of the EC's attempts at reducing food surpluses.

Social upgrading is an inevitable consequence of the types of economic activity which have been growing most rapidly. 'High tech', research establishments, corporate headquarters, producer services, all these employ a well-above average proportion of higher-paid male 'white-collar' staff. The purchase of country houses by the City high-fliers (Thrift *et al.*, 1987) merely represents the most remarkable example of a more general underlying trend towards the 'gentrification' of both town and countryside in the prosperous sub-regions. The emergence of the 'service class' has been noted as being particularly rapid in Berkshire and in the South East generally (Savage *et al.*, 1987; Fielding, 1989), but has also occurred elsewhere. In Cheltenham, for instance, the proportion of households headed by a person in a professional, managerial or intermediate socio-economic group grew faster than average between 1971 and 1981, when it accounted for almost a third of its population compared to a quarter for Britain as a whole (Cowen *et al.*, 1989). Nor has this process been confined to the South, as graphically described in the case of Lancaster, where 'Industry has departed . . . The city is being reconstructed as a post-modern consumption centre, as its occupational and industrial structure has become dominated by service industry and by those with middle class/higher education qualifications' (Bagguley *et al.*, 1989, 162).

As a result, it is the prosperous sub-regions that are leading the way to the new forms of life-style described in Chapter 3. Something of the essence of the evolving settlement structure is captured by the concept of the 'outer city'. In fact, according to Herington (1984, 9), 'There are two kinds of "outer city" in Britain: first, those whose social and economic life is still orientated to the city in whose regions they are located; second, those which have grown to develop strong internal functional linkages and rely much less on the dominant city.' It is, however, the latter that are gaining in importance, as employment has expanded at outer city nodes, economic linkages have become more complex there, and commuting patterns have become relatively more localized and varied (see, for instance, Ambrose, 1974; Herington and Evans, 1980). Patterns of social interaction are also becoming increasingly independent of the metropolitan centres, as the range of facilities provided in the prosperous sub-regions had increased through both town-centre developments and various forms of out-of-town schemes. The degree of traffic pressure on orbital motorways like the M25 around London, and on similar but more modest bypass routes round other large and medium-sized cities, bears witness to this reorientation of settlement. These changes appear to be leading to the breakdown of functional dependence between inner and outer parts of the urban system and to the emergence of the 'city beyond the city' (Herington, 1984, 1–11).

The 'price' of prosperity for people and firms

An aura of well-being has pervaded the prosperous sub-regions for several decades. As noted in Chapter 7, most of them fall into the categories of towns recognized by Donnison and Soto (1980) as the 'good city' – places where people of any particular characteristic are generally better off than their counterparts living elsewhere in Britain. Nevertheless, the wealth and rapid pace of change in these localities cause their own types of challenges. Certain types of people have not been able to adjust to the major shifts in skill requirements which economic restructuring has caused in the labour market – a problem which is greater in some places than others depending on the scale of de-industrialization, the dynamism of the new forms of employment and the strength of labour supply. In the mid 1980s it was the sheer scale of overall economic growth that emerged as the key disadvantage, as 'overheating' began to create difficulties for firms and as the greater development pressures affected both the cost and quality of life for residents.

The negative effects of economic restructuring on the labour force were more evident in the early 1980s, when redundancies in traditional industries were at their peak. Not surprisingly, the most severe problems facing the prosperous sub-regions occurred in some of their larger cities, though not necessarily all in the North. An analysis of socio-economic conditions based on 1981 Census data found that in Bristol the wards which exhibited 'the most adverse conditions' housed 62,000 people (Redfern, 1982) – significantly more than in metropolitan districts like Sheffield and Coventry, both of which have programme status under the Inner Urban Areas Act (see Chapters 8 and 10), and only just short of Newcastle which has Partnership status (Boddy, 1987a). The location of serious deprivation within the sub-regional context of above-average prosperity may indeed help to account for the social unrest which lay behind the urban riots at that time (Hamnett, 1983a).

Even within the prosperous sub-regions of the South East, significant contrasts in job opportunities were a dominant feature throughout the 1980s, with the eastern half of the region comparing unfavourably with the west and with coastal areas performing more poorly than inland (SERPLAN, 1989a). Resorts like Clacton, Thanet and the Isle of Wight were characterized by unemployment rates well above the regional average, despite – or perhaps because of – their strong population growth. So, too, were some other coastal towns including Southend, Harwich, Portsmouth, Folkestone and Dover, along with the Lower Thames Corridor which includes Rochester and Basildon New Town as well as several districts like Thurrock, Dartford and Swale which are classified as 'industrial' rather than prosperous.

Subsequent economic growth has only partially alleviated these problems, because a significant proportion of redundant workers and school-leavers has not possessed the high-level skills required for most of the new jobs. A study of older male workers made redundant from Lancaster's chemical industry showed that only about a third had been able to move up from their 'firm-specific skills', with a further third moving down to lower-skilled work and the remaining third taking early retirement or going on the dole (Bagguley *et al.*, 1989). The tight housing market has also tended to put a squeeze on lower-paid and unemployed 'locals', particularly those in the process of forming new households, forcing them to move away to areas with lower cost housing. This problem was highlighted most dramatically by the chairman of the housing committee at St Albans (Herts.) who likened the plight of those forced to live outside the city to that of a previous lost generation: 'Soaring house prices will decimate St Albans' young people are surely as the battlefields of the First World War' (*St Albans Review*, 1986, quoted by Champion *et al.*, 1987). Such out-migration obviously serves to mask the problem as far as the most prosperous areas are concerned, but equally obviously it takes place only at social costs to the individual and their families and it has implications for the most common destination areas (like the coastal resorts) where the easier access to housing reflects already less dynamic local economies.

The negative impacts on employers were already becoming noticeable in the early 1980s, but have subsequently become much more marked. The chief challenge is shortage of suitable staff, and not only for less skilled and lower-paid work (Parsons, 1987; Palmer, 1989). The housing squeeze in the most dynamic areas has restricted the inward migration of staff with 'high tech', computing and advanced managerial skills, as well as presenting a formidable obstacle to middle-income employees. House prices in London and the western crescent, extending out to embrace Bournemouth, Bristol and Cambridge, are the highest in the country and virtually doubled here during the economic recovery of the mid 1980s, aggravating the problems traditionally faced by potential labour migrants from further north, where prices were lower and rises occurred only later in the decade (Green *et al.*, 1986; NABS, 1987; Hamnett, 1988; see Chapter 7 for more details). As a result, firms have been faced with the 'poaching' of labour by other firms, higher rates of staff turnover and the need to pay higher wages.

Operating costs for firms in these areas have also been raised by higher land prices and increasing traffic congestion. Traditionally within southern England there has been a marked differential in commercial and industrial rents between the London area and the rest of the Greater South East (Fothergill *et al.* 1986; Hillier Parker, 1987a and b; Tyler *et al.*, 1988). In the 1980s, however, this gap narrowed substantially, with places like

Norwich, Bristol, Plymouth and Northampton experiencing a doubling of the real level of office rents between 1979 and 1989 and with Oxford, Milton Keynes, Luton and Bristol, along with the M4/Heathrow zone, leading the way for inflation in industrial floorspace costs (Figure 9.3). Transport problems have also become notorious in this part of the country, not only in relation to the M25, but also on the general network of roads which has seen relatively limited investment in the post-war period compared to the scale of motorway construction and trunk road improvement around and between the principal cities and growth points in the North (Hall, 1989a).

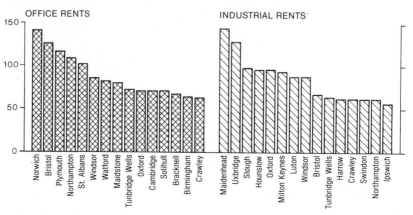

Figure 9.3 Towns with highest increases in real level of office and industrial rents, 1979–89.

The same types of factors also affect the cost and quality of life for residents. The 'price of prosperity' is readily evident in high house prices, traffic congestion, the disruption caused by new building, the erosion of open space in urban areas, and increasing levels of pollution – air, water, noise vibration and visual intrusions (Breheny, 1989). The differentials in living costs between northern Britain and southern regions, particularly the South East, widened significantly during the latter half of the 1980s. According to Reward Regional Surveys, the income required to support various standard living styles in the South East was already 10–20 per cent higher than the national average in 1986, but the margin has increased to 30–40 per cent higher by 1989, with the level for Greater London being 40–55 per cent above the average then (Table 9.4). Even in 1986 the list of the ten most expensive towns included in their study was dominated by places in the South East – London, Welwyn Garden City, Slough, Woking, Hemel Hempstead, Brighton, Berkhamsted, High Wycombe, and Crawley, the only exception being Aberdeen as third most expensive at that time (Reward Regional Surveys, 1986, ii).

These problems have, of course, not arisen overnight, nor – once again – should it be thought that they have arisen merely as a result of market forces. Development pressures and economic 'overheating' were major policy issues in south-east England in the 1960s. At that time, as Hall *et al.* (1973)

Table 9.4 Regional variations in gross annual incomes required to maintain different living standards, January 1989 (and January 1986)

Region/living standard	A		B		C		D	
Greater London	155	(133)	146	(127)	152	(128)	140	(124)
Rest of South East	125	(114)	115	(109)	118	(110)	115	(109)
All South East	140	(122)	130	(116)	135	(117)	127	(116)
South West	110	(102)	106	(100)	104	(98)	105	(97)
East Anglia	112	(97)	108	(98)	96	(95)	95	(92)
East Midlands	88	(85)	94	(88)	95	(91)	101	(94)
West Midlands	83	(86)	93	(90)	96	(91)	100	(95)
Wales	89	(92)	92	(95)	90	(92)	92	(90)
North West	74	(88)	84	(94)	83	(96)	87	(99)
Yorkshire & Humberside	77	(84)	84	(89)	84	(89)	85	(90)
Northern Region	72	(84)	75	(88)	76	(89)	85	(90)
Scotland	88	(113)	·84	(104)	77	(101)	79	(101)
Northern Ireland	72	(85)	72	(92)	66	(90)	64	(84)
UK survey average	100	(100)	100	(100)	100	(100)	100	(100)

Key to living standards:
  A = 3-bedroomed terraced private house bought on a 68% mortgage, 46 meals out, 1 000cc car, no telephone, coal and electricity for heating
  B = 3-bedroomed semi-detached private house bought on a 68% mortgage, 78 meals out, 1 000cc car, telephone, coal and electricity for heating
  C = 4-bedroomed detached private house bought on a 65% mortgage, 129 meals out, 1 600cc car, telephone, gas central heating
  D = 4-bedroomed detached private house, 3 reception rooms, medium-sized garden, 61% mortgage, 184 meals out, 2 000cc car, telephone, golf club, domestic help for 104 hours, daughter at fee-paying school, gas central heating
Note: the figures in brackets are those for January 1986. The UK survey averages of required income for each living standard are as follows: A £13,379 in 1989 (£9,528 in 1986); B £18,188 (13,213); C £31,741 (£21,841); D £49,159 (£37,127)
Source: calculated from *Cost of Living Report, Regional Comparisons*, March 1986 and March 1989, Reward Regional Surveys

demonstrated very convincingly, the social impacts were greatly aggravated by town and country planning policies and the way in which they were implemented. The overall strategy of 'urban containment', by restricting planning permissions for urban development, served to raise the price of housing and building land in the main urban areas and the 'protected' countryside, particularly in London's Green Belt. This forced people to seek homes further away from the metropolitan employment cores, causing longer commuting journeys and greater penetration of urban influence into essentially rural areas. These factors, together with underlying political differences between 'town' and 'country', contributed towards social polarization between the more wealthy and mobile who were able to decentralize and those who could not.

The chief differences between the 1960s and recent experience is that the problems have become more intense and have spread out to affect a wider area around the main cities, particularly London. In the South East, for instance, the most seriously affected places in the 1960s lay in the counties directly abutting on to the Greater London boundary, whereas now they comprise not only the prosperous sub-regions of the Greater South East, but also some of the more remote, rural areas beyond (see Chapter 11).

Strategic planning issues

The variety of problems arising from the rapid growth of the prosperous sub-regions during the 1980s adds up to some formidable issues requiring strategic policy decisions. The problems have led to arguments over the extent and location of new house-building and over the balance to be struck between the continuation of economic growth and the more even distribution of its benefits. Policy challenges also include the rash of proposals for out-of-town developments for retailing and business parks, the escalating scale of traffic congestion, and the whole question of protecting 'the environment'.

Not surprisingly in view of what has been outlined above, some of the most serious problems have arisen in the South East and so will be illustrated in this section principally by reference to the situation here. Figure 9.4 indicates the type and scale of the development proposals facing the planning authorities here at the end of the 1980s. Ironically, as noted

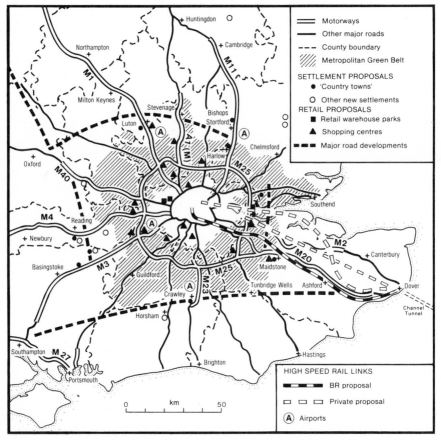

Figure 9.4 Urban development pressures in the South East 1988/89. Map shows existing network of motorways and major roads, together with proposals for new settlements, retailing, major roads, and high-speed rail links between London and the Channel Tunnel.

previously in relation to the abolition of the metropolitan county councils (Chapter 8), these issues have risen to prominence at the very time that the strategic planning system was being dismantled. The spirit of strategic planning, however, has been kept alive in this region through the work of the London and South East Regional Planning Conference (SERPLAN). Moreover, with the emergence of an environmental backlash from the Tory shires, by the end of the 1980s central government was beginning to show signs of a change of heart towards planning.

Housing land

The availability and cost of housing land have dominated planning debates in the prosperous sub-regions for decades and particularly since the property boom of the early 1970s. This issue is seen to be at the heart of problems such as house-price inflation, labour shortages, and accommodation difficulties for first-time buyers and the low paid (Evans, 1989). The main questions centre on how much new building should be allowed and where it should take place, and the green fields of the South East have formed the principal battleground.

The arguments over the scale of house-building requirements came to a head in the South East in 1988, with the upward revision of population and household forecasts. The number of dwellings to be provided in the region during the 1990s was raised to around 570,000, some 110,000 more than agreed between SERPLAN and the Department of the Environment three years before. This change put pressure on local planning authorities to identify additional land for house building, though several Councils have been attempting to limit their planned allocations to the amount required to meet the needs of local household formation only.

The chief locational issues have revolved around the merits of using 'brown-field' as opposed to 'green-field' sites. Since the decision was taken to wind down the New Towns programme and revive the inner cities (see Chapter 8), a heavy emphasis has been placed on peripheral extensions to existing settlements and the use of vacant and derelict land within the boundary of the main built-up areas. This policy has achieved a fair degree of success, with the annual national rate of agricultural–urban land conversion down from some 15,000 ha in the early 1970s to barely 5,000 ha in the 1980s and with nearly half of all new house-building taking place on non-agricultural land (Department of the Environment, 1989a). The degree of containment is substantially higher than this in the South East, where according to a survey by Tym (1987) 55 per cent of new housing starts were on urban land, a further 11 per cent were in the form of infill village development and only 34 per cent on green-field sites.

Recent years, however, have seen a surge of proposals for new settlements. The campaign was led by a group of property development companies called Consortium Developments, which proposed a ring of ten 'country towns' around London (Figure 9.4). So far (November 1989) two of these have been the subject of planning applications and public inquiries – Tillingham Hall in the Metropolitan Green Belt in Essex and Foxley Wood in north-east Hampshire. Both these were eventually turned down, as was one from another developer at Coombe Bassett in Oxfordshire. By the end of the decade, however, the list of proposals for new settlements had grown considerably, including schemes in Cambridgeshire, Leicestershire and North Yorkshire as well as in the South East (Table 9.5).

Table 9.5 Proposals for new settlements, 1989

County/site	number of houses	County/site	number of houses
Berkshire		*Kent*	
Great Lea	3 200	Bishop's Forstal	4 500
Hogwood Farm	1 000	Site between	
Spencer's Wood	2 500	Shadoxhurst &	
Upper Donnington	300	Bethersden	4 500
Cambridgeshire		*Leicestershire*	
Belham Hill	3 000	Bittersby Parva	3 400
Boum Airfield	3 000	Garendon Park	1 000–1 500
Crow Green	3 000–4 000	Six Hills	1 400
Denny Abbey	1 500	Stretton Magna	2 000–2 500
Great Common Farm	3 300		
Hare Park	3 000	*Perthshire*	
Highfields	3 300	Moneydie New Town	5 000
Nine Mile Hill	2 000		
Scotland Park	2 200	*Yorkshire*	
Swansley Wood	3 000	Acaster Malbis	4 500
Waterfenton	1 500	Forest of Galtres	1 200–1 600
Westmere	1 500	Thorp Arch	6 000
Hampshire			
Eversley Green	2 500		
Foxley Wood	4 800		
Hook	2 000		

Source: survey of local authority planning departments

Retailing

In the 1980s the scale and location of shopping facilities has emerged as the most powerful single threat to the continuation of traditional policies of urban containment. Not surprisingly, in view of their wealth and rate of growth, the prosperous sub-regions in southern England have been in the forefront of these changes. In the South East as a whole, 2.7 million m² of retail floorspace was completed between 1980 and 1988, and in October 1988 a similar amount was under construction or had received planning permission, including 70 superstores/hypermarkets and over 200 retail warehouses. Yet at this time the South East was still reckoned by the planners to be 'under provided' with retail facilities, giving encouragement for new proposals. Altogether, a further 2.3 million m² of retail floorspace was awaiting the results of planning decisions in 1988 (SERPLAN, 1989a).

Relatively little of this new development is being accommodated in existing town centres. Some 72 per cent of the retail floorspace completed in the South East between 1980 and 1988 was located out of centre, mainly in the form of retail warehouses. Most retail developers seek large sites with abundant parking and easy vehicle access (Teale, 1989). Particular pressures have occurred within the Metropolitan Green Belt, with many of the largest proposals being situated along the M25 corridor or on radial roads connecting with this orbital route (Figure 9.4). In addition, key problems are posed by development in suburban areas, principally as a result of the extra car and lorry traffic generated on local roads. There is also concern about the longer-term effects of these out-of-centre schemes on the viability of existing town centres, which are more heavily dependent on retailing than the CBDs of the large cities but are generally not so attractive as the latter. Clearly planners face a difficult task in enhancing town centres and maintaining some overall urban structure, while taking into account the needs of consumers and the environmental problems arising from new development (SERPLAN, 1989b).

Employment

The spatial variations in employment opportunities between the prosperous sub-regions within the South East constitutes another major planning challenge. As mentioned above, the principal issue is the contrast between the chronic labour shortages in many localities in the western half of the region and the relatively sluggish job growth in the eastern half – a key element of the so-called 'South–South Divide' (SEEDS, 1987). During the past decade, reliance has been placed on self-correcting mechanisms in the market place, reinforced by strict controls on new commercial development in the west and by the improvement of access to eastern areas through the opening of the M25 (Damesick, 1986; Simmons, 1986). The importance of transport infrastructure has been stressed in the study *Eastern Promise* (Breheny *et al.*, 1986), which paints a rosy picture of development prospects along the M11 corridor between London and Cambridge as a result of the motorway itself, rail electrification and the growth of Stansted airport. SERPLAN (1989b) is also studying the A12 corridor across Essex and the particularly problematic Lower Thames Corridor. Meanwhile, as argued by Vickerman (1989), the prospect of the opening of the Channel Tunnel in 1993 provides an opportunity for tackling the 'frontier region' disadvantages faced by Kent (see Figure 9.4).

A second question concerns the prospects for the prosperous sub-regions in the North. In general, their circumstances have changed markedly since the events of the 1970s, which led Townsend (1986) to remark on the 'surprising significance of dispersed centres'. Though they have continued to gain population since then (Table 9.1), their sluggish employment growth in the 1980s (Table 9.2 and Figure 9.2) reflects the adverse side-effects of the severe economic difficulties faced by the neighbouring large cities and industrial districts during the 1979–83 recession and the southern focus of the subsequent economic recovery. Breheny *et al.* (1987) have, however, argued that these localities constitute the 'Northern Lights' which, through their attractive environments and diverse economic bases, can provide the basis for the rebuilding of the North's economy. This study highlighted ten places – Congleton and Knutsford in Cheshire, Lytham St Annes and Clitheroe in Lancashire, Kendal in Cumbria, Hexham and Morpeth in

Northumberland, Thirsk and Harrogate in North Yorkshire and Beverley in Humberside – and proposed them as essential elements in a broader strategy for regenerating the North. On the other hand, their scattered distribution, their generally small size, and the antipathy of their residents to large-scale expansion suggest that they cannot be expected to provide a full panacea for the economic problems of the North, unless a major shift in strategic priorities takes place (Champion, 1989b; see also Chapter 12).

Transport

Transport issues are seen by many as the key to the future well-being of the prosperous sub-regions, particularly in the Greater South East (Breheny and Congdon, 1989; Hall, 1989b). Their importance has been highlighted in relation to the outward spread of development pressures from the large cities and in the context of securing new spatial patterns of economic development. The history of the recent past, however, is of inadequate investment in transport facilities and of the consequent congestion and costs. Some localities seem to have almost reached the 'suburban gridlock' nightmare feared in the USA (Cervero, 1986; Breheny, 1989). In the words of SERPLAN's chairman, Lord Carnarvon, 'Mobility is a dominant theme . . . the inadequacies of the South East's transport systems will limit its future prosperity unless means are found to overcome them' (SERPLAN, 1989b, iv).

   In the past greater emphasis has been placed on radial routes serving the large cities and linking them together, but in the late 1980s more attention was being given to orbital routes, parkway stations and cross-city services. Such developments are particularly necessary in the South East, not only to tackle the recent growth of the 'outer city' areas but also to provide alternative channels for the extra traffic expected to result from the advent of the Single European Market ('1992'), and the anticipated completion of the Channel Tunnel. A 1989 review of the M25's problems has stressed the need for action, including the widening of the motorway itself, the upgrading of parallel roads to reduce pressure on the motorway, and the more detailed study of options for outer orbital corridors and the possibilities for enhancing the road network near the fringe of the London conurbation (Department of Transport, 1989). With the White Paper *Roads for Prosperity* (HMSO, 1989) anticipating a doubling of traffic by the year 2025, key bottlenecks have been identified in relation to the Lower Thames crossing, the South Coast route and the M3–M40 link (Figure 9.4).

Conclusion

The prosperous sub-regions have experienced impressive growth over the last few decades, and particularly in the 1980s, but it has become increasingly apparent that there is a price to pay. The provision of extra housing land, the proposals for regional shopping centres and out-of-town business parks, the steering of economic development towards less rapidly growing localities and the enhancement of transport infrastructure all raise questions which are fundamental to the future well-being of these areas, particularly in the more heavily pressurized parts of the Greater South East. There are, in addition, many planning issues which, if not of such general importance, loom as large as these for particular localities; for instance, the need for the quarrying of building materials and for sites for the disposal of rubbish, the development of leisure facilities in the countryside, and the protection of sites of heritage and scientific value. These considerations all relate to the environment, either in the specific sense of nature conservation or more generally in terms of the full range of conditions which affect the quality of life for residents and the efficiency of operating conditions for business and industry.

During the past few years environmental issues have come to replace economic concerns at the top of the political agenda in the prosperous sub-regions. This has happened partly because the problems of unemployment have receded and partly because the new surge of economic growth has exposed bottlenecks and inadequacies in the infrastructure. At the same time, there is a growing feeling that economic prospects and environmental quality are closely related, as evidenced by studies that show how businesses in the 'new service economy' are attracted to high-amenity, or 'prestige', areas (e.g. Fielding, 1989). In the words of SERPLAN's chairman, 'Maintaining economic buoyancy and the improvement of the environment are inextricably linked; it is not merely the case that wealth is needed to pay for environmental improvement but that enhancing the quality of the environment is an essential pre-condition for preserving economic vitality' (SERPLAN, 1989b, iii).

It is the traditional task of the 'town and country planning' system to ensure that basic environmental standards are maintained. It is clear from the evidence of this chapter that a collossal challenge currently faces local planning authorities in the prosperous sub-regions, for there now exists a set of major issues which are crying out for strategic decisions and effective policies. At the same time, planners have become more sensitive to the political realities and negative side-effects which limit their scope for action, whether these relate to the NIMBY (Not In My Back Yard) opposition to new development or to the recognition that past planning solutions have had unintended impacts like lengthening commuting journeys or encouraging 'town cramming'. Finally, partly as a result of studies mentioned in this chapter, there is a growing awareness that not all the current issues can be dealt with adequately by land-use planning mechanisms alone, nor should the problems of the prosperous sub-regions be tackled without reference to events in other types of localities. For this reason we return to this subject in Chapter 12.

Further reading

The prosperous sub-regions, as a distinctive type of place, do not yet possess a large literature devoted to their own characteristics and dynamics. More commonly, they are highlighted in nationwide studies of population and employment growth, as referenced in Chapters 4 and 6. In relation to their population growth, therefore, see particularly Britton (1986); Champion (1987b); and Hamnett and Randolph (1983a). The latest population trends for each of the four OPCS district types included in our definition of prosperous sub-regions can be followed for England and Wales from OPCS Monitor PP1 and *Key population and vital statistics: local and health authority areas* (HMSO, annually).

Studies of economic growth which focus primarily on the prosperous sub-regions include Howells (1984); Gillespie and Green (1987); Marshall (1989); and Breheny and Hall (1987). A geographically more focused study of new growth processes is provided by Hall *et al.* (1987). Two studies have dealt with groups of more prosperous places in the North; namely, Townsend (1986b), and Breheny *et al.* (1987).

For the majority of literature dealing specifically with prosperous sub-regions, it is necessary to look either at case studies of individual places or at regional-scale accounts dealing with regions dominated by this type of place. SQP (1985) is a classic study of the modern research-orientated industrial complex, while a case study of the role of one particular industry is provided by Boddy and Lovering (1986). See also the wider results of the ESRC-financed case study of Bristol in Boddy *et al.* (1986). The subsequent ESRC initiative on the Changing Urban and Regional System included case studies of three places located in prosperous sub-regions: Cheltenham, classified (like Bristol) as a non-metropolitan city, and two 'resort, port and retirement districts', Lancaster and the Isle of Thanet. Good summaries of these three studies can be found in Cooke (1989).

The largest concentration of prosperous sub-regions is located in the South East of England outside Greater London. A useful introduction to this region is provided by Wood (1987). A series of detailed accounts can be found in Breheny and Congdon (1989), which includes chapters on the economy, employment, population and housing. Social restructuring in the region is examined by Hamnett (1986), and by Fielding and Savage (1987). Population, employment and development pressures are monitored annually by the London and the South East Regional Planning Conference in SERPLAN (1989a).

The key issues faced by the prosperous sub-regions at the end of the 1980s are illustrated by SERPLAN's (1989b) consultative paper on the review of the South East regional strategy. The main problems are elaborated with particular reference to the impact of London's growth and decentralization by Hall (1989). A set of three papers on the planning challenges raised by the M25 can be found in the 1986 volume of *Geographical Journal*, while the conflicts between pressure groups are explored by Munton (1983). The aims and outcome of past planning policies designed to restrict urban expansion more generally across Britain are the subject of Hall *et al.* (1973), and Herington (1984). The progress of development proposals relating to housing, retailing, roads and so on can be monitored on a weekly basis in the magazine *Planning* and through the monthly journals *The Planner* and *Town and Country Planning*.

10

Industrial districts: in decline?

The older industrial parts of Britain are often the forgotten districts of the world's first industrial country. The exposure given by television to inner cities (Chapter 8), or to the pressures on the environment in prosperous areas (Chapter 9), is more persistent than to the very different problems raised by, say, shipyard or coal-mine closures. There is considerable variety among industrial areas. The quiet decline of old industrial towns is less well known but is perhaps reflected by *Last of the Summer Wine* (a long-running television series set in the early Pennine mill-town of Holmfirth, W. Yorks.).

It is significant that most images projected of people suffering from industrial decline are extremely negative. For most of the 1980s, the sharply reduced importance of manual industrial skills and employment (Chapter 5) added prolonged high unemployment to the range of problems already being faced by these industrial districts. As that chapter showed, widespread increases in productivity in surviving industry meant that any net growth in employment was very patchy. In Chapter 6 we stressed that industrial areas were being partly recompensed by new forms of employment of lesser quantity and quality. Here we will review the variety of communities which have been dependent on industry, and the variety of measures to help them which have been evolved in central and local government. We will be forced to ask, however, whether 're-industrialization' is a viable strategy in the light of the international transformation of industry and the environmental and social image of these towns.

Diversity among 'industrial districts'

This chapter will bring together two heads of the OPCS district classification of England and Wales, and will take in comparable areas in Scotland (Figure 10.1). The three categories which have been identified for this book as delineating the 'industrial districts' of Britain (Figure 10.1) are

1 30 of the 36 metropolitan districts: that is, all the former metropolitan counties, less the 6 districts which are the cities at their centres (see Chapter 8). All these districts are independent planning authorities. They include an important continuous block from the Mersey to the Don (S. Yorks.).

2 the 73 non-metropolitan 'industrial areas' recognized by the OPCS.

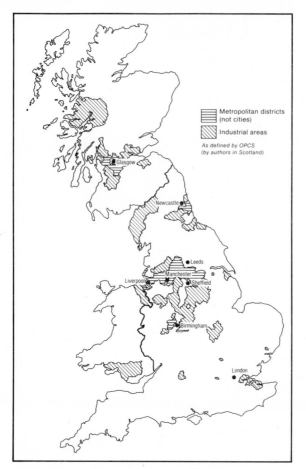

Figure 10.1 Industrial districts of Great Britain. The eight large cities (Chapter 8) are shown for reference purposes. Source: see text.

These comprise most coalfields, and industrial towns such as Stoke-on-Trent, but also include some southern towns e.g. Luton.

3 a further 18 districts of Scotland, identified by the present authors on equivalent criteria.

These three categories together comprise all our 'industrial districts'; they are closely congruous with more populated areas of the North, and with all areas with high dependence on industrial employment. Table 10.1 identifies the main sectors of manufacturing (Divisions 2–4) and combines them with the 'energy and water supply' industries (Division 1, which includes British Coal) to show the proportion of total employment, 1987, in industry. The average proportion for all industrial districts, of 36.7 per cent, is considerably lower than in the past, but nonetheless stands 40 per cent above the national average.

In considering this overall area, it may be objected that severing the six

Table 10.1 Structure of employment in industrial districts, 1987, by North/South groups (percentage of employees in employment)

Division	Metropolitan districts (not cities)	Industrial areas North	South	All industrial districts	Great Britain
1 Energy and water supply	3.0	3.9	6.1	3.8	2.3
2 Metal processing, other minerals	4.5	6.8	4.2	5.1	3.2
3 Metal goods, engineering and vehicles	15.0	13.7	12.8	14.2	10.8
4 Other manufacturing	12.5	14.5	14.9	13.5	9.9
Total 'industry'	35.0	39.0	38.0	36.7	26.2
Total all employment %	100.0	100.0	100.0	100.0	100.0
(000s)	(2 888.3)	(1 553.6)	(1 022.4)	(5 464.4)	(21 778.3)

Note: see Fig. 10.1 and text for definition of districts
Source: Census of Employment, NOMIS

cities from their commuting hinterlands is an artificial distinction. In all six former metropolitan counties and in Strathclyde, conurbation Passenger Transport Authorities have continued to co-ordinate and develop public transport facilities over a wide area. In all cases, radial rail routes have been improved. In Strathclyde, Tyne and Wear, Merseyside and Greater Manchester, new construction of track and electrification were undertaken. Over time, some of the official statistical 'travel-to-work areas' in these conurbations have been merged, and those of the 'central city' have been widened as more office staff have travelled in from surrounding areas. However, the logic of Part III of this book is to identify the different mixtures of problems which occur at different points on the urban–rural spectrum. Industrial districts are different from cities (Chapter 8) and from the wider regional territories which they serve, yet in discussion of 'urban and regional problems' they have often fallen between the two.

Questions of industrial change

It is only recent trends, chiefly those of falling industrial employment across many sectors, which have brought many common features to our areas of study, other perhaps than a social structure which tended to produce Labour MPs. These trends were superimposed on areas of varying age, density and diversity of industrial activity.

The legacy and intensity of areal specializations are best seen in terms of successive Kondratieff long waves of investment in the Industrial Revolution (Chapter 1). The earliest surviving areas of industry tended to build up the greatest manufacturing strength. In the West Midlands the Black Country took over the innovations in iron-making of the Shropshire Coalfield of the late eighteenth century and adjusted well to many changes in the product cycle until the 1970s; thus in 1987 the West Midlands still had 33 per cent of all their employment in metal goods, engineering and vehicles. The eighteenth-century innovations in factory textiles of Greater Manchester and West Yorkshire not only provided jobs for women, but also opened the market for later diversification into machine-making, engineering and chemicals, which afforded high levels of employment into the 1970s. Other industrial districts of the North West had also diversified into engineering etc., partly through conversion of cotton mills. Merseyside, by contrast, specialized in port activity until efforts began in the 1930s to bring light industry into its present outer areas. Coal and water power provided a base for early industry in South Yorkshire (metals) and industrial districts of the East Midlands (textiles and clothing), but the early-twentieth-century development of eastern parts of the Yorkshire, Derbyshire, and Nottinghamshire coalfield is apparent in the relatively high dependence still on 'energy and water supply' and in the number of large twentieth-century mining villages.

By contrast, the coastal, exporting coalfields of South Wales, Cumbria, the north-east coast of England and Scotland (Rawstron, 1964) developed mainly from the 1850s and specialized in shipping coal (from fields now largely uneconomic) and in narrower kinds of heavy manufacturing activity – shipbuilding (save in South Wales), heavy engineering, and iron and steel. Strathclyde has many surviving remnants of engineering activity in Division 4, and Cleveland (like the Yorkshire and Humberside 'industrial districts') attracted post-war investment in steel and chemicals (Division 2). Overall, however, these peripheral areas were the first to gain light *replacement industry* in branch plants of TNCs introduced under the main thrusts of regional policy in the 1940s and 1960s, as well as being the first to lose it (Chapter 5). As a result then of a later start and more specialized investment, their pattern of development, as well as their infrastructure and the texture of industrial landscape, was cruder than the other areas that we have considered; their 'social construction' depended on exploitation, initially of heavy male manual shift-work and latterly of semi-skilled females, and their occupational structure was ill-shaped for further 're-industrialization'.

Massey's (1984) concepts of the 'spatial division of labour' apply principally to the relationship of the *latter* areas to the South East. They tend to overlook the distinction that emerges between the industrial districts described in the last paragraph, the more 'peripheral' regions, and those described in the previous paragraph, in the 'manufacturing heartland'. (The distinction is a different one from that of 'metropolitan' and other industrial districts.)

The recognition of problems

The recognition of problems occurred at very different dates in the two kinds of area. First came the textbook 'assisted area' coalfields of South Wales, Cumbria and north-east England, with Clydeside in Scotland, where the interwar depression exposed common problems of over-specialization. 'Intermediate' or grey areas of the 'manufacturing heartland' in the North West, Yorkshire and Humberside, the West Midlands and East Midlands presented social and infrastructural problems later, in the 1960s. Commonwealth immigrants, for instance, had been attracted to all these by *labour shortages* in the 1950s and 1960s, but had met inadequate social and economic opportunity. In the 1960s and 1970s, regional policy for 'assisted areas' sought to create a climate of opportunity in most industrial areas. By 1984, this kind of assistance had been extended to the West Midlands. At the more local level, many industrial districts were designated 'programme authorities' under the Inner Urban Areas Act, 1978.

In the 1980s, problems extended well beyond the peripheral coalfields as major redundancies hit both the pre-war and post-war industry of *all* kinds of industrial districts. Convergence between the two types of industrial districts that we have discussed may be summed up as follows:

> While virtually no part of the country has escaped the pressures on the manufacturing sector, de-industrialization has been overwhelmingly concentrated in the north and west of Britain, *not only* in those regions with a long-established industrial base and long history of structural weakness, extensive labour organization and productive rigidities, namely the North, south Wales, central Scotland and all of the old industrial conurbations, *but equally* in what had been prosperous manufacturing regions during the post-war 'Fordist' regime, that is the West Midlands, the North West and Yorkshire-Humberside.
> (Martin, 1988, 223, emphasis added)

In the view of Hall and Markusen (1985), much of the uneven geography of socio-economic restructuring in contemporary Britain is accounted for by the technological transition between the fourth and fifth Kondratieff long waves. Industrial districts of the North West and West Midlands experienced some of the most rapid de-industrialization after the early 1970s. The new high-tech industries and activities, on the other hand, had begun to emerge out of quite different spatial concentrations of innovation in southern parts of the country (Chapter 9).

Recent critical analysis

There is nothing predetermined about the outcome of the recent manufacturing recession for weaker areas. There is the view that re-industrialization of industrial districts is difficult precisely because of their inherited characteristics. 'Areas, and social classes in them, associated with the older forms of product and production process are now seen as something of a drain on the capacity of firms to engage in the new competitive contest' (Cooke, 1988, 243). These characteristics were seen as a target of stringent government economic policies at the time of the early 1980s' recession, but 'the decline in many of these areas has been such that a sort of "economic hysteresis" effect has occurred, whereby the depth of contraction has retarded the process of economic recovery' (Martin, 1989a, 53). Old business premises, public buildings and housing, together with out-of-date skills, were not good 'market signals' for outside investment or local new firms.

There are many indications that industrial Britain was not prone to follow new international manufacturing trends in the 1980s. In terms of the alleged transition from ('Fordist') mass production of the 1960s and 1970s to more 'flexible' employment practices, production and sales, older industrial areas suffered all the job loss of the first phase without standing to benefit from the second. Hudson (1988) indeed questions whether the 'old industrial regions' fit the alleged transitions at all; he questions whether the 'Fordist' regime was ever applied to some industries, and stresses that the sectors most open to 'flexible accumulation' are notably absent. In the country as a whole the growth of new linked concentrations of industry is less evident than in Italy or France and 'this possibility must be treated highly tentatively' (Massey, 1988, 258). Although there was considerable re-investment in existing plants in the 1980s, the overall prospects of industrial districts appeared considerably worse than 20 years earlier.

The response in population trends

This long history of relative economic decline is expressed in different population trends between older and relatively newer industrial districts. Falling population in the coastal coalfield areas was endemic from the 1921 Census onwards. Districts which continued to lose population in both the periods 1971–81 and 1981–88 included the Rhondda (Mid Glamorgan), Hartlepool (Cleveland) and South Tyneside (Tyne and Wear). Elsewhere, districts with persistent decline in these two recent periods were largely concentrated in Greater Manchester, but also included Knowsley (Merseyside), Burnley (Lancs.) and Bradford (W. Yorks.).

Of the ten metropolitan districts recently most dependent on industry, Table 10.2 shows that nine experienced recent net outward migration of

Table 10.2 Industrial structure and migration, 1984–87

District/county	(1) Percentage of employees in industry, 1984	(2) Net migration of population, 1984–87, per cent
Leading metropolitan districts for (1)		
Knowsley (Merseyside)	56.0	−4.3*
Sandwell (W. Midlands)	51.4	−3.2
Oldham (Greater Manchester)	50.3	−0.6
Walsall (W. Midlands)	48.4	−1.8
Coventry (W. Midlands)	47.3	−2.2
Calderdale (W. Yorks.)	46.6	+0.9
Barnsley (S. Yorks.)	44.6	−1.7
Doncaster (S. Yorks.)	44.2	−1.0
Tameside (Greater Manchester)	43.9	−0.0
Rotherham (S. Yorks.)	41.9	−1.4
Leading counties for (1)		
Staffordshire	43.7	+0.7
Leicestershire	43.7	+1.1
Derbyshire	43.0	+1.1
Mid-Glamorgan	41.2	−0.7
Nottinghamshire	40.6	+0.3
West Midlands	39.5	−1.5
Gwent	37.6	+0.3
Fife	37.2	−1.2
Borders	37.1	+1.8
South Yorkshire	37.0	−1.2

Note: 'Industry' comprises Divisions 1–4 of the Standard Industrial Classification, 1980, including coal, energy and water
*includes St Helens
Source: National Online Manpower Information System (Census of Employment; National Health Service Central Register)

population. The most striking feature, however, lay in other non-metropolitan industrial districts. Only one (Bolsover, Derbys.) showed persistent decline, 1971–81 and 1981–88, among the 18 such areas of the East Midlands: that is, despite the dependence of those areas on industry for 51 per cent of employment in 1981. Staffordshire, Leicestershire and Derbyshire were the counties most dependent on industry in 1984 but had net migration gains, 1984–87. This suggests that there is a differential migration response to economic conditions as between regions, *and* between cities, metropolitan industrial areas and other industrial areas. Taking the last two together, as the subject area of this chapter, they had a 1988 population of 16.02 million compared with 16.14 million in 1981. Thus, dependence on industry is associated with fairly stable levels of population. It is *not* necessarily a cause of heavy outmigration, because poor employment conditions have been accompanied by a variety of labour-market responses including unemployment, part-time working and early retirement, in the absence often of suitable combinations of housing and employment in other parts of the country (Chapter 7).

Deprivation of industrial districts

Multiple deprivation

The overall structure and trends which we have so far discussed are strongly associated with social problems. Many features of deprivation reinforce each other in the national map of industrial districts. While one may recognize multi-variate deprivation most strongly in inner cities (Chapter 8), some of the worst areas on any one measure are often found elsewhere. For instance, from 1981 to 1988 three of the districts of the former West Midlands metropolitan country are estimated to have suffered worse rates of population decline than did Birmingham.

A consistent multi-variate analysis of deprivation is available only from 1981 Census data. Table 10.3 demonstrates the frequency with which industrial districts appear among the worst 50 districts of the 366 of England. The precise entries in the table depend on vicissitudes of geographical boundaries and statistical definition. Nonetheless, the table includes 13 of the 30 metropolitan districts and 10 of the 58 other English districts that we are considering here.

Clearly, multiple deprivation is more intense in metropolitan than in other industrial districts. However, the distinction is not exclusive, since the non-metropolitan districts of Blackburn and Burnley (Lancs.), together with Hartlepool (Cleveland), appear in the worst 11 districts. Unemployment, overcrowding and higher standardized mortality rates are the most frequently recurring elements in multiple deprivation, as defined here. They also provide the most frequent combinations of variables in the table, and are thus, statistically, at the centre of the structure of multiple deprivation.

The degree of causal connection between these variables, and between them and others, is more speculative. A principal thesis of this volume is the underlying role of the changing economic base and of employment. This is reflected in the prominence of 1981 unemployment in the above analysis.

Table 10.3 Multiple deprivation in industrial districts of England, 1981

Industrial districts appearing more than twice among the 50 worst districts of England (*)	Deprivation indicator (*see* Note)							
	1	2	3	4	5	6	7	8
6 appearances:								
Blackburn (Lancs.)	*	*		*	*		*	*
Salford (Greater Manchester)	*	*	*		*	*	*	
5 appearances:								
Coventry (W. Midlands)	*	*	*			*		*
Hartlepool (Cleveland)	*	*	*	*			*	
Knowsley (Merseyside)	*	*	*			*	*	
Sandwell (W. Midlands)	*	*		*		*		*
Wolverhampton (W. Midlands)	*	*		*		*		*
4 appearances:								
Bolton (Greater Manchester)		*		*			*	*
Burnley (Lancashire)			*	*	*		*	
Gateshead (Tyne and Wear)	*	*				*	*	
South Tyneside (Tyne and Wear)	*	*				*	*	
3 appearances:								
Bradford (W. Yorks.)		*	*					*
Grimsby (Humberside)	*		*				*	
Langbaurgh (Cleveland)	*		*				*	
Luton (Bedfordshire)		*	*					*
Pendle (Lancs.)				*	*			*
Rochdale (Greater Manchester)	*	*	*					
St Helens (Merseyside)	*			*			*	
Scunthorpe (Humberside)	*		*			*		
Stockton-on-Tees (Cleveland)	*		*				*	
Sunderland (Tyne and Wear)	*	*					*	
Walsall (W. Midlands)	*	*						*
Wear Valley (Co. Durham)	*	*					*	

Source: Department of the Environment
Note: key to deprivation indicators: 1 % unemployed, 2 % overcrowded households, 3 % single parent households, 4 % households lacking amenities, 5 % pensioners living alone, 6 % population change, 7 standardised mortality rate, 8 % born in New Commonwealth.

Nonetheless, as in inner city studies, housing and demographic variables have an independent input to the analysis (although an inheritance of poorer housing and health are in turn affected by the past economic roles of these areas). Donnison and Soto (1980), who undertook an analysis of 40 variables in 154 urban areas in the 1971 Census, lend credence to our view that social status and industrial structure, particularly the proportions of manual workers, lie at the heart of interrelationships between conditions in British towns. (Interestingly, the authors identified seven clusters of 'manual' towns, including three identified with engineering and one with textiles which were dubbed 'Middle England' and *then* considered strongly for the title of the 'Good City'. The exemplars were Doncaster (S. Yorks.), Bolton, Farnworth, Oldham and Stockport (Greater Manchester), Walsall (W. Midlands), Swindon (Wilts.) and Gloucester. (All except the last fall under the ambit of this chapter.)

Long-term unemployment in the 1980s

The 1981 Census, of course, showed worse unemployment than 1971. Later data show no basic change, but the proportions of long-term unemployed were still considerably greater in 1989. In that year 38 per cent of the unemployed (claimants for unemployment benefit) had been in this situation for a year or more. Variations around this figure largely reflected overall percentage rates of unemployment, with some of the highest proportions of long-term unemployed in Knowsley (Merseyside) and Wolverhampton (W. Midlands). Comparatively little was known about the long-term unemployed. A survey of 236 'Restart' interviewees in County Durham in 1988 found that the thesis of long-term unemployment being 'generalized' across a wide range of industries held true (although there were pockets of males made redundant by specific TNCs in 1979–81). A remarkable feature in Durham was the much lower rates of ownership of vehicles and telephones among the long-term unemployed than in the adult population at large. In general, economists concluded that the Durham sample did not seem to be unemployable; many were genuinely motivated to get work, and their background, experience and interests suggested that they were trainable.

Demand for craft and skilled workers is perhaps at the core of the issue, as it was among them that national unemployment increased most sharply. Not surprisingly, the 1981 Census showed that our industrial districts had an appreciably higher proportion of manual workers (62.4 per cent) among males than in the UK as a whole, a feature in virtually all our industrial districts. This is critical because, as noted by Cooke (1988, 244), 'there are signs of a restructuring which is jettisoning much of the low-skill operative labour – often female – taken on by manufacturing industry a decade or two earlier, and its replacement by new technology'.

Deprivation within industrial districts

Unemployment and housing conditions have led to increased social and political polarization within industrial districts. The local map of unemployment was and remains predominantly a map of housing areas, with the highest rates evident in council estates and poor housing. Thus in Bradford 'unemployment is highest in the inner city where it reaches 20 per cent or more, and less in the outer wards, except in the large council estates' (Dennis, 1986). Especially in the early stages of the last recession there was evidence of localized impacts from large factory closures. In the West Midlands conurbation, Spencer *et al* (1986) noted that, while high unemployment had been concentrated in inner-city locations, recession brought a wider dispersal with a concentration of high rates in some of the peripheral housing estates.

In general, most council estates of industrial districts were integral parts of the 'disadvantaged Britain of the 1980s', as the inevitable home of large proportions of manual workers, single parents and the aged. Segregation is especially marked in the newer, outer estates, which were built mainly in the 1950s and 1960s as parts of the slum-clearance drive but on the periphery of big cities, especially in the north of England, Scotland and South Wales. In some cases, these represent planned overspill from cities. Unlike many New Towns, they were built with the minimum of shops and industry, and had already been recognized by the 1970s as poor and overcrowded. In examining four major outer estates, Broadbent (1985) found that while the population of pensioners and New Commonwealth residents stood below the national average, the level of unemployment and proportions of low-skilled workers were over twice the national average.

Thus economic change and slum clearance have rarely changed the social status of areas. Old riverside industrial areas and industrial villages tend to remain working class in character, and to become more dominated by the unskilled underclass, even where later development has obliterated early industrial dereliction, or expensive landscaping has reduced pit heaps to grassy mounds. Several metropolitan industrial districts have developed 'ghettos' of Commonwealth immigrants and their descendants in older and poorly-maintained property notably in Bradford (W. Yorks.) and Wolverhampton (W. Midlands). The processes which trap people in such areas of high unemployment are similar to those of the cities, but it is difficult to see whether the same mixture of economic and physical planning policies (as used in the cities) can be applied across the wide range of districts and local areas considered here.

Physical planning needs of industrial districts

We now turn to the kinds of policies that are relevant to arresting and reversing the adverse trends of industrial districts, both occupational and industrial trends and the decay of the physical fabric of development. It is widely held that it is the social and industrial image of these districts which repels development. Massey (1988) suggested not only that the attraction of the outer South East for white-collar work was based on positive social class associations, but that the urban–rural shift reflected repulsion from industrial areas: 'What really seems to be at issue is distancing from manufacturing production and from the physical *and* social context that goes with it' (Massey, 1988, 269). Camagni (1985) looked internationally at the conditions of many old-established, highly urbanized and diversified urban areas which are suffering from a general maturity of the economic *and* environmental structure. Cooke (1988, 244) saw that 'the problem of the mature socio-spatial formations is to "de-mature" through environmental rejuvenation *and* new firm formation'. Thus, no one believes that the physical, social and economic heritages can in the end be separated, as they are all mentioned together. No one therefore imagines that the problem is simply one of the built and physical environment. However, industrial Britain was born at constricted water-power sites on the upland fringe of the Pennines in Greater Manchester, West Yorkshire, South Yorkshire and Derbyshire: it may be difficult to achieve modern development in the same travel-to-work areas today.

Infrastructure

Physical modernization of the infrastructure to promote growth in production attracted central government grants for pit clearance in the 'assisted areas' even prior to the provision of special funds from 1963 for motorway building, New Towns and airports in north-east England and central Scotland. Other authorities, such as the former West Riding County Council, planned new industrial estates in relation to motorway development. However, the addition of *new* infrastructure came to be seen internationally as only a partial measure, and motorway building as an unreliable tool of regional development. In 1969, the Hunt Report (Department of Economic Affairs, 1969) saw the whole physical and social environment of Lancashire and Yorkshire as detrimental to their economic future. Little new money, however, was forthcoming for these Intermediate Areas as such, and in 1986 a government report to the European Commission wrote about many areas as about Greater Manchester: 'Intensive action in some small areas has improved the general environment and operating conditions for many firms. The scale of the problem is, however, far in excess of the level of resources which are available' (Department of Trade and Industry, 1986). Derelict land is a continuing problem (Kivell, 1987).

Industrial improvement areas

After trial efforts in Rochdale (Greater Manchester), central government in 1978 introduced industrial and commercial Improvement Areas, in which loans and grants are available for clearing and landscaping land, improving access and modernizing buildings. Local authorities which qualified under the Inner Urban Areas Act (including some areas considered in the last two chapters) had set up 212 such areas by 1984. A report for the Department of the Environment (1986, 10) argued that 'The achievements of Improvement Area policy as evidenced by the case studies do not merit the proliferation of the number of IIA's and CIA's declared.' Ten of the schemes had produced only an additional 325 jobs in total. However, Etherington (1987) argued that the Areas were intended only as local palliatives, but nonetheless that they provided an invaluable opportunity in co-ordinated land-use planning.

Industrial buildings

'Britain's factory stock is old, often ill-designed for modern uses and offers only limited opportunities for significant expansion' (Fothergill *et al.*, 1987, 117). Nearly a fifth of buildings pre-dated World War One, and two-fifths World War Two; over two-fifths suffered the problem of having more than one floor. In Lancashire, many sound former cotton mills have been converted to successful use in other industries. In Yorkshire, the 16 mills of Dean Clough, Halifax have been converted into a successful business park. However, the same authors stressed how job prospects correlate inversely with the age of a firm's premises. They argue that regional policy (see below) has been concerned too much with building grants and the supply of *new* small units, when there is great need for public initiatives to alter larger existing properties. Thus there are gains to be made from physical planning, but Conservative ministers of the 1980s went out of their way to stress that land-use planning was not the clue to regional regeneration.

Trends in central government policies

Property and infrastructure are only one part of the *possible* armoury of central government in trying to arrest the decline of areas. At their widest, most kinds of government activity transfer taxpayers' money between regions, often without prospects of economic gain; thus large payments of unemployment benefit are one element of the greater than average levels of government spending per head in Northern Ireland, Scotland and Wales. This always provided a much greater element of regional redistribution than did 'regional policy' spending, but its significance was marginally reduced under Conservative policies of the 1980s. We have had good cause to refer at several points in this volume to regional policy as the principal explicit means of bringing industry and employment to defined problem areas. The policy had its origins in the recession years of the early 1930s, shown on the ground in government industrial estates which survive today, and gained most psychological support from the political memory of them.

The paradox is that this longstanding consensus of political support fell away at the very time of the next great recession, the early 1980s (Chisholm, 1987; Martin, 1989b). The most simple reason is that an essentially *redistributive* policy was irrelevant when there was little to distribute. Labour interests in the South were aware of high unemployment there, and Conservatives argued that it was dangerous to interfere with national growth. Further, in the same way that the Conservative government achieved economies in general public spending and welfare benefits by focusing down on the 'most-deserving targets', so too it both cut back on the scope and coverage of 'regional' policy (Townsend, 1987) and set up a whole range of locally-defined measures in many problem areas ('central government localism', see below). The overall decline of regional policy spending, compared with the growth of urban and European spending, is graphed at Figure 10.2. It is

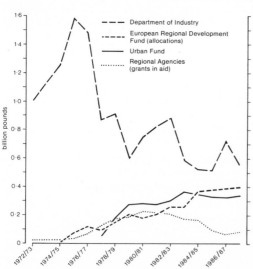

Figure 10.2 Annual central government expenditure on regional and urban policies, Great Britain, 1972/73–1987/88. Source: *Regional Trends* (various); *Economic Trends* (various).

very difficult to visualize all these trends combining in individual areas, but a very rare snapshot of relative kinds of spending in the Newcastle Metropolitan Region, 1978–84, is provided in Table 10.4. This shows the channels through which aid reaches an old industrial region; it does not specify the objectives, which increasingly moved from the direct support of job creation through direct industrial investment in plant and buildings on the ground to a wider range of assistance for business services and the unemployed, in improving the socio-institutional 'supply-side' of regional attraction. Help came through the (then) Manpower Services Commission in re-skilling the labour force; through revitalizing and modernizing the economy by help to mature industries; through modest but increasing support for the service sector and tourism; and, hopefully, through easing the availability of regional finance. The prevailing consensus itself moved away from 'traditional' regional policy of the Department of Trade and Industry to two different levels, to self-help through 'local economic initiatives', and to seeking European support. Nonetheless, the 'traditional' policy *remained* the leading financial element (Table 10.4) and we turn to that first.

Table 10.4 Types of government spending related to economic development in the Newcastle Metropolitan Region, 1978–84 (£m)

Department of Trade and Industry, incl.		204
Regional Development Grants	146	
Regional Selective Assistance	49	
Manpower Services Commission, incl.		187
Youth Training Scheme, Community Programme etc		
European Community, incl.		125
Regional Development Fund	49	
Social Fund	48	
Coal and Steel Community	28	
Local Authorities, incl.		61
Acquisition and servicing of land	24	
Factory building	20	
Loans and Grants	13	
Other agencies and schemes, incl.		65
English Estates (factory development and rent relief)	32	
Washington New Town Development Corporation	16	
Enterprise Zone (rate relief)	7	
Urban Development Grant	6	
British Steel (Industry) Ltd	1	
Total		642

Source: abridged from Robinson, Wren and Goddard, 1987, 54

'Traditional' regional policy

The term 'regional policy' is actually a misnomer: for most of its history since 1934 it has defined 'assisted areas' as smaller geographical units than a region, most of them similar in identity, character and shape to the industrial districts that are the subject of this chapter; the original definitions of 1934 actually excluded cities such as Glasgow and Newcastle; the core of the policy always focused on new factory building in industrial coalfields, and it was the run-down of coal-mining itself in the 1960s and 1970s which most spurred the revival of the policy then. Admittedly, that period also saw the extension of 'assisted areas' to coastal areas of unemployment resulting from problems in fishing or the holiday trade, and to the whole of Scotland and Wales. Much of the west coast of Britain still qualifies for assistance. However, a series of reductions after 1977 (Townsend 1980, 1987) produced the map of 1984 which is shown at Figure 10.3. Based on detailed assessment of unemployment and industrial structure, this remained in force in 1989. Its very stability brings in to question the role of regional policy in the 1980s. If policy was having any great effect, then some areas would surely have qualified for removal.

Regional policy built many new factories and was credited with bringing 604,000 jobs to 'assisted areas', 1960–81, of which 450,000 survived in 1981 (Moore *et al.*, 1986). One author castigates it for a much reduced role in the

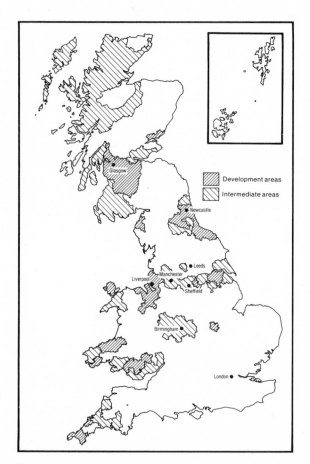

Figure 10.3 'Assisted areas' under Regional Policy, as defined from 1984. Source: Department of Trade and Industry.

1980s. 'The regional policy goal of reducing spatial unevenness has been relegated to the gesture politics out of which it emerged at the end of the 1930s' (Ward, 1988, 237). The rate of attraction of new firms indeed sank to low levels in the first part of the 1980s because of low levels of national manufacturing investment (Chapter 5), the ending of central restrictions on factory building in prosperous areas, and successive reductions in the scale of financial assistance. Total spending on regional preferential assistance fell from about £1,000m per annum in 1977/78 to £917m in 1982/83 and £553m in 1987/88. Regional Development Grants, providing 15 per cent of the value of a factory's approved capital expenditure, were no longer available from 1988. This left the bulk of regional policy conducted through applications for Regional Selective Assistance, generally regarded as less predictable and reliable for industrialists. There was evidence during the relative 'boom' conditions of 1988 of increased 'overspill' of industry from normally prosperous areas (Chapter 9) to 'assisted areas', and of a further concentration there of more TNCs from abroad. Dunning (1986) calculated that 92.5 per cent of Japanese-owned plants in the UK lay in areas of above-average unemployment. Electronics plants in industrial Wales were followed by the spread of plants to north-east England, associated with the development of Nissan's car-making plant at Washington New Town (Tyne and Wear). Toyota's decision of 1989 to locate near Derby fell outside the 'assisted areas', but the site is central to a wide area of industrial districts.

The power of policy to influence TNCs in 'green-field' developments provided some hope for industrial districts in general. Nonetheless, a geographer considering the prospects of any one area must always bear in mind the spatial competition for 'mobile projects' between the large number of problem areas of Europe, let alone the UK. The general post-war lesson on UK internal movement of industry is that it is the areas closest to the South East, such as South Wales, which achieve greater success. With male employment in industrial regions still in 1989 recovering at only very slow rates, and with labour shortages present in the South East, the arguments of the early 1960s were resumed that a strengthened regional policy could *improve national efficiency*. A decade of its operation had been largely lost, but the time was ripe for a partial return to past successes.

European Commission policies

The very survival of regional policy in the face of Conservative ministers' criticisms may largely be put down to international factors. Firstly it is necessary to provide financial assistance, as under regional policy, to compete with other countries in attracting foreign investments to, for instance, South Wales or north-east England. Secondly, grants from the European Regional Development Fund (Table 10.4) are limited 'to those aided areas established by Member States in applying their systems of regional aids'. The retention of UK-assisted areas thus ensured, for example, the spending there of 1.8 million European Currency Units in 1985 to 1987, principally on public infrastructure projects, including some approved for areas of decline in steel, shipbuilding, textiles, clothing and fishing. The approval of these and other schemes required the collation of forward regional plans by UK authorities, many of whom began to look more to Brussels than London for help.

Coal and steel areas

The existence from 1951 of the European Coal and Steel Community, as the precursor to the Commission, demonstrated international recognition of the most longstanding problem of restructuring in industrial Europe. As Table 10.4 shows, the Community's role continues in providing additional finance for infrastructure and training in areas of decline in coal and steel, almost all of them 'industrial districts' for this chapter. British regional policy, as we have mentioned, owed its existence to the job to be done to meet the persistent decline over several decades of the coalfields, particularly of Scotland, north-east England and South Wales; the success achieved by 1979 is not to be underestimated, as it included, for instance, the growth of Scottish New Towns and the basic conversion of central Durham to an engineering region. The critical feature then became the onset of massive closures in iron and steel, and the extension of heavy job losses to additional coalfields after 1985 (as introduced in Chapter 5).

The principal new measure was the establishment by the two (then) nationalized industries of companies to promote the diversification of closure areas, British Steel (Industry) Ltd. (BS(I)) in 1975 and British Coal Enterprise (BCE) in 1985, followed by British Shipbuilders (Enterprise) Ltd. in 1986 (Hudson and Sadler, 1987). BS(I) provided loans, capital and managed workshops in 19 areas. In some places it claims to have provided more jobs than were lost in steel; however, it is only one contributor to the moderate re-industrialization of these areas. As they were the prime target of several agencies in the early 1980s, they were on occasion among the most prominent of the few areas with manufacturing job increases by the period 1981–87.

The social costs of expected job losses were the prominent target of the miners' strike of 1984/85: yet the special organization to meet the problem, BCE, was widely seen as being inadequately funded (*The Economist*, November 22 1986, 30). Its target was to assist in replacing 15,000 jobs per year, but research reported by Bentley (1988) suggested that only 1500–2000 net permanent jobs per annum were being created on the ground. Given the additional problems of training, dereliction and transport in declining mining areas, it is not surprising that South Yorkshire and Nottinghamshire showed some of the scantiest reductions in unemployment of the 1980s (Chapter 7). In the country at large, there were 223 collieries employing 235,000 in 1979, whereas the Coalfield Communities Campaign (Bentley, 1988) forecast a reduction by 1992 to (a range of) 29–48 collieries and 27,000–44,000 people. Particular reasons for a continuation of the sharp decline after 1988 were a whole range of government policies: the privatization of the electricity industry, with the threat of increased use of cheap overseas imported coal in power stations and the protection of nuclear generation; the threatened privatization of the NCB itself, attended by government encouragement to reduced costs through further increases in productivity; and mounting government and private-sector interest in opencast mining, with, additionally, all its temporary disturbance to coalfield landscapes.

Government Development Agencies

In considering new organizations in this field, the main trend has been a departure from civil service bureaucratic management toward the financing of somewhat more autonomous public bodies. Like BS(I), the Scottish Development Agency was founded in 1975. It took over some existing tasks such as the running of government industrial estates in Scotland, which are mainly in the industrial districts. It is more noted for its strategies for individual industries, including the provision of investment finance and business advisory services, and for its involvement in urban renewal in the Glasgow Eastern Area Renewal Project (Chapter 8). The Welsh Development ment Agency was founded later on a similar model, but by 1987/88 was spending £44 million p.a. on land and factories. One reason for the retention of these interventionist state organizations in the 1980s was their control by the Secretaries of State for Scotland and Wales, whose relative autonomy within the London cabinet protected their countries from relevant cuts. The Welsh Office also boasted co-ordinated planning of the improvement of the industrial valleys of South Wales, including pit clearance, housing renewal and transport improvements. Several regions of England were jealous of the Agencies, most notably the North, which established the Northern Development Company as a strengthened promotional body.

'Central government localism'

Several new types of *local* designations were made by the Conservative governments from 1979 onwards. Ideologically they were meant to provide enclaves of free market activity: to geographers they represented whole sets of new boundary lines on the national map within which new ways of financing and building organized development took place (much of it in industrial districts). One precedent lay in the 'export processing zones' of Third World countries, in which exemption from customs duties was allowed for TNCs producing export goods. A similar exemption system was established in Freeports of the UK in 1984, shown in Figure 10.4, but has been of limited consequence.

Enterprise Zones, as their title implies, were meant to be zones in which the waiving of government planning and financial regulations would unleash business enterprise. In practice, while town planning rules were simplified, the most important incentive was freedom from the payment of rates for ten years and tax allowances on capital spending. Between 1981 and 1988, 26 Zones were established (Figure 10.4). Many writers identify the Zones with inner cities, but in fact the great majority fall outside the boundaries of the principal cities examined in Chapter 8 and within the 'industrial districts' category of this chapter. They represented political statements to areas of contemporary de-industrialization. In England, for instance, 11 of the Zones fall in our 'industrial districts', in metropolitan boroughs such as Salford/Trafford or in other industrial districts such as

Figure 10.4 'Central government localism': locations of designated areas and zones. Source: Department of the Environment.

Hartlepool. In Wales, the Swansea Enterprise Zone has achieved significant commercial development of an estate on the outskirts of Swansea (Bromley and Rees, 1988).

Was the experiment a success, considering the expenditure of nearly £300m between 1981 and 1986? According to the Department of the Environment (1988), of 63,300 jobs located in the Zones in 1986, 35,000 were there as a direct result of the policy, and 13,000 were net additional jobs supported by the experiment. That is, much of the development would have occurred anyway, and was merely encouraged to cross the Zone boundaries. These kinds of findings led the government to announce in 1987 that no new Zones would be created; the main beneficiaries were larger firms already in the Zones (Talbot, 1988); 'The most effective Zones have often proved to be those where one public sector agency owns much of the land and can effect an integrated overall development strategy' (Lawless, 1988, 531).

The greater use of Urban Development Corporations (UDCs) superseded Enterprise Zones in the second half of the 1980s. In the cities, the UDCs in London Docklands and Merseyside, both established in 1981, became 'flagships' of the Department of the Environment, principally because of mounting office development in London (Chapter 8). The approach was extended to defined derelict and other land at the heart of older industrial districts of the provinces when five were created in 1987, in the Black Country (W. Midlands county), Trafford Park (Greater Manchester), Teesside (Cleveland), Tyne and Wear and Cardiff Bay, followed by smaller ones in Bristol, Leeds and Manchester (Figure 10.4). By 1989, the UDCs presided over 40,000 acres and were expected to receive central government grant of over £200m per annum.

The UDCs were to act as catalysts creating a building environment in which the private sector could flourish, with powers to acquire and develop land and issue planning permission. In general, the provincial ones were more welcome to local planners and Labour councils than was the case in London. There can be little prospect, however, of the larger provincial ones attracting much office development; they have clear advantages as energetic property developers, but their success in adding new jobs to the economic base may vary considerably. For instance, the Teesside Development Corporation spoke in late 1989 of the creation of 6,000 jobs over the ensuing few years, when there were still 30,000 unemployed in the surrounding county of Cleveland. As of 1989, no more UDCs were intended before 1992.

Local economic initiatives

The roles of central government, working through regional policy and 'central government localism', have been supplemented and diversified by local economic initiatives. These are normally conducted by local government authorities, often those of industrial districts, and sometimes by local business groups. In the USA 'locally dependent firms form territorially-defined growth coalitions to encourage local economic development. Since the 1930s local governments have also increasingly intervened in pursuit of local economic developments' (Cox and Mair, 1988, 310). This competitive process has involved the attraction of large factories from elsewhere. Officials at the OECD now find much to imitate in specific American programmes to create new jobs – in particular, locally-based partnerships between public and private enterprise to stimulate growth in small and medium-sized firms (*The Economist*, May 28 1988, 58).

The use of local government money for economic development purposes did occur before the last war, but, except for instance in developing seaside resorts, it has traditionally been frowned upon in Britain (Ward, 1988), and still was by the Conservative government of the 1980s (Duncan and Goodwin, 1988). Nonetheless, the decade saw rapid diffusion of the practice of assisting development, for instance by providing sites or buildings, both by county and district councils. This has occurred mainly under provisions of the 1972 Local Government Act, which also sets limits on this spending. Recession conditions of 1980–81 left many councils feeling that they were 'trying to drain an ocean with a teaspoon' (Cochrane, 1983), but finding that they had to make a contribution (or at least, must appear to be doing something). Naturally, it was the worst-hit areas, usually our industrial districts and cities, which first adopted this activity. By 1986–87 the average metropolitan district had a staff of 19 concerned with economic development (Sellgren, 1989). In a survey answered by over 70 per cent of councils (Table 10.5), it was found that metropolitan districts in 'assisted areas' were the most active in industrial development policies, although two-thirds of councils in the South provided sites and premises for firms (Armstrong, 1988).

This latter policy reflects the traditional view of Conservative Britain, that it is in order to help private industry on property matters, which are reflected in the changing land-use map of a town. Many of the Labour industrial districts adopted more of a 'people-based' approach to redevelopment, which they referred to as 'new industrial strategies'. After 1979 they regarded the issue not merely as one of attracting new functions to town halls, but as one of social responsibility involving the authority's own direct employment level, the sectoral planning of local industry, and a concern with socially useful production and equal opportunities. This culminated in the establishment of Enterprise Boards in most of the former metropolitan counties. The Boards variously survived the abolition of those counties and continued with three main kinds of activity – developing and managing industrial property; providing finance in the form of loans for local companies; and providing training courses, as in new technology. Lancashire's agency supported more than 4,000 jobs and expanded into urban renewal – redeveloping old mill complexes and canal sites.

More than half of Britain's local authorities also came to support tourism, including the cultivation of urban tourism in the form of conference business

Table 10.5 The industrial development policies of district councils in the assisted and non-assisted areas of England and Wales, 1985–86

| | Percentage of responding districts operating policy | | | |
| | Metropolitan districts | | Non-metropolitan districts | |
Type of Policy	Assisted areas	Non-assisted areas	Assisted areas	Non-assisted areas
Provision of sites	92.0	70.8	91.9	69.0
Maintaining register of premises	92.0	91.7	64.5	47.5
Grants to firms	88.0	45.8	43.5	31.5
Provision of premises	84.0	70.8	90.3	66.0
Offering business advice	84.0	75.0	75.8	36.5
Maintaining guides to sources of finance	80.0	37.5	61.3	19.5
Loans to firms	76.0	45.8	43.5	18.0
Providing rate or rent free periods	76.0	45.8	62.9	30.0
Joint ventures with private sector	76.0	50.0	41.9	36.0

Note: The 'assisted areas' are those designated by the Department of Trade and Industry as at Figure 10.3
Source: Armstrong, 1988

and industrial archaeology in northern towns and cities. For instance, Bradford entered into one of the English Tourist Board's Tourist Development Action Programmes in order to refurbish an area of fine Victorian textile warehouses, in conjunction with expanding accommodation and exploiting the conference and exhibition market (Davies, 1987). Among other innovations of the 1980s, local authorities also contributed to the country's 80 technology and science parks.

Much promotional activity is, however, humdrum and difficult to measure. In the Tyneside Metropolitan Region, 1978–84, local authority expenditure on economic development was dominated by factory building and the servicing of land, and 45 per cent of all expenditure fell under the central government's conventional Urban Programme. In all, local authority projects in that area had generated only about 2,000 jobs, although at lower costs per job than from central government assistance (Robinson *et al.*, 1987).

In reality, the interventionist and 'free-market' approaches are not opposed. Local authorities have commonly contributed to the development of local Enterprise Agencies, normally run by businessmen. They aim to create employment in new and existing small businesses by providing help and counselling. Businessmen were also given the controlling lead in setting up sub-regional Training and Enterprise Councils to take over many former government training activities. The co-existence of these with many other forms of local agency would have been difficult to imagine a decade earlier. In many ways, Labour local authorities have a growing involvement with the private sector. On the other hand, some of their past initiatives which would have been considered 'radical' have been taken up by the mainstream of local authorities, in suitably modified forms by Conservative councils. Both Labour and Conservative councils are interested in 'co-operative' forms of organization of new businesses. Cochrane (1988) sees Labour authorities as increasingly developing alliances with local developers, financiers and industrialists in assembling openings for profitable local investment. This was, however, partly a response to the threat of 'the marginalization on offer from the centre' from the growth of Urban Development Corporations and repeated legislation which threatened to curtail severely the use of local authority spending powers.

A case study: the County of Cleveland, including Teesside

One of the areas chosen in the late 1980s to receive an Urban Development Corporation was the County of Cleveland, which includes Teesside. This area of the north-east coast of England enjoyed rapid growth from 1830 to 1920, but has never been classified as a 'metropolitan' area. It does, however, reflect many of the problems of peripheral industrial Britain, including that most characteristic feature of the Northern Region, a dependence on very large industrial plants (Buswell *et al.*, 1987).

The Teesside Development Corporation has responsibility for one of the largest areas of derelict industrial land in Europe. The surrounding County of Cleveland has been an area of exceptional problems since 1979, with higher unemployment rates than Merseyside in the peak years of the 1980s. The area owed its existence entirely to heavy industry: its large iron and steel industry, with later offshoots in heavy engineering, dated from the 1850s, and its chemical industry from the 1920s. In the 1960s and early 1970s it appeared still to have excellent prospects from investment in those indus-tries, which, using River Tees imports of raw materials (see Figure 10.5), set it among Europe's 'maritime industrial complexes'. Yet this very emphasis on manual shift-work in large capital-intensive process plants, supported by Regional Development Grants, proved the area's undoing in the fundamentally changed environment for manufacturing in the 1980s.

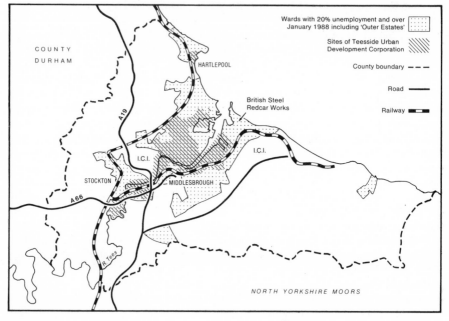

Figure 10.5 Cleveland County, in North-East England. Source: includes data of the County Council, 1988.

The especially acute depression of the Teesside economy was due to its being a steel-making area. Following the closure of Hartlepool Works in 1977, there occurred a process of 'technical change': the *new* Redcar iron and steel complex of 1979 superseded the work and jobs of lower productivity works, bringing (with other miscellaneous closures) a run-down of 60 per cent in the labour force by 1984 (Table 10.6). The decade saw not only the closure of the area's last two shipyards, but also the death of heavy engineering, replaced eventually by facilities making North Sea oil rigs. Large branch plants in other industries closed (e.g. GEC). More surpris-ingly, after a long period of investment in petrochemicals, ICI went through a period of heavier run-down in its labour force. The result was that the employment reduction in manufacturing was more severe than the national average, not only in the period 1978–81 (20.0 per cent) *but also 1981–87* (32.1 per cent). In the value of production per head, Cleveland fell from the fourth county of the country in 1977 to the rank of seventeenth in 1984.

Table 10.6 Employment and population in the County of Cleveland, 1978–87 (thousands)

	1978	1984	1987
Primary industries	5.0	4.5	4.2
Metal manufacturing	25.2	10.1	7.8
Chemicals	28.6	21.3	16.3
Other manufacturing	39.7	23.4	26.7
Construction	22.2	10.7	11.2
Services	114.5	114.1	118.5
Total employment	235.2	183.6	184.7
Total population	572.7	562.7	554.5

Source: Census of Employment (NOMIS) and OPCS

Added to all this, service employment ceased to grow. In the 1970s this was one of the leading examples of a northern, male-employing area catching up on the rest of the country through gains in female employment, particularly in the public sectors of health and education (Townsend, 1986a). In fact, health sector employment in this area had already fallen into decline between 1978 and 1981, and was then stabilized, partly through the privatization of hospital domestic work, and partly through the replacement of many older, small hospitals through the concentration of beds at the new South Cleveland Hospital.

Modernization of the Cleveland infrastructure in the 1970s had run ahead of the diversification of the economy, above all because then there were always worse problem areas in the north needing new investment from regional policy. In the early years of the 1980s, most of what was done to alleviate severe unemployment was the work of the MSC, voluntary organizations and the churches (Sadler *et al.*, 1989). Gradually, local economic initiatives came to fruition through the development of enterprise and technology centres. Enterprise Zones were, however, established in Hartlepool and Middlesbrough in 1981 and 1983, and then overtaken in 1987 by the foundation of the Teesside Development Corporation, responsible for no less than 19 square miles of territory. Some of its new successes lie in service and leisure development; significant projects included the Hartlepool marina, and the attraction of a large research establishment of the Ministry of Defence.

In short, a whole battery of initiatives were introduced to try to fill the area's vacant sites and the large hole which had been created in its employment structure. Meanwhile, the area became more notable for temporary employment, including, as in South Wales (Harris, 1987), the re-employment of ex-steel workers by contractors to British Steel. Recorded unemployment fell to the level of 12.9 per cent by the spring of 1990, but this was achieved only through declining activity rates, and increased outward migration of all kinds; this included movement on a weekly basis to jobs in the South, on longer turns on North Sea oil rigs, and on temporary contracts in foreign oil fields. The 1987 Census of Employment confirmed that job levels within Cleveland had been stabilized since 1984; that seemed the best to hope for, albeit in a productive and attractive environment.

The latest available trends

We conclude by attempting to answer the question raised by the title of this chapter, whether industrial areas remain 'in decline', considering the national economic recovery of the 1980s and the special efforts described above for some of the worst-hit areas.

It is certainly possible to identify local authority districts which showed a substantial gain in total employment from the economic low-point of 1981 to 1987 (in the latest Census of Employment at time of writing). Some of the leading gains fell in the industrial districts of the North, notably Derwentside (+20.7 per cent in total employment), the site of the Consett steel works closure in County Durham; Clydebank (+17.1 per cent), where government efforts at re-industrialization were concentrated in Strathclyde; and in closure areas of Clwyd which benefited from regional policy. There were also substantial recoveries of total employment in industrial districts of the South such as Luton.

However, any significant increases in metropolitan districts were few and far between; there were examples of serious decline in industrial districts of the South; many large industrial districts of the North were virtually untouched by efforts at 're-industrialization' and showed declines of 20 per cent or more.

The overall average of this range of outcomes was of continuing absolute and relative decline for the industrial districts as a whole. Total employment fell by 3.3 per cent, but this overall figure conceals a reduction of no less than 9.1 per cent in male jobs (compared with 5.5 per cent in Great Britain as a whole). The number of industrial jobs fell by no less than 19.2 per cent. Full details are provided in Table 10.7. As might be expected, the reduction in

Table 10.7 The structure of employment change in industrial districts, 1981–87, by North/South groups (percentage change)

	Metropolitan		Industrial: North		Industrial: South	
	Total	Diff. shift	Total	Diff. shift	Total	Diff. shift
Agriculture, forestry and fishing	− 9.4	+ 2.0	−16.9	− 5.4	− 2.1	+ 9.4
Energy and water supply	−41.1	−13.0	−46.8	−18.6	−29.8	− 1.6
Metal processing, other minerals	−28.0	− 3.7	−27.3	− 3.1	− 5.8	+18.5
Metal goods, engineering and vehicles	−23.2	− 4.5	−12.6	+ 6.0	−17.1	+ 1.6
Other manufacturing	− 6.8	+ 1.7	+ 2.4	+10.9	− 2.0	+ 6.5
Construction	− 2.0	+ 6.1	− 6.2	+ 1.9	− 7.7	+ 0.4
Distribution, hotels, catering, repairs	+ 1.8	− 1.9	+ 3.9	+ 0.2	+ 8.3	+ 4.6
Transport and communication	− 8.7	− 0.3	− 6.8	+ 1.6	+ 2.3	+10.7
Banking, finance etc	+33.9	+ 0.5	+25.4	− 8.0	+38.7	+ 5.3
Other services	+11.5	+ 0.8	+13.7	+ 3.0	+16.6	+ 5.9
Total, of which	− 4.6	− 1.3	− 3.5	+ 1.3	+ 1.1	+ 5.1
males	−10.3		− 9.3		− 5.4	

Note: see Fig. 10.1 and text for definition of districts. Diff. = differential
Source: Census of Employment, NOMIS

employment was greatest in metropolitan districts, followed by industrial districts of the North. Decline was concentrated in the industrial sectors of the table, the second to fifth rows, including a reduction of 140,300 in the 'energy industries', which include British Coal.

When we compare the performance of each sector with what would be expected from its national performance, by means of the 'differential shift', we find a variety of patterns. There has clearly been some diversification into 'other manufacturing', where there were positive gains in all types of area. Service industries generated jobs at a slightly faster *rate* than in the country at large in many entries. The 'differential shifts' were however predominantly negative in the most populated areas, the metropolitan districts (excluding cities).

The most striking feature of the performance of all these areas was the relatively small size of 'differential shifts'. This is to say that the relative decline of these areas as a whole, second only to that of the 'cities' (Chapter 8), is predominantly 'structural': that is, it was due to their dependence on industry at the start of the period. This feature is more accentuated by the urban character of the metropolitan districts (all in the North), and ameliorated by different characteristics of industrial districts of the South. There were renewed tendencies in 1987 and 1988 for industry to relocate from South to North. In general, however, it is difficult to see any general reversal in the 1990s of the decline in importance of industrial districts, due above all to their inherited industrial and environmental characteristics.

Further reading

The content of this chapter is drawn from several fields of writing rather than one. A theoretical approach is provided by Steiner (1985), and another is confronted by Hudson, in Massey and Allen (1988). The latter volume also includes valuable conceptual approaches and generalizations in separate chapters including those by Cooke, Martin, and Massey. General economic considerations are dealt with in Hasluck (1987).

The origins of government spending for development purposes are reviewed at district level by Ward (1988). An overall outline of 50 years' evolution is provided by Townsend in Lever (1987), and a policy review by Townsend (1985). Changing ideas of the 1980s are considered in Chisholm (1987), and in Paddison and Morris (1988).

The promotion of industrial employment in assisted areas is considered in Allen *et al.* (1986); in Roberts and Noon (1987); and in Willis and Saunders (1988). The acute position in areas of heavy industry decline is assessed in Hudson and Sadler (1987) and in Harris (1987).

The development of industrial districts and similar areas now has its own writing. The logic and scope of a wide field are considered in Morison (1987), and also in Chandler (1985) and Williams *et al.* (1987). These must be seen in the context of tension in the 1980s between the roles of central and local government, as reported by Duncan and Goodwin (1988).

An early prototype of the study of economic, political and social change in *localities* is provided by Murgatroyd and Urry (1983). A wide range of local case studies of industrial areas are available in Cooke (1986), while more extended studies of Middlesbrough (Cleveland), Kirkby (Merseyside) and Swindon (Wilts.) appear in Cooke (1989). A useful source of current articles is the journal *Local Economy*.

Conventionally, much of the interpretation of industrial districts is summarized at the regional level, for example Rhodes (1986) and Morgan (1986). All industrial regions are covered in Damesick and Wood (1987). Readers may wish to study volumes on individual regions including: Spencer *et al.* (1986); Hardill (1987); Robinson (1988); Hudson (1989); Morris (1987); Lever and Moore (1986); Keating and Boyle (1986); and Harrison (1986).

Statistical data are regularly available for regions, counties and metropolitan districts in the annual *Regional Trends* (HMSO); estimates of regional employment are available quarterly at Table 1.5 in the *Employment Gazette*, and statistics of unemployment for regions, travel-to-work areas, counties, districts and parliamentary constituencies are available monthly in the same journal.

11
Outer rural areas

At furthest remove from the cities lie sub-regions which we may define as 'outer rural areas', such as much of Scotland, the northern Pennines, mid Wales, the south-west peninsula and much of the east coast. These outer rural areas contain a great variety of landscapes and populations, yet have commonly started to recover from long-term de-population through a *reversal* of net migration flows. At first sight they have little in common with de-industrialized inner cities. Yet it is widely agreed that they are localities with extensive *social problems*: a number of authors, including Shaw (1979) and Moseley (1980), showed that outer rural areas, like inner urban areas, suffer from loss of the dynamic elements of their population, and from declining morale and community spirit and reduced availability of services of all kinds. For local rural people, these problems were in turn related to low wages and poor opportunities for school leavers, due in this case to falling demand for labour in the basic industry of *agriculture*.

Large reductions in the farming population, especially of farmworkers, since the mid nineteenth century were the cause of regional population decline in large areas including south-west England and East Anglia. Capital-intensive farming prospered for much of the post-war period; indeed, the needs of farming tended to block planning decisions both for the recreational use of the countryside and for housing expansion. Increasingly, farming trends became a positive threat, not only to employment levels, but also to the landscape itself; the ploughing of marginal hill-land, the draining of wetlands and the eradication of hedgerows encouraged the Conservative governments of the 1980s to amend the legislative balance between the interests of agriculture and conservation. Different problems, however, were threatened by the 1987 recognition that European Commission quotas and levies required a reduction of agricultural output, implying less inten-sive farming or, more likely, a reduction in the area of land in agriculture. Conservationists were worried by the resulting proposals to safeguard farmers' income and employment through promoting the use of their land for more forestry plantations, golf courses, riding schools and war games.

The *recreational* interest in outer rural areas is widely seen to have burgeoned from the spread of mass car-ownership after the 1950s, and is to some extent recognized by modest strengthening of the provisions for National Parks and other protected landscapes since the 1970s (MacEwen and MacEwen, 1981). Not surprisingly, what the OPCS (1981) classifies as 'remoter, mainly rural' districts (including our additions in Scotland, Figure

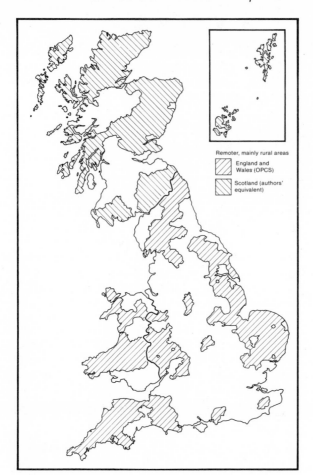

Figure 11.1 Outer rural areas of Great Britain. Source: see text.

11.1) coincides with or overlaps the Less Favoured Areas for farming recognized by the European Commission (The Arkleton Trust, 1982) and with all the National Parks and other treasured landscapes such as the Cotswold Hills or Norfolk Broads (Figure 11.2).

All definitions of extreme rural areas identify broadly the same parts of Britain. This is clearly a 'peripheral distribution', although some definitions also include a few more 'central' districts such as West Derbyshire. Cloke and Edwards (1986) identified two sets of 'extreme rural' areas for 1981. They used a wide range of factors including age structure, commuting patterns, distance from urban centres and the location of second homes. The Rural Development Commission also identify peripheral problem areas. The OPCS definition already introduced includes more inland districts in the agricultural belt from North Yorkshire to Essex (Webber and Craig, 1976).

Can these national playgrounds absorb, without permanent ecological loss, all the pressures placed upon them? Did the privatization of water

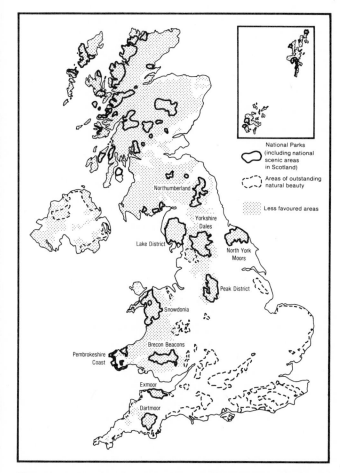

Northumberland

Yorkshire
Dales

Lake District

North York
Moors

Peak District

Snowdonia

Brecon Beacons

Pembrokeshire
Coast

Exmoor

Dartmoor

National Parks
(including national
scenic areas
in Scotland)

Areas of outstanding
natural beauty

Less favoured areas

Figure 11.2 The degree of coincidence of National Parks and agriculturally Less Favoured Areas, United Kingdom, 1988. Note that the Norfolk Broads have since been designated as a National Park. Source: *Regional Trends*, 1988, 71; Ministry of Agriculture, Fisheries and Food.

authorities in 1989 incorporate enough safeguards for walkers' access and for conservation in reservoir catchment areas? Should planning permission be given for increasing proposals for new holiday villages and 'time-share' developments?

Plural interests can be accommodated in the countryside. Green (1981) listed 26 activities carried on in the countryside including the exploitative (farming, forestry, mineral extraction, water supply and military training), the recreational (water sports, shooting, riding, bird-watching and rambling), and the 'protective' (the protection of wildlife, ecology, and sites of archaeological and geological interest). Of the 625 possible conflicts between the 26 activities, only 53 actual major conflicts and 55 minor ones were identified, suggesting that the great majority of uses are compatible with one another.

Nonetheless, the broader purposes of *social*, *recreational* and *agricultural* needs remain in conflict. The social need for employment and cheap housing is impeded by county planning policies. These are influenced by wealthier and landowning groups, which in the interests of 'amenity' (often in effect those of maintaining existing property values of the area) control the volume of house-building, factory-building and commercial development in villages. The ascendancy of wealthier groups is 'the political reality which underlies the neglect of council housing, public transport and the whole range of social, health and welfare services in rural areas' (Newby, 1980, 274). The development of recreation and tourism is criticized by landowners because of the nuisance created by visitors, and by local people because of the creation only of seasonal low-paid work. The agricultural interest can run counter to both landscape conservation and retention of jobs, even where support for Less Favoured Areas provides more support for sheep-farming than would otherwise be the case. Finally, all of these interests can be overridden by industrial needs for minerals and quarried stone, and by government support for the development of nuclear power stations and defence establishments.

One feature above all, however, has come to dominate the trends of an increasing number of outer rural areas: this is the influx of migrants of both working and retirement age. In addition to the continuing seasonal arrival of day visitors, and of tourists staying in hotels, guest-houses, hostels, field-centres and caravans, rural housing has been used by and expanded for an 'adventitious' population of 'second-home' owners, long-distance com-muters from cities, and retired people. As in much of western Europe, their opportunity has arisen partly from the initial depopulation of the countryside, providing cheap agricultural premises for purchase. The process has gone on, however, to create shortages of housing which local young people can afford, and has threatened the social and cultural cohesion of rural communities, notably in Celtic areas (Perry *et al.*, 1986). This added demand for housing has provided a further challenge to plan-ning policies, especially in the vicinity of National Parks. There are, how-ever, planners who welcome the refurbishment of old cottages, and the infusion of spending power thereby brought in.

It is clear that people from more urbanized parts are largely responsible for a progressive reversal of population trends in outer rural areas. This chapter will focus firstly on net migration to these areas, and then assess the future of the resulting *dual population*: is the long-established decline of employment and services in outer rural areas being arrested by the addition of the expanding adventitious to the declining indigenous population?

Population and migration trends

The outer rural areas are now amongst the fastest growing types of localities in Britain. In the 1970s the 'remoter, mainly rural' districts grew more rapidly than any of the other district types recognized by the OPCS, except those containing New Towns (OPCS, 1981; Champion, 1981) and considerably faster than the more urbanized categories of settlement (Table 11.1). In the 1980s, their performance was surpassed only by the 'resort, port and

Table 11.1 Population trends, 1971–88, for the three least urbanized types of districts.

	Remoter mainly rural	Urban and mixed urban–rural	Resort, port & retirement	Great Britain
Population 1971 (000s)	5 492.6	9 195.6	3 184.0	54 387.6
Population 1981 (000s)	6 050.5	9 881.3	3 369.3	54 813.5
Change 1971–81 (%)	+10.2	+7.5	+5.8	+0.8
Population 1988 (000s)	6 418.9	10 318.7	3 611.2	55 486.4
Change 1981–88 (%)	+6.1	+4.4	+7.2	+1.2

Source: Calculated from population estimates provided by OPCS and Registrar General Scotland

retirement' category of districts (Table 11.1). Moreover, their growth was achieved despite a surplus of deaths over births, with OPCS statistics (omitting Scottish districts) indicating a natural decrease of 31,000 between 1981 and 1988 as against a gain of 226,000 through migration and other changes.

Such trends, although compatible with continued de-population in a large proportion of parishes (Weekley, 1988), continue to create remarkable results. Thus, while the total population of the three northern regions of England declined between 1981 and 1988, that of Wales increased, chiefly due to the increases which occurred in all its rural counties. Increases of population in the adjoining rural counties of Shropshire and of Hereford and Worcester were even larger. In these cases the growth of long-distance commuting was a factor, as workers of the West Midlands conurbation are known to have taken houses as far west as Shrewsbury and Ludlow. There is a significant inflow of economically-active and pre-retirement migrants to areas such as Cornwall (Perry *et al.*, 1986).

Retirement migration, however, is a significant factor not only in the OPCS 'aggregate' of 'resort, port and retirement' areas, but also in the 'remoter, mainly rural' group. If we take the year 1988 and identify the ten counties of England and Wales with the highest *rates* of net inward migration (Table 11.2), we find that the list includes six counties that are dominated by rural districts, alongside counties composed mainly of prosperous sub-regions. For Cornwall, Gwynedd, Dyfed, Devon, North Yorkshire and Powys together, older people (55 and over) accounted for 30 per cent of net inward migration in 1988, but for no less than 41 per cent for Powys (see the case study below). Moreover, Devon and Cornwall were in 1988 the leading counties in terms of the absolute size of the net inflow of older migrants (Table 11.2).

The retirement of older people to resorts such as Bournemouth (Dorset) or Eastbourne (E. Sussex) is more familiar than retirement to, say, rural Wales. This extension of their movement may be construed as decentralization from traditional resorts at full housing capacity (Warnes and Law, 1984), as expressions of greater car ownership and road improvement, and above all as a statement of the increased longevity of people (Chapter 4) and the better provision of pensions. Never before has there been such a large and healthy population of older people, who are free to sell their houses in metropolitan suburbs and choose where to purchase a new home.

Table 11.2 Leading counties (England and Wales) for inward migration, 1988; contribution of the elderly

County	Net migration, all ages		Age 55 and over, thousands		
	Rate*	Thousands	In	Out	Net inflow
Cambridgeshire	+27.7	+18.1	4.5	3.2	+1.2
Cornwall	+22.1	+10.2	5.6	2.5	+3.1
East Sussex	+21.8	+15.5	7.8	5.7	+2.1
Oxfordshire	+18.0	+10.4	2.6	2.9	−0.3
Gwynedd	+17.2	+ 4.1	2.7	1.1	+1.6
Dyfed	+17.1	+ 6.0	3.2	1.1	+2.0
Devon	+16.7	+17.1	10.2	5.1	+5.0
Isle of Wight	+16.4	+ 2.1	1.7	0.9	+0.7
North Yorkshire	+15.4	+11.0	5.9	3.0	+3.0
Powys	+14.9	+ 1.7	1.4	0.6	+0.7

Note: * Rate per 1000 resident population
Source: National Health Service Central Register, NOMIS

Never before has there been a retired population with so much experience of holidays-with-pay, many of them spent with the advantage of the mobility of the private car.

> People can move to be nearer their relatives or friends, to return to their native or childhood areas, or to residentially, climatically, or socially more attractive areas . . . Most recently, the wide possession of the motor car and the extension of public utilities to most rural areas have encouraged retired migrants to move to less accessible coastal areas and to inland villages. The inland retirement districts include areas remote from the coast like the Cotswolds, the Welsh Borders (Herefordshire and Shropshire) and the Yorkshire Dales.
>
> (Law and Warnes, 1982, 53–4)

There are differences in the rates of out-movement from different conurbations (Chapter 4). Among 275,800 migrants (of all ages) from the rest of Britain to Wales, 1984–88, the greatest proportion moved from the South East (32.9 per cent), followed by the bordering regions of the North West (19.5 per cent) and the West Midlands (14.9 per cent). Among 210,600 migrants to the Northern Region, the greatest proportion again came from the South East (26.7 per cent), but it was followed more closely as a source by the bordering regions, in this case Yorkshire and Humberside (20.0 per cent) and the North West (16.9 per cent), including people familiarized with the Lake District by access on the M6.

This centrifugal redistribution of population has created a more elderly age structure in peripheral, mainly coastal, counties and districts of England and Wales, and in the Borders and Tayside Regions of Scotland. Added to the effects of selective *outward* migration among younger age groups of the *indigenous* population, the position by 1986 (OPCS, 1987) was that the 'remoter, mainly rural' areas of England and Wales had 23.1 per cent of their population in age groups of 60 and over, including 7.5 per cent of 75 and over. Only the more specialized 'resort, port and retirement' group have a greater proportion of older people. This is remarkable when one bears in mind the withdrawal of many consumer and welfare services in rural areas (see below) and the marked potential for further urban–rural migration. The implications of an ageing population for social and land-use planning are considerable (Greenberg, 1982; Taylor and Todd, 1982).

How do older people choose their retirement areas? One source of migrants' experience of destination areas lies in their earlier ownership (or loan) of second homes in 'seasonal suburbanization'. Their pattern of acquisition can be spatially modelled in similar fashion to that of migration itself, though the owners are not of course included in the above OPCS data for 'usual residence'. Evidence on the location of second homes is scanty, and could be found only by poring over a local authority's list of addresses of rating demands; dwellings whose rates are paid from a different address, in another local authority area, were deemed to be 'second homes'. A survey conducted by 'Shelter' in 1979 indicated that there were 115,000 second homes in England and Wales at that time. The county list was paradoxically headed by Greater London, which includes *pieds-à-terre* of wealthier people usually living elsewhere in Britain and abroad; it is followed by Kent. Most of the other counties high in this list contain outer rural areas.

Housing problems of outer rural areas

It is the limited pool of housing in rural areas which can set problems for the poorer part of the population. This general feature is accentuated by two institutional features, firstly by the existence of housing for farmworkers which is 'tied' to a job on a particular farm (problems arise on the redundancy, retirement or death of the farmworker), and secondly by the lower rate of provision of council houses in the countryside, which have often been concentrated in 'key' villages under long-established county policies.

The national extension of the sale of council houses in the 1980s illustrated these problems vividly, because council houses may sell better in rural areas and because they might readily be re-sold as second homes. These concerns led to two amendments to the Housing Act, 1980. Firstly, old people's dwellings were excluded from sale. Secondly, although tenants have just the same right to buy their council house in a rural area as anywhere else, there are restrictions on any future re-sale of the house in National Parks, Areas of Outstanding Natural Beauty (Figure 11.2) and other designated 'rural areas'. In the event, very few rural areas have been so designated by the Department of the Environment.

Two conclusions emerge from the juxtaposition of the 'adventitious' and 'indigenous' populations. The first is that in-migrants and second-home use may yield net benefits to the local economy where they occupy premises that would otherwise be vacant, due to out-migration etc. The second is, however, that planning authorities have been comparatively ineffective in implementing Structure Plan policies in areas of in-migration (Blacksell and Gilg, 1981), and that they are powerless to protect local people from the effects of in-migration on house prices and shortages in a period like the 1980s of limited building of council houses. In an area of strong attraction for in-migration, the Cumbria and Lake District Joint Structure Plan (Clark, 1982a) attempted to protect 'local persons' in the conditions attached to planning approval for new housing; approval would be given only for occupants who intended to dwell in the house for six months of the year. In 1984, however, the Secretary of State deleted this Lake District policy as being undesirable. The result in many rural counties, in the absence of much rented accommodation, is the concentration of the poor in 'winter lets', caravans and substandard property. 'If the proportion of households on the waiting lists is measured for particular areas, then certainly some rural areas do show equal amounts of housing stress to that found in inner city housing authorities' (Larkin, 1979, 78). In 1988 one in four villages of Lincolnshire was reported to have small caravan sites, mainly for the homeless. With attention to the problem mounting in 1989, the government finally produced a measure of backing for low-cost rural housing, by declaring that additional planning permissions should be given if arrangements could be made, as through housing trusts, to reserve the dwellings for local people.

The nature of rural deprivation

The problems of rural life are not confined to housing, or even to the 'indigenous population'. Indeed, there is an argument that the essential problem is one of 'multiple deprivation' which will justify an 'area-based approach' to the question, as in inner cities (whether or not the problems are as bad as in inner cities). This argument was first assembled towards the end of the 1970s, as by Shaw (1979). One reason for housing deprivation is certainly low income. If we take the average weekly earnings of adults in work in all counties (and Regions of Scotland) (Table 11.3), we find a remarkable correlation of low earnings with 'remoter, mainly rural' areas. The lowest average weekly earnings among males in 1988 were received in a dispersed group of peripheral (mainly coastal) areas led by Cornwall, Powys, Dyfed, Gwynedd, Dumfries and Galloway, and Lincolnshire. The list includes most of the areas of Britain which are most dependent for employment on agriculture, forestry and fishing, whose low wages drive down the overall level of earnings. The list also includes the areas of lowest female earnings.

Table 11.3 Leading areas for low pay, April 1988

County/ Scottish Region	Average gross weekly earnings (full-time) £		Per cent of employees in agriculture, forestry and fishing 1987
	Males on adult rates	Females on adult rates	
Cornwall	191.1	137.6	5.4
Powys	191.2	—	11.2
Dyfed	200.4	145.7	8.6
Gwynedd	204.0	147.7	4.6
Dumfries & Galloway	205.3	—	8.2
Lincolnshire	206.7	145.4	8.8
Devon	208.3	150.6	3.4
Tayside	210.1	148.7	2.1
Shropshire	211.6	141.6	5.6
North Yorkshire	216.4	152.1	5.4
Great Britain	245.8	164.2	1.5

Source: Department of Employment, *New Earnings Survey*, 1988, HMSO

> Evidence of both income profiles and other 'levels of living' indicators suggest that extensive rural areas suffer from many of the symptoms of household deprivation which characterise older industrial areas.
>
> (Shaw, 1979, 183)

Comparative use of indicators from the Census of Population is difficult because many Census measures, and forms of interpretation such as social area analysis, were designed for urban areas. Cullingford and Openshaw (1982) stressed that there was no agreement on the way in which deprivation differs between rural and urban areas. However, they did find it possible to identify Census enumeration districts of relative rural deprivation, characterized by low female activity rates, higher levels of unemployment, a high proportion walking to work, and higher levels of council housing, unfurnished tied dwellings and dwellings without toilets.

It is argued that, whereas rural 'household' deprivation is akin to that experienced by families in the cities (though it is evidently less serious in rural Britain), the second type of deprivation, based on a lack of opportunities, often takes a different form in rural areas (Shaw, 1979, 185). Shaw's view is that the distinctive feature of rural deprivation lies in *opportunity deprivation* – the lack of jobs and of choice of jobs, and the decline of private and public services – compounded by *mobility deprivation*: 'There is a consensus in all descriptive writing on rural problems, clearly validated by Moseley (1979), that the elderly, young children, teenagers, mothers at home, and the infirm, as well as the poor, all tend to be disadvantaged if they lack access to a car' (Shaw, 1979, 189).

In a policy definition of England's neediest rural areas made in 1984, the Rural Development Commission identified their 'Rural Development Areas' (RDAs) from many of the features which we have so far discussed. Their choice of areas focused on parishes where

1 unemployment is above the average for Great Britain, account being taken of changes in recent years;
2 there is an inadequate or unsatisfactory range of employment opportunities;
3 population decline or sparsity of population is having an adverse effect;
4 there is a net outward migration of people of working age;
5 the age structure of the population is heavily biased towards elderly people;
6 access to services and facilities is poor.

On this basis, the Commissioners identified groups of 25 or more parishes to form the Areas shown at Figure 11.3, similar to their earlier Special Investment Areas, which were for the reception of small factory projects. The RDAs also received Rural Development Programmes, designed with local authorities and other bodies. Their general aims contain an idealistic mention of 'integrated rural development' as between policies concerned with economic, social, community and voluntary projects. Many reports for the Development Commission stress the scope for much greater integration between government agencies in their work for rural areas: to that extent, linkage is recognized between different problems in the same area. There have been calls for wider RDAs and more intensive help for them. It would

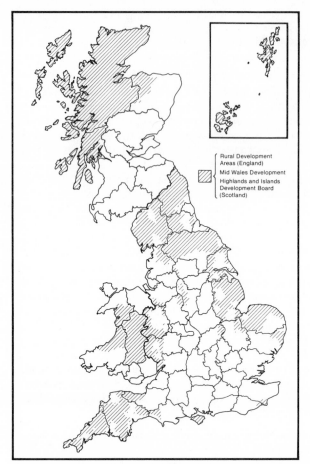

Figure 11.3 Rural priority areas. Great Britain. These include Rural Development Areas defined by the Rural Development Commission from 1984 onwards. Source: Rural Development Commission, Mid-Wales Development, Highlands and Islands Development Board.

be misleading, however, to suggest that there was the same mix of linked problems in all rural problem areas. For instance, by October 1987, unemployment rates varied between 19.8 per cent in the South Yorkshire RDA and 3.9 per cent in the Staffordshire RDA, while the average for all RDAs (8.0 per cent) was *below* the rate for England as a whole (10.3 per cent). This is largely because lower proportions of people attempt to enter the labour market in rural parishes. We may say, however, that, compared with urban areas, the outer rural areas now suffer more from low income than from unemployment.

Employment conditions in outer rural areas

Although there has been considerable employment change, the labour market in outer rural areas is characterized by a restricted sectoral and occupational range of opportunities as well as by low income. A survey of 93 young people in rural areas (Stern and Turbin, 1986) found that 86 had left school at or before 16 with less than five 'O' Level qualifications, that 37 were engaged on the Youth Training Scheme at the time of the survey, and that 79 had experienced periods of unemployment, 21 more than once. Employment problems were seen as differing from those of urban areas because of the role of agriculture, which recruits selectively from certain families and sets 'a low pay norm that affects an entire area' (Stern and Turbin, 1986, 68); because of the constraints of difficult and costly transport for firms and young people; and because of the limited range of local employers and jobs available. Local firms tend to be very small, while the branches of large national organizations tend to offer only a limited range of low-skilled or narrowly-skilled jobs, with seasonal peaks relying on part-time and casual labour. There is no suggestion that jobs in rural areas were any less segregated in terms of gender than jobs in urban areas.

The distinctive sectoral structure of jobs in 'remoter, mainly rural' areas is shown in Table 11.4, compared with equivalent data for Great Britain as a whole. The data exclude the self-employed, for instance many farmers. Agriculture and horticulture are found to provide less than 8 per cent of jobs, whereas the service sector provides 63 per cent of all work; this is a lower proportion than in Great Britain, and there is a marked bias in favour of hotels and catering. In some 'remoter, mainly rural' districts, hotels and catering represented nearly 10 per cent of employees in September 1987. Power stations and waterworks are important in some rural areas, but manufacturing is now almost as important as in the country as a whole. One systematic feature is the role of food manufacturing, which is almost twice as important proportionately in these areas as in England and Wales at large, and provides half as many jobs as the primary sector itself. Its most

Table 11.4 Structure of employment in remoter, mainly rural, districts, 1987 (employees in employment

	Remoter, mainly rural, areas		Great Britain
	000s	%	%
Primary industries	177.5	9.4	3.9
Agriculture and horticulture	146.0	7.7	1.5
Energy and water	31.5	1.7	2.4
Manufacturing, incl.	421.6	22.2	24.0
Food, drink & tobacco	92.1	4.9	2.6
Construction	102.0	5.4	4.7
Service sector, incl.	1 195.7	63.0	67.4
Retail distribution	179.7	9.5	9.7
Wholesale distribution	112.1	5.9	5.0
Hotels & catering	134.2	7.1	4.9
Transport & communication	102.9	5.4	6.0
Banking, finance etc	118.6	6.3	10.9
Public administration etc	142.8	7.5	7.5
Education	140.9	7.4	7.4
Medical services etc	111.8	5.9	6.4
Total	1 896.8	100.0	100.0

Source: Census of Employment, NOMIS

important sectors (in number of employees) are the processing of poultry and fruit and vegetables, followed by that of bacon and meat, milk and milk products, and bread and flour. These 'off-the-farm' jobs of the food industry may be significantly involved in future policy changes for agriculture.

This structure, of itself, barely appears conducive to the employment growth which has in fact occurred in outer rural areas over the last two decades. The 53 Rural Areas recognized by the Newcastle University Local Labour Market Area classification (see Champion *et al.*, 1987) expanded their aggregate number of employees by 7.9 per cent between 1971 and 1981, and by a further 3.2 per cent between 1981 and 1984. This record of course stands in marked contrast to the national (GB) *decline* of 2.5 per cent in the first period and 1.2 per cent in the second. Areas of growth in both periods were far flung; in the first period, the leading rural LLMAs for percentage rates of growth in Great Britain were recorded as Dingwall (Highland), Stornoway (Shetland), Truro (Cornwall), Lanark (Strathclyde) and Bangor (Gwynedd). In the period 1981–87, there is more differentiation between North and South: the leading rates of growth were attributable to Newmarket (Cambs.), Chard (Somerset), Truro (Cornwall), Northallerton (N. Yorks.) and Welshpool (Powys).

The overall performance of the 'remoter, mainly rural' areas of OPCS, 1981–87, showed a greater proportionate expansion of employment than did the 'prosperous sub-regions' of Chapter 9, taken as a whole. Table 11.5 demonstrates the extent to which the strong employment growth of rural Britain has resulted from the better performance of individual sectors rather than from any advantage of inherited economic structure. With reference to

Table 11.5 The structure of employment change in remoter, mainly rural, districts, 1981–87, by North/South groups (employees in employment)

	South			North		
	Total change		Diff.	Total change		Diff.
	000s	%	shift, %	000s	%	shift, %
Agriculture, forestry etc	− 9.7	−10.6	+ 0.9	−13.1	−17.1	− 5.6
Energy and water supply	− 3.3	−20.8	+ 7.4	− 4.7	−20.1	+ 8.1
Other minerals, etc	− 2.4	− 7.5	+16.8	− 4.4	−15.6	+ 8.6
Metal goods, engineering	− 7.8	− 7.1	+11.6	− 0.4	− 0.8	+17.9
Other manufacturing	+ 1.8	+ 1.3	+ 9.8	+ 1.1	+ 1.3	+ 9.8
Construction	− 2.3	− 4.1	+ 2.3	− 8.7	−15.3	− 7.2
Distribution, hotels, etc	+27.3	+12.0	+ 8.4	+ 4.8	+ 2.9	− 0.8
Transport etc	+ 4.4	+ 7.7	+16.1	+ 0.5	+ 1.2	+ 9.6
Banking, finance etc	+21.9	+42.2	+ 8.8	+ 6.9	+ 8.3	−15.1
Other services	+44.3	+17.4	+ 6.8	+34.1	+15.8	+ 5.1
Total, of which	+74.0	+ 7.2	+ 8.3	+16.1	+ 2.1	+ 2.6
Males	+ 2.8	+ 0.5	+ 6.3	−20.5	− 4.5	+ 1.3
Females	+71.1	+16.8	+11.2	+36.7	+11.3	+ 5.0
Full-time	+25.0	+ 3.2	+ 7.6	−18.7	− 3.1	+ 0.9
Part-time	+48.9	+20.4	+ 9.7	+34.9	+19.6	+ 8.5
Tourism-related industries	+12.4	+18.8	+ 9.6	+ 9.7	+15.7	+ 7.9

Note: Diff. = differential
Source: Census of Employment, NOMIS

northern and southern 'remoter, mainly rural' districts, the table partitions the net growth for the period 1981–87 between the sexes and sectors, and identifies the 'differential shift' of employment which is left after accounting for national sectoral changes. The overall picture might appear sluggish in predominantly male-employing sectors. However, the overall net increase of employment in both South and North (7.2 and 2.1 per cent respectively) was almost entirely due to positive 'differential shifts', that is to say, to smaller decreases and greater increases in different industries than would be 'expected' from the respective national performances of those industries. In the South, such favourable 'differential shifts' for rural areas are recorded in all ten industries of Table 11.5, notably in manufacturing sectors. In the rest of Britain, three sectors performed worse than in Britain as a whole and male and full-time employment declined. In both parts of Britain, the leading type of employment growth lay in a miscellaneous range of services, including banking and finance. However, the achievement of manufacturing in 'rural areas' in this period was to show only a 2.8 per cent decline, much smaller than the national contraction of 15.7 per cent.

A wide and miscellaneous range of industries was responsible for this 'favourable performance', including food industries, plastics and timber, and general engineering. The past growth of industries in rural areas from a comparatively low level has been attributed to improved infrastructure, the residential attractiveness of these areas for managers, and lower costs of premises and labour, amounting to a very different alternative socio-economic environment for investment from that of established industrial areas (as noted for Cornwall by Massey, 1984).

Increments of growth in these small economies have been sensitive to administrative action through government policies. For instance, Thetford (Norfolk) was among the areas of greatest manufacturing increase in Britain in the 1970s (Table 6.6 above), partly because of the role of its overspill housing scheme in inducing inward manufacturing movement; Dingwall (Highland Region) and Barnstaple (Devon) appear partly because of their designation as 'assisted areas' under regional policy.

What is the role of RDAs (and their predecessors, Special Investment Areas) of the Rural Development Commission and the formerly separate Council for Small Industries in Rural Areas (CoSIRA), which it now incorporates? Whereas the Commission used to operate throughout Great Britain, the establishment of the Scottish and Welsh Development Agencies in 1975 and 1976 restricted its activities to England, and focused there its building of factories (and conversion of other buildings). From 1974 to 1984, 921 factories were built, yielding by March 1984 an estimate of 'at least 4,740' jobs, including some relocations (Chisholm, 1985, 287). Similarly, ECOTEC Research and Consulting Ltd. (1988) estimated that about 4,050 job opportunities had arisen from the later total of 1,100 factory units developed by the Rural Development Commission.

In the context of Table 11.5 such policy efforts may be enough to help *stabilize* the level of manufacturing activity of outer rural areas. In the absence of disaggregated employment data after 1987, it is clear from later unemployment records that the 'remoter, mainly rural' areas enjoyed their full share of the national reduction of unemployment during the remainder of the 1980s. It would be wrong to see any major contribution to the employment question of rural areas coming from manufacturing *growth* (Fothergill *et al.*, 1985). All the evidence is that the 1980s growth of rural employment levels was attributable to service employment sectors.

Services: employment and facilities in outer rural areas

Providing services is the main function carried on in rural as in urban areas. To some extent, the outer rural areas are providing for people from other areas in the shape of the adventitious population of in-migrants and holidaymakers. The provision of services to a low-density population might be thought to require more service-workers per head of population than in urban areas. Both these factors would give the service sector a higher share of total employment than in the country as a whole. In fact, Table 11.4 showed that the outer rural areas had a marginally smaller share than average. This might then measure the deprivation which is frequently alleged to afflict outer rural areas, especially in connection with the lower representation there of most levels of the hierarchy of service centres, and the 'gravitation of services up the settlement hierarchy'.

Banking and finance are the service sectors least well represented in rural areas, whereas hotels and catering are over-represented (Table 11.4). All of these were prominent, however, in the absolute and 'differential' shift of employment to rural areas of the South in the period 1981–87 (Table 11.5). The growth of 32,100 jobs in 'distribution, hotels, catering and repairs' is fairly similar to the growth of female and part-time employment, but is difficult to identify precisely with the growth of tourism. Some of this growth is the work of farmers' wives (who are not employees in employment and are therefore not included in the tables), although the scale of farm tourism, and therefore its multipliers, is easily exaggerated (Winter, 1987). In Cornwall, tourism is seen as an industry as large as agriculture but,

> Tourism in Padstow cannot be seen simply as an 'industry' clearly defined by conventional means and producing calculable cash inflows and numbers of jobs. Rather, it has been, and remains, an amorphous, complex and fragmented economic activity, providing a main livelihood for a few, and only part-time, seasonal, casual, unpredictable or unofficial contributions to the income and employment of others.
>
> (Gilligan, 1987, 72–3)

The process of counterurbanization in Cornwall includes a net inflow of economically-active migrants (Perry *et al.*, 1986), some of them attracted to set up tourist businesses as in Looe (Shaw and Williams, 1988). For the latest available period (1981–87; Figure 6.2 above), Cornwall showed a slightly below average rate of increase in 'tourism-related industries'. Among 'other, outer rural counties' those which grew faster than the national average included North Yorkshire, Dyfed, Shropshire and Cumbria. However, Devon showed a decrease reflecting the decline in popularity of some traditional English resorts. Overall, Table 11.5 showed that the 'tourism-related industries' expanded by somewhat more than the GB average, 13.5 per cent, in the 'remoter, mainly rural' areas. Thus, special problems of definition, measurement and year-to-year variation make it difficult to record the growth of tourism, or therefore to claim that, as a favourite growth industry of government, it is the main salvation so far of rural economies.

On the other hand, while the *village* shop is clearly in decline, it is difficult to agree with rural 'pressure groups' that retailing is in disproportionate decline in rural areas as a whole. In market towns, shop rents rose between 1982 and 1986 by 12.1 per cent annually, compared with 8.8 per cent nationally (Hillier Parker, 1986). These points raise questions for the debate on the nature of rural problems. Campaigns of the 1970s originated from county and district councils:

> The effects of the 1974 local government reorganizations, linked to changes in the distribution of rate support grant, had provided a crisis of identity for many of these bodies. Consequently, in campaigning for rates-support to be adjusted in their favour they placed inordinate emphasis on the decline of rural services, with Rural Community Councils and planning departments vying to produce 'league tables of woe' for the eyes of the Department of the Environment.
>
> (Lowe, Bradley and Wright, 1987, 26)

However, when we consider only the smaller towns and villages, we can see a very systematic threat to all services in the 1970s (Standing Conference of Rural Community Councils, 1978) and in the 1980s. Essentially, a vicious circle is in operation, whereby village commercial facilities are unable to compete with the reduced unit costs of town competitors; increased car ownership takes trade away from village shops, with their limited sales population, to the towns, which thereby gain a cumulatively increasing share of rural business. A survey of five English rural areas (McLaughlin, 1986) found that only half of all households with a shop in their area actually used it for the bulk of their shopping requirements, due to higher local prices; those with no transport – the elderly and those on low incomes – were the main local shoppers. Only 17 per cent of households were in parishes with no shop; nonetheless, reports from most parts of the country indicate progressive decline in the number of shops; in County Durham, Weardale lost one in five of its shops between 1972 and 1982, and Teesdale 7 per cent. Particular problems arise from the closure of chemists' shops. Changes in the economics of petrol stations have had disproportionate effects in rural areas; national banks have had to review the retention of their smallest branches; brewery chains have reduced competition between their 'local' public houses.

In public services, the politics of the 1980s have challenged long-established modes of provision in rural areas. Upon the privatization of British Telecom, there were widespread fears, following the experience of de-regulation in the USA, over future levels of rural telephone charges and provision of public telephones. Sub-post offices have lost a considerable proportion of their work through the increased payment of state pensions through banks, so in 1987 the Post Office adopted new contracts which would convert about half the rural post offices to part-time opening. Most government agencies have begun the process of closing their smallest units; for instance, the closure of rural Job Centres and Employment Offices began in 1983. The Home Office recommended in 1986 the amalgamation of local benches of magistrates in a drive to cut costs, inevitably affecting RDAs. The availability of legal services in rural areas is difficult (Blacksell *et al.*, 1988). In certain rural counties the financial problems of the National Health Service have been manifested through closures of cottage hospitals. For instance in Shropshire, the District Health Authority announced proposals in 1988 to close ten hospitals, which would leave most acute services and much outpatients work located at only two centres, i.e. Shrewsbury and Telford. In general, people from rural communities are faced with much longer journeys to hospital (whether as patients or visitors) than town-dwellers. Rural access to hospitals by public transport is generally poor, and, in the case of some communities, impossible.

Of all the rural issues, however, few are more sensitive than the closure of schools, a responsibility, like libraries, of county councils. Following the closure of many rural secondary schools from the 1950s onwards, 90 per cent of secondary school pupils in rural areas lived beyond reasonable walking distance of their schools in MacLaughlin's (1986) survey; even the figure for primary school children had increased to 50 per cent following successive rounds of closures of small schools in many counties. Government proposals of 1986 urged the closure of all primary schools with fewer than three teachers, theoretically making 90 the minimum viable number of pupils. Even though Norfolk, with one of the most radical sets of proposals, set a minimum size of 60, this would have closed more than 100 primary schools. Parents are entitled to take objections to school closures to the central government. In the late 1980s there appeared to be fewer disputes as the government was taking a more flexible approach. For, in addition to providing problems for the pupils themselves in being 'bussed' to other schools, the loss of a village school removes a focus of identity, and a possible meeting place for social groups, and may deter the in-migration to the area of younger married couples.

There are many villages where the school bus is the only one ever seen. Increased car ownership and the low density of population made the conventional bus increasingly uneconomic from the 1950s onwards. Government legislation from the 1970s onwards increasingly tried to en-courage integration of public and school transport services, and the develop-ment of rural taxis, minibuses and community-based car volunteer schemes. There are examples of successful innovative schemes in different parts of the country; for example, the Post Office has operated over 160 post-bus services in different parts of the country, especially the Highlands of Scotland. The Transport Act of 1985, however, was a threat to rural areas because it removed general subsidies supplied by county councils to bus operators (which allowed cross-subsidization from urban to rural areas) and replaced them by specific subsidies for routes which, at a given time, operators were not prepared to run on a commercial basis. In general, this process of 'deregulation' did not appear to have as severe an effect on bus services as many critics anticipated. However, services can be curtailed and withdrawn much more readily than before. Official statements suggested that three years' worth of statistics would be needed to assess overall trends. The general trend of decline certainly means that it would be unwise for anyone (for instance, a retired couple moving to a rural area) to rely on the continuation of bus services to any but the very largest villages.

In England, these problems are monitored in each county by Rural Community Councils, in conjunction with the Rural Development Commission. There is significant scope for circulating advice to county and village organizations about taking action into their own hands (Woollett, 1982), for instance, in mobilizing support to keep a village school, in encouraging the growth of mobile service deliveries (Moseley and Packman, 1987) or in organizing car transport to town hospitals. In Scotland, many of the problems of remoter communities have a longstanding record of attention from the government's Scottish Office. The Highlands and Islands Development Board (Grassie, 1983) is generally recognized as a successful body, both in its prime task of assisting growth in new and existing businesses and in relating this to community and environmental needs. Many of the trends described in this chapter apply to rural Scotland; the demographic record is complicated by the far-reaching effects of North Sea oil development on small communities, yet it appears that forces of 'counter-urbanization' have been independently producing net gains through migration for a number of Highland districts (Jones *et al.*, 1986). In this chapter, however, we will illustrate issues facing outer rural areas with an example from rural Wales, where the distinctive institution is the Development Board for Rural Wales.

A case study: the County of Powys

One of the most remarkable reversals of population trends is that achieved by rural Wales, where expansions between 1971 and 1981 in Gwynedd (+9,900), Dyfed (+13,600) and Powys (+11,300) contributed to the principality's overall increase of 59,200 (2 per cent). After a century of depopulation, the original counties of Montgomery, Radnor and Brecon were merged in 1974 to form the County of Powys, still however with the smallest population of any county of England and Wales (including the Isle of Wight). Yet it stood among the leading five counties of England and Wales for its rate of population growth in the 1970s and showed the second highest rate of growth of all Welsh counties between 1981 and 1988, entirely due to migration which much more than compensated for the county's natural population decrease. Even more remarkably, Powys was recorded as achieving the greatest percentage growth of manufacturing employment of the counties of England and Wales, 1981–87, followed by its neighbours, Clwyd and Shropshire.

Powys remains central to the concerns of the Development Board for Rural Wales, a successor to the Mid-Wales Industrial Development Association (MWIDA), which in turn was founded in 1957, eight years before the Highlands and Islands Development Board. If we recall the low wages of outer rural counties (Table 11.3), it is not surprising that Welsh farmers regarded the proposed attraction of industry (which might raise wage levels) as an economic as well as a cultural threat (Levay, 1979; Broady, 1980). The Welsh Office from 1964, however, recognized depopulation as an urgent problem and the attraction of external industry was attempted through focusing development on Newtown, in the Severn Valley of Montgomery, and on 'Special Towns' and 'Key Towns'. The small size of most towns such as Llanfyllin and Builth Wells, and of most hamlets, meant that the planning philosophy of concentrating growth was adopted by MWIDA for economic and social reasons. Cloke (1983) applauds the Powys County Council Structure Plan for encouraging development both in and around designated growth centres and also notes, in the national context, that,

> We are thus presented with something of a paradox in terms of the fate of hinterland villages. On the one hand, reductions in life-style opportunities in these locations are well-documented. . . . On the other hand, in all but the most remote locations, there remains an element of in-migration (particularly of the retired and affluent) which, whether or not it is sufficient to counteract out-migration, changes the social structure of hinterland villages.
>
> (Cloke, 1983, 109–10)

This paradox, which spans the different themes of this chapter, is fully evident in Powys, where net inward migration has overtaken the negative trends affecting the tiny indigenous population. Between 1971 and 1981 the number of agricultural employees in Powys fell by 750 (16.7 per cent) and male employment as a whole increased by only 160 (1.0 per cent), compared with a female increase of 2,520 (26.3 per cent). In effect, efforts at industrial development simply stabilized male employment (which declined in Britain as a whole), and the record of population increase can be matched in employment data only by including females, to yield an overall increase of 2,680 jobs (10.2 per cent).

The growth of 1,600 in manufacturing employment was almost wholly concentrated in Newtown and Welshpool, under the efforts of the Development Board including the planned development of Newtown. Reappraisal was needed, however, in the 1980s (Wenger, 1980; Hedger, 1981; Pettigrew, 1987; Thomas and Drudy, 1987). The area was affected by recession in the 1981 closure of the largest new factory in Newtown, a branch of GKN of the West Midlands. Including the growth of the Laura Ashley group factory at Newtown, factory employment in Powys increased by 1,500 between 1981 and 1987, while male employment expanded by 800 and total employment by 2,400 (7.2 per cent).

The role of outside forces is clear. Of 134 factory lettings in 1986/87 in mid Wales, 70 were to outside businesses, with the largest number from the south east of England (Development Board for Rural Wales, 1987). Of 27,200 in-migrants to Powys in the five years 1984–88, 20,600 (75.5 per cent) originated elsewhere than Wales, including 6,100 (22.5 per cent) from the West Midlands Region and 5,700 (20.9 per cent) from the South East. These are proportionately very large flows, not only representing altogether 25.1 per cent of the county's 1985 population; but accelerating from a low point in the immediate post-recession years 1981–84. As usual in migration statistics there was a large counterstream, one of 20,400 for 1984–88, with many of the same spatial characteristics. Overall, there were net inward flows from all counties barring a handful of fellow rural areas (such as Dyfed, North Yorkshire and Devon; Figure 11.4), producing favourable balances with the rest of Wales (+600), the West Midlands (+1,000) and the South East (+2,200).

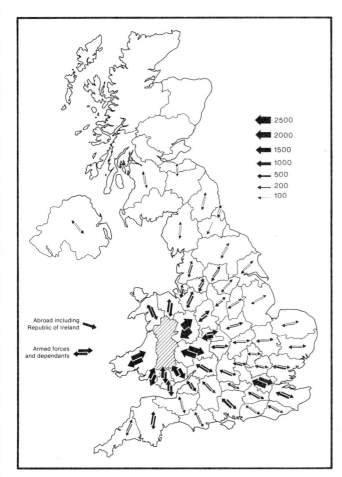

Figure 11.4 Migration flows to and from the County of Powys, 1984–88. Source: National Health Service Central Register, NOMIS.

What is even more diagnostic of the contemporary process of counter-urbanization is Powys' migration balance in different age groups (Table 11.6). Only in the age group 16–19 was there a net loss of population. Of the overall net gain of 6,800 people, nearly half (3,300) may be attributed to people aged 50 and over. For instance, in the ages 50–69, the county gained twice as many people by migration as it lost, and by the mid 1980s was among the leading twelve counties for the proportion of its population of pensionable age. It is this factor of the migration of the elderly, together with a resulting small excess of deaths over births, which will reconcile the population and employment trends of the area, and which suggests that the expansion of service employment is partly the result of population increase, rather than the cause.

We might expect, however, that the growth of services was affected by tourism. 'Mid Wales has an up-market tourism potential but a down-market tradition and perception' (House of Commons, 1986, 289). In the latest

Table 11.6 The age structure of migrants to and from the County of Powys, 1984–88

Age Group	In	Out	Net gain
0–15	6 000	4 200	+1 700
16–19	1 600	2 600	−1 000
20–24	3 300	3 300	+ 0
25–29	2 900	2 200	+ 700
30–39	4 300	3 100	+1 300
40–49	2 500	1 700	+ 800
50–59	2 300	1 100	+1 200
60–69	2 400	1 100	+1 300
70 and over	2 000	1 200	+ 800
Total	27 200	20 400	+6 800

Source: National Health Service Central Register, NOMIS

available employment data (for 1981–87), the 'tourism-related industries' increased employment by less than 100 (5.0 per cent), accompanying 'the first real signs of recovery in the mid-Wales tourism market' (Development Board for Rural Wales, 1987, 20). This is a modest contribution when it is considered that further job losses meant that the wider area of Powys, Ceredigion and Meirionnydd required 14,000 jobs to be created per annum, 1985–91; it would be a difficult task to provide a fifth of these from tourism (House of Commons, 1986, 290).

Powys has lower unemployment than the remoter areas (Ceredigion and Meirionnydd) to the west of the Cambrian Mountains; but even in Powys, the growth of a small new town, and proportionately heavy net inward migration, are thus not seen to have eliminated the socio-economic problems of local people, though the cultural problems of accommodating English people are much less than in the areas further west which have a more thoroughly Welsh-speaking tradition.

The future of land use and employment

The economy and landscape of outer rural areas were seen as being under renewed threat in the later 1980s. Re-evaluation of European farming quotas was seen to require less agricultural production, with a range of consequent land use and multiplier effects. For instance, 'agricultural uncertainties and cuts in production affect jobs "off the farm" just as much as those on it. The first round of milk quotas took its toll and the second round has revived speculation about the future of major processing plants in mid Wales. This was heightened by the collapse of Welsh Quality Lambs plc which had been a major consumer of local sheep stock' (Development Board for Rural Wales, 1987, 12–13).

There were visions of a new perspective for farming in which agriculture was seen not merely as a producer of food but as a multi-purpose industry, also capable of servicing the nation's needs for the protection of landscape and wildlife, tourism, forestry, energy and the revival of rural economies. In presenting the implications of market changes in 1987, the Minister of

Agriculture was concerned to compensate farmers once more for threatened losses of income, only this time by extending help and liberalizing regulations so as to generate non-agricultural income for farmers. Encouragement would be given to the establishment of golf courses, riding schools and paddocks. There were controversial proposals, deferred in 1989, to exempt all kinds of farmers' developments on farmland from planning controls, while the longstanding presumption against planning permission for housing was to be removed on all but the best agricultural land. While there would be an extension of payments to cultivate 'environmentally sensitive areas' in traditional, less destructive ways, it appeared that subsidies for forestry would extend the controversial planting of coniferous woodland.

In many ways the pace of change is likely to be more gradual than the debate suggested, but the regional impact of different European policy options varies considerably (Harvey, 1986). Bell (1987) argued that, although between 1.2 and 2.2 million hectares of land were already surplus to agricultural use, significant areas of land were unlikely to become derelict or unused in the immediate future. In general, a decline in Community Agricultural Policy support was forecast to have a *positive* effect on the environment. The Countryside Commission (1987) thought that land-use diversification could be specifically linked to 'creative' uses including new woodland, wildlife reserves, public amenity and recreation and improved access. In a 1988 scheme of support for private forestry, the government required new planting to respect rights of way, nature sites and ancient monuments, and provided higher grants for smaller woods and broad-leaved trees than for larger woods and coniferous stands. The target was to plant 12,000 ha a year, whereas applications in the first year would cover 7,100 ha.

The National Farmers Union argued that of 1.4 million ha taken out of agricultural use by 1995, only 285,000 ha would be taken up by woodland. There is some agreement that farm diversification, including forestry and farm tourism, can replace some employment. However, the Countryside Commission (1987) argued that the restructuring of the existing pattern of agriculture would require 150,000 new jobs by the year 2000. (On all of Bell's 1987 estimates, the majority of job losses would be from 'upstream' and 'downstream' linkages with farming, i.e. from suppliers and processing industries.) The Countryside Commission was critical that the Rural Development Commission's Programmes were restricted to RDAs and narrowly focused on issues of direct concern to itself. The Countryside Commission's statements leave the impression that many of the new jobs would have to be in the service sector.

The Rural Development Commission is much clearer that the solution to rural unemployment lies off the farm rather than on it. In emphasizing its role of making premises available, and providing advice and business development support, it is simply deploying the Conservative government's general emphasis on small-scale, indigenous industry. Whether any dramatic results or changes are possible is another issue. One view is that the thrust of 'counterurbanization' will be enhanced by modern telecommunications; former office workers might be able to undertake work from an outer rural location through use of telephone links to provide on-line communication of text and data with a parent office in another part of the country; businesses in rural areas might be able to function more effectively with special data links. An example of this, jointly by Powys County Council and British Telecom, is the new 'Mid-Wales City Connection', which brings together the latest telecommunications equipment by which 'a businessman can stay in touch from the heart of rural Wales'. Certainly, freelance writers provide examples of this possibility at work. Nonetheless, there are many fears that the competitive development of major trunk telecommunications routes between cities will only heighten the relative disadvantages of outer rural areas (Gillespie and Goddard, 1986).

The future for outer rural areas seems to show further relative improvement compared with other types of area. As stated in Chapter 5, it seems unlikely that manufacturing will actually yield net increases of jobs in rural areas. A gradual growth of service employment is the likely scenario, some of it in tourism, but much of it involved in servicing the incoming population of migrants. This will reflect the repopulation and restructuring that is going on in rural communities, creating a population of plural interests which requires sensitive integrated planning.

Further reading

There is now a very extensive literature on rural areas, even without including the European and world material, and many different standpoints are taken. One starting point of the approach taken in this chapter is reflected in Ashton and Long (1972). Traditional rural social life is analysed in Frankenberg (1966). A radical approach to the sociology of political power in the countryside is taken by Newby (1980, 1986, 1988). The associated issue of land ownership by capital was taken up by Massey and Catalano (1978).

Attention to social problems was led by Shaw (1979), with contributions from Knox and Cottam (1981); from Phillips and Williams (1984) and from Lowe *et al.*, (1987).

The implications of an ageing population have been developed by Warnes (1982), and by Rowles (1986). The related topic of urban–rural population shifts is examined by Cloke (1985); by Perry *et al.*, (1986); and by Champion (1989d).

Several books were addressed to the whole field of 'rural geography', by Pacione (1983, 1984), Gilg (1985), and Hoggart and Buller (1987). Rural settlement planning is considered by Blacksell and Gilg (1981); Clark (1982); and Cloke (1983, 1987). A more specialized issue has been assessed by Coppock (1977).

The wide topic of conservation and land use is exemplified by a number of volumes; MacEwen and MacEwen (1981); Green (1981); Open University (1985); Lockhart and Ilbery (1987); Mercer and Puttnam (1988); and Blunden and Curry (1988).

Factory farms and the growth of rural industry are considered in Healey and Ilbery (1985). The Scottish dimension is exemplified by Grassie (1983). Accessibility and transport are considered by Moseley (1979), and by Farrington (1985). The opportunities for villages to help themselves are collated in Woollett (1981).

PART IV

The Next Decade

12

Future directions and policy issues

Part III was concerned with the present characteristics and conditions of different types of places. It also looked at the ways in which these places have been affected by the underlying forces of national and international change, particularly with respect to economic developments and socio-demographic trends. Though we have referred there to the potential of these places and described the challenges which they currently face, we have left consideration of future directions principally to this final chapter. Not only does this require a different approach involving a greater degree of specu-lation, as opposed to description and historical analysis, but in addition it is of basic methodological importance that the prospects for individual types of places should be seen in relation to each other and in the overall context of the evolving map of Britain. Places are becoming increasingly interdepen-dent: what happens in one is likely to have major effects on another – something which is very important within the national territory, but which is also true on the global scale (Chapter 2).

Looking ahead, we see the final years of the twentieth century as particu-larly fascinating for geographical study, as previous chapters in this book have hinted. The 1990s follow ten years of major upheaval in Britain's economy and spatial patterns, involving more massive changes than any decade for over a century, the 1930s depression years notwithstanding. As shown in Part I the 1980s have been interpreted by some as the first stage of a fifth 50–60 year Kondratieff cycle associated with telecommunications, the 'information economy' and biotechnology, while others see the past decade as the dawn of a new 'post-industrial' era replacing the relatively short-lived industrial phase and re-introducing some of the spatial patterns of pre-industrial times. Every decade springs its surprises (see our Preface to this book), but the 1990s begin with us already aware of many forces for change: the introduction of the Single European Market ('1992'), the scheduled completion of the Channel Tunnel in 1993, the effects of the 'demographic time bomb' on staff recruitment and wages, the further growth of profes-sional and managerial occupations and of home ownership, the probability of further contraction in manufacturing jobs, the greater availability and use of telecommunications networks, the recently acknowledged need to find alternative uses for surplus farmland, the possibility of having to provide homes for thousands of Hong Kong residents before the colony's return to China in 1997, and so on.

In terms of spatial patterns, a wide range of questions is raised by these developments and by the trends noted in previous chapters, amongst them the following. Will they confer even greater advantages on southern England, or allow the wider dispersal of the new forms of growth? Will the South East end up with even greater 'town cramming' and 'gridlock', or will these problems be solved by a more favourable attitude to new settlements and road construction? Are cities like Liverpool and Glasgow going to see a significant revival, or are they doomed to slip further down the EC rankings? How fast will the revival of inner city areas proceed, and how far is this likely to provide new opportunities for ethnic minorities and low-skill workers and curb the development of an 'underclass'? Can a viable rural economy be maintained in the face of the further rationalization of agricultural holdings and the continued penetration of urban influences?

In this concluding chapter, we do not see it as our job to provide categorical answers to all these questions, even if we could. What we aim to do is provide a framework for anticipating events and identify the factors which we feel will have most influence on geographical developments through the decade. We begin by examining the official population projections for different areas and the questions which they raise, before going on to look at the expected trends in employment and their implications for regions and cities. The subsequent section focuses on environmental and 'quality of life' issues, which are likely to take on an even greater political prominence in the 1990s than in the last few years and have particular relevance for the future of the Greater South East and the balance of advantage between North and South. This leads us to believe that a revival of interest in spatial policy and strategic planning is inevitable during the decade, though at the same time a brief glimpse at Britain's changing fortunes on the international scene reminds us of the limits to state intervention. In sum, our biggest concern is that the degree of complexity and uncertainty which faces the UK should be seen as the justification for greater consideration of these matters rather than – as was the general attitude of the 1980s – as an excuse for ignoring them.

Population forecasts and their implications

Population constitutes one of the chief parameters for looking into the future. Just as we argued in Chapter 4 that population change poses many of the key questions for geographical inquiry, here too we can use it to set the scene for anticipating the trends of the 1990s and beyond and discussing the issues which they raise. Chapter 4 drew attention to the major changes which took place in the 1970s and 1980s in population distribution and composition in spite of the relative stability of overall numbers of people. What overall level of population change is expected in the next few years? Will London continue the recovery which it experienced in the 1980s or resume the high levels of population loss recorded in the previous decade? Will the greatest increases remain concentrated in the prosperous sub-regions of the Greater South East or spread out to bring even greater changes to the more remote rural areas? Are the provincial cities and industrial areas expected to decline further, or is some narrowing of the North–South divide anticipated?

The official population projections provide the starting point for answering these questions. At the time of writing (January 1990) national projections based on 1987 population estimates look forward as far as 2057 (OPCS, 1989), while at sub-national scales Wales and Scotland have 1987-based projections running up to 2006 and England has 1985-based projections to 2001 (Welsh Office, 1989; Registrar General Scotland, 1989; OPCS, 1988b). For the country as a whole (Table 12.1) it is expected that up to 2001, the population will grow at an annual rate approaching 0.3 per cent – considerably more rapidly than over the 17 years up to 1988 (cf. Table 4.1), but still modest by comparison with the 0.5–0.6 per cent recorded during the 1950s and 1960s. Thereafter, a slower rate of growth is forecast up to the late 2020s, but then in turn the entry of the 1960s 'baby boom' cohorts into retirement age groups leads to population *decline* through till at least 2057 (Table 12.1). The immediate prospects therefore are for stronger growth pressures than experienced recently, which – because they are due primarily to more births as opposed to fewer deaths or changing migration assumptions – will have their main short- to medium-term implications for maternity and child-care facilities, schooling and family-size housing. Trends in labour supply and numbers of households over the next few years relate, as we shall show below, to the demographic developments of the past two decades and to changes in behaviour amongst the existing population.

Unfortunately, it is impossible to calculate the population prospects specifically for the framework of locality types used in Part III, because sub-national projections for England and Wales are available only at county level outside Greater London and the metropolitan counties. Nevertheless, a reasonably clear indication of their separate prospects can be obtained from the county-level patterns shown in Figure 12.1. Cambridgeshire is expected to be the fastest-growing county over this decade, with some 15 per

Table 12.1 Population projections, 1987–2057, UK

Year/ end of period	Population (000s)	Index (1987 = 100)	Period change rate (% per year)
1987 (base)	56 930	100.0	—
1991	57 584	101.2	0.29
1996	58 522	102.8	0.33
2001	59 266	104.1	0.25
2006	59 714	104.9	0.15
2011	60 057	105.5	0.11
2021	61 247	107.6	0.20
2031	61 295	107.7	0.01
2041	60 605	106.5	−0.11
2051	59 722	104.9	−0.15
2057	59 208	104.0	−0.14

Source: OPCS, 1989

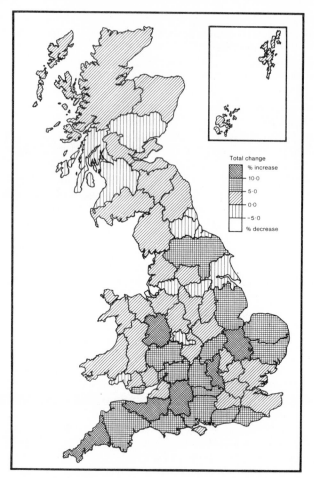

Figure 12.1 Projected population change, 1991–2001. Source: calculated from OPCS, 1988b; Welsh Office, 1989; Registrar General Scotland, 1989.

cent more residents in 2001 then in 1991. Increases of 10–12 per cent are forecast for Wiltshire, Buckinghamshire, Shropshire, Cornwall and Somerset, with Northamptonshire, Lincolnshire, Hampshire, and Hereford & Worcester next, at 8–9 per cent. At the other extreme, the most substantial population decreases over this period are forecast for Merseyside (−5.6 per cent) and Strathclyde (−4.3 per cent), with losses of around 2–3 per cent also calculated for Tyne and Wear, County Durham, South Yorkshire and West Midlands county. Amongst the large cities, Liverpool is expected to fare worse, with a decline of 47,000 people (−10.2 per cent), but significant losses are also projected for Glasgow (−56,000, or −8.1 per cent), Manchester (−24,000, or −5.5 per cent) and Sheffield (−25,000, or −4.8 per cent). Lower rates of loss are forecast for Birmingham, Newcastle upon Tyne and Leeds, while Greater London is expected to continue its recovery with an increase of 110,000 or 1.6 per cent over the decade.

These official projections thus anticipate a strong continuation into the next century of Britain's two main population shifts from North to South and from more urban to more rural. In itself, however, this observation raises questions about the likelihood of these patterns actually happening. It must be remembered that these projections are only as reliable as the assumptions on which they are based and that these assumptions are based on past trends, unless there are very sound reasons for departing from them (such as the designation of a New Town or major new growth zone). Since the unforeseen rise in fertility during the 1950s and early 1960s and their even more dramatic fall immediately afterwards, demographers have rightly been cautious about even short-term forecasts of births. Forecasting of natural increase has recently become subject to even greater uncertainty because of the spectre of AIDS hanging over mortality rates in the 1990s, but at regional and more local levels it is migration that is likely to remain the most problematic component of change. In this context, it is true, as we have noted in Chapter 4, that migration patterns are generally self-reinforcing and cumulative, tending to lead to higher rates of natural increase and employment growth. At the same time, however, the migration projections assume the continuation of existing government spatial policies. Moreover, the projection methodology is based on a limited model which does not take account of changes in the distribution of employment nor of changes in the relationship between migration propensities and job opportunities.

The assumption of 'no policy change' is important to bear in mind, because the trends indicated by the projections carry such major implications that some form of government intervention would normally be thought likely. The regional-level changes in population and labour supply provide ample illustration of this point (Table 12.2). The patterns in Figure 12.1 add up to overall population growth for 1991–2001 ranging from 8–9 per cent for East Anglia and the South West to population decline of up to 1.8 per

Table 12.2 Regional projections of population and labour force (per cent)

Region	Total population 1991–2001	Civilian labour force 1988–2000				
		Total	Male	Female	Under 25	25 and over
South East	4.1	5.9	3.9	8.7	−17	13
East Anglia	8.9	13.0	10.7	15.9	−20	23
South West	8.1	14.2	9.1	20.6	−15	22
East Midlands	4.7	7.0	3.9	11.1	−21	15
West Midlands	1.6	0.3	− 3.1	5.2	−27	8
Yorkshire & Humb.	−1.8	1.3	− 2.9	7.0	−23	8
North West	−0.8	− 2.6	− 5.9	1.7	−26	4
Northern	−1.7	− 3.2	− 6.2	1.0	−27	4
Wales	2.7	1.9	− 4.3	10.5	−19	8
Scotland	−0.3	− 1.9	− 4.1	0.9	−29	6
Northern Ireland	4.7	7.6	4.2	12.6	− 9	13
UK	2.6	3.7	0.6	7.9	−22	11

Source: *Population Trends* 58 (1989), 43–44, for population; *Employment Gazette*, January 1990, 9–18, for labour force

cent for Yorkshire and Humberside, the Northern Region, the North West and Scotland. Even more impressively, as a result of changes in activity rates as well as population trends, the total civilian labour force in East Anglia and the South West is expected to be 13–14 per cent larger in the year 2000 than it was in 1988, with that for the South East and the East Midlands up by 6–7 per cent. At the other extreme, the forecast for the Northern Region, the North West and Scotland is a fall in labour force by around 2–3 per cent. Much of the growth in labour supply in the four southern regions is due to the continued rapid growth of women in work, but the trend for males shows an even clearer distinction between increases of up to 11 per cent in these four regions and declines of 3–6 per cent in the six regions of northern Britain. (Northern Ireland does not fit this regional pattern, primarily because its rates of natural increase remain much higher than in the rest of the UK.) The final two columns of Table 12.2 show that no region will escape the effects of the 1990's 'demographic time bomb' of falling numbers of school-leavers, but its impact is proportionately smaller in the South, along with Wales, than in the North. The large increases in the South's labour force are of older, more experienced workers and, to the extent that they result from migration, are likely to be biased towards higher-income workers, particularly in professional and managerial occupations. This represents a valuable resource which will attract further business growth and lead to major expansion of consumer services in these areas.

Given the implications of these basic population projections, it is not surprising that questions have already been raised as to how much further existing trends are likely to continue, particularly in view of the build-up of political pressures for limiting new development in the prosperous sub-regions of the South (see Chapter 9) and the calls for greater governmental support for regeneration in the large cities and the industrial areas of the North (see Chapters 8 and 10). There is also the possibility that, following on from the major upheavals of the 1980s, the 1990s will be characterized by rather different patterns of employment growth. The remainder of this final chapter examines the main areas of uncertainty in relation to spatial developments, and assesses the scope that exists for the state to influence the course of events. Are the population projections likely to be self-fulfilling prophecies, or will they provide the warning signals for effective counter action?

Regional and urban trends in employment

Changes in the scale and distribution of economic activity and employment constitute the key parameter in the evolution of the space-economy, particularly in terms of the North–South divide. It is in this respect, as we have seen, that the 1980s left their most impressive mark. The legacy of that decade was a substantial widening of existing differentials and, put rather crudely, the growth of a distinction between 'de-industrialized Britain' and 'post-industrial Britain'. On the one hand, massive swathes were cut out of the most important sectors of the traditional industrial base, while certain new forms of employment experienced strong growth. Though not closely related to spatial processes as such, these changes manifested themselves clearly in geographical terms, with the strong economic recovery of the South in the mid-1980s and the persistence of severe difficulties in most northern and industrial areas through the decade, as shown in Part II. The central question for the 1990s is whether, either through the diversion of growth from the South or through its own indigenous efforts, the North will participate more fully in the 'post-industrial' economy or perhaps become 're-industrialized', or whether it will languish in its 'de-industrialized' state. In short, are places like Liverpool and Glasgow going to find new roles, or will they enter the next century looking increasingly like present-day Belfast? Similarly, will smaller industrial centres be able to establish new activities, or will they tend to fade away in the manner of the coal-mining villages in West Durham?

Unfortunately, the forecasting of employment trends is even more fraught with difficulties than that of population change. The pace of change can be much more rapid than for population, as was demonstrated by the effects of the 1979–81 recession. While even the most pessimistic seer is unlikely to predict a repetition of those traumatic events, considerable short-to-medium-term change in employment levels can take place as a result of developments in the global economy or alterations in domestic interest rates. Perhaps one of the most critical factors affecting regional prospects in the 1990s concerns whether employment in the manufacturing sector (as opposed to output) will continue to contract nationally and, if so, the extent to which these jobs will be replaced by growth in the service sector. To some, the continued transfer of workers from factories to services is inevitable. In 1987 67.8 per cent of UK economically active workers were in services, compared with only 47.8 per cent in 1961. Four OECD countries already had a higher percentage of workers in services than the UK in 1987 and were still increasing it, and the British proportion itself had increased further to 68.6 per cent by mid 1989. In the past, it has been suggested that there must be a ceiling to these figures: that services may level off at, for instance, 70 per cent of total employment. However, there is no firm sign of this from the international statistics. Indeed, 'In successful economies, employment gains in both goods-handling and information-handling services compensate for relatively modest manufacturing losses' (Hall, 1987, 98). Indeed, in relation to the USA, there has been at least one projection which generated too many jobs for the expected size of the labour force in the year 2000 (Leontief, 1985).

Others, however, attach much greater importance to the survival of a large manufacturing base. Hall's reference to 'successful economies' is not without significance, given that the UK's share of world trade in services declined from 12 per cent in 1968 to 7 per cent in 1983. Moreover, it should be noted that, in gross terms, manufacturing exports are still much larger than exports of services; for instance, as Sir John Harvey-Jones argued in his 1986 Dimbleby Lecture, if his then company, ICI, went under, 'You will need to entertain at least six million tourists per year, that is 40 per cent more than we now entertain'. In any case, Rajan (1987) argued that much of the 1980s growth of 'services' depended on the transfer of manufacturing firms' work to service-sector firms. Indeed, more than half the output of private-sector services – equivalent to 25 per cent of GDP – is directly linked to the production of goods, which itself contributed 43 per cent of GDP in OECD countries. With two-thirds of the economy thus involved in the production of goods, it would be foolish to separate the underlying dynamic of employment too much from industry. The further analysis of service-sector growth and its linkages at home and abroad is clearly a fundamental prerequisite for gauging the prospects for the nation's economic health more accurately.

Given the uncertainties, the best approach is to outline the assumptions on which forecasts are based and keep their results under review by reference to actual events. Moreover, it is perhaps not surprising that such forecasts provide an even lower level of geographical detail than the population projections. In fact, the most detailed sub-national economic projections – produced jointly by Cambridge Econometrics and the Northern Ireland Economic Research Centre – are for 'standard regions' and have been updated annually in the late 1980s. The third edition (1988) assumed an average annual growth of world industrial production of 3 per cent in the 1990s and a 2.4 per cent annual increase in the UK's GDP, following a lower rate (2.0 per cent) in 1988–90 because of the high interest rates correctly anticipated then (see Townsend, 1989, for a more detailed summary). On this basis, total employment in the UK was expected to resume the recovery of the mid 1980s, with the number of jobs some 5 per cent higher in 2000 than in 1988. This rate of growth is somewhat above the expected level of increase in labour supply, allowing some fall in the unemployment rate (Table 12.3). At *national* level, therefore, the balance of employment change in manufacturing and services over this period is expected to be positive – indeed, sufficiently large to offset continuing losses in the primary sector, most notably in agriculture and mining.

The same cannot be said, however, about the prospects for *individual regions* (Table 12.3). In particular, these forecasts suggested that the North

Table 12.3 Regional projections of employment and unemployment, 1988–2000

Region	Total employment		Unemployment rate	
	1988 000s	1988–2000 %	1988 %	2000 %
South East	8 839	3.8	5.0	3.4
East Anglia	989	24.0	4.7	2.5
South West	1 965	23.9	6.2	2.9
East Midlands	1 784	20.3	7.1	2.5
West Midlands	2 328	0.8	9.5	6.8
Yorkshire & Humberside	2 102	4.4	9.2	6.8
North West	2 575	− 8.6	11.8	11.8
Northern	1 208	− 4.3	12.0	10.7
Wales	1 045	− 0.3	11.0	8.0
Scotland	2 120	4.2	11.9	7.6
Northern Ireland	564	0.0	17.4	20.4
UK	25 523	5.2	8.2	5.9

Note: 1988 data do not necessarily agree with totals published elsewhere, due to differences in definition etc
Source: Cambridge Econometrics and Northern Ireland Economic Research Centre, 1988, unabridged version, Appendix C

West region will lose some 220,000 jobs between 1988 and 2000, an overall reduction of 8.6 per cent. The Northern Region will also be hit badly, while Wales, the West Midlands and Northern Ireland seem set for virtually no net change in employment level over this period, though with some variability between years. Despite better performances from Yorkshire and Humberside and Scotland (though these are still below the national average), these seven regions in aggregate are expected to lose some 80,000 jobs, a contraction by 0.7 per cent, and to see their share of the UK's total employment fall from 46.8 per cent in 1988 to 44.2 per cent in 2000. By contrast, the four southern regions together are forecast to gain 1.4 million jobs, an increase of just over 10 per cent. Huge gains of 20–24 per cent are expected for East Anglia, the South West and East Midlands, as congestion and high costs force more employers to look beyond the boundaries of the South East region (Table 12.3). The results of these projections, therefore, indicate a considerable further widening of the North–South divide (though in new forms) and an acceleration in the rate of spill over of jobs from London and the rest of the South East into the less heavily developed areas found in the adjacent regions, leading to the further extension of the 'prosperous sub-regions' of Chapter 9. The implications of these projections are even more dramatic than those for population, as evidenced by the predicted continuation of 11–12 per cent unemployment rates in the North West and Northern Region (and 20 per cent in Northern Ireland) co-existing with conditions of 'full employment' in the South (around 3 per cent or below in all four regions) as shown in the final two columns of Table 12.3.

Of course, projections are not the same as predictions. It is, for instance, very likely that the assumptions relating to underlying growth will prove wide of the mark, though presumably they are as likely to be revised downwards as upwards. Secondly, these and other such results may well stimulate concerted action aimed at avoiding the outcomes indicated by these projections. It is possible that new sources of economic growth can be harnessed in order to provide enhanced job opportunities in the less buoyant areas. In Part III mention was made of the considerable success in job generation which has been achieved in some places through the combined efforts of central and local government, special agencies and the business community. Though assessments of local potential (e.g. Figure 7.4B) paint a rather gloomy picture for the North in general, much depends on the particular circumstances of individual places and on the 'chemistry' of leading figures in a locality. Various commentators have attempted to sketch a scenario of the ways in which different types of cities are likely to develop in the future: one example is shown in Table 12.4. According to Begg and Moore (1987, 23–4), 'The role of urban areas in tradable activities will concentrate more on services and on specialist functions, while manufacturing activities gravitate to green-field sites or even to countries outside the advanced country bloc. This poses problems for many of the older industrial cities, some of which may find it very difficult indeed to manage the transition to a post-industrial future. Casualties are, therefore, to be expected . . . [but] what this typology [Table 12.4] indicates is that there is no single formula allowing the future of cities to be predicted.' Their prognoses for Liverpool, Newcastle and Belfast are hardly encouraging, though they

Table 12.4 Typology of future city development

Type	Example	Type	Example
Expansion or recovery		*Further decline*	
Diversified cities	Milan, Dusseldorf	Resource dependent	Duisburg, Charleroi
International role	London, New York	Loss of function	Liverpool, Bremen
'New wave' activity	Houston, Grenoble	Monolithic economy	Bochum,Liege
Regional centres	Bordeaux, Atlanta	Branch plant losses	Newcastle, Belfast
'Bottoming-out'		*Maturing*	
Specialization	Brussels, St Louis	Developing	Athens
Restructuring	Baltimore, Lille	Rural pressure	Palermo, Naples
Urban renewal	Pittsburgh, Glasgow		

Source: Begg and Moore, 1987

appear to hold out greater hope for Glasgow. In any case, major strides need to be made in the 1990s to prevent these places, and others like them, becoming the 'casualties' of the twenty-first century.

South East spill over and 'quality of life' considerations

Given the strength of the 1980s economic recovery in the South East and the inflationary pressure which have arisen as a result, one obvious and immediate potential source of jobs for the North lies in the diversion of growth from there. Indeed, by the beginning of the 1990s, there were signs that this process was underway. As this section goes on to show, however, commentators seem to disagree about the scale and extent of the benefits which would accrue to the North. One particular source of uncertainty concerns the degree to which the surge of interest in environmental ('green') issues and in 'quality of life' considerations might favour the North.

The available evidence on spill over from the South East comes from several sources. For instance, migration estimates suggest a major surge in net outward movement from the South East region in the latter half of the 1980s, rising from an annual average of around 5,000 in 1984–86 to 55,000 –60,000 in 1987–89. Secondly, Chapter 9 has already mentioned the squeeze imposed on manufacturing industry in the prosperous sub-regions and the substitution of higher-order activities for more routine operations on sites where low-cost land and labour were becoming scarcer. The latest employment estimates suggest that this process was beginning to have a measurable effect. The number of manufacturing jobs in the South East fell by over 50,000 (4.2 per cent) in the 21 months following the 1987 Census of Employment, primarily accounted for by Greater London, while in the East Midlands and all the regions of the North employment in the manufacturing sector increased over this period. Moreover, in the wake of more private sector decisions to decentralize from London, central government put dispersal of its own office firmly back on its agenda in the late 1980s, with plans for the relocation of 5,000 jobs being announced in November 1989 alone (for staff in Customs and Excise, Health and Social Security, and the Inland Revenue). By then, even local authorities in the South East were being forced to consider relocating office work to places with more readily available and lower-cost labour, with Sutton investigating the Sheffield area and Kingston upon Thames setting up its new computer unit in Barnstaple (Devon).

Opinion, however, seems to be divided with regard to the scale of the impact which this exodus from the South East is likely to make on the less buoyant economies of the North. There are some reasons to suggest that the benefits may be much more limited than those arising from the movement of factories in the 1940s and 1960s. In the first place, much of the recent office dispersal – just like that of factories – tends to involve 'branch' operations which provide relatively low-paid work. Secondly, the geographical impact of both office and factory relocation is likely to be over shorter distances than in the previous periods of planned dispersal. Much of the earlier movement of factories was targeted at the most depressed areas in Wales, Merseyside, the North East and Scotland, but now the West Midlands, Greater Manchester and much of Yorkshire share the weaknesses of the more peripheral regions. According to Townsend (1989, 23), 'The present pattern of spontaneous overspill from the South East is . . . likely to fill up weaknesses in the East and West Midlands and perhaps Cardiff; uncontrolled dispersal may stop at Doncaster and Harrogate before ever reaching Middlesbrough or Dundee.' In fact, the projections in Table 12.3 already take some account of this displacement process and, as was evident, conclude that the main beneficiaries will be the regions lying immediately adjacent to the South East, with their prosperous sub-regions and strongly growing rural areas. This is also the main message of the latest available migration statistics (for 1988–89), which show that the exodus from the South East is concentrated very largely on the South West, East Anglia and the East Midlands, with very modest net movement into Wales, the West Midlands and Yorkshire and continued net gains from the rest of the UK. Indeed, in relation to much of this development it is wrong – except in purely statistical terms – to talk about spill over from the South East, because, as mentioned in Chapter 9, what is occurring is in reality the outward extension of the Greater South East.

On the other hand, to be weighed up against these arguments is, first of all, the evidence of Leyshon and Thrift (1989), who demonstrate that the recent growth of financial and producer service employment within the provincial centres well beyond the real boundary of the South East has had a wide range of beneficial impacts upon the local and regional economies in which they are based. As mentioned in Chapter 6, these include the direct multiplier effects that result from increased corporate and employee spending and from the agency role that financial and producer service firms play in economic growth. Leyshon and Thrift feel that the increasing sophistication of the financial communities may well be bolstering the North's possession of key functions, including the development of local sources of venture funding. In addition, it appears that the influx of the branch offices of large financial organizations is allowing provincial centres to retain a local interest in large financing deals that otherwise would have gone to London, holding out the hope of increased local autonomy in industrial activity in the North.

Secondly, with the growth of concern for environmental and 'quality of life' issues during the latter half of the 1980s, it could be argued that the context of the 1990s contrasts substantially with the previous decade and could be expected to produce a different outcome. Mention has already been made in Chapter 9 of the increase in both the environmental and financial costs of living and working in the Greater South East. On the basis of current evidence, these are not likely to diminish in the next few years. On the contrary, we have already mentioned the massive growth in car ownership forecast for the next two decades. We have also noted the large scale of population increases expected here during the 1990s. Moreover, given the long-term trend towards lower average household size, these translate into even higher rates of growth in household numbers: 17–18 per cent for Buckinghamshire and Cambridgeshire between 1991 and 2001, 13–15 per cent for Wiltshire, Hampshire and Northamptonshire, over 12 per cent for East Anglia as a whole, and an average of 10 per cent for both the South East (excluding London) and the South West region (calculated from Department of the Environment, 1988c). As these pressures increase in the South, it could be expected that the attractions of the North will become more appealing.

In this context, it is relevant to note the amount of attention given recently to reports which highlight the 'quality of life' advantages of northern Britain. For example, Breheny *et al.* (1987) demonstrated how many of the local authority districts in northern England were significantly above the national average on an index based on such indicators as higher-income occupations, educational qualifications and unemployment rate. For its top ten 'Northern Lights' (see Chapter 9), that study went on to itemize their advantages in terms of provision of good hotels and restaurants, availability of golf courses and antique shops, and accessibility to motorways, commuter rail stations, major urban centres and National Parks. In the authors' own words, 'These ten places offer a quality of life at least equal to – and in important respects, such as access to the countryside, superior to – anything enjoyed by their equivalents in the South. And they do so at a fraction of the cost . . . of their competitors' (Breheny *et al.*, 1987, 38). Similar conclusions have been drawn by the University of Glasgow Quality of Life Team, which ranked the 38 largest cities in Britain by summing scores reflecting 20 dimensions of quality of life, including crime rate, health provision, education, shopping, pollution, housing and jobs (Rogerson *et al.*, 1988; see also Findlay *et al.*, 1988). Edinburgh came top, followed by Aberdeen, Plymouth, Cardiff, Hamilton-Motherwell and Bradford. It was clear that the North contains more than its fair share of places with the highest 'quality of life' scores and, moreover, that cities in southern and eastern England did not appear in nearly such a good light as they do on more conventional measures relating to economic performance, social status and material prosperity. London itself came in a miserable 34th position, while several other normally well-thought-of places like Bristol, Bournemouth and Norwich failed to get into the top half of the national rankings.

A key question for the 1990s is whether these 'quality of life' advantages, together with the scale of living cost differences shown in Table 9.4, have the potential for turning the North around. Some believe that this is very largely a matter of more effective advertising of the North's attributes (see, for example, Breheny *et al.*, 1987, 38). Several considerations, however, suggest that this attitude may be overly optimistic. First, the 'quality of life' studies tend to play down the importance of employment opportunities, which, for instance in the Glasgow University work, constitute only 15 per cent of the weighted index (see review by Champion (1989b) for further details). Would population movement result in the creation of an adequate number of new jobs, or would the people migrate despite limited employment opportunities? Secondly, in the towns identified as 'Northern Lights', there are already emerging signs of local resistance to the suggestion of rapid expansion; people there seem just as concerned about protecting the traditional character of their settlements as those in the shire counties of the Greater South East. Even if the jobs can be generated or attracted, it may be as difficult for developers to secure the necessary planning permission here as elsewhere. A further consideration is the extent to which political pressures will force action to improve the quality of life in the Greater South East, thereby diminishing the advantages currently believed to be held by the North. The attitude of central government towards regional policy and physical planning is likely to have an important bearing on the map of Britain in the 1990s.

Redistribution through spatial or social policies?

The revival of strategic planning in the 1990s?

In previous chapters, notably in relation to metropolitan government (Chapter 8) and regional policy (Chapter 10), we have referred to the demise of spatial thinking in the 1980s; in the words of Breheny and Hall (1984, 95), 'the strange death of strategic planning and the victory of the know-nothing school'. The primary focus of central government's activities during the 1980s was on restructuring the national economy with very little attention being paid to questions of spatial structure. This is not to say that spatial issues were entirely neglected, but to point out that government intervention tended to be restricted to 'fire fighting' – an Urban Development Corporation here, a Taskforce there, a Cabinet Minister charged with resolving a particular city crisis, or a 'country town' proposal turned down in response to local political pressures – rather than to emanate from the same strength of purpose that clearly underpinned economic and financial policy at this time.

A key consideration in anticipating the geographical trends of the 1990s is, therefore, whether and to what extent there will be a revival of the spatial perspective in policy making and planning. In our view, this change of attitude will occur sooner rather than later, irrespective of whether or not there is a change of political party in power at Westminster or even a change of Prime Minister. As long ago as 1986, the RTPI Working Party on Regional and Strategic Planning had satisfied itself 'that the circumstances of the late 1980s and the 1990s will create a pressing case for regional strategic planning' (RTPI, 1986, iv). In the late 1980s, the principal cleavages between 'have' and 'have not' places have continued to widen (Hudson and Williams, 1989; Smith, 1989) and, as shown in Part III of this book, the distinctive problems of different types of places are increasingly those arising from uneven development and the geographical mismatch between people and jobs. Indeed, it is now being recognized, as it was in the early 1960s, that failure to grapple with this issue could lead to a reduction in economic growth because of the inflationary pressures caused in some areas and the underuse of resources in others.

If we are broadly correct in this assessment, then the principal questions concern the forms which a revised spatial component in policy would take and how effective the measures would be. In relation to the challenge of redressing regional imbalances between North and South, one option would be the re-introduction of the 'stick and carrot' combination which formed a major part of the earlier phases of strong regional policy, including curbs on the amount of new industrial and commercial development in the South as well as larger incentives to attract firms northwards. In this connection, however, it has to be remembered, first, that in the last few years there has been rather little 'footloose' manufacturing investment seeking new UK sites compared with the 1960s and, secondly, that there is no real precedent for long-distance office movement.

A second option, which relevant organizations in the North have been campaigning strongly for, is the further improvement of communications links. The arguments here are not straightforward. Better links between North and South might serve to strengthen the latter's role in supplying northern markets rather than the other way round. Alternatively, they could help to extend the range of South East spill over and could have a beneficial effect, particularly if combined with other policy initiatives favouring the North. As regards roads, there are already in the pipeline a number of schemes for better North–South links, including the M40 extension and the M6 relief route, but there are a range of other possibilities which are only at the proposals stage or are merely private-sector recommendations, such as a new east-coast motorway (Figure 12.2). Similarly, though electrification of the east-coast intercity rail route to Edinburgh was begun in 1988, it appears according to current plans that direct rail links from the Channel Tunnel will be sparse, with only 5 out of the 35 daily passenger trains from Paris and Brussels being seen north of London. There is also concern that the North will be poorly served by new telecommunications infrastructure. Partly to tackle this problem and partly to ensure a strong basis for regional regeneration and attraction of South East spill over, certain groups including the Town and Country Planning Association (1987) have campaigned strongly for the development of the Greater Manchester area as a counter-magnet to London, with major new investment in airport facilities, a TGV North link to the Continent, a regional Metro rail system, and in particular the introduction of an integrated telecommunications system which would make Manchester the first 'wired up' city in Britain.

Equally important decisions, we feel, need to be made soon in relation to urban policy matters, if the present divisions in society and space are to be reduced. A key issue is the proper view to take on the growing congestion in the Greater South East. Parry Lewis's (1989) recommendation is 'Let the South East stew', thereby increasing the incentive for people and jobs to move northwards. Yet this hardly seems an economically or politically viable option. SERPLAN's chairman has pointed out, as we saw in Chapter

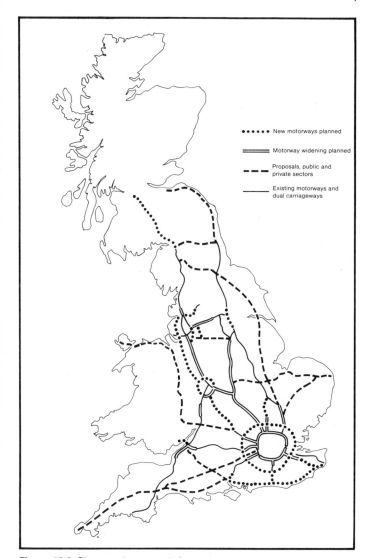

Figure 12.2 Plans and proposals for major roads, 1989.

9, that in the 'post-industrial society' economic growth and environmental quality go hand in hand. Failure to deal with the current 'quality of life' problems in the South East could result in new business investment being stifled or diverted to northern France or other parts of the EC. Somehow a way needs to be found to improve living and working conditions in the South East, without encouraging the even faster growth of population and employment. A rather similar dilemma faces government in relation to the large numbers of low-skilled people 'trapped' in inner urban areas. If planning restrictions on green-field sites were to be eased significantly, the degree of congestion within existing cities and towns and the competition for housing there would both become less intense, yet these areas might become even more distinctive in terms of their residual social composition and job opportunities.

These types of issues, are, of course, the *raison d'être* of planning beyond the local scale and it is because of their crucial importance now that we foresee the revival of regional and sub-regional planning in the 1990s. This is not to say, however, that the resolution of these questions will be easy, since by definition some types of people and places will stand to gain from certain decisions while others will lose out, just as there will be distinctive gainers and losers if these questions are ignored or solutions fudged (cf. Hall *et al.*, 1973). One immediate difficulty is that much of the machinery required for strategic planning simply does not exist. There has never been an effective regional tier of government or administration above the county level, apart from the 'national' branches of Whitehall in Wales, Scotland and Northern Ireland, and recent calls for even a minimum of regional devolution in the form of Regional Development Agencies in England have been stoutly resisted by central government. The abolition of the Greater London and Metropolitan County Councils in 1986 constituted the most conspicuous element in the general dismantling of strategic planning machinery which has taken place in recent years, giving greater powers to the 'suburban' and 'rural' authorities (outer metropolitan districts and shire counties) at the expense of the large cities (see Chapter 8).

A related difficulty is that the basic ethos of the local planning system remains firmly wedded to the principle of urban containment and continues to embody the traditional anti-urban prejudices of the British nation (Cameron, 1980a, 1–2; Robson, 1987c, 7–9). This is in spite of the food mountains which built up in the 1980s and the two previous decades of land-use monitoring and 'land budget' research which indicated that a faster rate of rural–urban land conversion would not produce a food supply crisis (Best, 1981; Edwards and Wibberley, 1971). Indeed, the recent calculations indicate that some 3 million hectares of agricultural land will become surplus to requirements over the course of the next 15 years under current 'set-aside' targets, equivalent to 16 per cent of the total farmland area including the upland rough grazings. Current proposals include the planting of extensive new 'forests' by the Countryside Commission in parts of lowland England, including green-belt locations round towns, but as yet no fundamental consideration of the implications for urban development patterns appears to have taken place.

At the threshold of the 1990s, there are indications that central government is beginning to pay greater attention to environmental and spatial policy. The replacement in 1989 of Nicholas Ridley as Secretary of State for the Environment by the 'greener' Chris Patten constituted a clear sign of the government's recognition of the importance of this electoral issue. This was reinforced in November 1989 by the publication of a draft guidance note on development plans and regional planning guidance, which reaffirmed the need for county structure plans and the leading role to be played by county councils in advising on regional planning matters (Department of the Environment, 1989c). So far, however, there has been no comparable change on questions relating to the North–South divide. This is unfortunate because, as stressed above, the prospects for significant changes are better now than for many years. Past experience has shown that greater success is achieved by those policies that attempt to channel market forces rather than oppose them; for instance, regional policy was most successful when labour shortage would have driven some firms northwards in any case. Attempts to implement regional policy under less favourable circumstances are more likely to reveal the limits of state intervention.

Redistribution through national spending policies?

There seems to be abundant evidence that central government is unable, due to its uncoordinated departmental structure, to take a wider geographical view in relation to its mainstream policies. Previous chapters of this book have referred to some explicitly spatial policies which have had only marginal effects on the main problems, and also to some instances where non-spatial policies have had marked local impacts, often running counter to the former. Examples are the increases in Urban Programme funding at the same time as much larger reductions in rate support grant, and the southern incidence of defence spending in contrast to regional policy aims. The latest example of such inconsistency is provided by the revaluation of commercial property for the uniform business rate, which looks like producing from 1990 much higher rate bills in the South than previously and a substantial reduction in the North, suggesting that for the past few years northern businessmen have been subsidizing their southern competitors.

Yet any government that is really serious about redressing regional imbalances in economic and social well-being, rather than pursuing spatial policies merely for political and electoral motives, should surely try to examine the redistributive effects of all its programmes, spatial and non-spatial alike. It is important to remember how miniscule is explicitly regional and urban policy spending compared with other sectors of central government spending, barely £1.5 billion in 1986/87 even after including European Regional Development Fund allocations (cf. Figure 10.2) compared with, for instance, over £37 billion paid out in the same year in the form of cash benefits (national insurance, supplementary and child benefit). Changes in the level of supplementary benefit payments would, for example, have important redistributive effects on total household incomes between North and South and between inner city and suburb. The same is true of the reduction in higher rates of income tax during the 1980s, which will presumably have had its greatest beneficial effect on our 'prosperous sub-regions', and no doubt this will also be the case with the change from domestic rates to the community charge ('poll tax') in April 1990.

In practice, it is extremely difficult to obtain data on, or even estimates of, the spatial incidence of all government expenditure (other than for Northern Ireland, Scotland and Wales). A major research effort by Short (1981) led to the production of a set of fairly comprehensive regional accounts which showed that the South East was then receiving rather more than its *per capita* share of 'regionally relevant' central government spending. No such detailed study, however, has been carried out since then because the data have been suppressed. Something that would change this state of affairs radically would be the introduction of Regional Assemblies in England, together with regional development agencies along the lines of those already operating in Scotland and Wales, as is currently advocated by the Labour party. Is it only through such a major administrative shake-up, probably involving the abolition of county councils and the redefinition of the role of central government, that a more co-ordinated approach is likely to be achieved? Would it affect the *inter*-regional movement of people and investment at all? What alternative mechanisms could be tried, and with what degree of success would they be likely to meet? These questions are not easy to answer, but as such they deserve much more attention from researchers than they have been given recently.

The changing national context

It has been a central feature of this book that, though our ultimate focus is on localities, we have laid great stress on the importance of the opportunities and constraints provided by the wider context, especially the fundamental role of the restructuring of the economic base and the underlying currents of social transformation. In looking forward through the 1990s to the next century, it is therefore appropriate that we should raise questions as to how these changes might affect the fortunes and characteristics of Britain's cities and regions, either directly through market forces or indirectly by influencing the scope of government and EC policy. Much hinges on the rate of national economic growth, which itself depends on trends in the global economy and partly on the UK's competitiveness in the international markets for goods and services.

The three-fold analysis of Britain's post-war record in tradables, developed in Chapter 2, provides a useful basis for anticipating the general trend in the national economy, in terms of the nation's ability to 'pay its way'. By the end of the 1980s there were some signs that Thatcherite policies avowedly aimed at producing a 'leaner and fitter' manufacturing sector had produced several years of consistent recovery of output, but the huge scale of the challenge is reflected in the long-term decline in trade balance of manufacturing goods (Figure 2.1) and the symbolic significance of the UK becoming a net importer and a 'post-industrial' economy. The economic recovery of the late 1980s seemed only to reinforce this picture, as it led to increased imports and record balance-of-payment deficits, resulting in the protective Treasury reaction of higher interest rates and thereby the discouragement of new investment in this sector.

At the end of the 1980s the oil and 'invisibles' sectors were both net earners for the UK economy (Figure 2.1). North Sea oil provided the mainstay of national prosperity during that decade, but the volatility of this sector makes the future contribution particularly difficult to gauge, depending as it does on the rate of domestic production, the level of national energy demand and oil's share of this, and the market price for oil. Following the commercially disappointing performance of nuclear power, however, current forecasts of a 45 per cent increase in Britain's oil consumption between 1985 and 2020 do not augur well for a long-term continuation of a trading surplus. As regards invisibles, the key consideration remains the status of the London Stock

Exchange in world financial markets, which was enhanced by the 'Big Bang' deregulation of 1986 but still faces strong competition not only from New York and Tokyo but also from other growing European centres. In this context, account needs to be taken of the implications of '1992' and progress towards a single European currency as well as of the anticipated dawning of the 'Pacific century' of economic hegemony. The net balance of investment income will also depend on the extent to which UK investors can take advantage of opportunities overseas, as well as on Britain's attractiveness to non-European firms which may decline after the introduction of the Single European Market.

In general, one cannot be anything but cautious about the prospects for the British economy after the restructuring of the past few years. This obviously means that the British government, whatever its future political hue, will have to think very carefully before providing the welfare provision and redistribution between income groups which would above all benefit the deprived regions and inner cities. On the other hand, the time is now right for a reappraisal of the resources which the country needs to secure its long-term future prosperity. Neglect of the spatial component in policy making during the 1980s has led to the development of mismatches and bottle-necks, which have impaired the efficiency of the national economy. The scarcity of urban land in the Greater South East, and the labour shortages arising partly from this and partly from demographic trends, serve to emphasize the importance of people and place in national planning. Unfortunately, however, the data sources which are needed to obtain the best use of the nation's resources have been progressively cut back during the 1980s in the efforts to reduce public expenditure and curb inflation, but the 1991 Census will soon provide the first clear picture of Britain's population for ten years and there is a growing pressure for a more complete record of the nation's land resources.

Conclusion: looking back and looking forward

The primary aim of this book has been the documentation of the patterns and processes of recent changes in the geography of Britain. Particular attention has been given to the traumatic events of the 1980s and the uneven way in which their effects have been felt across the nation. These developments have also influenced the way in which we have approached this task. In the first place, they have led us to put a heavy conventional emphasis on considerations relating to economic structure and employment. Secondly, we have laid stress on the extent to which trends within Britain have been related to changes on the international scene. Thirdly, in contrast with many previous treatments which have used the official 'standard' region, we have chosen to focus on sub-regional scales. This has allowed us to capture better the substantial differences between places within regions, which developed strongly during the period of rapid metropolitan decentralization in the later 1960s and 1970s. It has also helped us to take account of the often very place-specific nature of both the new developments of the 1980s and the policy responses to them. Bearing in mind these points, the book started by examining the key longer-term trends in the nature of the UK's economy and society and their links with international forces. In Part II the examination of the patterns of employment and population change led us to highlight the North–South divide *and* the urban–rural shift as the most important spatial dimensions affecting the relative fortunes of places within Britain. This perspective provided the basis for our identification of the four distinctive types of locality used in Part III for the more detailed accounts of the impacts of the changing patterns and the nature of the responses to them.

This final chapter has been forward-looking in the sense that we have used our knowledge of past and current trends to try and anticipate future developments and the way in which they will impact on the map of Britain. Trends in the national levels of manufacturing employment, unemployment, car ownership, household size, and so on, will have uneven effects on different types of places. The *outer rural areas*, for instance, now have almost as high a proportion of workers in manufacturing in Britain as a whole and are not likely to make further substantial net gains in factory jobs over the rest of the next decade. Multipliers from these gains, and the servicing of incoming migrants, will, however, produce employment growth in non-manufacturing sectors here. The *prosperous sub-regions* in the South are expected to profit increasingly from the dispersal and growth of financial offices, and as a result of their rapid growth will be greatly affected by the trend towards higher levels of car ownership and use. Their equivalents in the North are not seen to have a large enough population and economic base to contribute major economic growth to their respective regions, though some of the New Towns are likely to continue for some while to achieve stronger employment growth than their neighbours. For the *industrial districts*, particularly those in the North beyond the principal zone of South East spill over, structural effects may continue to cause employment reductions, even where differential shifts are more moderate. The available evidence suggests that the *large cities* in the provinces are bound to suffer continued negative trends, as they labour under their double disadvantages in relation to North–South drift and urban–rural shift, while the 'recovery' of London itself is seen by some as essentially a temporary phenomenon.

While it is tempting to put forward a more detailed scenario, this would be extremely foolhardy, given what we have said about the surprises produced by previous decades, the importance of underlying factors, and current problems over data sources. Instead, therefore, what we have done in this chapter is to provide a framework which the reader can use to monitor developments through the decade and be challenged to trace their likely impact on the ground, just as market researchers and government intelligence staff are expected to do in their task of providing information for policy making. With this goal in mind, we have identified what we consider to be the key parameters relating to the evolution of Britain's space-economy, indicated the degree of uncertainty over the way in which they will change, and identified the factors which are most likely to influence their trajectory. In particular, we urge close attention to the overall rate of national economic growth and its implications for unemployment, the impact of '1992' and other factors on the economic strength of London and the Greater South East, and the degree to which central government will accept the need for a clearer spatial perspective, not just in terms of explicitly urban and regional policies but also in relation to mainstream department spending programmes. In monitoring geographical trends, we consider the most important single element to be the future of London, because of its central place within the national economy and because of its pivotal position in both national and regional migration flows. Much also depends on the outcome of the battles currently being waged over the greenfield development in the Greater South East, because this will indirectly affect the prospects for the industrial districts and remoter rural areas of the North. We end by providing details of how these trends can be monitored over the years ahead.

Keeping up to date

In the spirit of this final chapter, we outline here the main sources which are *currently* (January 1990) available for monitoring employment, population and social trends at national and sub-national scales.

The *Employment Gazette*, published monthly by the Department of Employment, constitutes the best source for keeping up to date with trends in employment, unemployment, redundancies and vacancies. Each edition contains a central part (on coloured pages) with an extensive set of tables, most updated monthly but some included on a quarterly or annual basis. Monthly data on unemployment benefit claimants are provided for regions, travel-to-work areas, counties and districts, and parliamentary constituencies (section 2). Regional statistics are also given for redundancies (Table 2.30) and vacancies (Tables 3.2 and 3.3). Regional data on employment is published quarterly (Table 1.5).

Detailed local information on employment is collected through the Census of Employment, which is carried out at 2–3 year intervals. This book has been able to use the detailed results of the September 1987 Census, which were made available in September 1989. It is expected that the 1989 Census results will be produced during 1991. These, however, are not published, but can be obtained by users of the National Outline Manpower Information System, operated by the University of Durham for the Department of Employment, or by direct application to the Department's offices in Watford.

The *Employment Gazette* also contains national statistics on background economic indicators, including GDP, index of output, real disposable incomes, consumer expenditure, trade and balance of payments, employment in tourism-related industries, and earnings and spending from domestic and overseas travel and tourism. Another useful feature is the international comparison of labour force and employment by broad sector and sex (Table 1.9) and unemployment (Table 2.18). International statistics on labour force, employment and production can also be obtained from annual publications like the OECD's *Labour Force Statistics* and the World Bank's *World Development Report* (see bibliography for full references of their latest reports).

The principal source of population and social statistics at detailed spatial scales is the Census of Population. The next will be undertaken in April 1991 and will provide a huge range of information on population and household characteristics, which will largely be comparable to the data collected at the previous Census in 1981. A report on the preliminary results from the Census is scheduled for Summer 1991, followed over the next two years by a set of published volumes dealing, among other topics, with age/sex/marital status, household structure, housing and cars, ethnicity and country of birth, economic activity, journey to work and migration, with breakdowns to regional, county and district levels. Statistics for smaller areas are produced in machine-readable form.

Several sources provide population data between Censuses. The OPCS prepare estimates of population each year for regions, counties, districts and health areas in England and Wales, with the Registrar General Scotland performing the same task north of the border. These estimates are normally revised in the light of subsequent Population Census results. Migration between Family Practitioner Committee areas (counties, metropolitan districts and groupings of London boroughs) is monitored by the OPCS from records provided by the National Health Service Central Register. Data on population change and its components are updated quarterly in *Population Trends*, which also contains an annual review of the previous year and an annual summary of migration patterns.

The annual *General Household Survey* monitors trends in household and social characteristics, though being a sample survey the main emphasis is on the national picture. A wide range of national-level data can also be found in the annual publication *Social Trends*, which covers population, households and families, education, employment, income and wealth, household and public expenditure, health and personal services, housing, transport and the environment, and leisure.

Regional Trends constitutes the most comprehensive single source of geographical information. Published annually, this contains thematic sections on population, housing, transport and environment, health, law enforcement, education, employment, personal income and expenditure, regional accounts, industry and agriculture. The data are primarily for standard regions, though in many tables Greater London is shown separately from the rest of the South East. In addition, however, *Regional Trends* contains special sections with key statistics at sub-regional level: section 2 for counties or their equivalents in Scotland and Northern Ireland, and section 3 for 'urban areas' (i.e. local government areas with large urban centres). It also has a table showing comparisons with regions in other EC member states for a limited range of variables (section 14).

Finally, in order to keep up to date with developments in government policy and planning issues, the best single source is the weekly magazine *Planning*. See also the monthly journals *The Planner* and *Town and Country Planning*, and a new annual publication *Development and Planning*.

Bibliography

Adams, C.D., Baum, A.E. and MacGregor, B.D. 1987: Land prices and land availability in inner city redevelopment. In Robson 1987a, 154–77.

——1988: The availability of land for inner city development: a case study of Inner Manchester. *Urban Studies* 25, 62–76.

Allen, G.C. 1979: *The British disease.* London: Institute of Economic Affairs, 2nd edn.

Allen, K., Begg, H.M., McDowall, S. and Walker, G. 1986: *Regional incentives and the investment decision of the firm.* London: Department of Trade and Industry, HMSO.

Ambrose, P. 1974: *The quiet revolution: social change in a Sussex village, 1871–1971.* London: Chatto & Windus.

——1986: *Whatever happened to planning?* London: Methuen.

Amin, A. and Goddard, J. (eds) 1986: *Technological change, industrial restructuring and regional development.* London: Allen & Unwin.

Anderson, J., Duncan, S. and Hudson, R. (eds) 1983: *Redundant spaces in cities and regions?* London: Academic Press.

Arkleton Trust, The 1982: *Schemes of assistance to farmers in Less Favoured Areas of the EEC.* Langholm: The Arkleton Trust.

Armitage, R.I. 1987: English regional fertility and mortality patterns, 1975–1985. *Population Trends* 47, 16–23.

Armstrong, H.W. 1988: *A comparison of industrial development initiatives of metropolitan and non-metropolitan district councils in England and Wales.* Lancaster: University of Lancaster, Department of Economics.

Ascher, K. 1987: *The politics of privatisation.* Basingstoke: Macmillan.

Ashcroft, B.K. and Love, J.H. 1988: The regional interest in UK mergers policy. *Regional Trends* 22, 341–3.

Ashton, J. and Long, W.H. (eds) 1972: *The remoter rural areas of Britain.* Edinburgh: Oliver & Boyd.

Ashworth, W. 1954: *The genesis of modern British town planning.* London: Routledge & Kegan Paul.

Atkinson, A. 1983: UK trade in manufactured goods. *Barclays Review* LVIII, 4, 'centre spread'.

Atkinson, J. 1985: Flexibility, uncertainty and manpower management. *Institute of Manpower Studies Report* 89. Brighton: University of Sussex.

Atkinson, J. and McGill, D. 1981: *Geographical mobility in the labour market.* IMS Report 12. Institute of Manpower Studies, University of Sussex.

Atkinson, J. and Meager, N. 1986: Is flexibility just a flash in the pan? *Personnel Management,* September.

Bagguley, P., Mark-Lawson, J., Shapiro, D., Urry, J., Walby, S. and Warde, A. 1989: Restructuring Lancaster. In Cooke 1989, 129–65.

Barke, M. 1986: Newcastle/Tyneside 1890–1980. In Gordon 1986, 117–48.

Barlow, J. 1988: The politics of land into the 1990s: landowners, farmers and developers in lowland Britain. *Policy and Politics* 16(2), 111–21.

Beechey, V. 1986: Women's employment in contemporary Britain. In Beechey, V. and Whitelegg, E. (eds), *Women in Britain today* (Milton Keynes: Open University).

Beechey, V. and Perkins, T. 1987: *A matter of hours: women, part-time work and the labour market*. Cambridge: Polity.

Begg, I. and Cameron, G. 1987: When the chips are down South. *The Guardian*, 3 June, 22.

Begg, I. and Eversley, D. 1986: Deprivation in the inner city: social indicators from the 1981 Census. In Hausner 1986, 50–88.

Begg, I. and Moore, B. 1987: The future economic role of urban systems. University of Cambridge, Department of Applied Economics, mimeo.

Begg, I., Moore, B. and Rhodes, J. 1986: Economic and social change in urban Britain and the inner cities. In Hausner 1986, 10–49.

Bell, M. 1987: The impacts of CAP change: putting the pieces together. In Gilg, A.W. (ed.), *The International Yearbook of Rural Planning* 1 (Norwich: Geo Books), 33–43.

Bennett, R.J. 1980: *The geography of public finance*. London: Methuen.

Bentham, C.G. 1983: The changing distribution of low-income households in the British urban system. *Area* 15, 15–20.

Bentham, G. 1986: Public satisfaction and social, economic and environmental conditions in the counties of England. *Transactions, Institute of British Geographers, New Series* 11(1), 27–36.

Bentley, J. 1988: Coalfields in crisis. *Planning* 758, 10–11.

Berry, B.J.L. 1976: The counterurbanisation process: Urban America since 1970. In Berry, B.J.L. (ed.), *Urbanisation and counterurbanisation* (Beverly Hills: Sage Publications), 17–30.

Best, R.H. 1981: *Land use and living space*. London: Methuen.

Beynon, H., Hudson, R., Lewis, J., Sadler, D. and Townsend, A. 1989: 'It's all falling apart here': coming to terms with the future in Teesside. In Cooke 1989, 267–95.

Birch, D.L. 1979: *The job generation process*, Cambridge, Mass. M.I.T. Program on Neighborhood and Residential Change.

Black Report 1980: *Inequalities in health*. Report of a Research Working Group chaired by Sir Douglas Black. London: Department of Health and Social Security.

Blacksell, M., Clark, A., Economides, K. and Watkins, C. 1988: Legal services in rural areas: problems of acccess and local need. *Progress in Human Geography* 12, 47–65.

Blacksell, M. and Gilg, A. 1981: *The countryside: planning and change*. London: Allen & Unwin.

Bluestone, B. and Harrison, B. 1980: Why corporations close profitable plants? *Working Papers for a New Society* 7, 15–23.

Blunden, J. and Curry, N. 1988: *A future for our countryside*. Oxford: Blackwell.

Boaden, N. 1989: Merseyside Development Corporation: an evaluation. In Cross and Whitehead 1989, 99–102.

Boddy, M. 1987a: Bristol: sunbelt city? In Hausner 1987b, 44–98.

——1987b: High technology industry, regional development and defence manufacturing: a case study in the UK Sunbelt. In Robson 1987a, 60–83.

Boddy, M. and Lovering, J. 1986: High technology industry in the Bristol sub-region: the aerospace/defence nexus. *Regional Studies* 20, 217–31.

Boddy, M., Lovering, J. and Bassett, K. 1986: *Sunbelt City? a study of economic change in Britain's M4 growth corridor*. Oxford: Clarendon Press.

Booth, P. and Crook, T. (eds) 1986: *Low cost home ownership*. London: Gower.

Bover, O., Muellbauer, J. and Murphy, A. 1988: *Housing, wages and UK labour markets*. Discussion Paper 268. London: Centre for Economic Policy Research.

Bowlby, S.R. 1984: Planning for women to shop in postwar Britain. *Environment and Planning D* 2, 179–99.

Boyer, R. and Savageau, D. 1985: *Places rated almanac: new and revised*. Chicago: Rand McNally.

Bradford, M. and Burdett, F. 1989: Privatization, education and the north–south divide. In Lewis and Townsend 1989, 192–212.

Bramley, G., Doogan, K., Leather, P., Murie, A. and Watson, E. 1988: *Homelessness and the London housing market*. Occasional Paper 32. Bristol: School for Advanced Urban Studies.

Breheny, M. 1989: Southern discomfort: the costs of success in the south east. *The Planner* 75 (5), 14–15.

Breheny, M. and Congdon, P. (ed.) 1989: *Growth and change in a core region: the case of South East England*. London: Pion.

Breheny, M. and Hall, P. 1984: The strange death of strategic planning and the victory of the know-nothing school. *Built Environment* 10, 95–9.

——(eds) 1987: *The growth and location of high technology industires: Anglo-American perspectives*. London: Allen & Unwin.

Breheny, M., Hall, P. and Hart, D. 1987: *Northern lights: a development agenda for the North in the 1990s*. London: Derrick, Wade & Waters.

Breheny, M., Hart, D. and Hall, P. 1986: *Eastern promise?: development prospects for the M11 corridor*. London: Derrick, Wade & Waters.

Briggs, A. 1968: *Victorian cities*. Harmondsworth: Penguin.

Brindley, T. and Stoker, G. 1988: Partnership in inner city urban renewal – a critical analysis. *Local Government Policy Making* 15, 3–12.

Britton, M. 1986: Recent population changes in perspective. *Population Trends* 44, 33–41.

Broadbent, A. 1985: Estates of another realm. *New Society*, 410–11.

Broady, M. 1980: Mid-Wales: a classic case for rural self-help. *The Planner* 66, 94–5.

Bromley, D.F. and Rees, J.C.M. 1988: The first five years of the Swansea Enterprise Zone: an assessment of change. *Regional Studies* 22, 263–76.

Brown, D.L. and Wardwell, J.M. (eds) 1980: *New directions in urban–rural migration: the population turnaround in rural America*. New York: Academic Press.

Brown, P.J.B. 1988: A super-profile-based affluence ranking of OPCS urban areas. *Built Environment* 14, 118–34.

Buchanan, C.B. *et al.* 1963: *Traffic in Towns*. London: HMSO.

Buck, N. 1988: Service industries and local labour markets: towards an anatomy of service job loss. *Urban Studies* 25, 387–98.

Buck, N. and Gordon, I. 1987: The beneficiaries of employment growth: an analysis of the experience of disadvantaged groups in expanding labour markets. In Hausner 1987a, 77–115.

Buck, N., Gordon, I., Pickvance, C. and Taylor-Gooby, P. 1989: The role of Thanet: restructuring and municipal conservatism. In Cooke 1989, 166–97.

Buck, N., Gordon, I. and Young, K. 1987: London: employment problems and prospects. In Hausner 1987b, 99–131.

Buck, N., Gordon I. and Young, K., with Ermisch, J. and Mills, L. 1986: *The London employment problem*. Oxford: Oxford University Press.

Budworth, D. 1986: The making (and breaking) of a myth. *New Scientist*, 10 April, 70.

Burden, W. 1986: Economic and social change in the Medway towns. In Cooke 1986, 40–8.

Burkart, A.J. and Medlik, S. 1981: *Tourism*. London: Heinemann, 2nd edn.

Burrows, J.W. 1978: Vacant urban land – a continuing crisis. *The Planner* 64(1), 7–10.

Buswell, R.J., Champion, A.G. and Townsend, A.R. 1987: The Northern Region. In Damesick and Wood 1987, 167–90.

Cabinet Office 1988: *Action for cities*. London: HMSO.

Cadman, D. and Payne, G. (eds) 1989: *The living city*. London: Methuen.

Camagni, R. 1985: Industrial robotics and the revitalisation of the Italian North-West. Paper presented to an International Seminar on Technologies Nouvelles, Brussels.

Cambridge Econometrics and Northern Ireland Economic Research Centre 1988: *Regional economic prospects, analysis and forecasts to the year 2000 for the standard planning regions of the UK*. Cambridge: Cambridge Econometrics.

Cameron, G. (ed.) 1980a: *The future of the British conurbations*. Harlow: Longman.

——1980b: The economies of the conurbations. In Cameron 1980a, 54–71.

Cameron, S. and Gillard, A. 1983: Local authority economic development in Tyne and Wear. In Buswell, R.J. (ed.), *The North in the eighties: regional policies for a decade of development* (Newcastle upon Tyne: Regional Studies Association Northern Branch).

Camley, M. 1987: Employment in the public and private sectors 1981 to 1987. *Economic Trends* 410, 98–107.

Campbell, M. *et al.* 1988: Economic sense: local jobs plans and the inner city. *Regional Studies* 22(1), 55–60.

Cantle, T. 1986: The deterioration of public sector housing. In Malpass 1986, 57–85.

Carmen, H-K. 1988: *New life for city centres*. London: Anglo-German Foundation.

Cervero, R. 1986: *Suburban gridlock*. New Brunswick, NJ: Rutgers University Center for Urban Policy Studies.

Champion, A.G. 1981: Population trends in rural Britain. *Population Trends* 26, 20–3.

——1983: Population trends in the 1970s. In Goddard and Champion 1983, 187–214.

——1987a: Momentous revival in London's population. *Town and Country Planning* 56(3), 80–2.

——1987b: Recent changes in the pace of population deconcentration in Britain. *Geoforum* 18(4), 379–401.

——1989a: Internal migration and the spatial distribution of population. In Joshi 1989, 110–32.

——1989b: 'Quality of life' considerations and the prospects for the North. *The Planner* 75(5), 16–20.

——1989c: United Kingdom: population deconcentration as a cyclic phenomenon. In Champion 1989d, 83–102.

——(ed.) 1989d: *Counterurbanization: the changing pace and nature of population deconcentration*. London: Edward Arnold.

Champion, A.G., Clegg, K. and Davies, R.L. 1977: *Facts about the New Towns: a socio-economic digest*. Corbridge: Retail and Planning Associates.

Champion, A.G. and Congdon, P.D. 1988a: An analysis of the recovery of London's population change rate. *Built Environment* 13, 193–211.

——1988b: Recent trends in Greater London's population. *Population Trends* 53, 7–17.

Champion, A.G., Coombes, M.G. and Openshaw, S. 1984: New regions for a new Britain. *Geographical Magazine* 56, 187–90.

Champion, A.G., Gillespie, A.E. and Owen, D.W. 1982: Population and the labour market with special reference to growth areas in the UK. In *Population change and regional labour markets*. OPCS Occasional Paper 28 (London OPCS), 17–32.

Champion, A.G. and Green, A.E. 1989: Local economic differentials and the north–south divide. In Lewis and Townsend 1989, 61–96.

Champion, A.G., Green, A.E. and Owen, D.W. 1987: Housing, labour mobility and unemployment. *The Planner* 73(4), 11–17.

——1988: House prices and local labour market performance: an analysis of Building Society data for 1985. *Area* 20, 253–63.

Champion, A.G., Green, A.E., Owen, D.W., Ellin, D.J. and Coombes, M.G. 1987: *Changing places: Britain's demographic and social complexion*. London: Edward Arnold.

Chandler, J.A. 1985: *Local authorities and the creation of employment*. London: Gower.

Cheshire, P. 1987: Urban policy: art not science? In Robson 1987a, 22–39.

Cheshire, P., Carbonaro, G. and Hay, D. 1986: Problems of urban decline and growth in EEC countries. *Urban Studies* 23, 131–49.

Cheshire, P. and Hay, D. 1989: *Urban problems in Western Europe: an economic analysis*. London: Unwin Hyman.

Chiddick, D. and Dobson, M. 1986: Land for housing – circular arguments. *The Planner* 73(3), 10–13.

Chisholm, M. 1985: The Development Commission's employment programmes in rural England. In Healey and Ilbery 1985, 279–92.

——1987: Regional development: the Reagan-Thatcher legacy. *Environment and Planning C* 5, 197–218.

Chisholm, M. and Kivell, P. 1987: *Inner city waste land*. (Hobart Paper 108.) London: Institute of Economic Affairs.

Church, A. and Hall, J. 1986: Restructuring and current research in the London Borough of Newham. In Cooke 1986, 226–35.

Church of England 1985: *Faith in the City: a call for action by church and nation*. London: Church House Publishing.

Civic Trust 1988: *Urban wasteland now*. London: Civic Trust.

Clark, D. 1989: *Urban decline*. London: Routledge.

Clark, G. 1982a: *Housing and planning in the countryside*. Chichester: Wiley.

——1982b: Housing policy in the Lake District. *Transactions, Institute of British Geographers, New Series* 7, 59–70.

Clark, G.L., Gertler, M.S. and Whiteman, J. 1986: *Regional dynamics: studies in adjustment theory*. Boston: Allen & Unwin.

Cloke, P.J. 1983: *An introduction to rural settlement planning*. London: Methuen.

——1985: Counterurbanisation: a rural perspective. *Geography* 70, 13–23.

——(ed.) 1987: *Rural planning: policy into action?* London: Harper & Row.

Cloke, P. and Edwards, G. 1986: Rurality in England and Wales: a replication of the 1971 Index. *Regional Studies* 20, 289–306.

Coates, B.E. and Rawstron, E.M. 1971: *Regional variations in Britain: studies in economic and social geography*. London: Batsford.

Cochrane, A. 1983: Local economic policies: trying to drain an ocean with a teaspoon. In Anderson, Duncan and Hudson 1983, 285–312.

——1988: The future of local economic strategies. *Local Economy* 3, 132–41.

Coffield, F., Borrill, C. and Marshall, S. 1986: *Growing up at the margins: young adults in the North East*. Milton Keynes: Open University Press.

Coleman, A. 1976: Is planning really necessary? *Geographical Journal* 142, 411–36.

——1980: The death of the inner city: cause and cure. *London Journal* 6, 3–22.

——1984: Trouble in Utopia: design influences in blocks of flats. *Geographical Journal* 150(3), 351–8.

——1985: *Utopia on trial: vision and reality in planned housing*. London: Hilary Shipman.

——1987: The social consequences of housing design. In Robson 1987a, 142–53.

Coleman, D.A. (ed.) 1982: *Demography of immigrant and minority groups in the UK*. London: Academic Press.

Compton, P.A. 1982: The changing population. In Johnston and Doornkamp 1982, 37–73.

Congdon, P. 1988: Deprivation in London wards: mortality and unemployment trends in the 1980s. *The Statistician* 37, 451–72.

Congdon, P.D. and Champion, A.G. 1989: Trends and structure in London's migration and their relation to employment and housing markets. In Congdon, P. and Batey, P. (eds), *Advances in regional demography* (London: Bellhaven), 180–204.

Conway, J. 1985: *Capital decay: an analysis of London's housing*. London: SHAC, 2nd edn.

Conway, J. and Ramsay, E. 1986: *A job to move: the house problems of job seekers*. London: SHAC.

Cooke, P. (ed.) 1986: *Global restructuring, local response*. London: Economic and Social Research Council.

——1988: Spatial development processes: organized or disorganized? In Massey and Allen 1988, 232–49.

——(ed.) 1989: *Localities: the changing face of urban Britain*. London: Unwin Hyman.

Coombes, M.G., Dixon, J.S., Goddard, J.B., Openshaw, S. and Taylor, P.J. 1982: Functional Regions for the Population Census of Great Britain. In Herbert, D.T. and Johnston, R.J. (eds), *Geography and the urban environment: progress in research and applications* 5 (Chichester: Wiley), 63–112.

Coombes, M.G. and Raybould, S. 1989: Developing a local enterprise activity potential (LEAP) index. *Built Environment* 14, 107–17.

Coppock, J.T. (ed.) 1977: *Second homes: curse or blessing?* Oxford: Pergamon.

Countryside Commission 1987: *Countryside Policy Review Panel: new opportunities for the country*. Manchester: Countryside Commission Publications.

Cowen, H., Livingstone, I., McNab, A., Harrison, S., Howes, L. and Jerrard, B. 1989: Cheltenham: affluence amid recession. In Cooke 1989, 86–128.

Cox, K.R. and Mair, A. 1988: Locality and community in the politics of local economic development. *Annals of the Association of American Geographers* 78, 307–25.

Creigh, S., Roberts, C., Corman, A. and Sawyer, P. 1986: Self-employment in Britain. *Employment Gazette* 94, 183–94.

Cross, D. and Whitehead, C. 1989: *Development and Planning 1989*. Cambridge: Department of Land Economy/Policy Journals.

Crouch, C.S. 1989: The economic geography of recession in the UK; the early 1980s and historical perspectives. Unpublished PhD thesis, University of Durham.

Cullingford, D. and Openshaw, S. 1982: Identifying areas of rural deprivation using social area analysis. *Regional Studies* 16, 409–18.

Curtis, S. and Mohan, J. 1989: The geography of ill-health and healthcare. In Lewis and Townsend 1989, 175–91.

Damesick, P. 1982: The potential for and impact of office development in the inner city in London. *Progress in Planning* 18, 189–267.

——1986a: The M25 – a new geography of development? *Geographical Journal* 152(2), 155–60.

——1986b: Service industries, employment and regional development in Britain: a review of recent trends and issues. *Transactions, Institute of British Geographers, New Series* 11, 212–26.

Damesick, P. and Wood, P. (eds) 1987: *Regional problems, problem regions and public policy in the United Kingdom*. Oxford: Oxford University Press.

Daniels, P.W. (ed.) 1979: *Spatial patterns of office growth and location*. Chichester: Wiley.

——1982: *Service industries: growth and location*. Cambridge: Cambridge University Press.

——1985a: *Service industries: a geographical appraisal*. London: Methuen.

——1985b: The geography of services. *Progress in Human Geography* 9, 443–52.

——1986: The geography of services. *Progress in Human Geography* 10, 436–44.

Danson, M. (ed.) 1986: *Redundancy and recession: restructuring the regions*. Norwich: Geo Books.

Danson, M.W., Lever, W.F. and Malcolm, J.F. 1980: The inner-city employment problem in Great Britain, 1952–76: a shift-share approach. *Urban Studies* 17, 193–210.

Davies, L. 1987: If you've got it, flaunt it; making the most of city tourism. *Employment Gazette* 95, 167–71.

Davies, R.L. and Champion, A.G. (eds) 1983: *The future for the city centre*. London: Academic Press.

Davies, S.W. and Caves, R.E. 1987: *Britain's productivity gap*. Occasional Paper XL. National Institute of Economic and Social Research.

Davis, L.E. and Huttenback, R.A. 1987: *Mammon and the pursuit of empire: the political economy of British imperialism, 1860–1912*. Cambridge: Cambridge University Press.

Dawson, J.A. (ed.) 1980: *Retail geography*. Chichester: Wiley.

——1982: The growth of service industries. In Johnston and Doornkamp 1982, 203–26.

Dennis, C. 1986: The changing urban and regional system: the Bradford metropolitan area. In Cooke 1986, 55–9.

Department of Applied Economics 1980: Urban and regional policy with provisional regional accounts 1966–78. *Cambridge Economic Policy Review* 6(2).

Department of Economic Affairs 1969: *The Intermediate Areas*. Report of a Committee under the Chairmanship of Sir Joseph Hunt. London: HMSO, Cmnd. 3998.

Department of Education and Science 1987: International statistical comparisons in higher education. *Statistical Bulletin*, March.

Department of the Environment 1971: *Long-term population distribution in Great Britain*. London: HMSO.

——1985: *An inquiry into the conditions of local authority housing stock in England*. London: Department of the Environment.

——1986: *Evaluation of Industrial and Commercial Improvement Areas*. London: HMSO.

——1988a: *Evaluation of the Enterprise Zone experiment*. London: HMSO.

——1988b: *An evaluation of the Urban Development Grant programme*. London: HMSO.

——1988c: *1985-based household projections 1985–2001*. London: Department of the Environment.

——1989a: Land use change in England. *Statistical Bulletin* (89) 5. London: Department of the Environment.

——1989b: *Strategic guidance for London*. London: Department of the Environment.

——1989c: *Structure plans and regional planning guidance*. London: Department of the Environment.

Department of Trade and Industry 1986: *UK regional development programmes 1986–90* (17 vols). Submission to the European Regional Development Fund. London: Department of Trade and Industry.

Department of Transport 1989: *M25 review: summary report*. London: HMSO.

Development Board for Rural Wales 1987: *Mid Wales development 1986/87*. Newtown: The Development Board for Rural Wales.

Development and Planning. Cambridge: Policy Journals.

Dicken, P. 1986: *Global shift*. London: Methuen.

Dicken. P. and Lloyd, P.E. 1981: *Modern western society*. London: Harper & Row.

Docklands Consultative Committee 1988: *Urban Development Corporations: six years in London's Docklands*. London: DCC.

Donnison, D. and Middleton, A. (eds) 1987: *Regenerating the inner city: Glasgow's experience*. London: Routledge & Kegan Paul.

Donnison, D. with Soto, P. 1980: *The good city: a study of urban development and policy in Britain*. London: Heinemann.

Duncan, S. and Goodwin, M. 1988: *The local state and uneven development*. Cambridge: Polity Press.

Dunford, M. and Perrons, D. 1983: *The arena of capital*. Basingstoke: Macmillan.

Dunn, R., Forrest, R. and Murie, A. 1987: The geography of council house sales 1979–85. *Urban Studies* 24, 47–59.

Dunnett, P.J.S. 1980: *The decline of the British motor industry*. London: Croom Helm.

Dunning, J.H. 1986: *Japanese participation in British industry*. London: Croom Helm.

ECOTEC Research and Consulting Ltd. 1988: *Developing the rural economy: an assessment of the Development Commission's economic activities*. Birmingham: ECOTEC Research and Consulting Ltd.

Edwards, A.M. and Wibberley, G.P. 1974: *An agricultural land budget for Britain 1965–2000*. Ashford: Wye College.

Elias, P. and Keogh, G. 1982: Industrial decline and unemployment in the inner city areas of Great Britain: a review of the evidence. *Urban Studies* 19, 1–15.

Ermisch, J. 1983: *The political economy of demographic change*. London: Heinemann.

Etherington, D. 1987: Local economic strategies and area based initiatives – another view of Improvement Areas. *Local Economy* 2(1), 31–7.

Evans, A.W. 1989: South East England in the eighties: explanations for a house price explosion. In Breheny and Congdon 1989, 130–49.

Evans, A. and Eversley, D. 1980: *The inner city: employment and industry*. London: Heinemann.

Eversley, D.E.C. 1972: Rising costs and static increases: some economic consequences of regional planning in London. *Urban Studies* 9, 347–68.

Farmer, P. 1985: *The social and economic impact of unemployment, 1979–85; a select bibliography*. Letchworth: Technical Communications.

Farrington, J. H. 1985: Transport geography and policy: deregulation and privatization. *Transactions, Institute of British Geographers, New Series* 10, 109–19.

Fielding, A.J. 1982: Counterurbanization in Western Europe. *Progress in Planning* 17, 1–52.

——1989: Inter-regional migration and social change: a study of South East England based upon data from the Longitudinal Study. *Transactions, Institute of British Geographers, New Series* 14, 24–36.

Fielding, A.J. and Savage, M. 1987: *Social mobility and the changing class composition of Southeast England*. Working Paper 60. Urban and Regional Studies, University of Sussex.

Findlay, A.M., Rogerson, R.J. and Morris, A.S. 1988: Quality of life in British cities in 1988. *Cities* 10, 268–76.

Fleming, A. 1988: Employment in the public and private sectors, 1982 to 1988. *Economic Trends*, 119–29.

Flowerdew, R. and Salt, J. 1979: Migration between labour market areas in Great Britain, 1970–1971. *Regional Studies* 13, 211–31.

Flynn, N. and Taylor, A.P. 1986a: Inside the rust belt: an analysis of the decline of the West Midlands economy, 1. International and national economic conditions. *Environment and Planning A* 18, 865–900.

——1986b: Inside the rust belt: an analysis of the decline of the West Midlands economy, 2. Corporate strategies and economic change. *Environment and Planning A* 18, 999–1028.

Forrest, R. and Murie, A. 1988: *Selling the welfare state: the privatization of public housing*. London: Routledge.

Fothergill, S. 1986: Industrial employment and planning restraint in the London Green Belt. In Towse, R.J. (ed.), *Industrial/office development in areas of planning restraint in the London Green Belt* (London: Kingston Polytechnic), 27–39.

Fothergill, S. and Gudgin, G. 1979: Regional employment change: a sub-regional explanation. *Progress in Planning* 12, 155–219.

——1982: *Unequal growth: urban and regional employment change in the UK*. London: Heinemann.

Fothergill, S., Gudgin, G., Kitson, M. and Monk, S. 1984: Differences in the profitability of the UK manufacturing sector between conurbations and other areas. *Scottish Journal of Political Economy* 31, 72–91.

——1985: Rural industrialization: trends and causes. In Healey and Ilbery 1985, 147–60.

——1986: The de-industrialization of the city. In Martin and Rowthorn, 214–38.

Fothergill, S. and Guy, N. 1990: *Retreat from the regions: corporate change and the closure of factories*. London: Jessica Kingsley.

Fothergill, S., Kitson, M. and Monk, S. 1985: *Urban industrial change: the causes of urban–rural contrast in manufacturing employment trends*. London: HMSO.

Fothergill, S., Monk, S. and Perry, M. 1986: *Property and industrial development*. London: Hutchinson.

——1987: Trouble at the mill – Britain's deteriorating factories. *Local Economy* 2, 115–22.

Fox, A. and Goldblatt, P. 1982: *Socio-demographic mortality differentials from the OPCS longitudinal study, 1971–1975*. London: HMSO.

Frankenberg, R. 1966: *Communities in Britain: social life in town and country*. Harmondsworth: Penguin.

Friedmann, J. 1985: The world city hypothesis. Paper to the International Sociological Association, University of Hong Kong.

Froebel, F., Heinrichs, J. and Kreye, O. 1980: *The new international division of labour*. Cambridge: Cambridge University Press.

Gaffakin, F. and Nickson, A. 1984: *Job crisis and the multinationals: the case of the West Midlands*. Birmingham: Trade Union Resource Centre.

Galbraith, J.K. 1958: *The affluent society*. London: Hamilton.

Gershuny, J.I. 1982: Changing use of time in the United Kingdom: 1937–75, the self-service era. *Studies of Broadcasting* 1, 7–13.

Gershuny, J. and Miles, I. 1983: *The new service economy*. London: Pinter.

Gertler, M.S. 1988: The limits to flexibility: comments on the post-Fordist vision of production and its geography. *Transactions, Institute of British Geographers, New Series* 13, 419–32.

Gibbs, D.C. 1988: Restructuring in the Manchester clothing industry: technical change and interrelationships between manufacturers and retailers. *Environment and Planning A* 20, 1219–33.

Gilg, A.W. 1985: *An introduction to rural geography*. London: Edward Arnold.

Gillespie, A.E. and Goddard, J.B. 1986: Advanced telecommunications and regional economic development. *Geographical Journal* 152, 383–97.

Gillespie, A.E. and Green, A.E. 1987: The changing geography of producer services employment in Britain. *Regional Studies* 21(5), 397–412.

Gilligan, H. 1987: Visitors, tourists and outsiders in a Cornish town. In Bouquet, M. and Winter, M. (eds), *Who from their labours rest? Conflict and practice in rural tourism* (Aldershot: Avebury), 65–82.

Ginzberg, E. and Voyta, G. 1986: *The large corporation at risk*. London: Harper & Row.

Gleave, D. and Cordey-Hayes, M. 1977: Migration dynamics and labour market turnover. *Progress in Planning* 8, 1–95.

Goddard, J.B. 1987: Can new technologies bridge the divide? *Town and Country Planning* 56(12), 326–28.

Goddard, J.B. and Champion, A.G. (eds) 1983: *The urban and regional transformation of Britain*. London: Methuen.

Goddard, J.B. and Gillespie, A.E. 1987: Advanced telecommunications and regional development. In Robson 1987a, 84–109.

Goddard, J.B. and Marshall, J.N. 1983: The future for offices. In Davies and Champion 1983, 109–32.

Gordon, G. (ed.) 1986: *Regional cities in the UK. 1890–1980*. London: Harper & Row.

Gordon, I.R. 1988a: Housing and labour market constraints on migration across the North–South divide. Paper prepared for the NIESR Conference on Housing and the National Economy. December.

——1988b: Resurrecting counter-urbanisation: housing market influences on migration fluctuations from London. *Built Environment* 13(4), 212–22.

Gordon, R.L. (ed.) 1987: *World coal*. Cambridge: Cambridge University Press.

Gottmann, J. 1961: *Megalopolis: the urbanized northeastern seaboard of the United States*. Cambridge, Mass.: MIT Press.

Gould, A. and Keeble, D.E. 1984: New firms and rural industrialization in East Anglia. *Regional Studies* 18, 203–6.

Grassie, J. 1983: *Highland experiment. The story of the HIDB*. Aberdeen: Aberdeen University Press.

Greater London Council 1985: *The future of planning; planning for shopping*. GLC Conference. London: GLC.

——1986: *London Labour Plan*. London: GLC.

Green, A.E. 1988: The North–South divide in Great Britain: an examination of the evidence. *Transactions, Institute of British Geographer, New Series* 13, 179–98.

Green, A.E. and Champion, A.G. 1989: Measuring local economic performance: methodology and applications of the Booming Towns approach. *Built Environment* 14, 78–95.

Green, A.E. and Owen, D.W. 1989: The changing geography of occupations in engineering in Britain, 1978–1987. *Regional Studies* 23, 27–42.

Green, A.E., Owen, D.W., Champion, A.G., Goddard, J.B. and Coombes, M.G. 1986: What contribution can labour migration make to reducing unemployment? In Hart, P.E. (ed.), *Unemployment and labour market policies* (London: Gower), 52–79.

Green, B. 1981: *Countryside conservation*. London: Allen & Unwin.

Green, C.E.W. 1989: Congestion – a rail solution. *Modern Railways*, July, 351–2, 373–5.

Greenberg, L. 1982: The implications of an ageing population for land-use planning. In Warnes 1982, 401–26.

Greve, J. *et al.* 1986: *Homelessness in London: a statement and recommendations by the research team*. Working Paper 60. Bristol: School for Advanced Urban Studies.

Grigson, S. 1989: Development planning in London without the GLC. In Cross and Whitehead 1989, 51–4.

Hakim, C. 1987: Trends in the flexible workforce. *Employment Gazette* 95, 549–60.

Hall, P. 1971: Spatial structure of metropolitan England and Wales. In Chisholm, M. and Manners, G. (eds), *Spatial policy problems of the British economy* (Cambridge: Cambridge University Press), 96–125.

——(ed.) 1981: *The inner city in context*. London: Heinemann.

——1986: From the unsocial city to the social city. *The Planner* 73(3), 17–24.

——1987: The anatomy of job creation: nations, regions and cities in the 1960s and 1970s. *Regional Studies* 21, 95–106.

——1989a: *London 2001*. London: Unwin Hyman.

——1989b: *London 2001*. In Breheny and Congdon 1989, 252–60.

Hall, P., Breheny, M., McQuaid, R. and Hart, D. 1987: *Western sunrise: the genesis and growth of Britain's major high technology corridor*. London: Allen & Unwin.

Hall, P. and Markusen, A. (eds) 1985: *Silicon landscapes*. Boston, Mass.: Allen & Unwin.

Hall, P. and Preston, P. 1988: *The Carrier Wave, new information technology and the geography of innovation, 1846–2003*. London: Unwin Hyman.

Hall, P., Thomas, R., Gracey, H. and Drewett, R. 1973: *The containment of urban England*. London: Allen & Unwin, 2 vols.

Halsey, A.H. 1986: *Change in British society*. Oxford: Oxford University Press, 3rd edn.

Hamilton, A. 1986: *The financial revolution. The Big Bang worldwide*. Harmondsworth: Viking.

Hamnett, C. 1983a: The conditions in England's inner cities on the eve of the 1981 riots. *Area* 15, 7–13.

——1983b: Housing change and social change. In Davies and Champion 1983, 145–63.

——1983c: Regional variations in house prices and house price inflation 1969–81. *Area* 15, 97–109.

——1986: The changing socio-economic structure of London and the South East 1961–1981. *Regional Studies* 20, 391–406.

——1988: Regional variations in house prices and house price inflation in Britain, 1969–88. *The Royal Bank of Scotland Review* 159, 29–40.

——1989: The owner-occupied housing market in Britain: a north–south divide? In Lewis and Townsend 1989, 97–113.

Hamnett, C. and Randolph W. 1982: How far will London's population fall? A commentary on the 1981 Census. *The London Journal* 8, 95–100.

——1983a: The changing population distribution of England and Wales, 1961–81: clean break or consistent progression? *Built Environment* 8, 272–80.

——1983b: The changing tenure structure of the Greater London housing market, 1961–81. *London Journal* 9, 153–64.

——1986: Tenurial transformation and the flat break-up market in London: the British condo experience. In Smith, N. and Williams, P. (eds), *Gentrification of the city* (London: Allen & Unwin), 121–52.

——1988a: *Cities housing and profits: flat break-up and the decline of private renting.* London: Hutchinson.

——1988b: Labour and housing market change in London: a longitudinal analysis, 1971–81. *Urban Studies* 25, 380–98.

Hamnett, C. and Williams, P. 1980: Social change in London: a study in gentrification. *London Journal* 6, 51–66.

Hardill, I. 1987: *The regional implications of restructuring the wool textile industry.* Aldershot: Avebury.

Harris, C.C. 1987: *Redundancy and recession in South Wales*: Oxford: Blackwell.

Harrison, B. 1982: The tendency toward instability and inequality underlying the 'revival' of New England. *Papers of the Regional Science Association* 50, 41–51.

Harrison, R.T. 1986: Industrial development policy and the restructuring of the Northern Ireland economy. *Environment and Planning C* 4, 53–70.

Harvey, D. 1989: *The condition of postmodernity.* Oxford: Blackwell.

Harvey, D.R. 1986: *Countryside implications for England and Wales of possible changes in the Common Agricultural Policy: report to the Department of the Environment and Development Commission.* Reading: Centre for Agricultural Strategy.

Hasluck, C. 1987: *Urban unemployment, local labour markets and employment initiatives.* Harlow: Longman.

Hausner, V.A. (ed.) 1986: *Critical issues in urban economic development, Vol. I.* Oxford: Clarendon Press.

——(ed.) 1987a: *Critical issues in urban economic development, Vol. II.* Oxford: Clarendon Press.

——(ed.) 1987b: *Urban economic change: five city studies.* Oxford: Clarendon Press.

Heald, G. and Wybrow, R.J. 1986: *The gallup survey of Britain.* London: Croom Helm.

Healey, M.J. and Ilbery, B.W. (eds) 1985: *The industrialization of the countryside.* Norwich: Geo Books.

Healey, M.J. and Watts, H.D. 1987: The multiplant enterprise. In Lever, 149–66.

Hedger, M. 1981: Reassessment in mid-Wales. *Town and Country Planning* 50, 261–3.

Herington, J. 1984: *The outer city.* London: Harper & Row.

Herington, J. and Evans, D. 1980: *The social characteristics of household movement in 'key' and 'non-key' settlements.* Research Paper 4. Department of Geography, Loughborough University.

Hillier Parker 1986: *The market town shop rent index.* London: Hillier, Parker, May and Rowden.

——1987a: *Industrial rent and yield contours*. London: Hillier, Parker, May and Rowden.

——1987b: *Office rent and yield contours*. London: Hillier, Parker, May and Rowden.

HMSO 1989: *Roads for Prosperity*. London: HMSO, Cmnd. 693.

Hobsbawm, E.J. 1969: *Industry and empire*. Harmondsworth: Penguin.

Hogarth, T. and Daniel, W.W. 1987: The long-distance commuters. *New Society*, 29 May, 11–13.

——1988: *Britain's new industrial gypsies: a survey of long-distance weekly commuting*. London: Policy Studies Institute.

Hoggart, K. and Buller, H. 1987: *Rural development: a geographical perspective*. London Croom Helm.

Holliday, J.C. 1983: City centre plans in the 1980s. In Davies and Champion 1983, 13–28.

Hollis, J. 1982: New Commonwealth ethnic group populations in Greater London. In Coleman 1982, 119–42.

Holtermann, S.E. 1975: Areas of deprivation in Great Britain: an analysis of 1971 Census data. *Social Trends* 6, 33–47.

House, J.W. (ed.) 1982: *The UK space: resources, environment and the future*. London: Weidenfeld & Nicholson.

House of Commons, Committee on Welsh Affairs 1986: *Tourism in Wales, Minutes of Evidence, 19 February, Mid-Wales Development*. London: HMSO.

House of Commons, Employment Committee 1988: *The employment effects of Urban Development Corporations*. London: HMSO.

Howells, J.R.L. 1984: The location of research and development: some observations and evidence from Britain. *Regional Studies* 18, 13–29.

Howland, M. 1988: Plant closures and local economic conditions. *Regional Studies* 22, 193–208.

Hudson, R. 1985: The paradox of state intervention: the impact of nationalised industry policies and regional policy on employment in the Northern Region in the post-war period. In Chapman, R.C. (ed.), *Public policy studies: the North East of England* (Edinburgh: Edinburgh University Press).

——1988: Labour market changes and new forms of work in 'old' industrial regions. In Massey and Allen 1988, 147–66.

——1989: *Wrecking a region*. London: Pion.

Hudson R. and Sadler, D. 1987: National policies and Local Economic Initiatives: evaluating the effectiveness of UK Coal and Steel Closure Area reindustrialization measures. *Local Economy* 2, 107–14.

Hudson, R. and Williams, A. 1986: *The United Kingdom*. London: Harper & Row.

Hudson, R. and Williams, A. (eds) 1989: *Divided Britain*. London: Belhaven Press.

Hughes, G. and McCormick, B. 1981: Do council housing policies reduce migration between regions? *Economic Journal* 91, 919–37.

——1985: Migration intentions in the UK: which households want to migrate and which succeed? *Supplement to the Economic Journal* 95, 113–23.

——1987a: Does migration reduce differentials in regional unemployment rates? Paper presented at the International Conference on Migration and Labour Market Efficiency, October. Edinburgh/Southampton University, Department of Economics, mimeo.

——1987b: Housing markets, unemployment and labour market flexibility in the UK. *European Economic Review* 31, 615–41.

Humphrys, G. 1987: Public sector industries. In Lever 1987, 196–208.

Institute for Employment Research 1988: *Review of the economy and employment*. Warwick: University of Warwick.

International Labour Organization 1985: *Bulletin of Labour Statistics, 1985*. Geneva: International Labour Organization.

Johnson, D. 1988: An evaluation of the Urban Development Grant programme. *Local Economy* 2(4), 251–70.

Johnson, J.H., Salt, J. and Wood, P.A. 1974 *Housing and the migration of labour in England and Wales*. Farnborough: Saxon House.

Johnson, P. and Thomas, B. 1990: Employment in tourism: a review. *Industrial Relations Journal* 21(1), 36–48.

Johnston, B. 1980: Second homes threat averted. *Planning* 356, 7.

Johnston, R.J. 1985: *The geography of English politics*. London: Croom Helm.

Johnston, R.J. and Doornkamp, J.C. (eds) 1982: *The changing geography of the United Kingdom*. London: Methuen.

Johnston, R.J., Pattie, C.J. and Allsopp, J.G. 1988: *A nation dividing?* Harlow: Longman.

Johnston, R.J. and Taylor, P.J. (eds) 1986: *The world in crisis?* Oxford: Blackwell.

Jones, H., Caird, J., Berry, W. and Dewhurst, J. 1986: Peripheral counterurbanization: findings from an integration of Census and survey data in northern Scotland. *Regional Studies* 20, 15–26.

Joseph, A.E. and Phillips, D.R. 1984: *Accessibility and utilization: geographical perspectives on health care delivery*. London: Harper & Row.

Joshi, H. (ed.) 1989: *The changing population of Britain*. Oxford: Blackwell.

Kaim-Caudle, P.R. 1973: *Comparative social policy and social security*. London: Martin Robertson.

Kaldor, N. 1966: *Causes of the slow rate of growth in the United Kingdom*. Cambridge: Cambridge University Press.

Karn, V., Kemeny, J. and Williams, P. 1985: *Home ownership in the inner city: salvation or despair?* London: Gower.

Kay, J.A., Mayer, C.P. and Thompson, D. (eds) 1986: *Privatisation and regulation: the UK experience*. Oxford: Clarendon Press.

Keating, M. 1988: *The city that refused to die: Glasgow: the politics of urban regeneration*. Aberdeen: Aberdeen University Press.

Keating, M. and Boyle, R. 1986: *Remaking urban Scotland*. Edinburgh: Edinburgh University Press.

Keeble, D.E. 1968: Industrial decentralization and the metropolis: the North West London case. *Transactions, Institute of British Geographers* 44, 1–54.

——1980: Industrial decline, regional policy and the urban–rural manufacturing shift in the United Kingdom. *Environment and Planning A* 12, 945–62.

——1987: Industrial change in the United Kingdom. In Lever 1987a, 1–20.

——1990: Small firms, new firms and uneven regional development in the United Kingdom. *Area* 22.

Keeble, D., Owens, P.L. and Thompson, C. 1982: Regional accessibility and economic potential in the European Community. *Regional Studies* 16, 419–32.

——1983: The urban-rural manufacturing shift in the European Community. *Urban Studies* 20, 405–18.

Keeble, D. and Wever, E. (eds) 1986: *New firms and regional development in Europe*. London: Croom Helm.

Kelly, T. 1987: *The British computer industry: crisis and development*. London: Croom Helm.

Kennett, S.R. 1983: Migration within and between labour markets. In Goddard and Champion 1983, 215–38.

Kennett, S. and Hall, P. 1981: The inner city in spatial perspective. In Hall 1981, 9–51.

Kinnear, R. and Klausner, D. 1986: Southall's interaction with economic change. In Cooke 1986, 140–6.

Kitzinger, U.W. 1961: *The challenge of the Common Market*. Oxford: Blackwell.

Kivell, P.T. 1987: Derelict land in England: policy responses to a continuing problem. *Regional Studies* 21, 265–9.

Klausner, D. 1987: Infrastructure investment and political ends: the case of London's Docklands. *Local Economy* 1(4), 47–60.

Kleinman, M. and Whitehead, C. 1987: Local variations in the sale of council houses in England, 1979–84. *Regional Studies* 21, 1–12.

——1989: Demand for new housebuilding 1986–2001. In Cross and Whitehead 1989, 71–7.

Knox, P.L. 1974: Spatial variations in level of living in England and Wales. *Transactions, Institute of British Geographers* 62, 1–24.

——1982: Living in the United Kingdom. In Johnston and Doornkamp 1982, 291–308.

Knox, P.L. and Cottam, M.B. 1981: A welfare approach to rural geography. *Transactions, Institute of British Geographers, New Series* 6, 433–50.

Kondratieff, N.D. 1978: The long waves in economic life. *Lloyds Bank Review* 129, 41–60.

Labour Research Department 1987: Multinationals reduce UK investment. *Labour Research*, July, 19–20.

Larkin, A. 1979: Rural housing and housing needs. In Shaw 1979, 71–80.

Law, C.M. 1985: The spatial distribution of offices in metropolitan areas: a comparison of Birmingham, Glasgow and Manchester. *The Manchester Geographer NS* 6, 33–41.

——1986: The uncertain future for the city centre: the case of Manchester. *Manchester Geographer NS* 7, 26–43.

——1988: Public-private partnership in urban revitalization in Britain. *Regional Studies* 22(5), 446–51.

Law, C.M. with Grime, E.K., Grundy, C.J., Senior, M.L. and Tuppen, J.N. 1988: *The uncertain future of the urban core*. London: Routledge.

Law, C.M. and Warnes, A.M. 1982: The destination decision in retirement migration. In Warnes 1982, 53–82.

Lawless, P. 1981: *Britain's inner cities: problems and policies*. London: Harper & Row.

——1986: The changing urban and regional system in the U.K.: Sheffield case study. In Cooke 1986, 170–4.

——1988: British inner urban policy: a review. *Regional Studies* 22(6), 531–51.

Lawton, R. 1982: People and work. In House 1982, 103–203.

LDDC 1988: *Report and Accounts 1987–88*. London: London Docklands Development Corporation.

Lee, M. 1983: Property development in the 1980s. In Davies and Champion 1983, 29–40.

Le Grand, J. 1987: *Measurement of inequality in health*. London: Welfare State Programme, London School of Economics.

Le Grand, J. and Robinson, R. (eds) 1984: *Privatisation and the welfare state*. London: Allen & Unwin.

Leicester CC 1983: *Survey of Leicester 1983: initial report of survey*. Leicester: Leicester City Council, Leicestershire County Council.

Leontief, W. 1985: *The impacts of automation on employment, 1963–2000*. Oxford: Oxford University Press.

Levay, C. 1979: Farm viability in mid-Wales. *Town and Country Planning* 48, 197–8.

Lever, W.F. (ed.) 1987a: *Industrial change in the United Kingdom*. Harlow: Longman.

——1987b: Glasgow: policy for the post-industrial city. In Robson 1987a, 40–59.

Lever, W. and Moore, C. (eds) 1986: *The city in transition, policies and agencies for economic regeneration of Clydeside*. Oxford: Oxford University Press.

Lewis, J. 1987: The urban and regional consequences of the financial services revolution in the UK. Paper presented to the European Congress of the Regional Science Association, Athens, August.

Lewis, J. and Meegan, R. 1986: The impact of socio-economic change on Merseyside outer areas. In Cooke 1986, 129–39.

Lewis, J. and Townsend, A. (eds) 1989: *The North–South divide: regional change in Britain in the 1980s*. London: Paul Chapman.

Leys, C. 1983: *Politics in Britain*. London: Heinemann.

Leyshon, A. and Thrift, N. 1989: South goes north? The rise of the British provincial financial centre. In Lewis and Townsend 1989, 114–56.

Lloyd, P.E. and Mason, C. 1984: Spatial variations in new firm formation in the United Kingdom: comparative evidence from Merseyside, Greater Manchester and South Hampshire. *Regional Studies* 18, 207–20.

Lloyd, P. and Shutt, J. 1985: Recession and restructuring in the North West region, 1975–82: the implications of recent events. In Massey and Meegan 1985, 16–60.

Lockhart, D.G. and Ilbery, B. 1987: *The future of the British rural landscape*. Norwich: Geo Books.

Lowe, P., Bradley, T. and Wright, S. 1987: *Deprivation and welfare in rural areas*. Norwich: Geo Books.

LSPU 1986: *A city divided: London's economy since 1979*. London: London Strategic Policy Unit.

McArthur, A.A. and McGregor, A. 1987: Local employment and training initiatives in the national manpower policy context. In Hausner 1987a, 116–59.

McCrone, G. 1969: *Regional policy in Britain*. London: Allen & Unwin.

McDowell, L., Sarre, P. and Hamnett, C. 1989: *Divided nation: social and cultural change in Britain*. London: Hodder and Stoughton.

MacEwen, M. and MacEwen, M. 1981: *National parks: conservation or cosmetics*. London: George Allen & Unwin.

McGregor, A. and Mather, F. 1986: Developments in Glasgow's labour market. In Lever and Moore 1986, 22–43.

Mackenzie, S. and Rose, D.C. 1983: Industrial change, the domestic economy and home life. In Anderson, Duncan and Hudson 1983, 155–200.

McKinnon, A.C. 1989: Scotland's freight links with Europe in the 1990s. *Royal Bank of Scotland Review* 163, 33–43.

McLaughlin, B.P. 1986: *Rural England in the 1980s; rural deprivation study; summary of findings*. London: Department of the Environment, Development Commission (now the Rural Development Commission).

McRae, H. and Cairncross, F. 1984: *Capital city: London as a financial centre*. London: Methuen.

Malpass, P. (ed.) 1986: *The housing crisis*. London: Croom Helm.

Marshall, J.N. 1983: Business service activities in British provincial conurbations. *Environment Planning A* 25, 1343–360.

——1985: Business services, the regions and regional policy. *Regional Studies* 19, 353–64.

——(ed.) 1989: *Uneven development in the service economy: understanding the location and role of producer services*. Oxford: Oxford University Press.

Marshall, J.N. and Bachtler, J.F. 1984: Spatial perspectives on technological changes in the banking sector of the United Kingdom. *Environment and Planning A* 16, 437–50.

Marshall, J.N., Damesick, P. and Wood, P. 1985: Understanding the location and role of producer services in the United Kingdom. *Environment and Planning A* 19, 575–95.

Marshall, M. 1987: *Long waves of regional development*. Basingstoke: Macmillan.

Martin, J. and Roberts, C. 1984: *Women and employment, a lifetime perspective*. London: HMSO.

Martin, R.L. 1984: Redundancies, labour turnover and employment contraction in the recession: a regional analysis. *Regional Studies* 18, 445–54.

——1987: Mrs Thatcher's Britain: a tale of two nations. *Environment and Planning A* 19, 571–4.

——1988: Industrial capitalism in transition: the contemporary reorganisation of the British space-economy. In Massey and Allen 1988, 202–31.

——1989a: The political economy of Britain's North–South divide. In Lewis and Townsend 1989, 20–60.

——1989b: The new economics and politics of regional restructuring: the British experience. In Albrechts, L., Moulaert, F., Roberts, T. and Swyngedouw, E., *Regional planning at the crossroads* (London: Jessica Kingsley), 27–52.

Martin, R. and Rowthorn, B. (eds) 1986: *The geography of de-industrialisation*. Basingstoke: Macmillan.

Mason, C.M. 1985: The geography of 'successful' small firms in the United Kingdom. *Environment and Planning A* 17, 1499–513.

——1987: The small firm sector. In Lever 1987, 125–48.

Mason, C.M. and Harrison, R.T. 1985: The geography of small firms in the UK: towards a research agenda. *Progress in Human Geography* 9, 1–37.

Mason, C.M., Pinch, S. and Witt, S. 1988: Flexible employment strategies in British industry: evidence from the UK 'sunbelt'. Paper presented at Institute of British Geographers Study Group meeting, Birkbeck College, 5 July.

——1989: Inside the 'Sunbelt': industrial change in Southampton. In Breheny and Congdon 1989, 55–86.

Massey, D. 1983: Industrial restructuring as class restructuring: production decentralization and local uniqueness. *Regional Studies* 17, 73–90.

——1984: *Spatial divisions of labour*. Basingstoke: Macmillan.

——1986: The legacy lingers on: the impact of Britain's international role on its internal geography. In Martin and Rowthorn 1986, 31–52.

——1988; Uneven development: social change and spatial division of labour. In Massey and Allen, 250–76.

Massey, D. and Allen, J. (eds) 1988: *Uneven re-development: cities and regions in transition*. London: Hodder and Stoughton.

Massey, D. and Catalano, A. 1978: *Capital and land: landownership by capital in Great Britain*. London: Edward Arnold.

Massey, D.B. and Meegan, R.A. 1979: The geography of industrial reorganization: the spatial effects of the restructuring of the electrical engineering sector under the Industrial Reorganization Corporation. *Progress in Planning* 10(3), 159–237.

——1982: *The anatomy of job loss: the how, why and where of employment decline*. Basingstoke: Macmillan.

——(eds) 1985: *Politics and method: contrasting studies in industrial geography*. London: Methuen.

Mawson, J. and Miller, D. 1984: Local responses to unemployment: the Leeds approach. *Local Government Policy Making*, March, 13–21.

——1986: Interventionist approaches in local employment and economic development: the experience of Labour local authorities. In Hausner 1986, 145–99.

Meadows, P., Cooper, H. and Bartholomew, R. 1988: *The London labour market*. London: HMSO.

Meager, N. 1984: Job loss and the regions: how important is redundancy? *Regional Studies* 18, 459–68.

Mercer, D. and Puttnam, D. 1988: *Rural England: our countryside at the crossroads*. London: Queen Anne Press.

Metcalf, D. 1988: *Trade unions and economic performance: the British evidence*. Centre for Labour Economics Discussion Paper 320. London: London School of Economics.

Minford, P. 1985: *Unemployment: cause and cure*. Oxford: Blackwell, 2nd edn.

Minford, P., Peel, M. and Ashton, P. 1987: *The housing morass: regulation, immobility and unemployment*. London: Institute of Economic Affairs.

Mohan, J. 1988a: Spatial aspects of health-care employment in Britain, 1. Aggregate trends. *Environment and Planning A* 20, 7–23.
——1988b: Spatial aspects of health-care employment in Britain, 2. Current policy initiatives. *Environment and Planning A* 20, 203–17.
——1988c: Restructuring, privatization and the geography of health care provision in England, 1983–7. *Transactions, Institute of British Geographers, New Series* 13, 449–65.
Monck, C.S.P., Porter, R.B., Quintas, P. and Storey, D.J. with Wynarczyk, P. 1988: *Science parks and the growth of high technology firms.* London: Croom Helm.
Moore, C. and Booth, S. 1986: From comprehensive regeneration to privatization: the search for effective area strategies. In Lever and Moore 1986, 76–91.
Moore, B., Rhodes, J. and Tyler, P. 1986: *The effects of government regional economic policy.* London: HMSO.
Morgan, K. 1986a: Re-industrialisation in peripheral Britain: state policy, the space economy and industrial innovation. In Martin and Rowthorn 1986, 322–60.
——1986b: The spectre of 'two nations' in contemporary Britain. *Catalyst* 2, 11–18.
Morgan, K. and Sayer, A. 1988: A 'modern' industry in a 'mature' region: the remaking of management labour relations. In Massey and Allen 1988, 167–87.
Morison, H. 1987: *The regeneration of local economics.* Oxford: Clarendon Press.
Morrey, C. 1973: The changing population of the London Boroughs. *Greater London Research Memorandum* RM 413.
Morris, A., Findlay, A., Paddison, R. and Rogerson, R. 1989: Urban quality of life and the North–South divide. *Town and Country Planning* 58, 207–10.
Morris, J. 1987: The state and industrial restructuring: government policies in industrial Wales. *Society and Space* 5, 195–213.
Morris, J.L. 1988: Producer services and the regions: the case of large accountancy firms. *Environment and Planning* 20, 741–59.
Morrison, P.A. and Wheeler, J.P. 1976: Rural renaissance in America? *Population Bulletin* 31(3), 1–27.
Moseley, M.J. 1979: *Accessibility: the rural challenge.* London: Methuen.
——1980: Is deprivation really rural? *The Planner* 66, 97.
Moseley, M. and Packman, J. 1987: Mobile services and service delivery in rural Britain. In Lowe, Bradley and Wright 1987, 205–12.
Moser, C.A. and Scott, W. 1961: *British Towns.* Edinburgh: Oliver & Boyd.
Munton, R.J.C. 1983: *London's green belt: containment in practice.* London: Allen & Unwin.
Murgatroyd, L. and Urry, J, 1983: The restructuring of a local economy: the case of Lancaster. In Anderson, Duncan and Hudson 1983, 67–98.
Murray, R. 1988: Life after Henry (Ford). *Marxism Today* 10, 8–13.
NABS 1987: *House prices bulletin: the North–South divide.* London: Nationwide Anglia Building Society, August.
——1988: *House prices: highs and lows – a local view.* London: Nationwide Anglia Building Society.
National Audit Office 1988: *Department of the Environment: Urban Development Corporation.* Report by the Comptroller and Auditor General. London: HMSO.
Newby, H. 1980: *Green and pleasant land: social change in rural England.* Harmondsworth: Pelican.
——1986: Locality and rurality: the restructuring of rural social relations. *Regional Studies* 20, 209–16.
——1988: *The countryside in question.* London: Hutchinson.
North, J. 1989: How much land will be available for development in 2015? In Cross and Whitehead 1989, 29–34.
Northern Region Strategy Team (1977): *Strategic plan for the Northern region.* Newcastle upon tyne: Department of the Environment.

Noyelle, T.J. and Stanback, T.M. 1984: *The economic transformation of American cities*. Totowa, NJ: Rowman & Allanheld.

OECD 1989: *Labour force statistics*. Paris: Organisation for Economic Cooperation and Development.

Ogilvy, A.A. 1982: Population migration between the regions of Great Britain 1971–79. *Regional Studies* 16, 65–73.

OPCS 1981: *Census 1981, preliminary report, England and Wales*. London: HMSO.

——1983: *Recently moving households*. London: HMSO.

——1984a: *Census 1981: key statistics for local authorities, Great Britain*. London: HMSO.

——1984b: *Census 1981: key statistics for urban areas, Great Britain*. London: HMSO.

——1986: Ethnic minority populations in Great Britain. *Population Trends* 46, 18–21.

——1987: *Key population and vital statistics: local and health authority areas, 1986*. London: HMSO, series VS no. 13, PP1 no. 9.

——1988a: Mid 1987 population estimates for England and Wales. *OPCS Monitor* PP1 88/1.

——1988b: *Population projections, England, by area, 1985–2001*. Series PP3 no. 7. London: HMSO.

——1989: *Population projections, 1987–2027*. London: HMSO.

Open University 1985: *The changing countryside*. London: Croom Helm.

Openshaw, S. and Charlton, M. 1984: The urban face of Britain. *The Geographical Magazine* 56, 421–4.

Osborne, R.H. 1964: Changes in the regional distribution of population in Great Britain. *Geography* 49, 266–72.

Owen, D.W., Coombes, M.G. and Gillespie, A.E. 1986: The urban–rural shift and employment change in Britain, 1971–81. In Danson 1986, 23–47.

Owen, D.W., Gillespie, A.E. and Coombes, M.G. 1984: 'Job shortfalls' in British Local Labour Market Areas: a classification of labour supply and demand trends, 1971–81. *Regional Studies* 18, 469–88.

Owen, D.W. and Green, A.E. 1989a: Labour market accounts for travel-to-work areas, 1981–84. *Regional Studies* 23, 69–72.

——1989b: Spatial aspects of labour mobility in the 1980s. *Geoforum* 20, 107–26.

Owens, S. 1989: Agricultural land surplus and concern for the countryside. In Cross and Whitehead 1989, 35–8.

Pacione, M. 1981: Glasgow. In Pacione. M. (ed.), *Urban problems and planning in the developed world* (London: Croom Helm), 189–222.

——1983: *Progress in rural geography*. London: Croom Helm.

——1984: *Rural geography*. London: Harper & Row.

Paddison, R. and Morris, A. 1988: *Regionalism and the regional question*. Oxford: Blackwell.

Pahl, R.E. 1984: *Divisions of labour*. Oxford: Blackwell.

Palmer, D.J. 1989: The changing geography of the South East: housing and labour market constraints. In Breheny and Congdon 1989, 23–32.

Parkinson, M. 1985: *Liverpool on the brink*. Hermitage: Policy Journals.

——1988: Urban regeneration and Development Corporations: Liverpool style. *Local Economy* 3, 109–18.

Parry Lewis, J. 1989: Let the South East stew . . . and combat inflation? *Royal Bank of Scotland Review* 163, 3–14.

Parsons, D. 1987: Recruitment difficulties and the housing market. *The Planner* 73(1), 30–4.

Peach, C. 1982: The growth and distribution of the black population in Britain 1945–1980. In Coleman 1982, 23–42.

——1985: Immigrants and the 1981 urban riots in Britain. In White, P.E. and Knapp, B. van der (eds), *Contemporary Studies of Migration* (Norwich: Geo Books), 143–54.

Pearson, R. 1987: Rebuilding the Lower Don Valley, Sheffield. *The Planner* 73(6), 35–8.

Peck, F.W. and Townsend, A.R. 1984: Contrasting experience of recession and spatial restructuring: British Shipbuilders, Plessey and Metal Box. *Regional Studies* 18, 319–38.

——1986: Corporate interaction in oligopolistic markets: the role of case studies of rationalisation. In Danson 1986, 49–64.

——1987: The impact of technological change upon the spatial pattern of UK employment within major corporations. *Regional Studies* 21, 225–40.

Perry, R., Dean, K. and Brown, B. 1986: *Counterurbanisation: international case studies of socio-economic change in the rural areas*. Norwich: Geo Books.

Pettigrew, P. 1987: A bias for action: industrial development in Mid Wales. In Cloke 1987, 102–21.

Phillimore, P. 1989: *Shortened lives: premature death in North Tyneside*. Bristol: School for Applied Social Studies, University of Bristol.

Phillips, D.R. and Williams, A.M. 1984: *Rural Britain: a social geography*. Oxford: Blackwell.

Philpott, J.C. and Kraithman, D.A. 1986: Structural change in a New Town: the case of Stevenage. Hatfield Polytechnic, Local Economy Research Unit, mimeo.

Pinch, S.P., Mason, C.M. and Witt, S.J.G. 1989: Labour flexibility and industrial restructuring in the UK 'Sunbelt': the case of Southampton. *Transactions, Institute of British Geographers, New Series* 14(4) 418–34.

Planner, The. Gloucester: Ambit Publications.

Planning. London: Royal Town Planning Institute.

Pollard, S. 1981: *The industrialisation of Europe, 1760–1970*. Oxford: Oxford University Press.

——1983: *The development of the British economy, 1914–1980*. London: Edward Arnold, 3rd edn.

Power, A. 1982: *Priority Estates Project 1982: Improving problem council estates: a summary of aims and progress*. London: HMSO.

——1984: Trouble in Utopia: II. Rescuing unpopular council estates through local management. *Geographical Journal* 150, 359–62.

——1987: *Property before people: the management of twentieth-century council housing*. London: Allen & Unwin.

Rajan, A. 1987: *Services – the second Industrial Revolution?* London: Butterworth.

Rajan, A. and Pearson, R. 1986: *UK occupation and employment trends to 1990*. London: Butterworth.

Ravenstein, E.G. 1885: The laws of migration. *Journal of the Statistical Society* 48, 167–227.

——1889: The laws of migration. *Journal of the Royal Statistical Society* 52, 241–301.

Rawstron, E.M. 1964: Industry. In Watson and Sissons 1964, 297–318.

Redclift, N. and Mingione, E. (eds) 1985: *Beyond employment: household, gender and subsistence*. Oxford: Blackwell.

Reddaway, W.B. 1977: The economic consequences of zero population growth. *Lloyds Bank Review* 124, 14–30.

Redfern, P. 1982: Profile of our cities. *Population Trends* 30, 21–32.

Registrar General Scotland 1989: *Population projections: Scotland (1987–based)*. Edinburgh: Registrar General Scotland.

Reward Regional Surveys 1986: *Cost of living report: regional comparisons March 1989*. Stone: Reward Regional Surveys.

Rhodes, J. 1986: Regional dimensions of industrial decline. In Martin and Rowthorn 1986, 138–68.

Riddle, D.J. 1986: *Service-led growth; the role of the service sector in world development*. London: Praeger.

Robert, S. and Randolph. W. 1983: Beyond decentralisation: the evolution of population distribution in England and Wales, 1961–81. *Geoforum* 14, 75–102.

Roberts, P. and Noon, D. 1987: The role of industrial promotion and inward investment in the process of regional development. *Regional Studies* 21, 167–74.

Robertson, J. 1986: *Future work*. London: Gower.

Robertson, J.A.S., Briggs, J.M. and Goodchild, A. 1982: *Structure and employment prospects of the service industries*. Research Paper 30. London: Department of Employment.

Robinson, F. (ed.) 1988: *Post-industrial Tyneside*. Newcastle upon Tyne City Libraries and Arts.

Robinson, F., Wren, C. and Goddard, J. 1987: *Economic development policies: an evaluative study of the Newcastle Metropolitan Region*. Oxford: Oxford University Press.

Robson, B.D. and Pace, W. 1983: Renewal and employment. In Davies and Champion 1983, 85–108.

Robson, B.T. 1986: Coming full circle: London versus the rest 1890–1980. In Gordon 1986, 217–32.

——(ed.) 1987a: *Managing the city: the aims and impacts of urban policy*. Totowa, NJ: Barnes & Noble Books.

——1987b: The policy framework. In Robson 1987a, 211–15.

——1987c; The enduring city: a perspective on decline. In Robson 1987a, 6–21.

——1988: *Those inner cities: reconciling the social and economic aims of urban policy*. Oxford: Clarendon Press.

Rodgers, B. 1986: Manchester: metropolitan planning by collaboration and consent; or civic hope frustrated. In Gordon 1986, 41–58.

Rogerson, R.J., Findlay, A.M. and Morris, A.S. 1988: The best cities to live in. *Town and Country Planning* 57, 270–3.

Rogerson, R., Morris, A., Findlay, A. and Paddison, R. 1989: *Quality of life in Britain's intermediate cities*. Glasgow: Quality of Life Group, University of Glasgow.

Rose, E.A. (ed.) 1986: *New roles for old cities*. London: Gower.

Rose, R. and Page, E. (eds) 1982: *Fiscal stress in cities*. Cambridge: Cambridge University Press.

Rothwell, R. 1982: The role of technology in industrial change: implications for regional policy. *Regional Studies* 15, 361–70.

Routh, G. 1986: *Unemployment: economic perspectives*. Basingstoke: Macmillan.

Rowles, G.D. 1986: The geography of ageing and the aged: towards an integrated perspective. *Progress in Human Geography* 10, 511–40.

Rowthorn, B. 1986: De-industrialization in Britain. In Martin and Rowthorn, 1–30.

RTPI 1986: *Strategic planning for regional potential – a discussion document*. London: Royal Town Planning Institute.

Salt, J. 1985: Labour migration and housing: an overview. Paper presented at Conference on Labour and Housing Market Change, Parsifal College, London.

Savage, M., Dickens, P. and Fielding, A.J. 1987: The 'service class' in Britain: one class or several? Paper presented at Sixth Urban Change and Conflict Conference, University of Kent.

Schiller, R. 1986: Retail decentralisation – the coming of the third wave. *The Planner*, July, 13–15.

Scott, A.J. 1988: Flexible production systems and regional development: the rise of new industrial spaces in North America and western Europe. *International Journal of Urban and Regional Research* 12, 171–86.

SDA 1980: *GEAR: Strategy and programmes*. Glasgow: Scottish Development Agency.

SEEDS 1987: *South–south divide*. Stevenage: South East Economic Development Strategy.

Sellgren, J. 1989: Assisting local economies: an assessment of emerging patterns of local authority economic development activities. In Gibbs, D.C. (ed.), *Government policy and industrial change* (London: Routledge), 232–65.

SERPLAN 1989a: *Regional trends in the South East: the South East regional monitor 1988–89*. London: London and South East Regional Planning Conference, RPC 1430.

——1989b: *Into the next century: review of the South East Regional Strategy: consultation paper*. London: London and South East Regional Planning Conference, RPC 1500.

Shaw, C. 1988: Latest estimates of ethnic minority population. *Population Trends* 51, 5–8.

Shaw, J.M. (ed) 1979: *Rural deprivation and planning*. Norwich Geo Books.

Short, J. 1981: *Public expenditure and taxation in the UK regions*. London: Gower.

Short, J.R. 1982: *Housing in Britain: the postwar experience*. London: Methuen.

Simmons, M. 1986: The M25 – a new geography of development? III. The emerging planning response. *Geographical Journal* 152(2), 166–70.

Simpson, M. and Smith, P. 1986: Where the jobs are. *New Society*, 7 August, 51–2.

Sims, D. 1982: *Change in the city centre*. London: Gower.

Singh, A. 1977: UK industry and the world economy: a case of de-industrialization? *Cambridge Journal of Economics* 1, 113–36.

Smith, D. 1989: *North and South: Britain's economic, social and political divide*. Harmondsworth: Penguin.

Smith, N. 1984: *Uneven development*. Oxford: Blackwell.

Smith, R.D.P. 1968: The changing urban hierarchy. *Regional Studies* 2, 1–19.

Sparks, L. 1986: The changing structure of distribution in retail companies: an example from the grocery trade. *Transaction, Institute of British Geographers, New Series* 11, 147–54.

Spence, N.A., Gillespie, A., Goddard, J., Kennett, S., Pinch, S. and William, A.M. 1982: *British cities: analysis of urban change*. Oxford: Pergamon.

Spencer, K., Taylor, A., Smith, B., Mawson, J., Flynn, N. and Batley, R. 1986: *Crisis in the industrial heartland: a study of the West Midlands*. Oxford: Clarendon Press.

SQP 1985: *The Cambridge phenomenon*. Cambridge: Segal Quince and Partners.

Standing Conference of Rural Community Councils 1978: *The decline of rural services*. London: The National Council of Social Service.

Steiner, M. 1985: Old industrial areas: a theoretical approach. *Urban Studies* 22, 387–98.

Stern, E. and Turbin, J. 1986: *Youth employment and unemployment in rural England*. London: The Development Commission (now The Rural Development Commission).

Stillwell, J. and Boden, P. 1986: *Internal migration in the UK: characteristics and trends*. Working Paper 470. Department of Geography, University of Leeds.

Stoker, G. 1989: Urban Development Corporations: a review. *Regional Studies* 23(2), 159–67.

Storey, D.J. 1982: *Entrepreneurship and the new firm*. London: Croom Helm.

Storey, D. and Johnson, P. 1987: *Job generation and labour market change*. Basingstoke: Macmillan.

Storey, D., Keasey, K., Watson, R. and Pooran, W. 1987: *The performance of small firms*. London: Croom Helm.

Storper, M. and Walker, R. 1989: *The capitalist imperative*. Oxford: Blackwell.

Talbot, J. 1988: Have Enterprize Zones encouraged enterprise? Some empirical evidence from Tyneside. *Regional Studies* 22, 507–14.

Taylor, H. and Todd, H. 1982: British research on social gerontology and its relevance to policy: towards a geographical contribution. In Warnes 1982, 427–48.

Taylor, M.J. and Thrift, N.J. 1982: *The geography of multinationals*. London: Croom Helm.

——1986: *Multinationals and the restructuring of the world economy.* London: Croom Helm.

TCPA 1987: *North-South divide: a new deal for Britain's regions.* London: Town and Country Planning Association.

Teale, M. 1989: Retail shopping: the need for space. In Cross and Whitehead 1989, 78–80.

Thomas, A.D. 1986: *Housing and urban renewal: residential decay and revitalization in the private sector.* London: Allen & Unwin.

Thomas, D. 1970: *London's green belt.* London: Faber & Faber.

Thomas, I.C. and Drudy, P.J. 1987: The impact of factory development on 'growth town' employment in mid-Wales. *Urban Studies* 24, 361–78.

Thompson, J.H. *et al.* 1962: Towards a geography of economic health: the case of New York State. *Annals, Association of American Geographers* 52, 1–20.

Thrift, N. 1986: The geography of international economic disorder. In Johnston and Taylor 1986, 12–67.

Thrift, N., Leyshon, A. and Daniels, P. 1987: 'Sexy greedy': the new international financial system, the City of London and the South East of England. Working Papers on Producer Services no. 8. Bristol/Liverpool.

Tilly, L.A. and Scott, J.W. 1978: *Women, work and family.* New York: Holt, Rinehart & Winston.

Titmuss, R.M. 1976: *Essays on the welfare state.* London: Allen & Unwin.

Town and County Planning. London: Town and County Planning Association.

Townsend, A.R. 1980: Unemployment geography and the new government's 'regional aid'. *Area* 12, 9–18.

——1983: *The impact of recession, on industry, employment and the regions.* London: Croom Helm.

——1985: A critique of past policies of modernisation for the North East. In Chapman, R. (ed.), *Public policy studies: the North East of England* (Edinburgh: Edinburgh University Press), 97–118.

——1986a: Spatial aspects of the growth of part-time employment in Britain. *Regional Studies* 20, 313–30.

——1986b: The location of employment growth after 1978: the surprising significance of dispersed centres. *Environment and Planning A* 18, 529–45.

——1987: Regional policy. In Lever 1987, 223–39.

——1989: The future of UK regions. *The Planner* 75(5), 21–3.

Townsend, A.R. and Peck, F.W. 1985a: An approach to the analysis of redundancies in the UK (post 1976): some methodological problems and policy implications. In Massey and Meegan 1985, 64–87.

——1985b: The geography of mass redundancy in named corporations. In Pacione, M. (ed.), *Progress in industrial geography* (London: Croom Helm), 174–218.

——1985c: 'Multinational control': a misleading definition yields misleading results. *Area* 17, 327–30.

——1986: The role of foreign manufacturing in Britain's great recession. In Taylor and Thrift 1986, 282–310.

Townsend, P., with Corrigan, P. and Kowarzik, U. 1987: *Poverty and labour in London.* London: Low Pay Unit.

Townsend, P., Phillimore, P. and Beattie, A. 1988: *Health and deprivation: inequality and the North.* London: Croom Helm.

Trebilcock, C. 1981: *The industrialization of the continental powers, 1780–1914.* Harlow: Longman.

Trippier, D. 1989: *New life for inner cities.* London: Conservative Political Centre.

Tyler, P., Moore, B. and Rhodes, J. 1988: *Geographical variations in costs and productivity.* London: HMSO.

Tyler, P. and Rhodes, J. 1987: *South East employment and housing study*. Discussion Paper 15. Cambridge: Department of Land Economy.

Tym, R. 1987: *Land use for residential development in the South East*. London: Roger Tym & Partners.

Urry, J. 1987a: On the waterfront. *New Society*, 14 August, 12–14.

——1987b: Some social and spatial aspects of services. *Environment and Planning D: Society and Space* 5, 5–26.

Vickerman, R.W. 1987: The Channel Tunnel: consequences for regional growth and development. *Regional Studies* 21(3), 187–98.

——1989: After 1992 – the South East as a frontier region. In Breheny and Congdon 1989, 87–105.

Vining, D.R. and Kontuly, T. 1978: Population dispersal from major metropolitan regions: an international comparison. *International Regional Science Review* 3, 49–73.

Vining, D. and Strauss, A. 1977: A demonstration that the current deconcentration of population in the United States is a clean break with the past. *Environment and Planning A* 9, 751–8.

Wannop, U. 1986: Glasgow/Clydeside: a century of metropolitan evolution. In Gordon 1986, 83–98.

Ward, R. 1989: Minority settlement and the local economy. In McDowell, Sarre and Hamnett 1989, 111–27.

Ward, S.V. 1988: *The geography of interwar Britain: the state and uneven development* London: Routledge.

Warnes, A.M. (ed.) 1982: *Geographical perspectives on the elderly*. Chichester: Wiley.

Warnes, A.M. and Law, C.M. 1984: The elderly population of Great Britain: locational trends and policy implications. *Transactions, Institute of British Geographers, New Series* 9, 37–59.

——1985: Elderly population distribution and housing prospects in Great Britain. *Town Planning Review* 56(3), 292–314.

Watson, J.W. and Sissons, J.B. 1964: *The British Isles: a systematic geography*. London: Nelson.

Watts, H.D. 1989: Non-financial head offices: a view from the north. In Lewis and Townsend 1989, 157–74.

Watts, H.D. and Stafford, H.A. 1986: Plant closures and the multiplant firm: some conceptual issues. *Progress in Human Geography* 10, 206–29.

Webber, R. and Craig, J. 1976: Which local authorities are alike? *Population Trends* 5, 13–19.

Weekley, I. 1988: Rural depopulation and counterurbanisation: a paradox. *Area* 20, 127–34.

Weiner, M.J. 1981: *English culture and the decline of the industrial Spirit 1850–1980*. Cambridge: Cambridge University Press.

Welsh Office 1989: *1987-based population projections for the counties of Wales*. Cardiff: Welsh Office.

Wenger, C. 1980: *Mid Wales: development or deprivation?* Cardiff: University of Wales Press.

Whitehead, M. 1987: *The health divide: inequalities in health in the 1980s*. London: Health Education Council.

Williams, R.H., Cameron, S.J., Gillard, A.A. and Willis, K.G. 1987: *Promoting local economic development*. London: Croom Helm.

Willis, K.G. and Saunders, C.M. 1988: The impact of a development agency on employment: resurrection discounted? *Applied Economics* 20, 81–96.

Wilmott, P. and Murie, A. 1988: *Polarisation and social housing: the British and French experience*. London: Policy Studies Institute.

Winter, M. 1987: Private tourism in the English and Welsh uplands; farming, visitors and property. In Bouquet, M. and Winter, M. (eds), *Who from their labours rest? Conflict and practice in rural tourism* (Aldershot: Avebury), 22–34.

Women and Geography Study Group of the IBG 1984: *Geography and gender*. London: Hutchinson.

Wood, P.A. 1986: The anatomy of job loss and job creation: some speculation on the role of the 'producer' services sector. *Regional Studies* 20, 37–46.

Woollett, S. 1981: *Alternative rural services*. London: National Council for Voluntary Organisations.

World Bank 1989: *World Development Report 1989*. New York: Oxford University Press.

Wray, I. 1986: Wanted: a new partnership for development in the South. *The Planner* 73(3), 14–16.

——1987: The Merseyside Development Corporation: progress versus objectives. *Regional Studies* 21, 163–7.

Young K. 1989: Inner city policy: institutions, programmes and strategies. In Cross and Whitehead 1989, 81–7.

Young, K. and Mason, C. (eds) 1983: *Urban economic development: new roles and relationships*. Basingstoke: Macmillan.

Young, S., Hood, N. and Jamill, J. 1987: *Foreign multinationals and the British economy*. Cambridge: Cambridge University Press.

Index